In one sense, this book is history. The struggles described in it took place this year, or last year, or a decade ago. But it also hints of things coming. As we see that resources have limits while our appetites seem to have none, the stories in this book look more and more like a prelude to some epic struggle yet to come.

The message here — from people who know — is simple: If the environment is to be kept habitable, we must make it so. No one else will do it.

To those who have already put their hearts to the task, and to the others who must join them, we dedicate this book.

The editors

THE GRASS ROOTS PRIMER

edited by

James Robertson and John Lewallen

Sierra Club Books

San Francisco 1975

Editors
James Robertson and John Lewallen

Contributors
Steven Bundy, Blackbird, Linda Penn,
Dorothy Gray, Leila Mustachi, Joan Reiss

Staff
Colleen Carter, Carolyn Robertson, Cindy Boatwright,
Sharon Miley, David Weitzman, Marcia Smith

Photography
Eleanor Lewallen, John Lewallen, James Robertson,
Lee Harris. For other photographic credits, see
acknowledgements, page 5.

This book was edited and prepared for publication at
The Yolla Bolly Press, Covelo, California, between
September 1974 and June 1975.

The Sierra Club, founded in 1892 by John Muir, has devoted
itself to the study and protection of the nation's scenic and
ecological resources — mountains, woodlands, wild shores and
rivers. All Club publications are part of the nonprofit effort
the Club carries on as a public trust. There are some 50 chapters
coast to coast, in Canada, Hawaii and Alaska. Participation is
invited in the Club's program to enjoy and preserve wilderness
everywhere. Address: 1050 Mills Tower, San Francisco,
California 94104.

Printed in the United States of America

Library of Congress Cataloging in Publication Data
Main entry under title:

The Grass roots primer.

    Bibliography: p. 269-76.
    Includes index.
    1. Environmental protection — Citizen participation.
I. Robertson, James, 1935-   II. Lewallen, John.
TD170.G7   363.6   75-10017
ISBN 0-87156-142-5

Acknowledgements

The editors are especially grateful to these and other people without whose generous assistance and cooperation this book would not have been possible:

Cynthia Dietz, New York, New York
Larry Alaimo, Queens, New York
Joan McClure, New York, New York
Marcy Benstock, New York, New York
Phyllis Katz, New York, New York
Jo Ann Fluke, New York, New York
Aurora Gareiss, Douglaston, New York
Robert Brown, Hershey, Nebraska
Richard Dougherty, Salt Lake City, Utah
Joan R. Reiss, Sacramento, California
Wesley Chesbro, Arcata, California
Joseph Holaday, Eugene, Oregon
Forest Golden, Auburn, New York
Holway Jones, Eugene, Oregon
Richard Noyes, Eugene, Oregon
Marjorie P. Sheldon, Fair Haven, Vermont
Peter Smith, Belmont, Vermont
Harold Silverstein, Brooklyn, New York
Anne Taylor, Raleigh, North Carolina
Marty Gardner, Raleigh, North Carolina
Nancy Chirich, Charleston, South Carolina
Ben Gibbs, Charleston, South Carolina
Alex Duris, Hendersonville, North Carolina
Jane Novick, Eugene, Oregon
Susan Thornton, Littleton, Colorado
Sharon Leventhal, Arvada, Colorado
Bill Mitchell, Billings, Montana
John Duncklee, Tucson, Arizona
Joyce Griffen, Flagstaff, Arizona
Shirley Solomon, Pacific Palisades, California
Barbara Doe, Springfield, Illinois
Tom McKiernan, Keystone, South Dakota
Marlene J. Sandel, Alma, Michigan
Robert F. Morris, Santa Rosa, California
Barry Grimm, Wilmington, North Carolina
Ernest L. Youens, Alpine, Arizona
Herbert B. Rosenstock, Temple Hills, Maryland

Carolyn W. Baker, Omaha, Nebraska
Nancy Erb, Bloomington, Indiana
Norma Schaeffer, Munster, Indiana
Lowell L. Klessig, Madison, Wisconsin
Alan George, Visalia, California
Susan Wolf, New York, New York
Ingrid Lustig, Doyle, California
Art Downing, Grants Pass, Oregon
Bob Franson, Vancouver, British Columbia
Patricia I. Felton, E. Hartford, Connecticut
Charlotte M. Taylor, Escanaba, Michigan
Ray Kresek, Spokane, Washington
William W. Biddle, Plymouth, New Hampshire
Lee Botts, Chicago, Illinois
Nancy Jack, Kansas City, Kansas
Margie Cook, Lawrence, Kansas
Todd Tinkham, Maybee, Michigan
John A. Brigham Jr., Saratoga, California
James F. Redford Jr., Miami, Florida
Sylvia Retherford, Attica, Indiana
Molly Thomas, New York, New York
Louise Young, Winnetka, Illinois
June Viavant, Salt Lake City, Utah
Pamela R. Patton, Nashville, Tennessee
Jerry Friedman, Point Reyes Station, California
Mary Jean Haley, Oakland, California
Ellsworth Barnard, Amherst, Massachusetts
Lea Wood, Aptos, California
Louise Burton, Oakland, California
Paul T. Brady, Middletown, New Jersey
Laurie Chisler, Santa Paula, California
Dorothy Gray, Los Altos, California
David Pesonen, San Francisco, California
Jean Siddall, Lake Oswego, Oregon
Sally Hamburg, San Diego, California
Richard Marx, Jamesburg, New Jersey
Margaret Drury, Princeton, New Jersey

The editors also acknowledge the following who have given their permission to include in this book material which may have appeared elsewhere.

Page 18: Drawing by Robert Day. Copyright © 1966, reprinted by permission of The New Yorker Magazine, Inc.

Page 20: Cartoon by Dan O'Neill. Reprinted by permission of Chronicle Features Syndicate, *San Francisco Chronicle.*

Page 27: Photograph by Ernest Sisto. Reprinted by permission of *The New York Times.*

Page 39: Cartoon by Martin Stanton. Courtesy of the *Citizen-Advertiser,* Auburn, New York.

Introduction

This is a practical book for people whose world is threatened, and who want to do something effective to prevent the piecemeal destruction of Earth's natural environment. As most of us now realize, all of our world is threatened by constantly expanding environmental exploitation. As many do not realize, there is a growing grassroots movement which is stalling and slowing this human abuse of the natural environment.

In beginning this book, we interviewed grassroots environmental activists throughout the United States, and in Canada. A questionnaire sent out brought an astonishingly large response, from all sorts of people in all regions. Out of this reaction to our project emerged a simple and powerful fact: Successful grassroots groups, no matter where they are or what issue they are dealing with, are using similar methods. In other words, there *are* specific practical steps a grassroots environmental group can take to gain victory.

Since Earth Day 1970 the environmental movement has come of age. It has come out of the headlines and off the streets. The placards have been replaced by legal briefs and environmental impact reports. Instead of burying cars as symbolic rejections of pollution, whole industrial sources of pollution are being buried beneath legal restrictions. Most significantly, instead of decrying national or global problems that no human power could cope with, the people in the environmental movement are tackling local issues that they *can* handle.

Behind virtually every wilderness area and national park, each piece of urban open space, is a group of citizens who worked long and hard to create it and probably still are actively protecting it. Most of the federal and state environmental laws enacted in the past few years had no teeth until grassroots groups went to court to assert their — and our — rights under them. How do these grassroots groups work? How can you save some part of the environment that is vitally important to you? These are the questions answered by *The Grass Roots Primer*.

The physical act of assembling this book began last year — the interviews, the correspondence, the collecting of visual materials, the editorial consultations. . . . But the seeds of grassroots activity began long before — before the energy crisis, before Earth Day, perhaps before our generation. The ideas which underlie this book are not new; they have just languished until people — everyday people, working and raising families — decided quite by the force of circumstances to put them into action.

To see our lives (and needs) as part of the sustaining process of the entire planet required no sacrifice before now. Resources seemed to be illimitable, the GNP could know no bounds, progress was all. To do without was a spiritual exercise, not a practical necessity. To ask others to do without was the request of a lunatic, probably a dangerous one. *Times, they are a-changing.* No longer is it a question of have and have not, but rather what we shall do without in order to save that which the earth — and human dignity — must do with.

"Grass roots" in this book has taken on a meaning more closely allied with the words themselves. The phrase is still political, still attached to self-interest, albeit enlightened, but finally it has precisely to do with grass and with roots. It is about people's interest in grass and in roots. And about what they did to try to save them, and what they learned in the process.

The Grass Roots Primer comes out of the experience of many people, too many to acknowledge. It is the celebration of the experience of a determined few, and the application of their involvement in community problems to issues that face us all. The theme is action — learning by doing — and it salutes all those who are committed to a new relationship between our society and the resources of the earth which we draw upon.

A handful of energetic, dedicated people do not a movement make. Sharing of experiences — successful and unsuccessful — with persons holding similar hopes and fears can. This book aims then at much more than the celebration of those named in it; it sings the unsung, and heralds those who by will or circumstance soon will be struggling in their communities for values which are primary to our lives (and the lives of our descendants) in ways no system of measurement could ever delineate.

The editors

Contents

Grass Roots Heroes

Get Back in Your Kitchen, Lady, and Let Me Build My Road!

On a January morning in 1966, a half dozen housewives held a roadside meeting with the San Mateo County engineer and five reluctant county supervisors who had come to hear their complaints about the county's plan to widen the Alameda de las Pulgas in Menlo Park, California.

The plan called for making a 35-foot country road with a 60-foot right of way into a four lane thoroughfare with a right of way of 104 feet — at the expense of yards, flower gardens, trees, parking, and whatever else got in the way. Though the project had not yet been formally authorized by the board of supervisors, agents working for the county had already been quietly negotiating with property owners for land for the expanded right of way, and had managed to purchase two or three of the 198 parcels to be affected.

Claire Dedrick, post-doctoral student, housewife and self-declared political abstainer, was there only because she had promised an absent friend to attend and report back.

ABOUT THE NAME "ALAMEDA DE LAS PULGAS"

There are two old trails that run north and south along the Peninsula of San Francisco. Both are still in use today. One of them, built by the Spanish, was called by them "El Camino Real" or "The King's Highway." The other, much older, was used by the Indians of the area. The Spanish gave it a name too: Avenue of the Fleas, "La Alameda de las Pulgas."

"The ladies were not happy. Mrs. Van Goerder was saying, 'Look what you're going to do to my new garden! You can't do that! This is my home!' The supervisors hung back and let Don Wilson (the engineer) take the brunt of it. He was getting a trifle ruffled, so I spoke up:

'What's the existing right of way?'

'Sixty feet.'

'Well, what do you want to build a freeway through here for anyway?'

'It's not a freeway.'

'All right then, an expressway.'

'It's not an expressway. We are not building an expressway.'

'Well what in hell are you building then?' By that time I was was getting a little testy myself.

'It's a major arterial.'

'Oh. Okay, why can't you build your major arterial within the existing right of way?'

'It's not a standard road.'

'Well, what's a standard road?'

'A standard road is. . . .' And he launched into a long technical description.

"I kept trying to get him to answer my questions directly. He kept avoiding them. I was getting madder. And he was getting madder. Mrs. Van Goerder was getting madder. And the supervisors were getting in the car. The other ladies had each nailed one and had begun to state their own complaints. By the way, that's a good technique, but of course we didn't realize it at the time. About then Mr. Wilson said:

'You're getting too excited.'

'I'm not half as excited as I'm going to get.'

'Well, you'd better watch your blood pressure.'

'And you'd better watch your ulcers.'

"Then Mrs. Van Goerder joined the fray and hollered, 'But Mr. Wilson, *WHAT ABOUT MY GARDEN?*' To which he replied:

'GET BACK IN YOUR KITCHEN, LADY, AND LET ME BUILD MY ROAD!'

"Well — that did it."

What followed was a battle with the County of San Mateo that still isn't over. Claire Dedrick was propelled into the fight despite herself.

"In a way, it all started that day on the road. Because until Don Wilson lost his temper at Mrs. Van Goerder, there wasn't really any opposition to his road. He created it. And that's a good rule of strategy: Never lose your temper. When you let your anger say something dumb, you can count on being made to look foolish. That's just what happened. My husband, Kent, put Wilson's very words on a glorious big sign which we nailed to the back of a county sign down at the edge of the project. Later we

"In a way, it all started that day on the road. Because until Don Wilson lost his temper at Mrs. Van Goerder, there wasn't really any opposition to his road. He created it. And that's a good rule of strategy: Never lose your temper."

found out he had to drive by that sign every day on his way to and from work."

The proposed road project was one of only two or three public works projects in the county at that time, and was at least in part an effort to keep a staff of over twenty engineers and a big budget intact. The bond issue for road construction, of which the Alameda project was originally a part, had been defeated at the polls 4 to 1 a few years before. At the same time, less than a mile to the west, the state division of highways was at work on Junipero Serra freeway, a new interstate route intended to carry high speed traffic in the same direction. Moreover, an incorporated enclave called Atherton, which accounted for a half mile of the project near the middle of its length, would have no part of widening the road. Though the engineers knew this and must have realized it would create a bottleneck that would void all their efforts, the local residents at first did not. At the time, all Claire Dedrick and her neighbors knew was that in less than six months, the county was going to lop off their front yards, and in some cases, their homes.

"We were damn mad. And from then on, we didn't spend a whole lot of time in our kitchens!"

Getting Organized

"Very early in the fight we did two things that turned out to be exactly right, though we didn't know it at the time. None of us had ever done anything like this before in our lives. One was to find an experienced attorney who could contribute his time. We got Ted Carlstrom and he was just great."

Carlstrom made their legal position clear from the beginning. They didn't have one. The Public Works Act of 1911 and the right of eminent domain were the reasons. In San Mateo as well as other California counties, the board of supervisors establishes an assessment district which consists of the voters directly affected by the public works project. Not only were the residents along the Alameda to lose their front yards, they were also to pay for the privilege.

The county would attempt to buy the land, offering prices that were variable depending on the savvy of the owner. Failing a purchase, the property would be condemned. Residents' only hope lay in the public hearings that were required by law following the board's public notice of its intent to form the assessment district. At that time, opposing residents could file a formal protest in the form of a petition, which the board could override with a 4/5 vote. Since the board seemed to be unsympathetic there was little indication that such a vote would be difficult to muster. Though they were to delay the formation of the assessment district until late that year, it was clear that something had to be done to influence votes on the board of supervisors.

"And that was the other thing we did right. We got an inside track with the board. One of its members, Bud Harrison, had been appointed by Governer Brown to fill a vacant seat and was up for re-election in June. He faced tough opposition. We thought if we could interest him in our plight, we might get one of the votes we needed to avoid a veto and in return give him the visibility and good-guy status he needed. It was a slim chance, but worth trying. So I called him."

He went for it. That same evening, at a meeting of the Menlo-Atherton Democratic Club, incumbent Harrison fielded questions about the Alameda road project from a stacked audience of residents while the other candidates for the board sat by silent. At that meeting, Harrison promised that the project would be taken up at the next board meeting.

It was. At their next session, the San Mateo Board of Supervisors directed the county engineer to hold a public meeting for the purpose of informing residents about the project in detail.

"It was at that May 3rd public meeting that we had our next lucky break thanks to the engineers. There were about 250 people there. At the end of a tedious question and answer session during which he was obliged to listen to complaints from practically everyone in the place, deputy County Engineer Sid Cantwell was asked by someone if hearing so much opposition to the project had made any difference to him. Now Sid didn't want to be rude. He tried to point out that the situation was not at all unusual to him. But he was clumsy:

'I've been to many such meetings with many such people. What you're saying, I've heard a thousand times before. To me, you're just a sea of faces. . . .'

"God! Talk about a recruitment device. We were solid as rocks after that!

"A handful of us went home that same night and talked things over. Ted (Carlstrom) had advised us to draw up a set of resolutions that would state our objectives clearly, form a committee of all the residents and elect officers. We worked on the resolutions that very night.

Though this sign was eventually torn down by the engineer who is quoted on it (and had to drive by it every day on his way to work), his remark lived on as the battle cry of the residents of Menlo Park, California who fought his road-widening project. What his opponents may have lacked in experience, they more than made up for in imagination and wit.

"Then we called another meeting — without the engineers — and we formally created the Committee for the Improvement of the Alameda. We also adopted the resolutions we had written and elected just two officers. Phil Brown was made chairman and Tim Brush treasurer. We assessed each household $20 and everyone paid right up. We must have walked out of there with $1800 in cash. And except for a couple of big gifts later on, that's how we raised all our money. A few of us went around door to door later and collected from the ones who couldn't come to the meeting. We covered the whole length of the project — almost three miles — and for two blocks in either direction.

"We organized block by block. Each block had a captain who was responsible for about 50 households. Not just the 198 on the Alameda, but the people on the cross streets too. That brought the total up to around 2000."

Not only had the county planned to widen the Alameda itself, but the plan also called for going up the side streets for a distance of one lot with a 60-foot right of way. The project would also have severely reduced parking at a local shopping district. So virtually everyone in the area had a reason for supporting the Committee — and did.

The block-and-captain system was both the device for dividing work and also the method for communication. Bulletins were printed by mimeograph and taken around to each captain, who was to see that they got the rest of the way, usually via the children.

"I suppose the most famous bulletin was our warning about the county agents. Even before the assessment district was formed, they hired road agents who went around and tried to get owners to sell property for the right of way. They were very smooth characters. And they got a commission on each sale, so

"To arms! To arms! The bull-dozers are coming!"

Drawing by Robt. Day; ©1966, The New Yorker Magazine, Inc.

they didn't discourage easy. We found out about all this and sent around a bulletin. The headline was: 'Warning! Road Agents Are in the Area!' Every time there was to be a meeting, or we found out about a new development, we sent out a bulletin."

Going Public

At the May 3 public meeting, the county engineer had shown residents drawings that for the first time revealed the new road in frightening detail. Later calculations were to show that an average of 96 percent of the area between homes on opposite sides of the street was to be paved. The average setback was to be 6.5 feet. Hundreds of trees would be removed. A 14-foot-wide concrete divider was to run the length of the project separating 4 lanes of traffic and limiting left turns. Down the center of the divider were to be located power transmission lines — a particularly despised feature.

"At that time in this county, or in California for that matter, putting power lines underground was a laugh! Nobody was undergrounding 60kv lines. These were 60-kilovolt transmission lines, mind you, not just local lines. Well, our attorney was hooked on power lines. So he urged us to insist on undergrounding those lines. As a result, two of our most important resolutions were that we would not object to any road that could be built within the existing right of way; and that the power lines had to go underground.

"By June we were organized. We had everyone calling the supervisors and writing letters and we were generally raising a lot of fuss. But we couldn't get any press."

What followed were the Burma Shave signs. The need for some kind of newsworthy gimmick was pointed out by Bruce Brugmann who is now the publisher of *The San Francisco Bay Guardian* ("Print the Truth and Raise Hell"). At that time he was a reporter for *The Redwood City Tribune* and was sympathetic when he heard Claire Dedrick's story. He promised to bring out a photographer if she could provide the reason.

Kent Dedrick, Claire's physicist husband, who by now was as involved in the fight as everyone else in the neighborhood, is credited with having first thought of borrowing Burma Shave's famous signs for the purpose of fighting the county. The idea was an inspiration to his wife.

"On a Saturday morning, with a good deal of beer flowing, we laid out a hundred-plus plywood panels that had been donated, and using everybody's leftover latex paint and some rollers, we painted backgrounds. As they dried, we sent them up to where the sign painters were doing the lettering. We wrote the words on the spot. Most of them were unprintable but hilarious.

"Before the road fight, we didn't know a soul here and neither did anybody else. The threat of losing the neighborhood everyone had taken for granted, brought us together and created a bond that is still strong." The making of the Burma Shave signs was one of the first of many community gatherings. Claire Dedrick is the lady on the right in the lower photograph. Val Sassone, left, organized communications.

They pay you money
for your land
and take it back
with the other hand.
Bum Shave!

House to house
for 100 feet
all you'll see
is white concrete.

Road agents stay away.
My dog bit one
and died today.

Junipero Serra
a mile away.
They want this one anyway.

With a concrete divider
of 14 feet
how will you turn
across this street?

Atherton border
4 lanes to 2.
Tighten your seat belt
the jolt's on you.

Rural beauty
will be depleted
if we're wall-to-wall
concreted.

By then it was July and the ground was hard as a rock. Crews worked most of that night digging post holes. By the next morning there were 120 signs waiting on the Alameda.

"That morning traffic was at a standstill. It was just jammed. The photographer came and took pictures. People were stopping and laughing and backing up. Some would turn off and go around the block for a second look. The cops were there but they couldn't do a thing. And besides, they thought it was funny. Well, that's what got us in the papers.

"After that, we started visiting editors with more of the story. We tried hard to impress them. That's where the hundred-foot rag comes in — that 100 feet of torn-up-and-sewn-together bedsheet. The ladies got together and did that, and it was 110 feet actually. By that time, we had done a lot of homework. We knew exactly where that right of way would go and

Though part of the fight against widening the Alameda was waged with tongue in cheek, it was deadly serious. Residents were accused of fighting "progress." Actually, they were fighting for their homes and a semi-rural neighborhood which would have been permanently eradicated by the proposed project. Though their prospects for success were dim, residents managed to avoid sounding desperate. Instead, they exposed serious flaws in the county's plan using a combination of gentle ridicule and hard facts.

ODD BODKINS - - - - - - -

- - - - - - - **BY DAN O'NEILL**

what it would do. We stretched that sheet out along the edge of the right of way, and then took pictures and a statement we had written down to the *Palo Alto Times*. The editor ran our pictures and statement on the editorial page, and that was when the letters to the editor started coming in."

Doing Battle

1966 was election year. Though Harrison had won his June race, he faced a run-off against Supervisor Robert St. Clair in the November elections. St. Clair's sympathies were well known. It was important to retain Harrison. The strategy of the board seemed to be to stall for time. The strategy of the Committee was to raise hell and attend every meeting.

"All during this period the board was continually calling meetings and we were continually packing those meetings. We would get on the phone and call all the little old ladies who didn't have rides. Peggy Brown and Val Sassone and Penny Peterson and all the gals would collect up a carful of ladies and dragoon everyone else. The board chamber holds about 60 people. Well, you'd walk in there and we'd have the chamber filled and people out in the hall. There was never a meeting during that whole fight that we didn't have that hall over half full.

"We had a friend in the county office who would tell us every time the name Alameda de las Pulgas appeared on an agenda. And every time, we'd be there. We attended dozens and dozens of board meetings and hearings. We could rustle up 35 people with no notice at all, day or night. And that's important. They were really frightened of us. They kept trying to talk us out of our position but we had defined it in those resolutions and had agreed we would not settle for less."

On the first Tuesday of November, Harrison lost to St. Clair, though he would remain in office until January first. Later in November, after months of delay, the board of supervisors served notice of its intent to form the assessment district. Now it was possible for the Committee to file its petition of protest. Ted Carlstrom drew it up.

"Ninety seven percent of the proposed assessment district signed the protest. Now that's a little spooky to a board of supervisors. It meant they would have to condemn 192 of 198 parcels. It meant all that legal action. It meant they were opposing a fairly large block of the community. Because even though they wouldn't admit that the rest of our people existed because they didn't live on the road, they really did know they were there. They noticed them!"

What followed was a public hearing on December 6, at which the board was to make its ruling concerning the Committee's protest.

"Well, the logic we used went this way — and I think it could be thought of as another basic rule of strategy: We are the public. Our only legal recourse was to file that lawsuit."

"It was the critical part of the whole fight. We'd done one hell of a lot of hard work. We were really in a bad spot: Bud (Supervisor Harrison) was going off the board. Finally, at the meeting, they made the following agreement with us: The road would be restricted to a 60-foot right of way, 4 lanes within that width; there would be no concrete divider; and the power lines would be put underground. That agreement passed the board by a vote of 3 to 1 with one abstention.

"Now this was simply a routine vote of the board. Then they very carefully explained to us that they would next adopt a resolution of public intent and necessity, which would form the assessment district and override our protest — in order to build the road we had all just agreed on. Which they proceeded to do. But what was binding on the board was not their agreement with us. What was binding was their resolution to override our protest. That was their only legal action. What it meant was that they could ignore their agreement with us and build anything they damn pleased. But at the time, we thought we had won!"

It was lawyer Carlstrom who left the hearing that day and went home feeling uneasy. The next day he called Claire Dedrick to tell her he had decided they still weren't out of the woods.

"Right away, we called another meeting of the Committee. Now the statute of limitations on this board action was 30 days. This meant that if we did not file a lawsuit to contest the assessment district by January 5, we would never be able to do such a thing. We'd have lost our only chance.

"We were ready to sue, but we worried about it. Would they or would they not honor their agreement with us? If we went ahead and filed the suit, would they harden up and fight against us?

"Well, the logic we used went this way — and I think it could be thought of as another basic rule of strategy: We are the public. Our only legal recourse was to file that lawsuit. We weren't assuming that the board would be dishonest, but we'd have been irresponsible if we didn't protect our people in every way possible.

"So we wrote a letter to the board saying essentially those things. We thanked them for their willingness to make the agreement with us — and then on the 5th of January, we filed a lawsuit."

Fights like the one over the Alameda are never finally won. "You can lose conclusively, but no victory is ever final."

Ted Carlstrom telephoned the county's attorney, hired to handle legal work for the yet-unformed assessment district, to inform him of the Committee's decision.

"When Ted told him what we'd done, he was just furious! And it was then that we knew we were right. They were absolutely going to chuck the whole affair! No question about it. They would have gone ahead with their original road design and every bloody thing we had done all year would have been lost. Ted called me back afterward and said: 'Well, we sure did the right thing!' "

The county's attempt to out-maneuver the Committee had failed. The lawsuit had the effect of reopening discussion concerning the road's specifications. It forced the county to offer a compromise design in which the existing right of way was increased by ten feet — to 70 feet. The residents met and voted to accept the county's offer. The lawsuit was thus settled out of court. Construction of the new road was divided into three phases and phase one, accounting for approximately a third of the total length, has been completed.

Aftermath

Claire Dedrick, who began by trying to keep out of the fight, is now an inspired and full-time conservation activist, and has gone on to wage other battles. Which just goes to show — you can never be quite sure what will come from a conservation fight. The effects are seldom limited to the turf over which battle is done. And it never leaves the combatants in exactly the same state as at the beginning. In fact, you could extrapolate Dedrick's Law from her experience: Lives are changed in direct proportion to their involvement.

She makes it clear that fights like the one over the Alameda are never finally won. "You can *lose* conclusively, but no victory is ever final."

As this is written, there are signs that the county of San Mateo intends soon to complete phases two and three of the Alameda widening project. It looks as though another fight, or another round in the same fight, is ahead. Claire Dedrick and her roadfighting neighbors are ready. They regret their 70-foot compromise. Accidents on the completed portion of the road are on the increase. Traffic anticipated in the county's projections has never materialized. This time, the engineers may not get their road.

When asked what was most important in their fight against the road, Claire Dedrick describes something that sounds like being stubborn and thorough at the same time.

"We worked like crazy. We never missed a meeting — theirs or ours. We did homework — theirs and ours. We did traffic counts. We didn't trust theirs. We did tree counts. We did pedestrian counts. We even counted bicycles. Kent (Dedrick) made a study of power lines in the area and discovered there was a loop near here which reinforced our argument for undergrounding. We measured the setback on every parcel to arrive at that 6.5 median figure. We knew where every bulldozer cut would be made and how many trucks would be required to haul away the fill. We hired our own firm of engineers to design a road that would carry the county's traffic estimates within the existing right of way. We drew up tables and charts for presentation at hearings and board meetings. We never let go.

"But you know, we never really minded all that hard work. Somehow, in spite of it all, we managed to have a hell of a good time.

"And it turned us into a neighborhood, besides!"

The two diagrams below indicate the scale of the road widening project along the Alameda, but fail to show its impact on the semi-rural road. Neither drawing is to scale. The widest set of parallel lines shown in the street map directly below are what the county engineer intended to build. The dark line in the center indicates the original 30-foot-wide roadway.

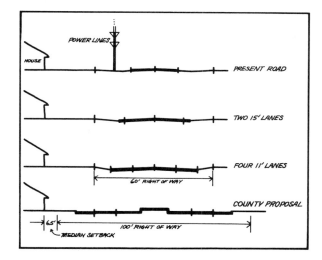

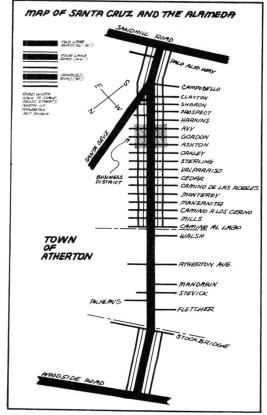

The Seemingly Miraculous Survival of the Udalls Cove Marsh

The Huck Finn scene you see above is taking place within the city limits of New York. Besides providing relief for asphalt-tired eyes and entertainment for small boys, the Udalls Cove marsh is one of the few remaining saltwater tidal marshes left on the eastern coast. Over half of these life-generating habitats have been dredged, filled, or otherwise destroyed.

If you're one of the tens of thousands of commuters who ride the Long Island Railroad's Port Washington line, you have a chance to view one of nature's most intricate ecological creations. In Udalls Cove, on the Little Neck Bay side of the peninsula that was the "West Egg" of F. Scott Fitzgerald's *Great Gatsby,* is a saltwater marsh. Teeming with fish and fowl, Udalls Cove is one of the few pleasant sights offered to the Long Island commuter. But the commuter must look quickly and in the right direction: on the other side of the tracks sprawls an auto graveyard.

The seemingly miraculous survival of the Udalls Cove marsh on the very edge of New York City, when such marshes have been dredged and filled all along the Atlantic Coast, is largely due to the persistent efforts of one 65-year-old woman. Aurora Gareiss was 14 years younger when she began her conservation battle.

In 1960 Aurora Gareiss began writing letters, asking that the marsh be preserved in its natural state. She didn't know who to write to, so she wrote to everybody she could think of.

The Gareiss residence in Douglaston, New York, overlooks Udalls Cove. From an aging pier in her back yard, Mrs. Gareiss can commune with ducks, kingfishers, snowy egrets, and other sojourning species in this way station on the North American flyway. During the 1960's, she could also watch as the 100-acre marsh was being gradually filled with refuse. The marsh seemed to lie in the path of inexorable forces. Various uses for the area were discussed: boat marinas, golf courses, and parking lots were suggested as uses of the future.

In 1960 Aurora Gareiss began writing letters, asking that the marsh be preserved in its natural state. She didn't know who might help save Udalls Cove, so she wrote to everybody she could think of.

For the first nine years she was largely ignored. Her legislative representatives did not respond. The U.S. Fish and Wildlife people told her the marsh was too small for them. The U.S. Army Corps of Engineers issued an order to restore the marsh, but made no effort to enforce the order or to prevent filling under the Refuse Act of 1899.

The Inescapable Dilemma

In 1969 the Village of Great Neck Estates, which owns 57 acres of the marsh, decided to fill it in and make it into a golf course. Almost desperate, Mrs. Gareiss stood on a hot September day of that year beside the car of Philip Finkelstein, local chairman of Mayor John V. Lindsay's Urban Task Force. Confronting Finkelstein, as he hurried from one engagement to drive to another, Aurora thrust into his hand a sheaf of marsh photographs taken by her husband Herbert. "You must save this marsh!" she insisted. Startled, Finkelstein mumbled that he would call her, then drove off into the smog.

Finkelstein did contact Mrs. Gareiss. Moved by her plea, he insisted on one thing before taking action: that Mrs. Gareiss organize a force for the marsh. "If you can get ten people together," he told her, "I'll come down and tell you how to fight this battle."

As an article in the 1973 yearbook issue of the *National Fisherman* put it: "The inescapable dilemma of all conservation movements was hitting home to Mrs. Gareiss. Those who would rather move quietly among the reeds and through the waters must get into the thick of political persuasion and organization."

EDITOR'S NOTE

The following was written by Homer Page and appeared under · the title "View from New England" in Not Man Apart, *vol. I, no. 10, October 1971. Reprinted with permission of Friends of the Earth.*

WHAT'S IN A COASTAL SWAMP?

Tidal wetlands are by far the most important biological regions along our coastlines and contain, in fact, the most productive soil on earth. Sadly, they are also the most benighted of our lands. It is estimated that an acre of salt marsh produces as much food as an acre of prime beef cattle grazing land, and is equal in protein production to seven acres of good Kansas wheatland. Fish amounting to two-thirds of the value of the entire Atlantic Coast catch depend upon the eastern tidal marshlands for their survival. Yet from 1960 to 1965, commercial catches of Atlantic coastal fish declined as much as 50%. Why? To a major degree because dredging, draining, and filling had destroyed about one-half of the original wetlands by 1955, and one-fifth of the remainder have succumbed since then, defaced by refuse, smothered by fill, and polluted and paved to death.

The salt marsh, long considered a nuisance by the uninformed, is one of the most dynamic ecosystems to be found anywhere. Grasses growing on the boggy ground die and decay during the winter to provide nutrients for the sun-warmed, saline waters. Algae consuming this food are eaten in turn by the myriads of tiny fish and shellfish who then fall prey to larger fish, waterfowl, and aquatic mammals. This cycle of air, land, water, and living things interacts continuously with other cycles of sunlight and seasons, tides and temperature, to form a delicate inner harmony that has taken thousands of years of evolution to create, and only a

Udalls Cove, in the words of a *New York Times* article, was viewed by some as "a dismal, brackish swampland, a breeding place for mosquitos, gnats and rodents."

She responded by calling Ralph Kamhi, a neighbor and fellow bird watcher. The two of them wrote letters to other neighbors, and got 20 people together for a meeting. True to his word, Finkelstein appeared and spoke, and a local professor lectured on the essentials of wetland ecology. The Udalls Cove Preservation Committee was born, with Aurora Gareiss as its president.

Swamps suffer from a bad public image. Tidal wetlands such as Udalls Cove are not only the most productive ecosystems on earth; marine fish, migratory birds, and a host of other creatures depend on marshes for their survival. Marshes are beautiful, too, in the intricate profusion of their life. Yet Udalls Cove, in the words of a *New York Times* article, was viewed by some as "a dismal, brackish swampland, a breeding place for mosquitoes, gnats and rodents."

The Udalls Cove Preservation Committee set out to acquaint their neighbors with the marsh. Presentations, using maps, diagrams, photos, and slides, were given before local organizations. A local teacher took children on nature walks through the marsh. An anonymous $900 donation financed a mailing of copies of the November 1969 *Audubon* magazine, which featured marshland ecology, to every household in Great Neck Estates.

An Unusual Confrontation

These initial efforts set the stage for an unusual confrontation. Douglaston is not the sort of community from which acts of civil disobedience usually emerge. In the words of Mrs. Gareiss, "We are an upper middle-class residential community, unique in New York City. All one-family homes with curved streets, lovely trees, on the North Shore of Queens County. The people are mostly lawyers, dentists, doctors, high school and college teachers. As we are a peninsula, we are surrounded by water. On one side the Cove and marsh, and the other side Little Neck Bay." These people wouldn't hit the streets and put their bodies in the path of dump trucks, right?

Wrong. On February 6, 1970, dozens of dump trucks suddenly appeared, laden with fill intended to convert part of the Udalls Cove into a parking lot. By noon, a small band of women were standing, arms linked, between trucks and cove. Then the men came, leaving their jobs and putting their reputations on the line for Udalls Cove. "We confronted police from two counties," Mrs. Gareiss wrote, "and almost were arrested."

For six hours the doughty band of suburbanites held their line. Finally the dumpers agreed to knock off for the day. The Udalls Cove protectors moved swiftly to get a court injunction against further dumping.

Press coverage of this confrontation greatly increased support for preservation of the Cove. Less than a month later, the Committee invited everyone from local communities to take a "Walk on the Marsh." Over 300 people came. One of them, an American Indian, was approached by a television interviewer. "What should we do to save the marsh?" the interviewer asked the Indian. "Do?" the Indian replied, amazed. "Leave the marsh alone, and it will do for itself what it has done before for all time!"

Later in the spring of 1970, the Udalls Cove Preservation Committee invited all the residents around the Cove to the first annual marsh cleanup. Hundreds showed up and pulled eighteen autos, a hundred tires, dozens of shopping carts, and several tons of other trash from the ooze. This, perhaps, was the day on which salvation of the Cove became certain. Neighbors who have had the sharing — and back-wrenching — experience of cleaning up a natural area together will not easily let it be destroyed.

Neighbors who have had the sharing — and back-wrenching — experience of cleaning up a natural area together will not easily let it be destroyed.

hydraulic dredge to destroy. With its destruction goes not only an indispensable nursery for young fish, but also a bird refuge, a wildlife habitat, a natural erosion control, a storm buffer for the mainland, and one of the most subtle, intricate, and lovely works of nature.

Local townsfolk take to the streets. When the Udalls Cove marsh was threatened by a landfill operation (to make a parking lot), the residents of Queens and Nassau counties bordering the Cove staged a public outing at the marsh to attract attention and gain support. Below, residents walk the streets of Little Neck, Queens, on their way to the marsh. Over 300 attended. (Photo credit: *The New York Times*/ Ernest Sisto)

On the theory that vigilance is enhanced by hard work, the Udalls Cove Preservation Committee each year stages a marsh cleanup for the purpose of rallying public interest and removing accumulated trash. At the first of these, workers dragged no less than 18 derelict automobiles from their muddy graves, not to mention tires and shopping carts. Locals provided the labor, all of it volunteer, and much of it from neighboring high schools.

This is Aurora Gareiss, who started it all. Though the object of her attention is not visible to us, it is probably safe to assume that she is watching for shorebirds, or land developers — or both.

A Cooperative Effort

The citizens of Great Neck Estates voted against construction of a golf course on marshland owned by the Village. This left the fate of the marsh in limbo. The administration of New York City Mayor John V. Lindsay was receptive to the idea of preserving the marsh; but most of the Cove lay in Nassau County.

The Preservation Committee persevered, and in December of 1972 was victorious. As Ralph Kamhi, vice-president of the committee, reported: "Three years and two months after it was formed, the Udalls Cove Preservation Committee got it all together. At City Hall last Thursday, privately owned and city-owned properties in Douglaston-Little Neck were formally remapped by the New York City Board of Estimates as a new city nature and wildlife sanctuary."

In announcing the new Udalls Cove Preserve, Mayor Lindsay said: "The preservation of the Cove represents a cooperative effort between New York City and the Village of Great Neck Estates. In all, the Udalls Cove Wildlife Preserve will cover 91 acres, including 33 acres within New York City."

Someone asked Aurora Gareiss if this meant the end of the Udalls Cove Preservation Committee. Silently she turned her gaze to an old fill site, and to the place that would have been a golf course but for the Committee. "To Aurora Gareiss watchers," wrote Ralph Kamhi, "the message was clear: for one who calls home Bit of Bay, the marsh and its creatures are going to need a lot of looking after. The end was not yet in sight."

"He was right, we are still fighting!" Aurora Gareiss wrote in October, 1974. "We are now in the process of fighting against the Department of Housing and Urban Development and the Town of North Hempstead, Nassau County, who want to build low-income housing right on top of the best fresh water stream that feeds into our cove. Also, on the New York City side we are trying to preserve a necessary watershed from development. Definitely, we must watchdog the area. Last week I had to call the Coast Guard, the police, and the sanitation department. Some vandal had dumped a Volkswagen into our creek."

"What should we do to save the marsh?" the interviewer asked the Indian. "Do?" the Indian replied, amazed. "Leave the marsh alone, and it will do for itself what it has done before for all time!"

The saltwater marshes teem with life. Tall grass hides the skittery muskrat and the nesting red-winged blackbird. Below in the rich muck, fish and crabs are spawned. This is a womb of the sea man must not disturb. If it is lost, billions of marine creatures will also be lost and so, eventually, shall we.
— From the Long Island Press, June 1, 1971

How Are You Going to Fight Blackberry Jam?

This cartoon from the November 6, 1973 issue of the Eureka *Daily Standard* exaggerates only somewhat a county-wide wrangle of the first magnitude. The issue: whether or not to permit the U.S. Corps of Engineers to dam the Mad River and inundate one of northwest California's coastal valleys.

Up the Mad River from Eureka, the capital of Humboldt County in northern California, lies Butler Valley. The Mad meanders through the Valley, creating spawning grounds for salmon and steelhead, and deep holes well stocked with summertime skinnydippers. Maple Creek, ghost of the mill town that stripped out the redwoods and Douglas fir decades ago, decays as the new forest emerges. A handful of year-round residents graze cattle, pick blackberries, fish, and in general cohabit this sylvan retreat with the peregrine falcons, bald eagles, and other untamed creatures.

Until the fall of 1970, everybody in Humboldt County— with the probable exception of Harvey Maples, Butler Valley resident and last surviving speaker of the Whilkut Indian language — either wanted the U. S. Army Corps of Engineers to cover Butler Valley with 550,000 acre-feet of water, or were willing to let the Butler Valley Dam go up without a squabble.

"They said, 'Well, if you were standing right here in about three years, you'd be looking up at the bottom of a fisherman's boat, about 150 feet over your head.'

And I said: 'Wha-a-a-at!' "

Then, true to the tradition started by the crusty prospectors who had named the Mad River after a furious argument that had attended their crossing of it, somebody got mad — vocally, insistently mad. What followed was an increasingly colorful, vituperative melee, underlain by some even-handed rationality and careful political work.

The opening scene of this rural environmental drama occurred amid the blackberry brambles of Butler Valley, where an unusual woman was doing an ordinary thing: teaching school.

"I was teaching the experimental science program at Maple Creek school," recalled Donna Hankins, a bundle of energy in a thick sweater. "We were on the playground one day, and I was calling the kids' attention to the view — to the way the beautiful river had cut the valley.

"The kids said, 'Well, you'd better enjoy it now.'

"I said, 'What do you mean?'

"They said, 'Well, if you were standing right here in about three years, you'd be looking up at the bottom of a fisherman's boat, about 150 feet over your head.'

"And I said: 'Wha-a-a-at!' "

Donna Hankins was raised on an Iowa farm, where she learned the regenerative value of solitude in nature. She is very insistent, and very emotional; one might think she is also impulsive and irrational, until discovering that she is a scientist with a persistent, tenacious character. She is, in short, just the sort of person required to get environmentalists interested in an issue they might otherwise ignore. As another opponent of Butler Valley Dam put it, the anti-dam campaign was like a relay race. Donna Hankins carried the baton from the starting line.

Humboldt County traditionally has been dominated by the lumber industry. In recent years, the growth of Humboldt State University in Arcata and the College of the Redwoods south of Eureka has introduced a large academic population into this timberman's preserve. The university community in Arcata supported a number of small conservation groups, which in 1970 were beginning to band together to form the Northcoast Environmental Center. To Arcata came Donna, seeking converts to her campaign against the Butler Valley Dam.

"I'd go up to people: 'Hey, you've gotta listen to me! You can stop this stupid dam.'

EDITOR'S NOTE

The following is excerpted from an article which appeared originally in the Osprey, student newspaper at Humboldt State University, for October 31, 1973, an edition devoted largely to the arguments concerning the Butler Valley Dam. It was written by Barry Allen and raises in dramatic fashion the question of the conservation of historic and human resources.

MY PAST IS BURIED IN BUTLER VALLEY

When discussion turns to the proposed Butler Valley Dam, ecological and economic questions nearly always arise, but there is a historical consideration to be made as well.

Ancient home of the Whilkut tribe, the valley is dotted with long abandoned village sites, burial and hunting grounds, and areas held sacred by the tribe and its descendants. The Whilkut have a long history in the valley dating back nearly 5,000 years. Only one member of the tribe — Harvey Maples — still lives in the valley. Although he is almost 80 years old, he still lives alone in a trackless part of the valley, miles from the closest road.

Maples has been involved in Humboldt County history throughout his life. As the county's first pilot, he made the Northcoast's first landing when he landed his frail airplane on a Samoa beach. In addition to this active past, Maples is probably the only person who retains knowledge of many of his tribe's traditional skills.

Maples' land is only a fraction of the area he once held — perhaps ten acres remain of more than one hundred granted him in the Allotment Act of 1880. The act was a government attempt to make restitution for the land grabs and violence visited upon the tribe in the years between 1850 and 1880. During that period, the main trail between the mines in Weaverville and the coast ran through Butler Valley, and the White men using the trail were less than fair with the Whilkut. At various times, Indians were killed, their lands taken and villages destroyed.

This slaughter, along with new illnesses introduced by the White man, drove the Whilkut from their ancient homeland.

As the last remaining member of his tribe, Maples is the only person who knows the locations of most of the historically significant sites in the valley.

Once the locations of 17 village sites were quite easy to find. The traditional site for a covered, pit style home was on the bank of a stream, close to fishing and hunting grounds. But today, only Harvey Maples knows their whereabouts — and he isn't talking.

Why? Because following repeated instances of grave robbing and disputes between Indians and the state over archaelogical rights to the burial and village sites, Harvey Maples has quit telling or showing anyone where these sites are. Without his help and guidance, finding the sites is impossible, for their locations are mapped mostly in Maples' mind, the physical areas having been long abandoned to become overgrown and indistinguishable from their surroundings.

That these sites should be preserved is a widely agreed upon fact; the means to their salvation is not. Although several documents dealing with the Butler Valley Dam project mention plans to excavate ruins and "salvage valuable Whilkut Indian sites," not everyone agrees that excavation and salvage are the proper methods to use.

The strongest objection comes from those with the most to lose — the last few direct descendants of the tribe, who do not want their ancestral villages and burial grounds dug up for any reasons, least of all the White man's. This small group has some strong legal tools to back their beliefs. Among these are a

"They'd say, 'Hey, go away Hankins, out! Wasn't that decided back in 1968 or something, by Congress? There's a document that thick up in the library.'"

The conservationists were busy fighting a whole system of proposed dams and aqueducts which would draw off the waters of Northern California for the benefit of Southern California. They were not interested in the Butler Valley Dam, a strictly local-use project. That is, they weren't interested in Butler Valley until Donna's insistence induced a few of them to read the Corps of Engineers' report on the project.

Calling the Colonel's Bluff

Chuck Kennedy, an owner of the Arcata Transit Authority (which deals in bicycling and backpacking supplies), had been active in a number of local conservation issues. He recalled that the Corps' report was the thing that woke him to the Butler Valley Dam issue: "I read it, and got some other people to read it, and that was the beginning. I found out what a pile of baloney the whole thing was."

Kennedy explained that the Butler Valley Dam was supposed to be justified on three grounds: water supply, recreation, and flood protection. The water supply figures, he noted, were based on the needs generated by an impossibly large population growth, and by pulp and aluminum industrial development which was not certain to occur. To get their recreation figures, Kennedy said, the Corps had every one of their massive population visiting the lake six times a year. And to get figures for money saved by flood prevention, the report writers assumed a tremendous flood; then had that flood, raging down an undammed Mad River, wipe out those industries which they had earlier assumed would be built because of the dam!

At a Mad River Symposium co-organized by Donna Hankins early in 1971, Colonel Roberts of the Corps of Engineers confronted some conservationists who were ready with probing questions. Kennedy recalled, "I started asking key questions about the report in the symposium. Colonel Roberts had to answer them; and he didn't *have* the answers. And he kept fudging, and we kept pushing. Finally he challenged the fledgling Northcoast Environmental Center. He said, 'We'll be glad to have a workshop and sit down with you, and we can answer your questions, if you will organize these workshops.' Looking back on it, I think this was his bluff."

The Local Cost

Meanwhile, Ray Peart, chairman of the county board of supervisors, had changed his mind about the dam. This event was notable because by simple majority vote, the five supervisors were to decide whether or not there was to be a Butler Valley Dam.

Peart had supported the dam in his campaign for supervisor. Then, as the facts were brought out, Peart saw that the dam would be both more costly and more environmentally damaging than he had expected. He first became undecided, and later was the only supervisor to publicly speak against the dam. He also began maneuvering within the county government to stop the dam, looking for ways to overcome the fact that three supervisors remained solidly in favor of it.

Peart concentrated on the local costs of building the dam, which were being clarified gradually by the Corps as the time slated for construction approached. "Local share costs kept rising," he recalled. "They went from 13 million, to 33, then to 48 million — that was our local share. You have to pay all the operating and maintenance costs after it's built; you pay about 50 percent of the construction costs. You pay this over a period of 100 years."

Ray Peart impressed his fellow supervisors with the truths that the dam not only would transform Butler Valley for all time; it would mortgage the county's financial future for 100 years. "They always give you today's prices," he said of the Corps. "Finally I asked the county public works department, 'What's the total local commitment in dollars over 100 years?' Public works came in with 305 million dollars, which blew everybody's mind."

The Facts Reach the Public

The Northcoast Environmental Center held seven workshops on Butler Valley Dam, at two-week intervals, in the fall of 1971. Simultaneously, a citizens' advisory committee of 20 members was chosen by the county supervisors to pass judgment for them on the Butler Valley Dam.

The Corps of Engineers tried to evade participation in the workshops, saying that they would deal with the citizens' advisory committee. Chuck Kennedy, a member of the advisory committee, initiated advisory committee endorsement of the workshops. The Corps, because of Colonel Roberts' earlier words, was then locked into a series of informal hearings which it could not control.

Chaired by an impartial citizen, the workshops involved representatives of local and state agencies as well as a wide range of local groups and citizens. Each workshop covered a certain topic area: wildlife habitat, recreation, flood control, geology, and so on. Opponents of the dam presented expert testimony on all these topics, drawing much of their expertise from the Humboldt State University community. By the last one, the Corps was committed to doing a new, much improved environmental impact statement.

county ordinance and a (state) senate bill which call for consultation with and clearance from the Northwest Indian Cemetery Protective Association (NICPA) before the go-ahead can be given on any project which would endanger areas that hold historic or sacred significance for Native Americans.

NICPA was formed about 3 years ago by Milton Marks of Orick. Marks realized that he and other Native Americans needed such a group when he witnessed two men, with the full legal backing of the state, exhume his grandmother's grave.

To a certain extent, the NICPA's opposition to the Butler Valley Dam project is a front for an emotional position difficult for many non-Indians to understand. Though the opposition to destruction, excavation, archaelogical "salvage" or inundation of historic and sacred areas is an honest and true position, it is at best only a small facet of the Native American's attitude toward the land.

For most Indian tribes, the land and all its creatures are the embodiment of their religion. The birds, fish, and animals are the Indian's brothers; the land, his father; the natural phenomena of wind, rain, sun, moon, sky and sea, his gods and spirits.

Thus, the Indian does not need the Anglo's reasons for opposing a lake which will cover and destroy his land — all he needs to know is that it will destroy his brother.

Their new impact statement drew on the evidence provided by workshop participants. "All the facts were there," Chuck Kennedy said of the statement. "Even the tone was against the dam. But the conclusion did a 180, saying that the dam wouldn't have a bad environmental impact, that the dam should be built."

The citizens' advisory committee recommended that the dam be built, by an 11 to 7 vote. By pure chance, however, the county grand jury at that time was a "blue-ribbon panel" of local conservationists; and *their* report recommended against the dam. The supervisors, who still held all power to decide the issue, were showing no eagerness to use it.

Build It Now

In 1972, the political battle over Butler Valley began to shape up; and new characters emerged in leadership roles. The local chamber of commerce formed the Build It Now Committee, with Dick Denbo as leader. Denbo, long-time promoter, was described by former Eureka journalist Richard Harris (Harris was fired for sympathizing with anti-dam forces) as "the only man in Eureka who still wears a straw hat."

The dapper Denbo collected signatures, each on a separate card, calling for an immediate vote of approval for the dam by the supervisors. He took these coupons in a big cardboard box and, with a flourish, dumped them on a table before the bemused supervisors.

The anti-dam forces evolved the Concerned Citizens Committee, a group of professional people lending their support to efforts to put the dam issue up for a county-wide vote. Wesley Chesbro, director of the Northcoast Environmental Center, was a leading force in the new phase of dam opposition.

If Denbo has an opposite, Chesbro is it. Young, long-haired, a college dropout and conscientious objector, Chesbro had already managed two environmental initiative campaigns in the county. He saw the initial political situation as being quite favorable: "We had the Concerned Citizens Committee advocating democracy, and the Build It Now Committee advocating a very narrowly based decision made by a few people."

The supervisors could not legally delegate their decision-making power to the electorate, even though they may have dearly wanted to. They could, however, call for an advisory vote of the people. "I argued that it was proper for citizens to express their wishes on this vital matter which would obligate the county for 100 years." said supervisor Ray Peart. "The vote would also get information out about the dam. The ballot results would not be binding on the board; but as an expression of the will of the people, it would carry a lot of weight."

Since the board remained solidly 3 to 2 in favor of the dam, an advisory vote seemed the only hope of dam opponents. By a

WESLEY PAUL CHESBRO

Wesley Chesbro, executive director of the Northcoast Environmental Center and councilman of the City of Arcata, California, came north to attend Humboldt State University from his home in South Pasadena. A conscientious objector to war, he dropped out of his course of studies to direct a recycling project as his alternative service.

"I've learned more from community involvement than from school," he says. "I intend to finish college as soon as the balance tips back."

Elected to the Arcata City Council in March 1974, Chesbro is settling down in his adopted home. "I've found a community I really care about," he says. "The environment that really matters is the one close to home." Still in his early twenties, Chesbro is buying a house in Arcata, and is well known locally as an environmentally aware community leader.

3 to 2 vote, the board called for an advisory vote. At that point, the Build It Now Committee disappeared, and the Your Economic Survival (YES) Committee appeared in its place.

One-Third, One-Third, One-Third

In September 1973, on behalf of the YES Committee, Eureka mayor Gilbert Trood took the arm of a bathing beauty and guided her into a plastic wading pool adorned with happy fish. The Concerned Citizens responded with the Reverend Doctor Phillip Nesset, who poured a bucket of muddy water into another plastic wading pool. Thus opened the YES Committee and Concerned Citizens campaign headquarters. These events also were marked by restraint in the use of vitriol and mud by both sides.

Wesley Chesbro, coordinator for the Citizens Committee, saw his task as being quite clear. "Judging by Humboldt County voter preference on other environmental ballot issues," he said, "it was fairly obvious that only about one-third of the voters could be said to be environmentalists. On the other end were one-third of the voters who are extremely against environmental issues. That leaves a nebulous one-third in the middle that had to be reached in order to win. This is of course a super-generalization, but I think it is a fairly accurate one."

Chesbro set out to spark ad hoc committees, each arguing against the dam from its own point of view. Commercial salmon fishermen were early converts, since the dam would destroy salmon spawning grounds. A group of union members publicly attacked the Central Labor Council for supporting YES, saying that no union votes had been taken on the issue and that the dam was for the benefit of "fat cats."

The Concerned Citizens printed "$300 million boondoggle bills" and handed them out, to raise the issue of local cost. In fact, they took the offensive on the issue of cost from the outset. Soon there was a taxpayers' committee arguing against the dam.

The three thousand Indian residents of Humboldt County were also solidly against the dam. Harvey Maples, 74, is one of

"Have we got a deal for you! frankly, at $325 million... it's a 'STEAL!!'"

Dam opponents issued these "Boondoggle Bills" to dramatize what they regarded to be the real costs of the project. Corps estimates of the local share ran from 13 to 48 million, to be paid over 100 years. When the county public works department computed the local commitment it came to more like 305 million. The news made headlines.

For all-stops-out mud and guts political vitriol, the ads pro and con in the local papers were something to behold. Huge and noisy, what they lacked in gentility, they made up in brawling spirit. Though the ad above gets honors for most outstanding in its field, neither side gets any awards for good sportsmanship.

the last surviving members of the Whilkut Tribe, which was centered in Butler Valley until being decimated by white settlers early in this century.

For over 20 years Maples has lived a hermit's life in Butler Valley, surrounded by the graves and ceremonial sites of his vanished people. Maples refused to move or to disinter his relatives. California state environmental protection law prohibits disturbance of recent Indian burial sites without Indian approval. The Northwest Indian Cemetery Protective Association was prepared to sue should the county try to proceed with dam construction.

Hippies and Fat Cats

One day Wesley Chesbro discovered a true star: Joe Sikora. "He was digging a ditch in front of the office," Chesbro recalled. "I handed him one of those boondoggle bills. I asked him how he felt about the Butler Valley Dam, and he started fumin' and fussin' about those fat cats ripping us off, and I thought: gold mine! 'How would you like to be on TV?'

"We have local TV stations, which are quite small and financially accessible. We'd been talking about making ads with ordinary people. He went on TV, and he was just beautiful — so enthusiastic, standing in front of his ranch-style home, talking about how hard he'd worked to bring it about. He pretty much expressed a fear of a threat to his own lifestyle, an economic threat, and a threat to the environment he liked. It was all his own words."

In general, the Concerned Citizens put out amateur publicity, while the YES Committee did slick ads that branded it as an old-line pressure group. The ads of both sides increased in imaginative vituperation as the November balloting date approached.

The crowning piece was by Bonnie Benzonelli Gool. It ran on October 28. Among other accusations, the anti-dam people were denounced as "hippies, dopers, a self-satisfied clique."

Chesbro thinks this ad gave the Concerned Citizens a real boost. "Bonnie, who owns a very pleasant antique store, was speaking in favor of the dam at a meeting I was at," said Chesbro. "She told me she ran the ad to make people think. Well, it livened things up." As for its effect on the hippies and pot smokers, he said, "They may have been too stoned to even know the issue was happening, but suddenly it was their issue. The ones who weren't hippies or pot smokers were really insulted. The people who were neutral said, 'Hey, these guys are overtly playing on my prejudices, they think I'm stupid.' "

The Concerned Citizens did not overlook the details of running an election campaign. Jim Moore, a young veteran of the McGovern presidential race, organized a thorough precinct coverage on the eve of the election. Roberta Allen led the fund-raising effort, following up mailed solicitations with personal phone calls.

(The YES Committee spent about $30,000 to the Concerned Citizens' $8,000.)

End Game Psychosis

In the last days of the campaign, Chesbro noted a certain madness stealing over a few of the anti-dam workers. "There's a feeling you get in a campaign," he said. "You can't sit still, you have to do something, you might lose by one vote. You get wired. Some of the people in the last few days, they were on the verge of psychosis. I'd come into the office at nine in the morning, they'd have this crazed look on their faces. They were like speed freaks.

"I knew the intensity of the moment, and I was afraid I was going to blow it. I had a list of key people I'd check things out with. It's important in a political campaign to have all your facts straight; because if they can attack one of your facts, all the others are in question."

During these final days, some of the campaign members did things which were not cross-checked and approved by the Citizens Committee. The worst, a mailing of facsimiles of inflated county tax bills, caused widespread criticism. The bills could have been confused for genuine tax bills, and they bore no return address. "I think the trust of the people on the Committee was abused," Chesbro said. "It didn't affect the vote much, though."

The Circle of Wagons

The vote was decisive: 70 percent, eighteen thousand voters, against the dam. The Corps dropped the project even before the board of supervisors voted against it.

One year later, two conservation-minded candidates, including Ray Peart, were defeated in county political campaigns. Don Peterson, a supervisor who had supported both the dam and the people's right to vote on it, believed that voters had "perceived that issue narrowly."

Peterson believed that underlying the "no" votes was a feeling that the "dam would basically alter lifestyle in the county; lifestyle in its broadest sense. People don't live here to get rich," he added. "There's a general feeling that we only want enough growth to keep our heads above water economically. The vote was caused by a 'draw the wagons in a circle and fight off the enemy' kind of mentality."

Most observers believed that the economic issue — the issue of taxation — was decisive. Peterson observed that the big timber and agricultural interests did not back the dam, probably because of the increased taxation it would require.

Early in 1973, Donna Hankins had countered the Corps' economic development projections with development plans based on a preserved Butler Valley. High on her list was a blackberry jam industry. When she finished her presentation, a dam supporter had sighed, "How are you going to fight blackberry jam?"

In any environmental conflict, the real issue, even if there is only one, is always hard to find. To the earth moving equipment dealer, it was a matter of jobs. But after the dam was defeated, local observers were more inclined to think it was taxes. When put to the vote, taxpayers apparently put greater faith in the threat of rising taxes than in either the arguments of conservationists for preserving nature, or the vague promises of plenty from public works.

The Man in the Can-covered Car

How does Forest B. Golden's wife feel about the fact that he has spent a good part of the past four years trying to get a beverage container deposit law enacted in Cayuga County, New York?

"She never has been enthusiastic," Golden says carefully, "but she has grown in favor of my activities. She now realizes the importance of the issue."

There are many aspects of Golden's campaign which would give pause to almost anyone. Not only has he put in long hours; he and his family have been harassed. Flares have been thrown onto their lawn. Bags of cans have flown out of the darkness into their front yard. His job has been threatened.

There are powerful, nationally organized forces which are totally opposed to laws banning throwaway containers. The chief opponent of container deposit legislation, according to Golden, is the U. S. Brewers Association. "They have been very forceful," says Golden. "They have at least two full-time lobbyists in New York State. One of their lobbyists was heard to say that they didn't use enough force in Cayuga County. A lobbyist also threatened the life of the chairman of the Cayuga County Legislature who supported our bill. Somebody threw a brick through his front window, too."

This is Forest B. Golden, who in the tradition of Rich Chambers of Salem, Oregon, and other environmentalists around the country, led the fight for a container ordinance in his county in New York state. He is also the owner of the car pictured on the next page. The illustration above — only a mild exagger-

39

ation according to bottle bill statistics — appeared in the Auburn, New York, *Citizen-Advertiser* on September 18, 1973 and is reprinted here by permission.

"The cans can be attached using a five-minute epoxy and silicone rubber (purchased in caulking tubes). Remember, though, that this will be permanent."

What keeps Golden going in his effort to abolish the beer can and the "no deposit, no return" bottle? "The more pressure, the more resolute I become," he says with feeling. "It has become a matter of ethics to me. I can't tolerate the American people having the wool pulled over their eyes any longer."

An Abundance of Shortages

Golden's can crusade began quietly in the summer of 1971, when he learned of the container deposit law that had been passed in the State of Oregon. The topic came up at a meeting of the Cayuga County Environmental Management Council, a unique institution that was to become a major source of support in Golden's effort to ban non-returnable containers.

Environmental management councils may be set up in any New York State town, city, or county if the local government's law-making body so wishes. Guidelines for such councils are set by the state department of environmental conservation, which provides 50 percent of their funding. The councils advise their respective governmental units concerning environmental matters, particularly issues involving open space and land use in general. Forest Golden estimates that there are 30 or 40 environmental management councils in New York State.

Here is Forest Golden's famous 1970 Simca, a measure of his commitment (would you do it to your car?) and his wife's forbearance (would your wife drive it shopping if you did?). Though the epoxy he used to glue the cans formed a permanent bond with the car, and must have somewhat affected its resale value, his idea worked — the car did attract attention — particularly that of the local media. "Fortunately," says Golden, "I'm an extrovert." *Photo from Auburn, New York* Citizen-Advertiser.

In Cayuga County, the council has one paid employee, Bob Brower, a young man sympathetic with environmental protection measures in general and bottle bills in particular. It also has 16 or 18 volunteer members who, as Golden puts it, are "environmentally enlightened." Forest Golden, as leader of the council's Beverage Container Deposit Legislation Study Committee, spent a year and a half studying the cans and bottles of America. The result was a book, *Social, Economic, and Environmental Impacts of the Beverage Container.* *

Golden identifies four major issues which convinced him that non-returnable containers should be banned. First, there is the economics of litter, the tremendous waste of throwing away something valuable. Golden estimates this amount to be about $10 or $11 per American family per year. Second, there is the visual ugliness of litter. Third, the cost of disposing of cans and bottles as solid waste is also great. And fourth, the fact that beverage containers use scarce, non-renewable, and increasingly expensive resources. "Since the oil crisis came along, and shortages became abundant — that is, we have an abundance of shortages — this issue has become more important," remarks Golden. "We could make one million 4,000-pound cars with just the steel in the throwaway containers every year. There are 60 *billion* beverage containers thrown away in America every year. End-to-end, they would go around the world 160 times."

County Target

Having decided to act against the one-way container, Forest Golden very carefully mapped a political strategy. His strategy, very well described in his book *Citizen's Action Manual for Container Deposit Legislation,* was shaped by his position and his personality.

Cayuga County is a rural, upstate New York area, with industrial employment in the county seat, Auburn. "I'm 150 miles from Albany, the capital of the state," Golden notes. "They have a hot line to Washington up there, so it's tough to influence that many legislators. I decided I did have a good chance of getting my hands and arms around 20 county legislators."

Besides being accessible, the county level had other desirable features as Golden's "target." He had the support of the County Environmental Management Council, which was financing the publishing of his books (though later he had to start buying his own paper).

* Editor's Note: If you're thinking of doing battle against the formidable throwaway container, you might well put out the $2.50 this book costs. Golden's Citizen's Action Manual for Container Deposit Legislation ($1.00) is also excellent, though it reflects his lone-wolf operating strategy. Both are available from: Cayuga County Environmental Management Council, 160 Genesee Street, Auburn, New York 13021.

EDITOR'S NOTE

The following is excerpted from the Rodale Press' Environment Action Bulletin *for December 22, 1973. It is reprinted here by permission of the publisher.*

ALICE IN WONDERLAND

Under the new federal energy allocations, manufacturers will get all the petroleum fuel they used last year, plus 10 percent to allow for growth. It doesn't make any difference what they make — the rule covers all manufacturers, even those making throwaway bottles and cans.

Home heating oil is placed in a third order of priorities, and it's very likely that homes will be cold this winter in order to keep the throwaways coming. "They *are* a convenience," as one spokesman for the industry has said.

THE POP-TOP ENERGY RIPOFF

The packaging of beer and soft drinks in approximately 60 billion throwaway containers rather than in returnable bottles wasted 211.5 trillion British Thermal Units of energy during 1972, according to Crusade for a Cleaner Environment, 2000 L St. NW, Washington, DC 20036.

That energy wastage is the equivalent of:

18.2 billion kilowatt hours of electricity — enough to supply the electrical needs of 9.1 million relatively affluent Americans for a whole year;

1.69 billion gallons of gasoline — enough to operate 1,690,000 automobiles averaging 10 miles per gallon for a typical driving year of 10,000 miles;

enough energy to heat approximately 2 million three-bedroom brick homes in the Middle Atlantic region with natural gas for an entire eight-month heating season.

While throwaway containers are tremendous energy wasters, returnable bottles conserve energy by functioning as their own recycling system. Each returnable bottle travels the natural closed loop from container manufacturer to bottler, to retailer, to consumer and back again for reuse an average of 15 times.

With fuel shortages, brownouts and gasoline rationing real possibilities, American industry and consumers must change their habits of energy consumption to "waste not, want not." The perfect place to begin is by returning to the returnable bottle system of distribution for soft drinks and malt beverages.

One might wonder why there's a headlong rush of the American bottling industry towards conversion to one-way, disposable containers. The answer is *monopoly*. It becomes obvious to any competent observer that the returnable deposit bottle system imposes a natural limitation on the market area served from any bottling plant — the limitation being how far delivery trucks can carry the filled bottles and return with the empties. This back and forth distribution system is an efficient system of recovering and recycling, with the costs internalized within the industry.

The national brand franchise companies (Coca Cola, Pepsi Cola, 7 UP, Canada Dry and others) recognized the advantages accruing to themselves from a system whereby they could ship out their products and forget about the empties. A one-way system eliminated the need for large investments in returnable bottles, it required less capital than a diversified plant arrangement, it offered huge reductions in labor costs incidental to rehandling the empties, but most of all it provided the medium through which monopolization of the soft drink industry would be achieved.
— *Peter Chokola, Soft Drink Bottler, Wilkes-Barre, Pa.*

"If the county passed a container deposit law," he says, "it would encourage other counties to do the same and attract attention at the state level. And the opposition lobbyists would be outsiders coming in to interfere with local politics."

The Catalytic Activist

Golden, a professional engineer employed by a large electronics firm, is a genial but very independent soul. When he is out to do something, he does not like to be hassled by a lot of busybodies. Or, as he put it in his *Action Manual:* "If you must get an okay from an organization every time you turn around, you are better off working apart from the organization. The organization must give you a vote of confidence and critique only your final results. In other words, you can't get the job done with back seat drivers or Monday morning 'hot air' quarterbacks constantly harassing you."

Many people, rather than setting up a single-purpose environmental group, prefer to get the support of already existing groups. Forest Golden carried this form of "catalytic activism" to a state of fine art.

Golden, in his *Action Manual*, advises others to obtain endorsements from as wide a range of groups as possible, as he had done:

Prepare a 15 minute slide program or other presentation. Emphasize only the very major points such as consumer dollar savings, litter, and raw material and energy savings. Be sure to include the Oregon success story, and end by calling for action in the form of:
(1) endorsement by the group
(2) distributing bumper stickers
(3) signed petitions
(4) commitments to help conduct surveys

In getting endorsements, as in all his other activities, Golden never lost sight of his final objective: to influence a majority of county legislators to vote for a returnable container bill.

Surveying

Golden organized three opinion surveys and one litter survey. The opinion surveys were done by telephone, with the aid of the League of Women Voters and the Senior Citizens. They came out about 3 to 1 in favor of container deposit legislation.

The litter survey involved a wide range of community groups. About 1,000 students loaded litter into city and county trucks, enjoyed refreshments served by senior citizens and Jaycees, and listened to three rock bands sponsored by the Cayuga County Sportsmen's Association. Participants raised funds by taking pledges for contributions based on the number of bags of

"We could make one million 4,000-pound cars with just the steel in the throwaway containers every year. There are 60 billion beverage containers thrown away in America every year. End-to-end, they would go around the world 160 times."

litter picked up. Proceeds were donated to the Association for Retarded Children.

Golden notes that litter surveys are vital to counter the on-going "Keep America Beautiful" surveys, which always state that cans and bottles are a small percentage of roadside litter. This they do by counting each item — cigarette butts, labels, etc. — as one unit, the same as bottles and cans. Keep America Beautiful, says Golden, is "a front for the beverage interests and their suppliers." A far different survey result is obtained if the litter is by *volume*. In Golden's Cayuga County survey 66 percent of the volume of litter collected was found to be beverage cans and bottles.

A price survey also is often very useful, Golden reports. Comparing supermarket prices of beverages in throwaway containers and those in returnables often shows the "throwaways" to be more expensive. For example, a 1974 survey by the League of Women Voters in Onondaga, New York, found that beverages in returnable bottles averaged four cents cheaper per bottle than beverages in throwaway containers.

The Canned Car

Perhaps Golden's leading contribution to the anti-throwaway movement is his apparent origination of the "canned car." With the aid of the YMCA, Golden glued 1,000 cans to his 1970 Simca compact wagon. "The cans can be attached using a five-minute epoxy and silicone rubber (purchased in caulking tubes)," according to his *Action Manual.* "Remember, though, that this will be permanent."

The canned car greatly increased his appeal to television and other media. Of course it attracts a lot of attention wherever he (or Mrs. Golden) goes. "Fortunately," he says, "I'm an extrovert. I wave and smile at everybody."

Golden's other publicity and public relations activities were quite economical, effective, and within the means of a person with a full-time job. "I got to the press very early," he says. "I spoke with the editor of the local paper, going over all the facts with him, and got his support. After that we had good coverage for our events, and cartoons and editorials supporting us.

What has happened in Oregon poses serious problems for beverage industries nationwide. Bottlers, brewers and container suppliers seem to be on the unfortunate side of a substantial credibility gap. Claiming all along that the law would wreak havoc on their businesses and fail to stop litter, they seem for the most part to have been proven wrong. Sales are steady in Oregon, with some bottlers even admitting that sales and profits are better than before the bill was enacted . . . the major responsibility for this situation falls on the shoulders of those who have made inaccurate claims in the name of proving the law unfair.
— *Softdrinks magazine, November 1973*

RICH CHAMBERS, BOTTLE BILL GURU

The container deposit legislation movement in the United States owes a lot to Rich Chambers of Salem, Oregon, who died last year at the age of 52. "Chambers, since he lived in the state capital there, could lobby the bottle bill through," says Golden. "After it passed he could have rested on his laurels. Instead, he corresponded with people all over the country, putting out his information sheets, doing a hundred copies or so every week."

Golden visited Chambers a couple of times in Salem. "He was a friendly, outgoing guy," says Golden. "He was a salesman of veneer equipment, and traveled all over the country with his business. He was quite an outdoorsman. Like the rest of us, I guess he'd just had it up to his ears with the abuses of the throwaway container industry.

"He never graduated from college, but he could pack an amazing amount of information into his leaflets. He typed with one finger, hunt and peck, using all capital letters. Whenever I had a question about anything, Rich would help me out."

Excerpts from Rich Chambers' weekly bulletins are reprinted on the facing page.

"Letters to the editor were very useful. I wrote about 40 or so of them, got other people to sign them, and sent them in one at a time."

From Rich Chambers of Salem, Oregon, who was a main inspiration to Golden, he got the idea of sending out information sheets to legislators and the media. These were on sheets of various colors. Golden mailed 40 of these, one at a time.

A Positive Position

After doing this extensive groundwork, says Golden, "we had a pretty positive position to go to the legislature with." This, as he wrote in his *Action Manual*, is the crucial stage at which two facts must be brought home to legislators:

First, citizens are awakening to the environmental cost of throwaways. Second, energy and the economy cannot sustain the burden of throwaways while allowing us to keep food on our tables, a roof over our heads, and providing energy for heat, manufacturing, lighting, and transportation. Container Deposit Activists must communicate these two facts over and over again, in as many different ways as possible, to Legislators. It's hard, but it can be done.

"I got to be on a first-name basis with all the county legislators," says Golden. "Our real break came when the chairman of the legislature decided a delegation should go to Oregon, to see for themselves if container deposit legislation really works."

Three county lawmakers went to Oregon: one who favored the container law, one opposed to it, and one who was neutral. They had a long list of people to interview there, but threw it away and just drove around the state, talking to grocery store owners, policemen, and others. They saw little roadside litter.

"One of the delegation to Oregon, the one who opposed the law, owns a liquor store," says Golden. "He decided the law wasn't a disaster; that it was working." The three returned to report that Oregon's container law was a success.

"I took the Oregon bottle bill to a third-year law student," says Golden, "and he wrote up a similar one for Cayuga County. Later, a local attorney helped revise it."

The key provision of Oregon's bottle bill is that all beverage containers offered for sale in the state have a refund value of not less than five cents. The Cayuga County bill also requires beverage containers — including non-returnable cans — to carry the stamp, "Cayuga County - Five Cents." Under the law, a beverage may still be sold in an aluminum can, as long as the buyer can get a nickel back for the can.

Doing a lot of person-to-person lobbying, Golden guided the bill through approval by the Environmental Management Council, then to the county legislature, where he got approval for a June 1973 public hearing on the measure.

```
TO :  ANYONE INTERESTED IN BEVERAGE CONTAINER DEPOSIT LEGISLATION
FR :  RICH CHAMBERS / LOMBARDY LANE / SALEM, OR 97302

THE ALUMINUM CAN FOR BEER AND SOFT DRINKS IS AN ECONOMIC, ENVIRON-
MENTAL AND ENERGY-CONSUMPTION [DISASTER] IN THE UNITED STATES.
WITNESS :  THE 1970 BASIC DATA BOOK FOR THE U.S. ALUMINUM INDUSTRY
           LISTS ALL ALUMINUM USED IN THE U.S. ACCORDING TO 72
DIFFERENT CATEGORIES. LISTED HERE FOR YOUR EDIFICATION ARE THE 6
TOP CATEGORIES AND THE WEIGHTS CONSUMED :

  1 - METAL CANS ----------------->  878,000,000  POUNDS
  2 - POWER TRANSMISSION & DISTRIBUTION  864,000,000  POUNDS
  3 - PASSENGER CARS                 675,000,000  POUNDS
  4 - "OTHER IDENTIFIED END USES"    376,000,000  POUNDS
  5 - RESIDENTIAL SIDING             330,000,000  POUNDS
  6 - PRIMARY DOORS AND WINDOWS      318,000,000  POUNDS

THE ECONOMIC FACTS OF LIFE FOR ALUMINUM ARE QUITE SIMPLY THAT
NINETY PERCENT ( 90% ), OF THE RAW MATERIAL FROM WHICH ALUMINUM
IS MANUFACTURED, ( BAUXITE ), REACHES THE UNITED STATES FROM A
FOREIGN COUNTRY. EVERY OUNCE OF BAUXITE IMPORTED DAMAGES OUR
ALREADY VERY BAD BALANCE OF PAYMENTS.

THE REASON ALUMINUM IS USED SO EXTENSIVELY IN PRIMARY DOORS AND
WINDOWS, LISTED ABOVE, IS THE STABILITY OF THE METAL AND THE
LONGEVITY UNDER ALMOST ANY WEATHER CONDITIONS. THESE CHARACTER-
ISTICS ARE EXACTLY WHAT MAKE ALUMINUM JUST EXACTLY THE WRONG
MATERIAL FROM WHICH TO MANUFACTURE CONSUMER CONTAINERS. THIS
METAL DOES NOT RUST AND OXIDIZES SO SLOWLY AS TO BE MEASURED IN
HUMAN LIFETIMES. UNDER WATER THERE IS SIMPLY NO MEASUREABLE
DETERIORATION AND, OF COURSE, NO DESTRUCTION.

AS FAR AS ENERGY CONSUMPTION IS CONCERNED, PERHAPS A LOOK AT THE
POWER SOLD BY THE BONNEVILLE POWER ADMINISTRATION IN THE NORTH-
WESTERN UNITED STATES WILL HELP UNDERSTAND THE PROBLEM. DURING
A RECENT YEAR 39.6% OF THE ELECTRICITY SOLD BY THE BONNEVILLE
POWER ADMINISTRATION WENT DIRECTLY TO THE ELCTRO-PROCESSING
INDUSTRIES OF THE "BROWNOUT THREATENED" NORTHWEST. THE ELECTRO-
PROCESSING INDUSTRIES ARE ALMOST EXCLUSIVELY ALUMINA REDUCTION
PLANTS ALONG THE COLUMBIA RIVER IN OREGON AND WASHINGTON. AS
UNBELIEVABLE AS IT SEEMS, THEN, WE ARE THREATENED WITH BROWNOUTS
OR WORSE IN ORDER TO CONTINUE TO PRODUCE 878 MILLION POUNDS OF
ALUMINUM CANS.

THERE IS AN ALTERNATIVE, AND IT INVOLVES THE USE OF GLASS MADE
FROM FREELY AVAILABLE SILICA SAND. GLASS MADE INTO RETURNABLE
BOTTLES, AND A RETURN TO THE SYSTEM THAT WORKED IN AMERICA FOR
TWO HUNDRED YEARS PREVIOUS TO 1940 AND IS THE NORM IN THE REST
OF THE WORLD TODAY ...   THE DEPOSIT AND RETURN FOR RE-USE SYSTEM.
```

```
TO :  PERSONS INTERESTED IN BEVERAGE CONTAINER CONTROL
FR :  RICH CHAMBERS / LOMBARDY LANE / SALEM, OR 97302
RE :  LITTER COMPOSITION DATA

THE "STUDY" USED CONSISTENTLY TO SHOOT DOWN ANY AND ALL ATTEMPTS
AT LEGISLATIVE ATTEMPTS TO CONTROL BEVERAGE CONTAINERS IN THE
UNITED STATES IS THE ONGOING "KEEP AMERICA BEAUTIFUL" STUDY, AS
CARRIED ON UNDER THE AUSPICES OF THE HIGHWAY RESEARCH BOARD OF
THE DIVISION OF ENGINEERING, NATIONAL RESEARCH COUNCIL, NATIONAL
ACADEMY OF SCIENCES - NATIONAL ACADEMY OF ENGINEERING.

DO NOT LET THE TITLES FOOL YOU. THE STUDY IS VIRTUALLY MEANINGLESS
BECAUSE OF A SINGLE GLARING WEAKNESS THE AUTHORS ARE WELL AWARE OF
BUT DO NOT CHANGE BECAUSE THEY KNOW IT MIGHT BRING THINGS INTO
PROPER PERSPECTIVE. THIS WEAKNESS IS QUOTED HERE DIRECTLY FROM THE
INSTRUCTIONS ISSUED TO THE VARIOUS STATE HIGHWAY DEPARTMENTS :

  "OTHER PIECES OF PAPER ARE COUNTED IN ITEM 21 PROVIDED THEY
  ARE OF SUFFICIENT SIZE TO BE PICKED UP IN NORMAL CLEANUP
  OPERATIONS"

SINCE THE SAMPLING AREAS ARE ONLY 2/10 MILE LONG, AND THE MEN IN THE
FIELD ARE TOLD THAT THIS IS TO BE A SCIENTIFIC ANALYSIS YOU MAY BE
CERTAIN THAT THE MEN IN THE FIELD ARE GOING TO MAKE A THOROUGH
CLEANUP. THE RESULT IS THAT THE FIGURES OF THIS PIECE COUNT
ANALYSIS ARE ALL COCKEYED AND "OTHER PAPER ITEMS" COMPRISES 46%
OF THE LITTER AND ALL PAPER 59%.

UNLESS YOU CONSIDER A BUTT OR A 1" SQUARE PIECE OF NEWSPAPER
THE SAME ENVIRONMENTAL PROBLEM AS A GLASS BOTTLE OR AN ALUMINUM
CAN, THEN, IT IS EASY TO SEE THAT IT IS POSSIBLE TO BE SORT OF
HONEST BUT VERY, VERY UNSCIENTIFIC AT THE SAME TIME, AND THIS IS
EXACTLY THE NATURE OF THE KEEP AMERICA BEAUTIFUL STUDY, WHICH IS
FULLY FUNDED BY CONTAINER FILLERS AND MANUFACTURERS.

IN ADDITION TO THE ABOVE WEAKNESS, THERE IS THE OBVIOUS FACT THAT
A VERY SIGNIFIGANT AMOUNT OF THE PAPER FOUND IN LITTER IS BEVERAGE
CONTAINER RELATED. NO ACCOUNTING IS MADE OF THIS IN THE STUDY.
THIS PAPER WOULD NOT BE IN THE LITTER STREAM IF THE CONTAINERS
WERE NOT IN THE STREAM.

IF YOU CONTEMPLATE A LITTER ANALYSIS, IT IS SUGGESTED THAT
YOU UTILIZE BOTH A LITTER VOLUME AND A LITTER COUNT BASIS,
AND ANALYZE ONLY BEVERAGE CONTAINERS AND PAPER, SINCE TOGETHER
THEY COMPRISE THE BULK OF ALL LITTER. USE FIBER DRUMS OF KNOWN
CUBIC FOOTAGE VOLUME AND AVERAGE NUMBER OF BEVERAGE CANS AND
AVERAGE NUMBER OF BEVERAGE BOTTLES SMALLER THAN NOMINAL QUART.
THUS YOU HAVE NUMBERS TO SHOW THE SCOPE OF THE ANALYSIS AND
VOLUME TO GET THINGS IN PERSPECTIVE. RUN EVERYTHING THROUGH THE
BARRELS BEFORE PILING IN SEPARATE PILES FOR : GENERAL PAPER,
CONTAINER-RELATED PAPER, LARGE BOTTLES, SMALL RETURNABLE BOTTLES,
SMALL THROWAWAY BOTTLES AND -  IT WILL SCARE YOU -  CANS.

ABOVE ALL, HAVE YOUR SURVEY CONTINUOUSLY MONITORED BY A LOCAL
JUDGE OR DISTRICT ATTORNEY WHO WILL SIGN HIS NAME TO THE
RESULTS, AND BE SURE THAT NEWSPAPER COVERAGE IS COMPREHENSIVE.
```

Brewers' Blitz

"About one month before our public hearing in June 1973, the beverage industry got active," Golden recalls. "They even flew in people from outside the state."

The U. S. Brewers Association, with an annual budget of about $130 million, according to Golden, led the blitz. "It's a consortium of the major brewers," he says. "Not all the brewers, but the major brewers. They're against container deposit legislation because they're in the can-making business."

During the next few months, Forest Golden learned what it means to take on a $3 billion industry. His advice in the *Action Manual* reflects this experience:

Hearings - get your people out early and in force. The opposition will try to pack you out of the hearing room. Suggest the hearing procedure limit the time of each speaker to 5 minutes maximum. The opposition speakers are on a regular hearing circuit and are prepared to speak for an hour or more at a time, complete with movies. You should expect fair treatment at the hearing. Get college and high school students to the hearing early (90-120 minutes) to save seats for your adults.

Be prepared to save some of your best news releases for the final week preceding the vote. Industry lobbyists will literally

The picture at the top was taken March 13, 1973. The one below it was taken 54 weeks later. The lower one has about a quarter inch of snow. The one above it has about a foot of beer cans. It was a little warmer in 1973 and Vermont had a a container deposit law in 1974. *Caption and photographs (A. J. Marro) reprinted from the* Rutland (Vermont) Daily Herald, *March 27, 1974.*

move into your area and use every trick in the book to get publicity, including 11th hour press releases whose reliability will be difficult to check, and movies on TV as well as full page newspaper ads, whose validity may sometimes be questioned.

"They lied and lied and lied," Golden says of the container industry lobbyists. In countering them, he found that use of facts taken from industry trade journals was most effective, because the lobbyists could hardly attack their own journals. "For example," Golden recalls, "the industry lobbyists were always saying that the cost of beverage containers is not large relative to other costs. Yet *Beverage Industry* magazine reported on August 24, 1973 that packaging is 56 percent of the total cost of making beer — *the* major cost in production of beer."

No Laurels to Rest On

The law was due to go into effect on November 26, 1974; but the beverage container industry was not ready to give up. First they tried to get a repeal of the law. Golden went on talk shows and "wrote continual letters to the editor," in opposition to this move. Although the county legislature went 11 to 9 in favor of repeal, the two-thirds necessary for repeal was not there.

Then, on the very eve of the date the law was to outlaw the throwaway in Cayuga, an industry group filed a lawsuit attacking the law on a technicality of its passage, and alleging that it was vague. An injunction stopped the law from going into effect. As of early 1975 the case has not been decided.

Golden believes that the suit has "about a 50-50 chance," and is biding his time. "I'd rather not work people up, then lose," he says. "I'd rather just pass it again."

He notes that a number of New York counties were considering container deposit bills, and that many New York State bills had been written. He is joining with one other person to form a coalition for a state bill. "The organization will be very, very informal," he quickly added. "Newsletters and all those things — I can't stand it."

The Cayuga County container deposit law was the first passed in New York State. Three states — Oregon, Vermont, and South Dakota — have container deposit laws in effect. Washington, D.C. passed a container deposit law which will go into effect *if* neighboring local governments enact similar legislation.

The more local container deposit laws that are passed, the more likely it is that a national bottle bill, such as the one proposed by Senator Mark Hatfield of Oregon, will be passed. Such a national law, Golden believes, would save about $1 billion per year and end a monumental eyesore.

Bird-watching
in the Smoke-filled Room

By Joan Reiss

EDITOR'S NOTE:

Joan Reiss offered us this "first person" murder mystery free of charge. It was an offer we couldn't refuse. We thank her for her generous assistance.

The committee sat in a raised semicircle. A solo voice muttered,

"Move the bill out."

"Second."

"All in favor?" asked the chairman.

A chorus of ayes rang out.

"All opposed?" he countered.

An equal chorus of nays followed.

"The bill is passed," pronounced the chairman.

Prior to 1972, this scene was reenacted thousands of times during committee hearings of the California State Legislature in Sacramento. The muffled choruses of ayes and nays, as well as the silences of quieter souls who said neither aye or nay, all disappeared within the vast abyss of governmental secrets.

In California, the committee system provided anonymity for legislators. Although committee members were free to request roll call votes, thereby establishing a permanent record, this rarely occurred since a member requesting roll call might easily incur the wrath of a chairman who preferred secrecy. Special-interest lobbies were well served by this process; but public-interest groups were becoming increasingly frustrated in attempts to track committee votes.

Two major conservation groups active in Sacramento battles were the Sierra Club and the Planning and Conservation League (PCL). PCL's sole purpose was lobbying conservation legislation at the state level. Both groups felt that legislative awareness could be raised immeasurably if an observer corps went to committee hearings and recorded environmental votes.

The leader of our fledgling observer group was to be Virginia-Jane Gleadall, a math instructor at American River College, long involved in conservation matters and fresh from a University of California public lobbying course. Notification of the first observer meeting was printed in the Sierra Club newsletter, and notices were mailed from the PCL office. Although the Audubon Society was not involved, the group became known as "Legislative Birdwatchers."

Fledgling Observers

The first meeting of the flock was held on April 29, 1970, less than ten days after the first Earth Day. The assembled group was composed of businessmen, retired citizens, students, teachers, and, predominantly, activist women. Although our backgrounds varied, a common goal linked us: preservation of the environment through the governmental process.

As we listened to Virginia that first night, I marvelled at her knowledge of the intricacies of the legislature. From this first introduction, and through the subsequent years, I learned government is not complex; but it is complicated! Deep down I have always suspected that this complication exists to keep the public just a bit intimidated.

My first committee hearing will never be forgotten. I walked up the capitol steps and between the awesome, immaculate pillars into the building and under the huge glass dome — now considered an earthquake hazard. Finally, I found the committee room and timidly sat in the second row. In front the committee members sat around in a semicircle, quite oblivious of me; some were even oblivious of committee business! They were slightly raised above the floor level of the audience, a position I am certain was by design and not chance.

In the days to come we fledgling observers learned that government was not always what it seemed. Agendas at committee meetings were rarely followed. Bills were cancelled or "put over." Votes were rarely taken at a first hearing of a bill. Committees often operated with less than a quorum. When the vote was taken we all had great difficulty in determining who was "aye" and who was "nay." These early committee hearings were a study in frustrated confusion.

Legislative Murders Solved

At the conclusion of that first year, we published an Environmental Voting Index (EVI), which was to contain major floor and committee votes on environmental issues. Our inexperience showed grimly, for we had few reliable committee votes. Still, newspapers were quick to publish the results when the voting index boldly stated:

Subject: A Dozen Murders Solved
This is an expose — of a dozen legislative murders and of the bipartisan killers and accomplices. And particularly of the killings that occurred in the quiet committee chambers where no public record of the votes is maintained. This is what the witnesses saw. .

This index placed the Birdwatchers firmly, if not credibly, on the Sacramento map. But it also created problems for both Birdwatchers and PCL. Imagine PCL's attempts to lobby the "murderers" and the "accomplices" in the early part of the 1971 legislative session! The Birdwatcher effort had seriously hampered the lobbying effort. It became clear that an effective lobbying organization could not also be a rating group. What could be done?

Birdwatchers decided to incorporate and "officially" separate from PCL. A small subscription service was begun through which organizations and individuals supported the Birdwatchers, and a separate phone was installed; but in fact Birdwatchers did not physically leave the PCL space, for there was no money and nowhere to go. Virginia-Jane became further involved in her teaching and other Sierra Club activities, and I became "Chief Birdwatcher."

A Formidable Flock

We trained many new volunteers who flocked to join us as the next legislative year began. Joan Janson, a Sierra Club activist, became phone coordinator, and for key committee votes managed to get two and even three people into committee. She established the practice of phoning a legislator ahead to find out if a bill was to be heard. Dobbie Patterson, who had become a superb Birdwatcher, used her past secretarial skills to run our office in a businesslike manner. The entire operation remained

The somnambulistic ritual of legislative committee work is the subject of this cartoon, used by the Birdwatchers to poke fun at the do-nothing attitude of many lawmakers. Once attention was called to committee methods, many of the guilty ones began to pay more attention to their work. Drawing by Jim Snider.

JOAN REISS

Joan Reiss was born in New York City in 1937. She set out on a science career and completed a master's degree in chemistry at the University of Connecticut. This was followed by several years of work in the fields of chemistry and biochemistry.

She settled in California in 1969, and viewed her new home, Sacramento, as a fine "halfway" place between San Francisco and the Sierra Nevadas, where she and her family enjoyed backpacking, skiing, and biking. Joan continued her science career as a high school biology teacher.

Living in the state capital, she soon became aware of politics. In 1970, she had already been contemplating a career shift. Her commitment to environmental politics began after hearing Phil Berry, then Sierra Club president, address a chapter meeting.

Active participation with the Sierra Club eventually led to Legislative Birdwatchers. Today Joan is both president of Legislative Birdwatchers and Sacramento vice-president of the Planning and Conservation League.

During the past years, her major political concerns have been with the environment and all governmental activities which encourage citizen participation.

volunteer. We raised some money, but it has always been PCL's low rental policy that has enabled us to continue.

Attending committee hearings in 1971, we were a far cry from the intimidated souls who had begun a year ago. Our presence was announced by the bright yellow bird tag we wore. We learned to "split" a committee in order to accurately lip-read from two to four legislators per Birdwatcher.

When confronted with unsure votes we would phone the lawmaker's office. Occasionally these enquiries led to humorous responses, such as "Assemblyman Dunlap thinks he voted *yes* in committee yesterday." Assemblyman MacDonald's secretary responded, "I can't ask him how he voted in committee, he never tells me that!"

In January 1972 we assembled a solid EVI containing a good compendium of recorded committee votes in one area. We had established a priority list of environmental bills by concentrating on legislation lobbied by the PCL, Sierra Club, and the Clean Air Coalition. After a press conference in Sacramento, newspapers throughout the state printed the environmental percentages of their own legislators. The Birdwatchers were no longer sensationalist; we were a true, credible environmental conscience.

The Smoke Clears

January was also a significant month for Senator Peter Behr (R) from conservation-minded Marin County. He introduced a measure to permanently record all committee votes. Lawmakers are good reformers of other groups; but self-reform requires courage, and Peter Behr was indeed courageous.

Joan Reiss is shown here with students who attended a workshop sponsored by the Birdwatchers. The workshop was offered to anyone who wanted to participate in public-interest work in California's state capitol. Two hundred fifty people showed up.

Although Birdwatchers do not lobby legislation, we gathered support for recorded committee votes. We contacted as many public interest groups as we could, asking them to write letters favoring the resolution. We spoke on the radio in public service announcements. The media came in loud and clear with editorials, announcements, and articles on recorded committee votes.

Two weeks later the California Senate responded with a 34-3 vote of approval. Eventually the Assembly drafted an "adjusted" version of recorded committee votes, which passed the Assembly by an overwhelming 67-0. On March 20, 1972 the California Assembly began recording committee votes. On April 10 the Senate too began recording all committee votes. With that, a 100-year-old practice of voice votes in committee was laid to rest. The prestigious *California Journal* wrote in their February 1972 edition, "If any one organization can take credit for making the recording of committee votes 'an idea whose time has come' it is the Legislative Birdwatchers."

California became the eighth state in the union to have recorded committee votes. Legislative Birdwatchers made it happen. What about making your state the *ninth* to have recorded committee votes?

Volunteer Birdwatchers observing their state government at work in committee are given scorecards similar to this one for keeping track of the action. The results are tabulated and issued at the close of each legislative session.

John Dewey's Giant Killers

"The Army Corps of Engineers won't send us their project listings anymore. We call them and call them and they just won't send their listings. I'm sure it's fear. It's got to be fear."

The speaker of this bold line is a student at John Dewey High School in Brooklyn, New York. He has reason to speak boldly. He is part of the unique marine biology program designed and taught by Harold Silverstein and Lou Siegel.

Afraid of Kids

"Let's put it this way. We were two New York City school-teachers without administrators around, starting from scratch, doing it on our own. We raised the question: Could high school students take marine biology? Typically, a high school sophomore takes biology, then is retrained in college. We wondered if we could train students properly in the first place."

Harold Silverstein, portly and bursting with energy, speaks in swift clusters of concepts punctuated with laughter. In 1969, he had been teaching biology for 19 years. Far from being jaded by endless beakers and Bunsen burners, he was about to expand his own professional world.

"There was a great concrete wall around Brooklyn. There were millions of people, and thousands of graffiti."

"Lou Siegel, another biology teacher, and I got together and designed a course, and wrote a lab manual," recalls Silverstein. "The principal went right along with us. Essentially, what we needed at first was longer class periods and the facilities to take field trips. We wanted to base the program on laboratory and field work. We got 1 hour and 20 minute periods, instead of 40 minute periods, and we got approval to take buses down the parkways."

Silverstein believes that the milieu of student rebellion at that time helped him organize a marine biology program. "Everyone was very cooperative in 1969," he says. "I guess the kids going on strike helped a great deal. Because the administrators were afraid of the kids, they permitted me to do what I knew was correct."

At that time, Silverstein had no idea that the program was going to enter the arena of environmental action. "In 1969 I wasn't interested in ecology. To me, then, an ecologist was somebody who was a very specialized scientist, or somebody who went out on street cleanup days. I was interested in basic science, because it has something to offer in terms of training young minds."

Graffiti Surrounding Brooklyn

"In 1971, Lou Siegel got wind that the U. S. Army Corps of Engineers wanted to build a wall around Coney Island. It would be huge. It would be a hulking deterrent against the ocean. There have been only four major hurricanes in this area since 1760. We didn't think the problem justified the solution. The Corps' answer to hurricanes and floods is to build a concrete wall around the United States."

Lou Siegel, Harold Silverstein's younger colleague, was about to get the veteran teacher involved in the ecological problems of the day.

"The *New York Times* did an editorial with a cartoon," recalls Silverstein, hugely amused. "There was a great concrete wall around Brooklyn. There were millions of people, and thousands of graffiti. There was graffiti from one end of Brooklyn to the other. And there were these little holes that people could go through to get to the beach.

"We decided to do an ecological report on the project; in other words, what would happen ecologically in building this thing. Lou did a lot of research, and I did a little. We came up with certain negative effects on the food web, besides which the wall was esthetically unpleasant."

A glimpse of Harold Silverstein. This photograph was taken early one morning, minutes before he was to leave for another wetlands hearing. Mr. Silverstein is framed by a small number of the tanks in which the marine creatures he and his students are trying to protect are studied. Though much of their work is done in the field, close observation of specific animals over long periods can only be done in controlled conditions.

"It is apparent that the wetlands near the major waters of the Atlantic coast are considered by some to be zones of specialized successions: Natural Marsh — Landfill — Spoil Area — and finally, the climax community — a Housing Development."

Then Silverstein was exposed to his first Corps of Engineers hearing. "We gave our report at a Corps of Engineers hearing at the New York Aquarium. You ever seen the Army Corps of Engineers? They're very polite, they listen, they tape everything, and they never respond. We learned that you can go through the official channels, but unless you have some political or social input nothing happens.

"They scrapped that idea because they couldn't get money appropriated for it. Then they developed another plan, for what are called jetties and groin walls. Lou and I wrote a paper on that, and sent it to congressmen, newspapers, and others, just to inform people on the issue. A congressman picked up our report and made it into his program. The Corps was stopped again.

"At this time, Lou and I were doing most of the work. We were new at it, so we couldn't teach the kids."

Low Viability Study

The next year, 1972, the marine biology class at John Dewey got involved in ecological studies of marshlands, a subject it was to become very knowledgeable about.

"Somebody wrote a letter from Queens, which is 15 miles away, saying, 'Help,' " Silverstein says. "We were so hot with intellectual ego that we decided to do it. It was a marshland called Spring Creek. I didn't know anything about marshlands at that time. I thought they smelled. Now I think marshlands offer the best place to teach marine biology, and to have a socially worthwhile project as well.

"It was the New York City Environmental Protection Agency (EPA) that wanted to fill the marsh. We did a salinity study of the area, looked for some chlorides, identified some organisms, and that was it. We went to the EPA hearing with our study. The EPA is really the sanitation department, in a sense, concerned with water and air facilities of New York City.

"Our side consisted of a couple of kids, myself, my son who is a Columbia Law School student, a Sierra Club lawyer, and an environmental group leader. In walked 12 lawyers and biologists for the EPA. We had sent them our analysis, we wanted them to know everything. Without hearing our testimony they said: 'The

Spring Creek area will not be touched. We sent out our biologists and they agree with you.' They sent out their biologists because they had seen our study. It was a very low viability study, quite frankly. Knowing what I do now, if I was the opposition I could have shot it full of holes.

"So we defeated the Army Corps of Engineers twice, and we we won Spring Creek. Then we took on Laurelton in Queens."

Specialized Successions

Laurelton, a partially filled marsh in front of a public school, was slated to be totally filled by the New York EPA. "By then we were getting to be really heavy," says Silverstein. "We met with the EPA on the site, and discussed an alternative to their plan. We traded off twelve acres, which would be left alone, for three they could fill. We suggested a walkway through the marsh-land under the auspices of the department of parks. The residents loved that."

In their formal letter on the Laurelton case to New York's commissioner of environmental conservation, the marine biology classes opened on a pungent note: "It is apparent that the wet-lands near the major waters of the Atlantic coast are considered by some to be zones of specialized successions: Natural Marsh — Landfill — Spoil Area — and finally, the climax community — a Housing Development."

Again, the proposal of the John Dewey High School marine biology classes was accepted. A little later in that month, on February 24, 1974 to be exact, they singlehandedly took on a phalanx of oil companies that might give pause to the Shah of Iran. The issue: discharge of waste oil into Jamaica Bay.

The home of the Giant-killers. John Dewey High School sprawls near the terminus of one of New York's subway lines, just a sniff away from "Nathan's Famous" at Coney Island. Though it looks like most other postwar urban schools, it houses an unusual faculty and unorthodox instructional programs, of which the Silverstein-Siegel marine biology effort is a standout example.

Death on Coney Island

It was the marine biology club versus Exxon, Texaco, Shell, Chevron, and 20 other petroleum firms. This time, the U. S. Environmental Protection Agency was holding hearings on the maximum concentration of oil which was to be allowed in the waterway operating areas of these companies.

Silverstein, Siegel, and students presented a detailed survey of just what was known about the biological effects of oil in a marine environment. The survey concluded:

Based upon research findings of independent investigators who have studied the effects of oil pollution on the marine environment, it has been credibly established at the anatomical level and the microscopic level that the components of oil pollutants are toxic to the organisms which comprise our marine food chain. It has also been found that bottom sediments contain oil which settles down to the organisms which live in said areas, further resulting in long-term toxicity to marine life.

The survey of scientific literature was backed up by field observation:

Our observations of the accidental oil spill in 1972 off the Sea Gate and Coney Island area indicate where oil can be detected in the sediments there has been a kill of animals. Bottom sediments contain many dead clams, crustaceans and snails. The affected areas have not been repopulated. Mussels that survived the spill, at this point in time, are almost incapable of developing eggs and sperms.

The marine biology club also had data supplied by one of the oil companies which showed that "concentration of oil pollutants presently exceeds the levels prescribed by regulatory agencies."

As one of the students recalls, "We found that 1/10 parts per million (ppm) of oil in the water has a killing effect. We got their standards down from 40 to 10 ppm." The U. S. Environmental Protection Agency officials were very impressed by the students' approach. One official told a *New York Times* reporter that hard biological data was a two-edged sword: it both gave the agency ammunition in fighting pollution, and could be strong evidence if the agency wasn't doing its job.

Truly Competent Work

"In June 1974 we did our first truly competent work," says Silverstein. "What we do is a total productivity study. One mistake that environmental groups make is that they concentrate on the legal and ignore the biological. We do a total biological and physical analysis of an area, so we can show that that area is highly productive, and is involved in energy exchange."

"We found that 1/10 parts per million (ppm) of oil in the water has a killing effect. We got the oil companies' proposed standards down from 40 to 10 ppm."

The Fresh Creek marshland, subject of the June hearing, was extensively studied by students and teachers from John Dewey. By then, their laboratory at school was similar to a professional research lab. Silverstein and Siegel had obtained $18,000 in National Defense Education Act money to buy advanced equipment. They had required each equipment supplier to send a technician for at least one day to train students in use of the equipment.

"We do a very extensive microbiological study," says Silverstein, "using various types of media to check ourselves. People can't believe the quality of work we do. We tend to validate the work done by Odum, that an acre of marshland supports about 1,200 pounds of fish per year."

The Fresh Creek case was the first time the marine biology class used the Tidal Wetlands Act as a research basis. The Act, which became a state law in June 22, 1973, establishes a Tidal Wetlands Agency under the state Environmental Conservation Department. The Tidal Wetlands Agency holds hearings on proposed developments in marshlands, recognizing eight values of marshes: marine food production, wildlife habitat, flood and storm control, recreation, treating pollution, sedimentation, education and research, and open space and esthetic appreciation.

"We are the only group in New York City that has attempted to follow the mandate of the Tidal Wetlands Act of 1973 from a biological consideration," according to Silverstein. Their studies document a particular area's value from the eight points of view.

The Environmental Law Council of Columbia University aided the marine biology class in the hearing on Fresh Creek, particularly in cross-examination of witnesses. The result of the hearing has not yet been announced.

A Hundred Schools

At this time, Harold Silverstein and Lou Siegel teach 240 students in sophomore marine biology, 30 in advanced marine biology, and 130 in the optional summer marine ecology course. They have applied for a grant to support an environmental law institute at John Dewey, which would involve lawyers teaching high school students. They have also asked for money to buy more laboratory equipment, a calculator, and a boat. They'll probably get it.

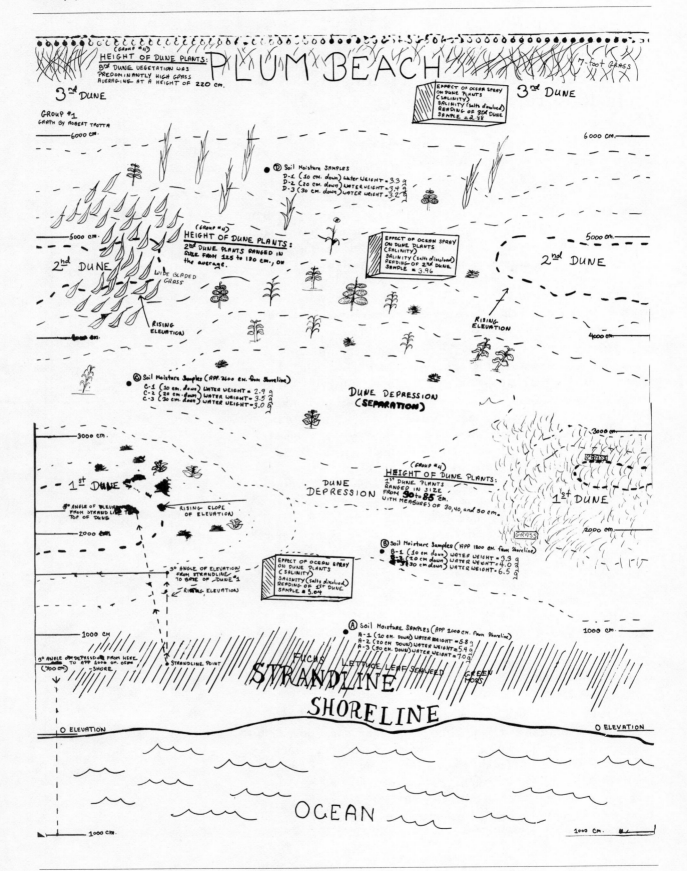

PLUM BEACH

"What we want to do now is get more involved." Silverstein is expansive. "We'd have 100 schools studying marshlands, and a data bank that would have more information on marshlands than has ever been collected before in human history. Any time a hearing came up, we would have the data. At the same time, in the same package, we want to study the question: how do you design an outdoor wild area for use by the community? Kids would study the area, make a plan, take it to the community, get feedback, make a new plan, and take it to agencies of the government."

The city of Robert Moses and the Empire State Building has now spawned a man who dreams great dreams of protecting the little wild places in its midst.

The chart on the facing page is tangible evidence of one student's awakening. What looks like deserted beachline washed by the polluted waters of Jamaica Bay, turns out to be a whole world of life he discovers for himself. After studying the beach and making a drawing like the one shown here, it is never possible to look at a sand dune in quite the same way.

"I've lived here all my life. Plum Beach is nearby, nobody ever goes there, the water is polluted and everybody knows that. We went there and did a study. There's so much life there! I'm learning more than A plus B, more than just paperwork."

A Certain Feeling

"It's a certain feeling, a rapport with the teacher. Things like, there's a class where, after we do a full external analysis of a lobster, we boil it and eat it."

The students speak of their marine biology course with genuine enthusiasm, a rare quality in high school biology students. Silverstein and Siegel may have found a good way to win environmental hearings on marshlands; but if the comments of their students are any standard, their main achievement is a great method of training socially aware biologists. Here are some statements offered by a group of students:

"We get into it because of the field trips. There's a carry-over from what you see in the books and what you learn in the field. It's a matter of sacrificing free time. The philosophy is that the equipment is there, it should be used. As a result we've had more than ample opportunity to use very advanced equipment."

"I've lived here all my life. Plum Beach is nearby, nobody ever goes there, the water is polluted and everybody knows that. We went there and did a study. There's so much life there! I'm learning more than A plus B, more than just paperwork."

"Yesterday I was in court with Mr. Silverstein, on a case involving a sea wall. You get a feeling for the carry-over from the laboratory to the courtroom. In court, you get so mad you want

Lou Siegel and friends. Something about taking on opponents like 20 major oil companies has welded a bond between Siegel, Silverstein, and their students that goes far beyond the conventional teacher-student relationship. Though the prevailing mood is jocular and the affection is palpable, there is a large measure of respect and esteem that seems to move in both directions. Siegel's friends in this picture are, *left to right*, Phillip Bernstein, Steve Storch, Marlene Zichlinsky, and Mike Lazar.

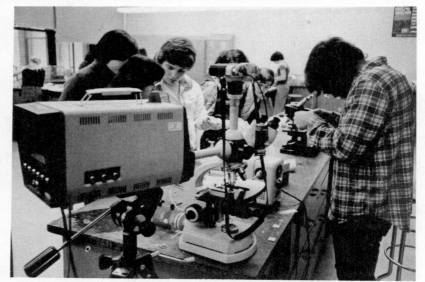

Though the marine biology classrooms at John Dewey High School are filled with the most elaborate and sophisticated professional equipment, the attitude of faculty is that it is "here to be used." After a short period of instruction, students are permitted to use even the most to jump up and scream, 'Liar!' A typical example: Mr. Silverstein was cross-examining a biologist, asking him about dune grasses, which build up land without a sea wall. The biologist was evading the questions; he was not interested in the truth, he was interested in the $400 he was getting to testify. You lose your respect. Whereas really he should have been concerned about the best method, he was only concerned about the method that was going to benefit him the most."

"There is a credibility gap between me and people who have known me for a long time. Like, your life rotates around marine biology, you have no social life; or, you work for the faculty, how can we tell you anything. But through time you can re-establish communication. It's fun."

"We go out, lecture teachers and students at other schools, show them slides, try to get them interested."

"What discouraged me was when we went out on a boat from the dock where they pipe the sewage onto a 200-foot boat, it looks like a small tanker. They just take it out and dump it. If people knew what this stuff was, if they could see it, I'm sure they would never get away with it!"

"We're doing a Coney Island pier study. We go out, test the water, ask people fishing there what they're catching. We've done it for two years, and want to measure changes over a period of years. Now I look more closely at things. Like, there's one tank at the aquarium, most people walk by and say, 'What's in there? They forgot to put something in the tank.' That tank has everything that grows in this area. I stood there for two hours once. There's so much life!"

"You really sense what's going on as you walk around. You get down, and you get hope, in the same breath."

expensive lab equipment with minimal supervision. "Their confidence in us makes us more careful," one student says, "and besides, we know if we break something, it won't be there when we really need it." The students seem eager to match their teachers' commitment: "They (Silverstein and Siegel) will even come down here on a Saturday or Sunday, just to open up the place so we can use the equipment!"

"The biologist was evading the questions; he was not interested in the truth, he was interested in the $400 he was getting to testify. You lose your respect. Whereas really he should have been concerned about the best method, he was only concerned about the method that was going to benefit him the most."

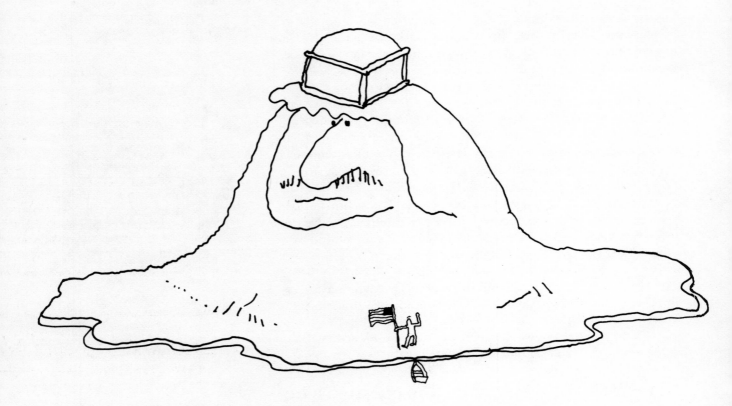

Nobody Walks Away from Twenty Million Dollars

Within artillery range of Fort Sumter — the island base off Charleston, South Carolina from which the opening shot of the Civil War was fired — another battle is taking shape. On one side is a young but rapidly growing environmental movement; on the other, land developers working for the Kuwait Investment Company. The prize in this confrontation between preservationists and petrodollars is Kiawah Island, a ten-mile-long barrier island a half hour's drive from Charleston — one of the precious few natural areas left in the southeast.

Even in the chill of February, Kiawah seems to be an island removed from time and place, a deserted tropical paradise. Strangely enough, very few of the quarter of a million people in the Charleston metropolitan area have any concept of the wonderful beach that lies an easy thirty minute drive from their doors.

The True Pacific

One has to see Kiawah Island to believe it. Unfortunately, that's not very easy to do. In February 1974 the island was bought, for a cool $17.4 million, by the Kuwait Investment Company — a Kuwaiti corporation, 50 percent of whose stock is owned by the Sheikdom of Kuwait. Although a causeway and bridge connect the island to the mainland, a locked gate, supplemented during the day with private guards, excludes the casual visitor from the Arabs' isle. Aside from people connected with the Kiawah Beach Company — an American firm the Kuwaitis have hired to turn the island into a resort community — only the residents of the 21 or so vacation homes on the island can bring in guests.

One of these island residents is Ben Gibbs. Ben is a leader of the Kiawah Defense Fund, a group incorporated in December 1974 to oppose development of the island. Now in his mid-20's, Ben has lived on the island for much of his life since he was eight. He probably knows the island better than anyone else, and his sensitive photographs of its flora and fauna testify to his deep attachment to it.

On a February night in 1975, Ben Gibbs took a visitor for a walk along the Kiawah Island beach. Only one light, a mercury vapor lamp placed atop a pole by the Kiawah Beach Company, cut the starlight with its metallic blue glow. Leaving it behind, eyes gradually became able to use the delicate illumination of stars.

The fantastic Kiawah beach stretched out ahead and behind, seemingly endless. Smooth as if it had been graded and swept, it gently sloped into the ocean. Soft, low waves lapped the sand.

"You call that ocean out west the Pacific," Ben Gibbs said quietly. "Well, this is the true Pacific. This is the most peaceful place you can imagine."

The history of Kiawah Island is entwined with the history of South Carolina. The island was named after the Indian tribe that once lived on the profusion of marine and marsh life there.

In February 1974 the island was bought, for a cool $17.4 million, by the Kuwait Investment Company — a Kuwaiti corporation, 50 percent of whose stock is owned by the Sheikdom of Kuwait.

INVOLVING BEN GIBBS

Ben Gibbs was raised on Kiawah Island and in Charleston, where his father practices law. His parents took him on trips all over the United States, giving him a perspective on the whole country. As he grew older, Gibbs wandered around the country on his own.

"I was going to college in Vermont when I got a call from Denny Royal, one of the heirs to the island, who wanted to make it into a nature preserve," says Ben. "He was going to do a topographical survey of the island, and asked if I wanted to work for him. I said yes, and dropped out of college. I started in September '73 and worked until March '74, when Denny came down to the trailer and said, 'Sorry, fellows, I'm going to lay you off tomorrow, I'm out of the deal,' and that was that. Fraser had made the deal between the Kuwaitis and the Royal heirs.

"For about three months after being laid off by Denny Royal, I worked for the Kiawah Beach Company. I was resident custodian and fire guard. Then I quit. I didn't like the people I was working for, and I didn't like the whole thing that was going down. I went back a little later for my W-2 form, and my former supervisor there sat me

In the eighteenth century, planters and their slaves cleared the forests from the land and made the island into one of the first coastal cotton and indigo plantations. A four-story wooden manor house still stands, now surrounded by forest; although built in 1772, its floors do not squeak and the staircase is still usable.

After the plantation was abandoned, sometime in the nineteenth century, the land went back to forest. Black families had small farms on it, as they do along much of the South Carolina coast. Through various devices, whites regained control of the land.

In 1951, C. C. Royal, an enterprising pulp mill operator from Aiken, South Carolina, bought the whole island for $125,000. Royal selectively logged the island, built a vacation home there for his family, and allowed a few others to do the same.

At present, no signs of the logging can be seen. Most of the island is thickly forested with oaks, palmettos, loblolly pines, magnolias, and other species of the Southern coastal forest. The forest is protected from salt spray by a "pruned shrub thicket," a dune ecosystem trimmed by saline winds from the ocean. At the ocean front, grasses give way to the magnificently clear beach, which is a good hundred yards wide in most places.

The island is separated from the mainland by a marshy river. There are extensive brackish-water marshes on it, as well as large fresh-water ponds. A profusion of wildlife — deer, wild turkeys, bobcats, alligators, eagles, egrets, ducks, and other species — are joined in this richly productive natural environment by feral goats and pigs, run wild from the plantations of the past.

Even in the chill of February, Kiawah seems to be an island removed from time and place, a deserted tropical paradise. Strangely enough, very few of the quarter of a million people in the Charleston metropolitan area have any concept of the wonderful beach that lies an easy thirty minute drive from their doors.

A Natty Alligator

"There is no public beach access available of any significant size in the Charleston area," says Steve Walker, a young statistician who is part of the Kiawah Defense Fund group. "The ideal thing for Kiawah would be wildlife protection for environmentally sensitive areas and beach availability for public use."

"The trick," says Ben Gibbs, "is to make the connection in people's minds between the beach — which is held in trust for the public — and access to that beach. If the beach is there and you can't get to it, it doesn't make any difference if it's there or not. After the next 20 years, there are probably going to be about three-quarters of a million people here. This area of the country is growing really fast. There's going to be a lot of pressure to get to the beach, and all of a sudden people will see all these obscenities that have been perpetrated up and down the coast by the politicians, the businessmen, the real estate interests, and they're not going to be able to get to the beach!

"For so long, South Carolina has been a rural state. It's been *so* rich in natural resources. People who wanted could just get in their car and go for an hour or so — they could go fishing, hunting, hiking, camping. Whatever they wanted to do, they could get to a place that was unspoiled and untouched. Suddenly all the areas are getting *creamed*. Big developers are sewing up the coast, little developers are running all around in between, selling half-acre lots."

One of the biggest of the big developers is Charles Fraser, head of Sea Pines. Fraser, a South Carolinian, has built developments throughout the southeast and in other parts of the country. One of his most famous works is Hilton Head, a resort community he built on another South Carolina barrier island.

"Charlie Fraser is known as a very aggressive sort of developer," says Steve Walker. "He wins a lot of design and conservation awards from questionable sources, self-serving kinds of things, which get a lot of headlines. He's in his mid-40's, and a graduate

down. I'd just been interviewed by CBS television news. He said he wasn't threatening me, and he said it so often that I got the message that he was. He said it was morally reprehensible of me to have done that interview. He said that I had been seen in the part of the island controlled by the company, wearing my hunting jacket — implying that I had been hunting — and said he couldn't guarantee my safety back there anymore. He said he'd gotten calls from members of his company, saying not to let Ben Gibbs get away with that again. I couldn't believe it.

"I don't remember what I told CBS. I kind of clutch in front of a camera. I usually talk about serenity. Apparently I didn't come off very well. Twenty million people saw the thing, and we only got one letter, from a guy in Washington State."

After quitting the Kiawah Beach Company, Gibbs worked as a steelworker and surveyor. He began giving a slide show and talk, in favor of preserving Kiawah Island. In the fall of 1974, he met and joined forces with the Audubon group interested in saving the island.

of Yale. At Hilton Head, people were told development would be low density, just like he's saying about Kiawah. Now Sea Pines is coming in at Hilton Head and putting in condominiums all over the place, jamming up the island; the homeowners' association there is mad at Sea Pines. At Hilton Head, on the golf course, Fraser has ponds with signs that say 'Please do not disturb the alligators.' And he really does have alligators there. He posed once with an alligator in a Brooks Brothers suit as a promotional stunt. That is, the alligator was in the Brooks Brothers suit."

It was Charles Fraser who arranged the sale of Kiawah by C. C. Royal's heirs to the Kuwaitis. The Kiawah Beach Company, which is developing the island, is not a corporation, so no public records exist of who owns how much of it. However, the company is staffed with Sea Pines personnel, who readily acknowledge that Sea Pines is providing the people who are developing the island.

"Sea Pines is in a tight situation because of the general economic situation," notes Steve Walker. "Fraser probably views Kiawah as a salvation, because he doesn't have any money tied up in it. He's just been retained to come in and develop it. And the Kuwaitis have all the money in the world. It would hurt Sea Pines if development was halted, but it wouldn't hurt the Kuwaitis. The Kuwaitis are believed to be very sensitive about public opinion, and might pull out if it were clear that local opinion is against the development."

Voice from The Citadel

The core of Charleston is an old city on the point between the Ashley and Cooper rivers. Here narrow streets, some gaslit and cobbled, trap sea mists between restored buildings dating to the 1600's. Family associations dating back that far are still highly influential in governing the city and the state.

A short ride from the city center is The Citadel, South Carolina's military college. Similar to West Point, The Citadel blends military with academic training. Its male students in grey-blue uniforms walk smartly around the quadrangle, between its fortress-styled buildings, changing direction with sharp right-angle turns.

In this milieu, it is no wonder that the Kiawah Defense Fund's most powerful voice is that of Dr. Richard Porcher, assistant professor of biology at The Citadel. "I'm a low-country native, raised in Berkeley County, which adjoins Charleston County," says Dr. Porcher. (The coastal plain of South Carolina is locally called the "low country.") "My ancestors were here in 1682. I'm from a long line of planters and noted botanists. I'm primarily a field botanist, and am familiar with the plants of the coastal plain area."

Dr. Porcher is vice president of the Charleston Natural History Society, the local chapter of the Audubon Society. Prior to the spring of 1974, the Society had not been active in conservation issues. Then, with fellow member Ann Pratt, Porcher formed a conservation committee within it. The first issue they tackled was the Kiawah Island development. "Three things happened at the same time then," recalls Porcher. "I finished my doctoral dissertation, we formed the conservation committee, and the Arabs bought the island. I've always had a love for the woods, and don't equate progress with concrete. I want my children to enjoy the same quality of natural areas that I do."

Porcher points out that, in South Carolina in general, and Charleston in particular, the environmental movement is in its infancy. Besides the Audubon chapter, only the Sierra Club is organized as an environmental group locally — and the Club has only been in Charleston for two years. Their work is cut out for them.

"In South Carolina," says Porcher, "a small group of people runs the state. Bankers and real estate people control the legislature. They want to develop every river, every swamp, every island. Some have been quoted as saying, 'We'll bulldoze those b—— environmentalists into the ocean if they give us any trouble.' They have the power to run roughshod over everything. Trails of economic involvement in Kiawah and other development projects run through the whole structure. We have no official state support whatsoever for saving the island."

Bid for Moratorium

Porcher and Ann Pratt started out by making public statements and writing letters to the editor, pointing out the values of the island and the losses its development would cause. "Our coast is now being developed in such a way that people are being denied access to the beach," remarks Porcher. "The Kiawah developers plan to put just one small parking lot at the end of the beach, which is ten miles long. Numerous states are now passing beach access laws. Not South Carolina."

Their efforts attracted much national attention to the issue. Major stories were written on Kiawah for the *Washington Post, New York Times, Wall Street Journal, London Daily Mail, Los Angeles Times,* and other huge dailies. They held frequent informal meetings at private homes. But their local reception was lukewarm, and they hadn't worked out any clear alternative to development of Kiawah.

In the summer of 1974, Porcher went to a regular Audubon Society meeting in Atlanta, Georgia. There he met people who had drawn up a successful proposal to make a national seashore out of Georgia's Cumberland Island.

"Cumberland Island," Porcher explains, "is an 18-mile-long barrier island that was owned by a few families. Sea Pines moved in, bought land on it, and was going to develop. The whole state of Georgia literally rose up against them: congressmen, senators, everybody. The island is now designated as a national seashore. They had state help there, which we don't have here right now."

If a senator and a congressman were to introduce a bill to make Kiawah into a national seashore, development would be halted while the National Park Service studied the feasibility of the idea: a process that would take about a year and a half. Thus far, Kiawah's defenders have had no support from congressional representatives.

Porcher says, "We are trying to raise the issue: 'If a proper and thorough study were made, would it reveal that a Kiawah National Seashore might be a better alternative, for South Carolina and the nation, than another development project?' "

Preparing for Action

In December 1974 the Kiawah Defense Fund was formally incorporated, and the small group of dedicated defenders of Kiawah began planning for a long-term campaign to save the island from development. Their first arena of confrontation appears to be the Charleston County Council, before which the Kiawah Beach Company was preparing to apply for rezoning of the island from "agricultural-general" to "planned unit development."

The Charleston Planning Board, which advises the county council, is receiving preliminary plans from the Kiawah developers. Kiawah Defense Fund lawyers say that these preliminary documents are public; the planning board says they're not, and won't show them to the island's defenders. "In January 1975," says Steve Walker, "the only professionally trained environmental planner on the planning board staff quit in disgust, because he said doors were being closed in his face and he wasn't being given any input on the planning process for Kiawah. The planning board is dominated by real estate interests; the majority of people on it are realtors."

"There are nine members of the county council," says Ben Gibbs. "We've taken two of them on a tour of Kiawah. We'll take two more next week."

The timing of the zoning hearing before the county council is up to the developers. Meanwhile, the site is being bulldozed and prepared for initial construction. The developers hold that under present zoning, they can do much of their construction without any zoning changes or public hearings.

Kiawah's defenders will try to get a lot of people to the zoning hearing, but have little hope of rallying much significant expert testimony to buttress their case. "The only experts who know about Kiawah Island are members of the Environmental

Research Center," says Ben Gibbs. "This is a group, composed largely of professors from the University of South Carolina, which is under contract to the Kiawah Beach Company to do an ecological survey of the island. Their survey is the only one that has been done of the island."

"Sea Pines is notorious for spending enormous amounts of money," adds Steve Walker. "Even their own money. Now they have the Kuwaitis' money to spend."

The Kiawah defenders briefly circulated a petition, asking that the county council deny rezoning and that the National Park Service study the island for possible national seashore designation. "The opposition was saying that we were just a handful of radicals trying to stop progress," says Richard Porcher. "We had to prove to ourselves that we weren't just a handful, so we got out the petition. We have five or six thousand signatures. Now we've stopped the petition campaign; it did show there's support."

Two lawyers are now working with the Kiawah Defense Fund, preparing for possible legal action if all else fails to stop the Kuwaitis and their American developers. Porcher concedes that possibly the development can't be stopped, and thinks they may sue for beach access.

"We're starting to fight the state power structure," says Porcher, "doing the groundwork for many battles to come. We've got to stop special interest groups from completely dominating and controlling what's going on in the state."

The Developers' Tour

Strained geniality was the order of the day on February 8, 1975, as the Kiawah Beach Company played host to the local Sierra Club chapter in the natural paradise both groups are so intimately concerned about. For obvious reasons, the developers had not been eager to squire Sierra Club members around their island domain; but a letter to the editor in a Charleston paper written by Nancy Chirich of the Club, in which she suggested that the company was trying to keep people off Kiawah, brought a phoned invitation a few days later.

Frank Brumley, in charge of the development for the Kiawah Beach Company, began the day with a flawlessly affable air. The tour, limited to about 20 conservationists by the developers, proceeded by pickup and jeep to the proposed marina site (now an area of live oyster beds), the manor house, the ponds with their egrets and palm-fringed tropical look, and a very tastefully constructed boardwalk dotted with placards bearing brief ecological descriptions of the surroundings. Brumley and his associates were courteous and helpful. The conservationists asked discrete and polite questions, generally evading sensitive areas of difference.

By lunch the amiability was developing cracks. Developers and conservationists were all together on the sun deck of the company's guest house. It isn't a very big sun deck. On one corner of it Brumley was explaining how the 150-car parking lot they were going to give the public on one end of the island was plenty of beach access, and more than they were required to provide. In the other corner Ben Gibbs was explaining that it wasn't too late to stop the whole development, and make a national seashore out of the place.

Finally Gibbs asked Brumley if they were going to visit the site being cleared for the motel, which is among the first buildings the developers plan to erect. Brumley said of course, that's what they had planned all along.

The cleared site looked as bulldozed forests look. Brumley climbed onto the seat of a tractor to address the conservationists, making a bizarrely appropriate tableau.

"It would be a mistake to oppose rezoning the island," said Frank Brumley. "The present zoning, called agricultural, is a misnomer. Actually, we can develop under the present zoning.

Ben Gibbs photograph

THE LOGGERHEAD TURTLE

The beach of Kiawah Island is one of the few remaining spawning grounds of the loggerhead turtle, an endangered species. "Loggerhead turtles are three or four feet in diameter, huge sea turtles," explains Ben Gibbs. "The females come in to the beach from the end of May until the first part of August. They come up at night, dig a hole in the sand on the dune line, and lay eggs — 100 to 150 eggs — in a hole. And they cover up the hole and go back in the water, and that's the last you see of them.

"It turns out that the turtles are extremely sensitive to light. When their eggs hatch, the young turtles use the reflected light of the full moon to find their way to the ocean. They hatch under a full moon. If you turn on a flashlight for one or two seconds, the mother turtles don't come at all. That's the reason they're an endangered species — all the lights up and down the East Coast.

"I have a friend who's working on a turtle study for the Kiawah Beach Company. He says he's disillusioned because beside the ocean front motel they're building now will be a parking lot, with mercury vapor lamps on 25-foot poles. This will keep turtles from going up on one-fourth to one-half of the beach. Their environmental advisors had recommended no lights on the ocean front. The environmental portion of the company puts out favorable statements; then the profit-making portion overrules them, and that's the end of it."

We're filing a planned unit development for the entire island, however. The rezoning will allow clustering, which is more ecologically sound. The alternative, under present zoning, is subdivision development. Our company wouldn't be associated with that type of development, but we'd probably sell it to somebody who would subdivide.

"A national seashore here is not a realistic possibility. The National Park Service is $500 million behind in acquisition. Besides, there are already 114 miles of coastline owned by the National Park Service in North Carolina, South Carolina and Georgia."

"How much of that is in South Carolina?" asked Ben Gibbs. (There is no national park land at all in South Carolina.) Brumley turned to an associate who said, well, none of it was actually in South Carolina. Gibbs kept pressing Brumley with sharp questions, some of which related to all the oil money in Kuwait.

Finally Brumley retorted: "The Kuwaitis have put $20 million into this development so far. Nobody walks away from $20 million, no matter how much oil they're pumping out of the ground. The real estate industry is one of the most depressed in the nation right now; developers are going broke. We couldn't go on without the Kuwait Investment Company. We expect a second-home demand in the spring of '76, and we're developing for that."

Abruptly, but still politely, Frank Brumley terminated the tour. Beneath his thoroughly professional job of public relations, he must have had a sinking sensation of *deja vu;* for, as one of his young associates had earlier said, Frank Brumley had been in charge of the Sea Pines development at Cumberland Island, until it was turned into a national seashore.

On the way back to the guest house, Ben Gibbs and other conservationists engaged in a rather heated exchange with a couple of young Kiawah Beach Company employees.

"Why do we suddenly need this island for beach access, just after the Arabs bought it?" asked one of the company employees. "Why didn't we need it before? The Arabs are businessmen; they have as much right as anybody else to engage in free enterprise."

Gibbs responded that the population was growing, more beach access was needed. "We're really trying to save one of the last natural areas left," he added.

"I hope there are no hard feelings on your side," Gibbs said on arrival at the gate. "I know there are none on mine." The two company employees turned silently and coldly, and walked away. Gibbs looked at their backs. "Their backgrounds are diffenent from mine. They have families to feed," he said. "I can understand their attitude." Then Ben Gibbs drove back to Charleston, to tell a radio audience that Kiawah Island should become a national seashore.

Will Giraffes Spoil Vermont?

"It started the way things start in small Vermont towns, with rumors: you know, somebody's going to bring in zebras and antelopes and so on. You tend to ignore it. Then on July 9, 1973 it developed reality rather quickly."

That was the day that Peter B. Smith of the village of Belmont (which is part of the town of Mount Holly) drove home from an outing to an encounter which would lead to the first constitutional test of Vermont's strong environmental protection law, Act 250.

A Polished Presentation

Smith, a Vermonter in his mid-30's, had just returned from an outdoor jaunt with a group of vacationing teenagers. He wasn't eager to attend the Mount Holly Planning Commission meeting scheduled for that evening, but, since he was one of the five commission members, he went.

What he saw was an anomaly in that tiny town. A poised young man named James D. Kinsey, a veterinarian from Manchester, Vermont, was proposing to set up a "Wildlife Wonderland" within the town's zoning jurisdiction.

"It was a very polished presentation," Peter Smith recalls. "He had maps, charts, and an artist's conception of what the buildings and pens were going to be like. He explained that the corporation he headed owned 630 acres or so, on which he wanted to put imported animals of various kinds, a barnyard, a miniature railroad, and that sort of thing. He said he wanted people to develop appreciation for nature and the outdoors. It sounded nice, initially."

Then Dr. Kinsey came to traffic. "He was talking about three hundred thousand visitors in one hundred thousand cars," says Smith. "Belmont is a one-street village. It has a church, a town hall, an Odd Fellows hall, and a general store. About 100 yards from the store, across the road, is a lake with a beach. In the summer, kids and dogs are constantly on the road. Kinsey's projections, which were probably realistic, figured out to about

If you don't slow down, you miss it. Tiny Belmont, Vermont, is on the edge of the Green Mountain National Forest, and on the main access to Dr. James Kinsey's proposed "Wildlife Wonderland," which would attract tourists down the road you see in this photograph. Although it appears that the zoo may be defeated, the controversy it stirred up has led to a challenge to Vermont's model land-use legislation, Act 250.

four or five cars a minute; but they would probably all come at once."

Smith, who is trained to be a high school biology teacher, is a woodsy sort of fellow. He lives in a log cabin with his wife Stephanie, who runs a nursery school. He wears thick woolen shirts, old blue jeans, and well-worn leather moccasins. He works in the oldest cheese factory in Vermont, where the cheese is lovingly hand-raked and kneaded. Peter Smith did not want to see his town overrun by herds of tourists bent on seeing giraffes in Vermont.

"I asked Kinsey if he would put up a directional sign in Ludlow, to keep people from going through Belmont," recalls Smith. "That was the first time I thought he wasn't dealing with me honestly. He never answered that question, except by avoiding an answer to it."

The Tax Question

In order to get a necessary zoning variance, Kinsey would have to get approval from the town selectmen. The planning commission, members of which are appointed by the selectmen, could only make recommendations to the selectmen. Owing to the importance of the issue, the planning commission scheduled a town meeting for August, so Kinsey's pitch could be heard by a wider audience before the planning commission voted.

Smith immediately saw that taxes would be the main concern of the townspeople. "Everybody was looking at a $400,000 project — he had advertised that figure — and said, 'Hey, we can make a bundle out of this.'" Smith prepared an analysis of the taxes the game farm would bring in, and the impact it would have on municipal services.

The town meeting was attended by about 130 people, a significant portion of the 500 or so voters in Mount Holly. "The developer made his presentation," says Smith, "and remained standing, taking questions, in effect beginning to chair the meeting. So I stood up and delivered my tax revenue estimates. I raised questions. For example, livestock is taxed at a low rate; would his zoo animals be considered livestock? Woodland is taxed at the lowest rate, and he would have 550 acres of woodland. He could argue he was being discriminated against if we taxed him at higher rates. Kinsey challenged my estimates, said that taxes could be three times higher than I estimated — not *would, could.* Subsequently, before the district environmental commission and under oath, he gave my exact figures to the penny."

Smith recalls that a poll of the crowd after the meeting ran 2 to 1 against the game farm. The planning commission voted 4 to 1 against it. Nevertheless, there was strongly stated support

EDITOR'S NOTE

We asked Peter Smith to write a description of the landscape over which the fight described on these pages took place. We did so because we think it is as important to know what was being fought over as it is to know how the battle was conducted. And besides, few of us are fortunate enought to know a Vermont mountain intimately. Here is what he sent us.

The lower slopes of the Green Mountains were once covered by great massive sugar maples, yellow birches, and beeches, their canopy high above a forest floor almost devoid of underbrush. Only an occasional opening — the result of some minor catastrophe — let in sunlight enough to release the seedlings, producing a thicket of saplings to repair, eventually, the hole above. The exceptions were valleys and high basins where beaver dammed the streams, flooded a few acres, and let in sun. When the trees were cut back too far to make harvesting them safe or efficient, the beaver moved on, leaving the dam unattended. Eventually the dam would release its water, providing a meadow deep in the forest.

Among the mosaic of autumn reds, golds, and yellows, and the winter grays, an occasional dark green hemlock protruded; but the evergreens, red spruce and balsam fir, usually provided a dark green cap seldom extending far down the mountain slopes, though often to be found in low, wet, cold pockets between hills.

As a result of the diverse habitats, early explorers found game plentiful, and in the years following the Revolutionary War, log cabins began to appear in their own self-created openings. Given a few more years, a small sawmill on a nearby stream, and frame buildings, their supports the hewn trunks of a virgin forest, replaced the cabins, thus pushing the forest back still farther. Stone walls were thrown up next, as much to keep stock from wandering as to delineate a boundary and clear the land. There's a saying among Vermonters. "God made the earth in six days and threw stones at Vermont on the seventh. Further, my ancestors are all dead from having picked up after Him." And pick up they did. Farther and farther the forests were pushed back to make room for sheep, pigs, chickens, a team of horses or oxen, and a few cows; with the aid of a small garden, these were almost all the necessities a family needed.

The growing season was short, frost to frost, the soil thin and the slopes steep, as often as not facing north. Winter never really let go; rather spring sun pried it loose, finger by finger, gaining by day and losing by night but each day gaining a little more than it lost, and in the exchange starting the sap to flow in the sugar maples beyond the walls. No diligent family let that pass without catching what they could to boil into syrup and sugar for the year ahead.

And then it was over, in scarcely a hundred years people had cleared the land, built a way of life, and lost it again. One by one these hill farms melted back into the woods as sons and daughters found easier work in neighboring towns. Each year their fathers cut the brush back on the stone walls a little less thoroughly until they, too, were gone, leaving winter snows and winds, and a few people who could not move, to finish the work.

Deer mice were probably the first to reclaim the empty buildings, followed by porcupines gnaw-

Despite the planning commission's opinion, the selectmen voted to grant Kinsey the zoning variance and allow him to create Wildlife Wonderland. Smith says, "They saw it as taxes, jobs, and getting rid of that road."

for Kinsey. "One basic feeling expressed," says Smith, "was that since the man owns the land, he can do what he wants with it. We also ran up against the small-town Vermont prejudice against 'outsiders.' I came here as a baby, but I'm thought of as an outsider. Outsiders should be seen and not heard. That was the cause of a great deal of dissension at the meeting, directed against myself and a number of others who were opposing the development."

Vermont towns are required by state law to maintain existing roads. There are many old unused roads in Vermont which, when brought back into use, nearly bankrupt the towns required to maintain them. One such road lay on Kinsey's land; and Kinsey promised to maintain it himself. Despite the planning commission's opinion, the selectmen voted to grant Kinsey the zoning variance and allow him to create Wildlife Wonderland. Smith says, "They saw it as taxes, jobs, and getting rid of that road."

Act 250

Vermont's Land Use and Development Law, commonly called Act 250, is a model piece of legislation designed to protect that happy state from the ravages of unwise development. Before a developer can proceed, he has the burden of proving that his project will not be damaging to the environment, nor damaging to the community for which it is planned. The act sets ten stringent criteria, and establishes district environmental commissions to hold hearings on these criteria. Decisions of the district commissions can be appealed to the state's environmental board.

The act offers the option of ruling on criteria 9 and 10 first (which require that any development conform to local or regional plans); then, if the development passes these hurdles, going on to hearings on criteria 1-8. Kinsey took this option. Smith thinks this decision saved the day for opponents of Wildlife Wonderland. "If the developer had started out by going through criteria 1-10, district first, then state, we would have been in a bad position. We hadn't generated enough support around town, or enough fear that the thing was going to go through. But because he chose what turned out to be the longer route, we had time."

Perhaps even more telling at this phase, the opponents of Wildlife Wonderland had no expert testimony prepared with which to combat Kinsey's testimony in the environmental hearings. Peter Smith, representing the Mount Holly Planning Commission, testified over and over in the hearings, lugging his "office" with him in an increasingly heavy, ancient, cracked leather satchel.

Kinsey didn't solicit expert testimony. He chose to provide most of it himself, and for a while it worked. He won approval at the hearings on criteria 9 and 10 at the district commission. His opponents appealed to the state environmental board. The state board then asked the district commission to rule first on criteria 1-8. Kinsey won the ruling on criteria 1-8 at the district commission.

By the spring of 1974, says Peter Smith, "it became obvious that we were going to have to get a lot more expert testimony, and a lot more local support."

A Tiger in Your Town

That spring, another event occurred which looked like it would pave the way to the Wildlife Wonderland: one member of the Mount Holly Planning Commission resigned, and was replaced by a strong supporter of the game farm. Now the planning commission was split 2 to 2 on the game farm, with one member (who earlier voted against the game farm) undecided. It seemed that Smith's only supporting organization against Kinsey's development was about to abandon the issue.

At this crucial point, Smith and his fellow game farm opponents did a number of things without which their earlier efforts probably would have been in vain. "I asked friends to circulate a petition asking the planning commission to oppose the game farm," he says. "In essence, since I was on the planning commission, I was getting up a petition to pressure myself to vote! I didn't actually go out and pass it around, of course. It worked; we got 200 signatures, and the petition was presented at a planning commission meeting. It convinced the undecided member that we were right."

Just after that planning commission meeting, in early May 1974, Smith got together with a few friends to set up a more formal organization to oppose Wildlife Wonderland. Besides the Smiths, the "working group" eventually shook down to Dan and Elizabeth Dunbar and Jim and Bette Kaufmann of nearby East Wallingford, Mrs. Grace Smith (Peter's mother), and Bob Broderick the attorney, who joined later.

Choosing the goal posed no problem. "What we wanted to accomplish was to stop Wildlife Wonderland," recalls Elizabeth Dunbar. "We thought we'd all be directly affected by it, adversely."

"We expected many growth-related changes if the Wildlife Wonderland was built," Dan says. "What would be next? Restaurants, probably, and a stoplight in town, and so on. As it is

ing at door frames and sills which sweaty hands had flavored with salt, until, with their underpinnings gone, barn and house collapsed into their stone-lined cellar holes, to become fertilizer for the wild raspberries which soon would take over. Only a lilac bush remained above ground to mark the spot, and perhaps some old maple still stood in the yard, bored round with tap holes from all the springs passed. The fields beyond disappeared equally fast.

[Continued on page 81]

Photographs of the site taken by Lee Harris. The track in the lower photo was made by an otter.

Peter Smith, *right*, biologist and cheesemaker, here with part of his band of zoo-fighters. *From left:* Lee Harris, photographer and leather-worker; Elizabeth Dunbar, nurse, and husband Dan Dunbar, paperhanger; Stephanie Smith, nursery school director (and Peter's wife).

now, we can sit on the front porch and wave to two or three tourists passing by every day. With Wildlife Wonderland around, we were planning to put up a six-foot fence."

The handful of people at that initial gathering formed Citizens Against Wildlife Wonderland (CAWW). "We had to have a group to share the load," notes Peter. "Forming an organization also gave us the appearance of having more strength than we otherwise would have appeared to have. We could type up letterheads, have an address. And, along with the Mount Holly Planning Commission, it meant that two groups were against the game farm."

Dan and Elizabeth went from door to door explaining the issue and asking for support and contributions. "We got into some arguments with people, but we tried to keep it short," says Elizabeth. "We still regularly talk to people, old people who can't get out, and keep them up-to-date. Also, we can hear rumors that are going around."

The door-to-door visits proved to be a good way to raise money ($4,000 was eventually collected). They also helped CAWW to mobilize people later to attend the state environmental board hearings. Because the board wanted to test local sentiment on the issue (and look good), the first hearing was held in Belmont; the hall was packed with opponents of the development. Smith recalls with a grim smile that the board members' nine cars created their own traffic jam in the tiny village, and that they had to make a round trip of six miles to find lunch. The CAWW followed up by getting townspeople to other hearings held at other locations in southern Vermont.

The Dunbars, who live on one of the main roads through the area, put up a sign in their yard which read, "Want a tiger in your town? Oppose Wildlife Wonderland." Elizabeth says, "People would slow down, stop, back up, wave, and smile. One man said he drove miles out of his way just to see it."

Lawyers and Experts

In the spring of 1974, Smith was looking for a lawyer and a number of experts to help fight Wildlife Wonderland in the state environmental board on behalf of the Mount Holly Planning Commission.

"The first attorney I approached gave me a bad weekend," Smith recalls. "He told me we didn't have a case."

The second lawyer, Bob Broderick from nearby Rutland, turned out to be much more useful. "He came in to one of our planning commission meetings even before we hired him and said, 'You don't owe me a dime, but I just covered you on a deadline for filing an appeal.' We'd had a different idea of when the appeal of the district environmental commission's ruling on criteria 1-8 was due. He asked for $500 in two weeks, and about $2,000 in all, and a guarantee that expert witnesses would be available for the hearings. We hired him."

The geologist Smith contacted in Burlington at the University of Vermont gave a response typical of other experts who eventually testified against the Wonderland. "You can't afford me," the geologist says. "Whatever you can pay, I'll work for that."

Smith's advice to anyone who is going to orchestrate opposition at a hearing is to "call anybody and everybody to testify." You never know who might make a difference. For example, Smith got a noted Vermont ecologist to testify on very short notice. It turned out that the ecologist knew a botanist who was on the state environmental board. "The ecologist could see just exactly what sort of evidence the board needed to hear," Smith says, "and he provided it."

Smith cautions users of state employees as witnesses. "With them," he says, "you are likely to get the 'how do I keep my job?' syndrome. How do you do that? Well, you don't antagonize anybody in any way. One of our witnesses, a state employee, testified that the wastes from the animals would cause water pollution. Then he reversed his testimony in cross-examination. Eventually he was called as a witness by the other side!"

[Continued from page 79]

With abandoned fields and return of the forest, deer and bear, bobcat and snowshoe hare reclaimed their homes. Gone were the wolf and mountain lion, but in their place came a newcomer, the coyote. And the otter and beaver, along with the mink, reclaimed the waterways. Often the beaver simply added to a mill dam long since abandoned, backing the water up to the advancing trees. Overhead, goshawk and broadwing, pileated woodpecker and arctic three-toed, winter wren and nuthatch, veery and hermit thrush claimed, through song, these woods for their own.

Such is the wildlife wonderland we have inherited. And such is the land a developer would have sable antelope and yak, llama and camel, wallaby and eland grazing upon and call *it* "Wildlife Wonderland" — three hundred animals on some ten acres of steep land, with shallow soils, winter temperatures occasionally approaching thirty degrees below zero, and an annual snowfall of over twelve feet. For a mile or more in either direction, no houses break the forest wall; and across the road lies the boundary for twenty thousand acres of one of the wildest sections of Green Mountain National Forest. Two hundred thousand people would inundate the nearby town and a miniature train would drown out the songs of our birds.

A pristine stream flows through the center of the area and, despite its use as a trail and slide by a wandering otter, or an occasional bath by a bird, still provides a clear cold drink with virtually no contaminants of any sort. Yet if the development were to proceed, it would become as high in nitrates, phosphates, bacteria, and, eventually, algae, as the worst streams in the state. It would be comparable to farm streams draining manure piles. Further, soil compaction by animal hooves on the surrounding slopes, and resultant destruction of the vegetation, would cause erosion of approximately 300 tons of topsoil per acre per year — nearly three inches from the entire surface to be washed into a stream scarcely six feet wide and two feet deep.

All of this, according to experts from the Departments of Botany, Geology, and Zoology at the University of Vermont, would irreparably destroy the area. Other experts testify that, in addition to simply driving out the native wildlife, there is the very real possibility that exotic diseases could be introduced into native populations. An engineer for the developer denies all of this, then explains away the possibility of damage with the comment, "Well, it won't affect us in our lifetime." With any kind of luck, he'll be correct because it will never be built and no one's life will have to suffer the effects. Land and economics being what they are, someone will sooner or later find another use for this land, but hopefully one more gentle. Hopefully one which will neither destroy the land and its wildlife, nor the tiny community of which it will be a part.

An Open Letter to Catamount Customers

The state environmental board hearings ground on through June and July of 1974, with Kinsey trying to prove that his game farm would have no undue impact on various environmental elements, and the CAWW witnesses arguing that it would. It all began to wear on the CAWW activists.

"You get so doggone wrapped up in it that it stops being fun," says Peter Smith. "When it gets so boring you hate to get up the next day and do anything, you're defeated. You've got to keep coming up with stuff just to keep yourselves amused. That's where the ad came in handy."

"We will carry this project through; we won't be done in by a group of bigoted people and rich people. I won't be harassed by people like that, and I won't be out-talked by them, and I won't be out-spent by them. I've always told them that they're doddering old people and I'll outlive them if I don't do anything else."

The "ad" was "An Open Letter to Customers of Catamount National Bank," which ran prominently in the August 27, 1974 issue of *Vermont News Guide,* the town paper of nearby Manchester. It read, in part: "We don't want a zoo in our town any more than the people of Manchester wanted a zoo in their area. The man responsible for this ecological disaster is Dr. James Kinsey, a Manchester veterinarian. He tried to put his zoo in Manchester, but gave up when people told him they didn't want any part of it."

Though some members of CAWW objected to it, the ad served to crack Kinsey's professional cool. A friend of Elizabeth Dunbar's was in the *Vermont News Guide* office when Kinsey burst in, irate, and began denouncing the paper for running the ad.

Soon after, the Manchester Chamber of Commerce scheduled a debate on the topic. Peter Smith and the Dunbars drove over for the event. "We put out about 100 information sheets in a stack," Dan Dunbar recalls. "Five minutes later we discovered they had disappeared. Somebody had just taken them away. Fortunately, Peter had some more in his car. We put those out and stood guard over them."

After the debate, Elizabeth says, "We felt mauled. We were really down." They had learned a trick from Kinsey's supporters, who had asked Kinsey prepared questions from the floor, thus giving Kinsey a forum to which Peter Smith could not respond. "We should have had questions for Peter that he could have answered brilliantly," says Elizabeth. "Kinsey's shills, who were dispersed in the crowd, did have good questions for Kinsey."

But the next day, Kinsey's anger boiled out into the press. A news article reported a number of vituperative insults he uttered after the debate, the first of a long series of bitter remarks. For example, recalls Smith, the article said that "Kinsey lambasted Congressman Lloyd, a popular local legislator, saying how Lloyd often acts in local playhouse productions and after leaving the stage has a hard time relating with the real world."

Kinsey's splenetic statements worked to the advantage of his opponents. Perhaps his classic curse was reported in the *Ver-*

James Kinsey, *far left*, stands on the site of his proposed zoo and describes its operation to members of Vermont's Environmental Board and local observers. *Rutland Herald* photograph.

mont Times and reprinted on a CAWW fund-raising flyer: "We will carry this project through; we won't be done in by a group of bigoted people and rich people who don't want their property changed when it isn't their property. I won't be harassed by people like that, and I won't be out-talked by them, and I won't be out-spent by them. I've always told them that they're doddering old people and I'll outlive them if I don't do anything else. If I can't out-talk them and I can't out-spend them, then I'll still be here when they're not."

Green Mountain Boys

The state environmental board decision was expected in the fall of 1974. Kinsey, confident that his permit would be granted, moved equipment to his proposed game farm site in October, ready to start without delay.

The CAWW, not at all confident that the environmental board would rule against Kinsey, asked for a 30-day stay of decision. "We wanted to make it difficult for him to proceed even if he got the permit, by generating statewide opposition," says Smith.

Much to Kinsey's surprise, the state environmental board ruled unanimously against granting him a permit to build Wildlife Wonderland. "They ruled against him on all the hard criteria, too," says Smith. "Not municipal services, but water pollution, soil erosion, and so on. Our expert testimony had worked."

James Kinsey was not done for. "The environmental board is just a bunch of over-zealous Boy Scouts," he said, unconsciously complimenting two worthy organizations. Then he filed an appeal of the Vermont State Environmental Board decision to the Vermont Supreme Court, challenging the constitutionality of part of Act 250 and the correctness of the environmental board decision.

With other parties, CAWW is now filing a brief for the state in in the Supreme Court case. A statewide group, Citizens for a Better Vermont, has formed to support Act 250 and oppose the sort of development the act is designed to eliminate.

Peter Smith figures that Kinsey's backers are more interested in the Supreme Court case than is Kinsey. According to Smith, "The southern part of Vermont is loaded with developers. Now, with the economy in trouble, these guys are out of work. The easiest scapegoat is our environmental laws. They set up an organization called Green Mountain Boys to fight against the environmental laws. Ethan Allen would turn over in his grave."

An Unexpected Conclusion

After the Wildlife Wonderland fight had become a public issue, Edward F. Kehoe, fish and game commissioner, called the game farm "a farce." Peter Smith says, "It turned out that, personally, he doesn't like zoos." The Vermont legislature gave the fish and game board authority to regulate the importation and management of non-native animals into Vermont. The fish and game board scheduled a hearing in Manchester on the content of the regulations.

"I went to the fish and game board hearing with proposals drawn up with the idea of stopping Wildlife Wonderland," says Smith. "Kinsey and his lawyer were there. They presented their case, then left, saying, 'We've heard enough from this guy in the past 15 months.' That was a bad, *bad* mistake on their part.

"I proposed that all animals in captivity be kept in buildings as well as cages to reduce the likelihood of escape. That would rule out any open-air game farms. Mostly as a public relations thing, I proposed that all imported animals be inspected by a veterinarian who is neither the person selling them nor the person keeping them. The third thing I proposed was that there should be no contact areas — that is, areas where animals and people mingle. Kinsey wanted to bring in European deer that you could put your kid on the back of. I argued that this was the wrong attitude toward wildlife to encourage.

"The fish and game board bought all three of my recommendations, incorporating them into law. The result is that the game farm has had the course."

Now, suddenly the battle has shifted. Peter Smith and his friends have won their fight. Or have they? The challenge to one of the few well-conceived environmental laws this country has yet produced still stands. At the time of this writing, the larger fight is still undecided and the stakes are much higher.

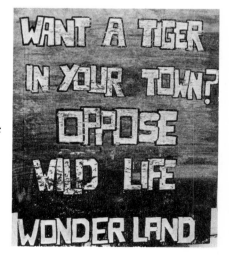

Second Thoughts on Future Power

EDITOR'S NOTE

Background for this article is largely from the working draft of "History of the Eugene Future Power Committee," by Rhoda Love. We are grateful to Ms. Love for the use of her material.

In August 1968, the Eugene Water and Electric Board (EWEB, pronounced "E-web" in Eugene), a public utility governed by an elected five-member board, announced that it would ask the voters in this Oregon city for a $225 million bond issue to finance the construction of a nuclear power plant. The power plant would have a one million kilowatt capacity.

The site had not been chosen; but in October, a month before the bond issue ballot, EWEB announced that it favored a site on flat farming land to the north of Eugene. Since nuclear plants discharge a lot of heated water, EWEB proposed to build a lake about 2,000 acres in size, into which the 80-degree discharge water would flow.

"The thing that really got me was that the hazards are so serious. The problems of radiation containment have not been solved."

Eugene, a city of about ninety thousand, is surrounded on three sides by mountains. Lush forests cover the slopes around the city, where they have not been cut to sustain the city's main industry: lumber. The city itself has a green, refreshing appearance. The University of Oregon, located in Eugene, has an enrollment of about sixteen thousand.

The people of Eugene were the first in the United States to vote on whether a nuclear power plant should be built. Also, the bond issue was the largest that had ever appeared on a Eugene city ballot. No opposition to the bond issue arose. In November 1968, the nuclear plant bond issue was approved by an overwhelming 4-to-1 margin.

Second Thoughts

Soon after the balloting, a few individuals scattered throughout Eugene began to have second thoughts about the nuclear power plant. Among these were three people who took action on their second thoughts: Jane Novick, Chris Attnaeve, and Joseph Holaday.

Jane Novick, artist and housewife, is a voluble and energetic person. Her husband, physical organic chemist Aaron Novick, worked on the Manhattan Project, which developed the atomic bomb, and later worked to try to keep the bomb from being used on a populated area. Chris Attnaeve, a housewife active in a number of civic causes, speaks with the authority of experience in many grassroots efforts. Joseph Holaday, a lean, soft-spoken retired nurseryman, provides quite a contrast to the women, both in his more advanced years and his carefully modulated style of speech.

Why didn't they raise questions about the plant *before* the bond issue ballot? Chris Attnaeve explains that at that time there was no critical factual information on nuclear plants available to the public. She had been out of town, and returned to read all the ads and stories in the local paper, the *Eugene Register-Guard*.

"What the voters saw," Chris recalls, "was a set of stories about how we needed power; how there was this marvelous, inexpensive technique we could use, because we didn't have any other source of power readily available. The only problem drawn out again and again was the problem of hot water, and that this hot water might be used for recreation and irrigation, converting a minus into a plus."

JOSEPH A. HOLADAY

Joe Holaday, first president of the Eugene Future Power Committee, is a third generation Oregonian. Reared in the Pendleton area of eastern Oregon, he moved to Eugene as a young man. For ten years he was a secondary school teacher, instructing students in politics, economics, and sociology. Then he set up his own business, the Holaday Nursery, which he operated for 20 years. Forced by rising taxes and assessments to sell his nursery in 1968, he is now semi-retired; he teaches horticulture part-time at Lane Community College.

"I've had a lifetime interest in social, economic, and political questions, as an observer," he says. "As a small businessman, I felt I shouldn't get actively involved. I'm glad that some of the small businessmen nowadays do get involved."

Joe's commitment to the campaign to stop the nuclear plant in Eugene began one day when he was lunching on the campus of the University of Oregon. "Have you heard where they're going to put that nuclear plant?" asked his young companion, who went on to tell him that they were going to put the plant on farmland that Joe knew well.

"Oh no, they can't do that!" said Joe Holaday.

Now that Joe is involved in social action, he has no intention of backing out. "I am opposed to further industrialization of the Willamette Valley, this beautiful valley in which we live," he says. "We regard every energy-intensive industry as an enemy."

Now in his late sixties, Joe Holaday says he will remain active in the Eugene Future Power Committee "as much as my strength, energy and time permit. These issues will be fought as long as my lifetime," he says to an interviewer less than half his age. "And they'll be fought as long as your lifetime, too."

"We all began to feel we had been tricked, that we had been the victims of a very deliberate campaign. We'd been told that there was nothing negative about the plant."

It was all this hot water that first aroused Chris' doubts. Eugene rests in a geological bowl, where temperature inversions (cool air overlain by warmer air) often trap dense smoke and fog. Chris says, "I began to wonder if an 80-degree lake, two-thirds the size of the town, would not produce fog."

Other individuals scattered throughout Eugene began to have second thoughts about nuclear power. Joseph Holaday read about the Atomic Energy Commission (AEC) taking federal land in Amchitka Island — land that was a wildlife refuge — to use as an atomic blast site. He became suspicious of AEC intentions in Eugene, wondering if they might be using subterfuge to gain access to land for dangerous activities. Jane Novick happened to have been reviewing *The Careless Atom,* a book by Sheldon Novick (no relation), for a women's group. Reading it, Jane recalls, "The thing that really got me was that the hazards are so serious. The problems of radiation containment have not been solved. Radioactive waste loomed large in my mind."

It was a group of farmers, however, who voiced the first public opposition to the nuclear plant. In February 1969, 115 landowners jammed a meeting north of Eugene, near the proposed site of the plant. Calling the location of a nuclear plant on farmland "the crime of the century," the farm group voiced formal opposition to the use of agricultural land for the plant. "With the farmers," says Joe Holaday, "it was a matter of protecting their way of life, as well as an economic matter. Their land would have been affected by roads, discharge water, and other activities connected with the plant. And many of them are third generation farmers in that area, to whom sale of farmland for the plant would have been an outrage."

The farmers and concerned citizens got together for the first time at a panel discussion held on April 16. Utility representatives on the panel told of great power needs to come. Professors from the University of Oregon spoke of the dangers of nuclear plants, and of the paradox of the utility's advertising campaign to get people to use more power. "One by one the people in the audience got up," Jane says, "and expressed tremendous reservations."

Joseph Holaday says, "Important to any group is a sense of being wronged, of indignation."

"And frustration!" Jane adds.

"We all began to feel we had been tricked," Chris notes, "that we had been victims of a very deliberate campaign. We'd been told that there was nothing negative about the plant."

The Atomic Stone Wall

The EWEB board refused repeated requests for public hearings. The intransigent refusal of the EWEB board of directors to answer questioning citizens added fuel to the fires of frustration.

In fact, the questioning citizens seemed to plunge some EWEB board members into a state of rage. Jane observes, "They loathed us with such a passion that you could see their teeth grinding in their jaws; they were *livid* with rage when they'd see us walk into the room. They really lost their cool."

In July 1969 the situation came to a head. The Eugene City Council called a meeting to discuss whether a public hearing on the nuclear plant could be held. The whole EWEB board was present, along with city council members. Jane recalls, "All the familiar faces were there, and some new ones: Joe, Chris, me, the farmers, private citizens, and students and faculty members from the University, who were all becoming more and more frustrated by EWEB's stubborn refusal to discuss their nuclear plans. Members of the audience were not allowed to testify at this meeting, but we all felt certain that at last EWEB would agree to follow the city council's suggestion and schedule a hearing."

The EWEB board again refused to schedule a public hearing. At that point, the audience — composed of a very irate group of people full of doubts about the nuclear plant — walked out and held a rump meeting in the hall.

It was then, Joe Holaday recalls, that the organized opposition to the plant was born. "I passed around a notebook," Joe says, "asking that all those who would be willing to undertake further study of this matter please sign." Sixteen people signed; three were farmers, and the rest were citizens with doubts about the plant.

Jane Novick thinks that it was EWEB's stonewall attitude that was their undoing. "If EWEB, instead of refusing to talk with us, instead of refusing to publicly discuss this issue, had given the appearance of being reasonable; if they had held meetings and had answered questions, even in their own deceitful way, they would've co-opted the whole movement."

The Politics of Inversion

During July and August the new group met, elected officers (Joseph Holaday, president; Jane Novick, secretary), chose the name Eugene Future Power Committee, and began developing a mailing list. They discussed the possibility of an initiative campaign — a common tactic in Oregon — but decided to wait until the hearing EWEB had finally agreed to hold on September 9.

Late summer is a stifling season in Eugene. Farmers are burning their fields to form fertilizer for new crops, and temperature inversions hold down hot, smoky air with even hotter air.

The EWEB hearing, held to "answer" questions asked two months before, turned out to be a public-relations-type presentation on the wonders of nuclear power. EWEB had a panel of seven experts, whose presentation of charts, slides, and speeches in defense of the nuclear plant droned on for four hours. By then, the audience had dwindled from 150 to a hard core of 50.

That afternoon, EWEB had reluctantly agreed to accept questions for their experts, but only if the questions were in writing. These questions were answered in a way that obscured serious issues about the dangers of nuclear plants. A typical example was a question that was intended to spark discussion of the fact that, in 1966, the Enrico Fermi Breeder Reactor near Detroit was shut down for four years because it nearly suffered a runaway chain reaction:

Question: Why was the Fermi Breeder Reactor near Detroit closed down?

Answer (by panelist Morton Goldman, staff member of the NUS Corporation, a nuclear consulting firm): The Fermi Breeder Reactor near Detroit is not closed down or certainly not closed down by the AEC. It is shut down at the present time for repairs and it will be started up again when the repairs are completed.

Joe Holaday and Jane Novick were angry, but cool-headed enough to issue the first of many nicely phrased press statements: *"The EWEB panel accepted the rapid increase in power demands without comment or critical evaluation of the real causes of demand (deliberate efforts to further industrialize the Pacific Northwest). Neither did the panel address itself to the overriding issue: the effects of such energy consumption on the liveability in the Valley. We further regret that far too much irrelevant material was introduced which was not in dispute. We regret that the panel appeared to be promotional rather than informational."*

A Modest Proposal

In October the new Future Power Committee began mapping an initiative petition campaign. Their first problem was to decide what to ask for. Opinion in the group was vigorous and diverse. Finally they chose an objective they could all agree on: a four-year moratorium on nuclear power development by EWEB, while further study on the effects of nuclear power on the local environment and economy could be made.

The initiative campaign was announced at a press conference on October 29. At the same time Charles Porter, a lawyer on the Future Power Committee, said they would sue EWEB if public monies were used to oppose the initiative. The battle was on.

The selection of this modest goal was a key element to the success of the campaign. "The goal was expedient and reachable," says Jane. Chris adds, "It was the goal everybody could agree on, though many were for total ban."

Calm Precision Meets Modern Witchcraft

"There is a vague, undefined emotional feeling about these nuclear plants," says Joe Holaday. "We don't understand it. Splitting the atom is modern witchcraft. It went all the way from the fear that a man would lose his virility if exposed to radiation — and that is true, as was found in a plant in the Soviet Union."

Jane and Chris contested the state of knowledge about radiation and virility with Joe. Their debate underlined two related problems which anyone opposing a nuclear plant must face squarely: the complexity of the technical facts, and the emotional responses evoked by atomic power.

"We did not have the credentials of nuclear physicists as did some of the people who were going to oppose us," Chris notes, "so we thought we'd better be totally accurate in everything we said."

They kept tight control on the content of everything put out by the Future Power Committee. Whenever possible, their board of directors would vote on policy. "Day to day, there was never anything that went out by just one person," Chris says. Three or four people would read each statement and tear it apart.

They eschewed controversial sources, even if those sources had good scientific credentials. Chris says, "We always tried to quote the AEC, or EWEB, or Westinghouse."

Adopting as a slogan the phrase, "We Can Wait . . . We Should Wait," the Future Power Committee set out to raise doubts in people's minds about the safety of nuclear plants, and about their environmental and economic desirability. They lost no opportunity to have speakers appear before service clubs, on talk shows, at schools, and wherever else they could get a hearing.

In the process of informing the people of Eugene about nuclear plants, members of the Future Power Committee gained some interesting insights into the minds of the people around them. "People believe what they're told," says Jane. "They identify with the establishment. When they're told they've been misled, when we say, 'No, it's not safe, we don't need it,' they're thrown into a very uncomfortable state of confusion."

Chris adds, "We took something away from them in a sense, which they should have known was too good to be true. They were told they were going to get this absolutely perfect thing, that it wouldn't cost anything."

One thing they felt they should have done earlier and more strongly in the campaign was present an alternative to nuclear power. When they circulated a *Christian Science Monitor* article on the feasibility of solar power, they won a number of votes. "The simple thing of giving them some other authoritative source seemed to work," Jane says.

"Women tend to say that they don't know what to think about the plants, or to object to them. Men tend to say that they know they're fine, and they have a lot of confidence in their knowledge. Your average male does not like to think that the technical world might have something wrong with it."

Chris believes that she detected a difference in attitude between the men and women she encountered: "Women tend to say that they don't know what to think about the plants, or to object to them. Men tend to say that they know they're fine, and they have a lot of confidence in their knowledge. Your average male does not like to think that the technical world might have something wrong with it."

Passing Petitions

To get their initiative on the ballot, the Future Power Committee had to get a number of signatures of voters equal to 15 percent of those who had voted in the most recent election for mayor — about 4,500 signatures. They mailed out 350 petitions to people who had agreed to help, asking them to pass them around door-to-door, at their offices, on street corners, or anywhere else.

They soon found that this was the wrong way to pass petitions. Returns were slow, and signatures not notarized. They then organized a well-monitored coverage of supermarkets and shopping center malls, with greater success.

They also found that personal style was all-important in passing petitions. "Jane was useless as a petition passer," Chris jokes. "You should do an instructional film on how to pass a petition." She then stands and holds out a notebook and pencil at arm's length, advancing and all but blocking the path of the would-be signatory, smiling genially. One feels gently compelled to grab them and sign.

One young mother with her child could fill two whole petitions while others got only two signatures. Another was so timid, says Chris, that "in order to sign the petition she was clutching, first of all you would have to make an indecent gesture!" On the other hand, when put in charge of dispatching and monitoring petition passers, the timid young lady proved to be marvelous.

By late February 1970, the requisite number of signatures was turned in and verified; and the measure, Ballot Measure 52, was added to the primary ballot for the May 26 election.

A Civilized Campaign

During the three months or so between completion of the petition campaign and the vote, the Future Power Committee smoked out EWEB officials into a number of face-to-face debates, and kept hammering away at EWEB's allegations.

They researched the power situation of the whole Pacific Northwest, and found that the nuclear plant initially was *not* intended to supply power to Eugene citizens. It was, in fact, part of a ten-year plan to further industrialize the whole area; its power would go elsewhere, largely to supply industries such as aluminum, which uses tremendous quantities of electricity. They confronted EWEB officials with these facts, in light of the EWEB warnings of brown-outs in Eugene if the power plant were not built.

Unfortunately, the farmers' group was no longer active. The previous October, EWEB had announced a siting change which moved the plant out of their neighborhood. Jane said, "The farmers were extremely helpful, extremely active, and very, very clever; and the minute we got the siting change they dropped out like that! It is difficult to motivate people in environmental campaigns unless you can show that they have a direct economic interest in your side winning."

A Cunning Canvass

In the final days of the campaign, EWEB and their allies in the local business community (who were operating as the Committee for Orderly Development of Electricity — acronym, CODE), unleashed a heavy salvo of advertisements, raising specters of economic stagnation and electric toothbrushes failing if measure 52 passed. The Future Power Committee countered with rational, doubt-raising flyers and ads of their own. The Committee also countered with the most imaginative tactic of the campaign: what might be called the "loaded questionnaire."

The loaded questionnaire was not exactly an original idea. "EWEB had put out a questionnaire that was heavily loaded on the 'we need the power' side," says Jane. "They simply reinforced propaganda they had been pouring out." The voters were asked questions about the major reasons they had for voting for a nuclear power plant.

The Future Power Committee canvass, a door-to-door coverage of Eugene near election day, presented voters with a questionnaire loaded the other way. People who showed little enthusiasm for the matter were simply asked four questions, one of which was:

Here are four areas that people are concerned about. Which ones are you concerned about?

1. radioactivity
2. hot water killing fish or other marine life
3. major accident or plant sabotage
4. economic risks

More interested respondents were left a longer questionnaire, offering a list of statements to which they could respond yes or no. The statements were designed to gauge how well people were informed on the issues, as well as how concerned they were about them; they presented a smorgasbord of horrors, all based on established fact about nuclear plants.

The canvass not only brought the issues raised by the Future Power Committee to the voters in a powerful and subtle way. It also indicated that they had at least an even chance of winning in the election. In some areas near the University of Oregon, opinion was running 4 to 1 in their favor. This gave the Future Power Committee workers heart to carry on to the end. "You've got to fight right to the last minute," says Chris. "You've got to do everything you can think of."

Housewives Reading Science

Measure 52 squeaked through by about 850 votes out of over 22,000 cast. The four-year moratorium proved to be the doom of EWEB's plans to build a nuclear power plant in the foreseeable future. In November 1974, EWEB formally abandoned its plans for a nuclear plant, saying that it would cost about $1 billion to build it at that time.

True to his word, Future Power Committee lawyer Charles Porter sued EWEB for the money they spent on the campaign. Adding insult to injury, the court ordered EWEB to repay that money (about $6,500) to their customers.

As of early 1975, the Eugene Future Power Committee was still vigorously in existence. They were concerning themselves with the future of power development in the whole Pacific Northwest, and aiding other groups in battles against nuclear plants. They lobbied to establish the Nuclear and Thermal Energy Council of Oregon, an official state body which sets criteria for siting nuclear and thermal power plants. Some of their members, having become experts on nuclear power during the campaign, testify in various hearings.

Existing loosely with no members, but an active mailing list, they can count on broad support whenever anything arises. Jane Novick and Chris Attnaeve regularly attend EWEB board meetings. There, they are still regarded with discomfort.

"I think what really drives them up the wall," Jane says, "is when Chris and I go to an EWEB meeting and we're reading *Science* magazine during the dull parts. They can't stand seeing housewives reading scientific magazines."

"I think what really drives them up the wall," Jane says, "is when Chris and I go to an EWEB meeting and we're reading *Science* magazine during the dull parts. They can't stand seeing housewives reading scientific magazines."

No Single Reason

The three leaders of the Eugene Future Power Committee agree that there was no single reason for their success in the initiative campaign. Chris Attnaeve emphasizes the importance of dedicated people — a factor that is either present or absent whether or not there are good "action manuals" around. She cites the examples of anti-nuclear plant groups in Florence and Roseburg, Oregon. "In both cases people, without access to good libraries, without skills, in a matter of a couple of months worked up a factual knowledge of nuclear power and became very competent in debating the issues with power company officials. One of the women in Florence had never finished high school. After the campaign she finished high school and got a job."

"They have to have stamina," Jane Novick adds. She focuses on the choosing of a reachable goal. "Doubts were raised in people's minds. We said, 'Let's wait, let's have a four-year moratorium and have the questions answered.' "

"A group should never leave any source untouched in terms of financing," says Joseph Holaday. First, he says, they had passed the hat; then they put a place for name, address, and contribution on everything they sent out. They accepted donations of rummage of any sort. After the campaign, they held a barn sale, an event that netted $900 in two days.

Joe sees three factors in Eugene as crucial to their success. "First of all," he says, "we won that moratorium because there was a group of highly dedicated people who were willing to take the abuse — and there was considerable verbal abuse — people that were almost invulnerable to economic reprisal, which came in the form of vague threats of cancellation of business contracts." Second and third were the support of the community around the University of Oregon, and the editorial support of the *Eugene Register-Guard*. "The *Register-Guard* is a unique local newspaper," says Joe. "The publisher lost revenues and took considerable abuse."

The tone of the Eugene Future Power Committee is summed up by Jane and Chris, in three phrases that come together in spontaneous harmony:

Jane: We accept that the system exists . . .

Chris: . . . and that we won't win everything . . .

Jane: . . . and we try to work through it.

Saving a Few Little Things

"Everything was set to move, and it didn't."

Richard Marx is describing the current status of the Jamesburg Environmental Commission, an institution he thought he had caused to be created in his New Jersey town. (Richard's account of the Jamesburg Environmental Commission appears on the opposite page.)

In a word, the commission is in limbo. An ordinance creating the commission was passed in the summer of 1974, but no funds were appropriated to cover its miniscule expenses. And nobody was appointed to serve on it, even though Richard had carefully lined up a group of excellent members.

Very few teenagers have even attempted what Richard did, and not many people of any age have learned as much as he has about the "do's" and "don'ts" of practicing local environmental politics. What sort of person is Richard Marx? How did he get so involved in keeping silt out of an obscure Jersey pond?

For an answer to these and other questions, we take you to the ordinary suburban house where Richard lives with his parents, brother, three sisters, and pet boa constrictor.

Snails Came First

"I've been interested in animals as far back as I can remember. When I was four we lived in California. All they had around were snails, so I collected snails. Later, I collected anything I could catch. I release the animals after keeping them awhile, and take care of sick ones. I use 'Havahart' traps that don't hurt the animals."

In the downstairs of the Marx home in Jamesburg is a room about six by eight feet in size. There, Richard has had as many as 100 animals at a time, wriggling, scuttling, and splashing in cages and tanks.

Richard collected many of these animals in and around Wigwam Pond. "I'd put on old clothes after school," he says. "I'd go down to the pond, pick up some animals that I wanted, and look at the rest. I'd do that about every day. Now I don't collect as many animals."

Wigwam Pond wasn't particularly outstanding, but Richard grew to love it. "It's a natural place," he says. "The whole one bank is completely natural. There are deer back there. It's actually a marsh, and more life lives in a marsh than anyplace else. There are a lot of birds, reptiles, and mammals there. It's a nice place to go."

Sand Pit Spinoff

It was silt flowing into Wigwam Pond from the adjacent Glen Rock sand pit that led to the series of events Richard describes in his article on the Jamesburg Environmental Commission. Though the commission was never formally appointed, Richard organized ten *de facto* meetings of it during the winter of 1973 and spring of 1974.

Of his fellow members in the potential commission, Richard says, "They thought it was a good idea; they were willing but not eager." The rump commission discussed a development project planned for the vicinity of Wigwam Pond. As a result of these discussions, plans of that project were modified to prevent run-off into the pond.

In April 1974, a lady called Richard and asked if he was going to be on the new Environmental Commission. When he replied that he was, she requested that he oppose the spraying of the insecticide Sevin on Jamesburg's trees in order to kill gypsy moths.

Richard researched Sevin, with the help of a concerned neighbor who had already studied insecticides. "It prevents cal-

EDITOR'S NOTE

Richard Marx was sixteen years old when he wrote this first person account for the March-April 1974 issue of The Jersey Sierran. *Now he's a little older and a lot wiser, having learned some hard lessons in environmental politics.*

THE JAMESBURG ENVIRONMENTAL COMMISSION
By Richard Marx

In Jamesburg, a small town in central Jersey, I have been working on the formation of an environmental commission for my town, and as of this month things have been looking good for its completion early in the spring.

The ordinance allowing the commission to be formed, is being written up so that the commission will have the maximum amount of power allowed by state law, and we intend to use it. There is one shortcoming though: the commission will have no money appropriated to it by the city government in 1974; but we can and will work around this.

The members of the commission will include a member of the town council, a member of the planning board, a corporate lawyer, an ex-mayor of Jamesburg, a chemistry teacher, and myself — six members in all.

This is the story of what motivated me to seek the power an environmental commission can wield in saving the local environment.

In the winter of freshman year high school, I built many small anti-erosion dams across many of the gullies which lead from a sand pit into adjacent Wigwam Pond. When the spring rains came the dams were either buried or washed away by the uncontrolled run-off. After a few failing attempts to control the erosion myself, I went to the foreman in charge of working the sand pit, with a few plans and maps I had drawn up showing where large anti-erosion dams could be placed in or-

[Continued on page 99]

Raccoon

cium from forming in the bones of birds, kills all insects, and has other ill effects," he notes. He presented his findings to the town council, and asked that a more expensive but less harmful spray agent be used. To his disappointment, the council decided to go ahead and use Sevin.

Quite casually and unexpectedly, the problem that had sparked Richard Marx's interest in city government was solved. "I was always asking the town council about the sand wash," he says. "Finally a member of the town council told me that the pit operators had been mining sand there for 20 years without a permit. They stopped mining then, so I guess they really didn't have a permit. I don't think they would have stopped mining if they had had one."

Young and Alone

Richard Marx is not satisfied with the results of his efforts in Jamesburg. "I'm disappointed," he says. "I might work on it more when I come back from college and am over 18. I can't have a strong say now because I'm too young.

"I'm glad I went through it now instead of later. Now I know what I did wrong and what I did right. I shouldn't have done it alone. All the people I got on the commission, I didn't really know. They were older people. I couldn't come in with a bunch of kids."

Richard feels that his cause lost momentum when he went to summer camp in 1974. Despite repeated assurances from the town council that they would carry the commission through, they contented themselves with creating a paper commission with no members or funds.

"If I could do it again," says Richard, "I would try harder to find somebody else who was truly interested in the issue, somebody who would have carried on the fight while I was away."

What is it about Richard Marx that caused him to take strong initiative against the polluters of Wigwam Pond? He's not the only young person who collects animals. He is a hard worker: he held down a full-time job while both attending high school and organizing the commission. He has won the Hornaday Award, a high Boy Scout honor. He is a cadet in the Jamesburg first aid squad, and in general has a record that will look good on his college application form.

None of this explains that peculiar independent fighting spirit it takes to raise and push environmental issues the established community would rather ignore.

His parents neither encourage nor discourage his activism. His mother calls him "the family Ralph Nader." He says, "They sit back and watch, and let me do my thing."

Canada Geese

[Continued from page 97]

der to divert the run-off away from the pond and back into the pit.

All throughout the spring and early summer the dams were being placed in the right places by the men and heavy machinery the sand pit had at its disposal. These dams held well during the summer of 1972, but they began to deteriorate in the late fall and winter. When the spring rains of '73 came, the erosion process had begun again. I went to the foreman throughout the spring but the meetings were useless since as far as he thought, he had done his bit for ecology.

It was at this time, late in the spring, when the sand pit had changed foremen; but the change was not for the better since the new foreman had no knowledge of the pit beyond his office. The foreman also repeatedly said that he had no power to do anything, even though he did seem to want to help.

I then turned to the Fish, Wildlife, and Shell Fisheries Department of the state government to see what they could do to the pond which was dying. They said they would send a man down to check out the pond, which they had been stocking for years. I guess someone did look around because about two weeks later, during a discussion with the foreman, he said he was told that if the department did do anything, it would be to stop stocking the pond because it was so dirty.

That seemed to be a dead end so I turned to the local U. S. Soil Conservation Service. I told them about the problem. This time I was lucky enough to get hold of the person in charge and he said that he would personally come down to check the place out as long as I came also. Of course I did.

I gave the conservationist a tour of the pit and he agreed that there was a problem and that he would send a letter to the owner, but after that any action would have to be taken by the owner himself in the form of asking for help from the service.

[Continued on page 101]

The drawings on these pages are evidence of Richard Marx's skill as an artist. The animals are some of the creatures Richard has observed at Wigwam Pond: screech owls, bullfrogs, racoons, box turtles, and Canada geese. In addition he has seen painted turtles, ducks, water snakes, deer, and many others.

This is Richard's house in Jamesburg. At the far left of the picture is a retired bread truck which Richard has rescued from an uncertain future by converting it into his rolling domicile. He did this in anticipation of leaving Jamesburg for college and a course of study in wildlife management. The truck has been restored with great care and when outfitted will accommodate Richard and whatever creatures he has in attendance at that time.

Richard is concerned about his future. He has been around enough to know that many of the kinds of jobs he might get are do-nothing positions. He hopes to find work that meets his high standards of dedication and action. He is not satisfied to go through the motions. We think there must be a lot of people around who need Richard Marx. His resume is already impressive.

Richard, in fact, seems rather shy and reserved, as though he would rather be at Wigwam Pond observing wildlife. He mentions that, long ago, the land the pond is now on was an Indian reservation. He mentions the name of the tribe: Lenni Lenape.

Then, with rare passion in his voice, Richard Marx says: "We've got a lot of little problems. People don't care about that. One thing goes, then another thing goes. Like when we pushed the Indians off our land — off *their* land. A hundred people go. You knock off one tribe, then another, then another one. . . ."

Here is a drawing Richard made to show what was going on at Wigwam Pond. The trouble was caused by erosion from the sand pit *(L)*, which was depositing silt in the pond *(D)*, and during winter months caused damage downstream *(J)*. Richard believes it was downstream flooding that may have had much to do with the closing of sand pit operations.

A	*woodland*
B	*Hidden Lake*
C	*gully erosion system*
D	*Wigwam Pond*
E	*sand washing complex*
F	*sludge pond*
G	*Wigwam Brook*
H	*Wigwam Road*
I	*waterfall*
J	*off-site flooding*
K	*Forsgate Drive*
L	*sand pit*

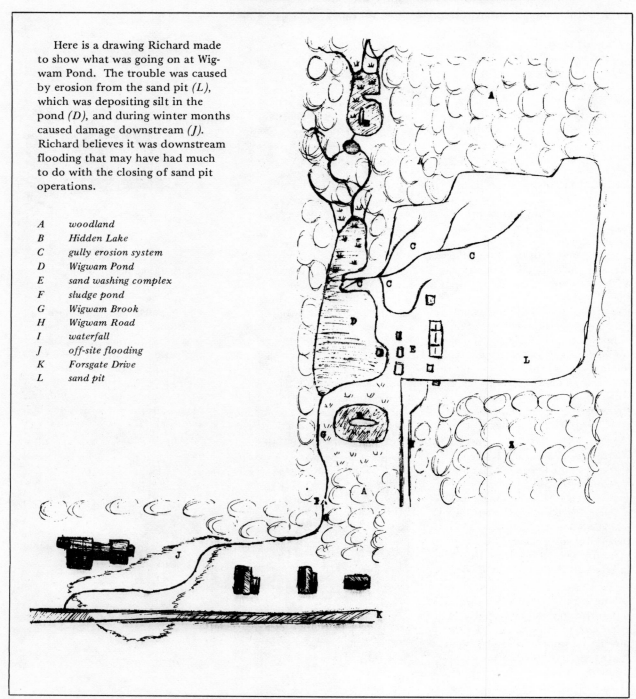

[Continued from page 99]

About once every other week after that I called the owner asking him to call the conservationist, and he said he might, but he never did. Then I wrote a few letters to the conservationist asking him if there were any laws broken. He said he didn't know of any, but if there was some off-site damage he might be able to do something.

I then went looking for some off-site damage due to the sand pit, and I found some in the front yard of a former mayor of Jamesburg. I showed him the erosion of the pit and told him how it would affect his yard downstream. The damage wasn't anything more than an annoyance so the conservationist wasn't contacted; but the ex-mayor did call the owner and told him about his problem. The owner then had the peninsula of silt dredged out of the pond and large retaining walls built. These dams are still holding today but they are showing the same signs of deterioration that the dams two years ago showed before being washed away.

I called the owner to ask him to build the dams stronger, but he didn't because he had already gone out of his way to help and he didn't feel like doing it again.

This time I turned to the Sierra Club. Before I joined the Club I called to see if they became involved in small-town pollution problems. It was then that the lady taking the call mentioned the usefulness of the environmental commission, and she explained how I could get one started.

I called Trenton (the state capital) the same day, asking for any further information they had on environmental commissions. By the time the next town council meeting was in session, I was ready to present my ideas for forming an environmental commission in Jamesburg. At that meeting, which was on the third Tuesday of November, the town council said that they would probably allow the commission to be formed but they also said they couldn't do anything until the first of January, 1974. Between November and January I was busy

getting some of the best men around to be in the future commission. By January I had submitted their names and they were accepted. On January 22 the mayor appointed a chairman for the future commission, and on February 13 we had our first environmental committee meeting.

Last winter, during a visit to the pond, Richard Marx pointed out that the water level was down because the little dam he had made at the foot of the pond was in need of rebuilding. Just as final preparations were being made to send this book to the printer, we received the photograph below and a note from Richard: "I have finished the dam like I promised. The water level is back up to where it was five years ago, and the sunnies have returned to their old nests." All we can add is that if every natural place had a friend like Richard Marx, this book would be unnecessary.

In Love With French Pete

When Dick Noyes set eyes on French Pete, it was love at first sight.

It was in 1961. Dick, a professor of chemistry at the University of Oregon in Eugene, was hiking on the Lowder Mountain Trail in Willamette National Forest. Suddenly he saw an expanse of undulating green before him: the French Pete Valley. In an instant he realized what the whole of the Oregon Cascades must have looked like before clearcutting lacerated and scarred the mountainsides.

For a long time it just seemed inevitable that French Pete would, like most of Oregon's forests, fall to the axe. Holway ("Holly") Jones, a librarian at the University of Oregon, has worked with Dick Noyes in a continuing battle to save French Pete that now spans nearly a decade. He sets the issue in historical perspective.

During the early 1900's, Jones explains, French Pete was used only to graze the sheep of Basque shepherds, one of whom probably left his name on it. In 1937 it was made part of the Three Sisters Primitive Area, a U.S. Forest Service classification which, unlike officially designated Wilderness Areas, the service can change at will.

By the mid-1950's, timber on private land was getting very scarce, and pressure was heavy to log Forest Service land. So fifty-three thousand acres were removed from what was proposed as the Three Sisters Wilderness Area, which was to have been protected by an act of Congress.

French Pete was part of the area removed from the proposed wilderness area. It contains about 700 million board feet of commercially valuable Douglas fir, the prime raw material of the relatively small logging firms which depend on public lands for their timber.

Eugene, Oregon, is known as the Lumber Capital of the World. Twenty-five percent of government timber receipts goes to the counties, earmarked solely for roads and schools. The federal share of Forest Service timber receipts goes into the general fund. Because of this, the Forest Service must seek annual appropriations for all its operations, including reforestation. The more it produces in timber sales, the more it is given for operations.

In the early 1960's, these facts suggested to Dick Noyes and Holly Jones that they would get little support in an effort to save French Pete. "The Forest Service has become a captive of the lumber industry," says Dick, "which by now has so little timber left on private land in this area that if they don't get access to public land the mills will close up."

In 1964, cutting began in the fifty-three thousand acres that had been removed from the Three Sisters Wilderness Area. Jones and Noyes would rather sadly walk over areas slated for cutting, but did little else. They felt, and still feel, that public support was lacking for a fight against that logging. "We let those areas slide by," Noyes says. "We couldn't fight for them all."

Just loving wilderness won't save it. "You have to care," says Dick, "and you have to think there is a chance to do something. For a long time we didn't."

Then, in 1967, Dick Noyes stopped in to pick up a Forest Service map of French Pete, and saw projected roads and sales for the area he loved.

"I still remember that rainy meeting at the Noyes house in 1967," says Holly. "There were ten or so of us; and Brock Evans, the Sierra Club regional representative, woke us up. He told us we *could* do it."

EDITOR'S NOTE

The following description of French Pete Valley — which may be seen on the left side of the aerial photo opposite — is taken from a proposal for Backcountry Management written to the U. S. Forest Service by the Save French Pete Committee. We reprint it here because it is one of the best descriptions of a natural area we have run across, and for that reason may be useful to other people who are groping for words to describe what can seldom be adequately expressed that way.

Like great white clouds, the ancient volcanoes of the Oregon Cascades march down the horizon of the entire state. Dominating the plateaus and ridges around them, towering high above their necklaces of alpine flower-gardens, they are the most impressive features of Oregon scenery. Once, before the white man came to Oregon, a magnificent green train of unbroken forest stretched from the base of these giants down across the plateaus and deep valleys all the way to the sea.

Down in the valleys and on the ridges in the Oregon mountains there grew a type of forest unequaled in size, extent, and luxuriance, anywhere else on earth. Giant fir, cedar, and hemlock, towered over a forest floor soft with ferns and mosses, and spliced with the color of rhododendron. This forest was not dark, but rather suffused and enveloped everywhere with a soft green light; everywhere was the sound of water from streams running clear and undisturbed. The valley of French Pete Creek was one of many similar valleys in the Oregon Cascades where grew this type of forest.

Once there were a great many of these green forested valleys in the Oregon Cascades — nearly 300 of them — all untouched, all deep and rich, all existing in their own right and serving also as green gem-settings for the giant cloud-peaks above.

Now, little of the Oregon forest remains as it once was, untouched by the works of man. A large and vigorous timber industry has consumed most of the virgin forest. Of the nearly 300 original, unmanaged valleys, over five miles in length, only seven now remain. Of this total, 65 valleys were major drainages of over ten miles in length. Only three of these remain in all of Oregon.

The three remaining major untouched valleys in the Oregon Cascades are Eagle Creek Valley, flowing into the Columbia River from near Mount Hood; Separation Creek Valley, flowing from the slopes of the Three Sisters Volcanoes westward through the Three Sisters Wilderness Area; and the valley of French Pete Creek, just to the west of the Three Sisters Wilderness Area.

Geologically speaking, the Oregon Cascades are divided into two distinct parts: "The Old" or West Cascades, and "The Young" or High Cascades. These parts are directly joined to each other, the High Cascades consisting of the string of volcanoes and surrounding plateaus which were formed in much more recent geologic times. The Old Cascades consist of heavily forested, deeply indented ridges, valleys, and peaks, representing the remains of the original Cascade Range. The two areas are distinct and different, geologically, esthetically, and from a scientific point of view.

Most of the valley of French Pete Creek is of the Old Cascades type. It is the only remaining valley in Oregon's Old Cascades over five miles in length which has not been logged or roaded; it is still completely undisturbed. Because its upper portions abut directly on the high plateau of the Young Cascades formation of the Three Sisters Wilderness, the valley of French Pete Creek affords the only opportunity remaining in Oregon for display of a continuous transition of

Brock Evans, a fireball new on the job, galvanized them. With Holly Jones, a long-time conservationist himself, the human resources were present to set up the formidable Committee to Save French Pete.

Dick recalls that their goal was carefully chosen. "We decided that, given the climate of public opinion at that time, we wouldn't go for wilderness designation. We had wilderness, we had logging roads and clearcuts, but there was nothing in between. French Pete is at a low elevation; you can get into it almost every day of the year. It's near Eugene. We decided to ask for an intermediate status, a roadless recreation area where scout troops could go in and find some camp sites and the like."

Early on, they also realized that they could take three routes toward their goal: the administrative, through the internal processes of the Forest Service; the legislative, seeking a law to protect French Pete; or, as a last resort, the judicial recourse of filing a lawsuit. Holly said, "When you've got a battle like this that involves a federal agency, you had better go all three routes."

A Testimonial for David Gibney

Dick and Holly were sitting in the downstairs office of the Noyes residence in Eugene, a house solidly constructed with plenty of timber and surrounded by mossy trees soaking up winter rain. Both are rather reserved men, perhaps introspective, certainly at home in the groves of academe and the solitude of wilderness.

Dick's eyes twinkled. "I have said that if we did win French Pete, I'd be willing to give a testimonial dinner for Dave Gibney, without whose help we'd have never accomplished it."

"That's right," Holly agrees, laughing.

David Gibney, supervisor of the Willamette National Forest until his early retirement, was one of those public officials who function by being a broad, stationary, obvious target.

In a paper delivered to a Sierra Club wilderness conference in 1971, Brock Evans testified to the inspirational effect Gibney had had on his conservation career:

I have never forgotten my first meeting nearly five years ago with the supervisor of the Willamette National Forest in Oregon. He put his feet up on the desk, leaned back and said, 'I don't like you people. I'm not going to let you lock up any more wilderness.' And he referred to the Oregon Cascades wilderness as a 'forest slum.'

I came out of that meeting full of fight, determined that he was not going to succeed.

Refusing to discuss French Pete at all, refusing to debate the issue publicly, refusing even to put a Forest Service exhibit alongside a Committee to Save French Pete exhibit at the University of

Oregon library, Gibney was the stolid, insensitive bureaucrat from beginning to end. "He made a number of tactical mistakes because he didn't understand what we were doing," Noyes recalls fondly.

Starting out on the administrative route, the first step taken by the Committee to Save French Pete was the formal presentation of a detailed intermediate recreation plan to David Gibney. Dick says, "I think it was good that there was something in writing that had been submitted as a proposal to the Forest Service as of this date, which was April 1, 1968." Gibney, of course, pretended the proposal did not exist.

That rare and wonderful newspaper, the *Eugene Register-Guard,* had been giving sympathetic coverage to the protectors of French Pete. Low-keyed events such as exhibits and debates had brought the issue to some public attention.

By May 1968 the matter had aroused enough public attention that Congressman John Dellenback, though he supported the Forest Service plans, requested that the proposed French Pete sales be withdrawn pending further study. The Committee had made its first breach of the bureaucratic stone wall.

In March 1969, a game of charades was arranged by Gibney to announce his decision about the future of French Pete. The public was excluded. An ad hoc committee of 23 people — three of whom were French Pete Committee supporters, the rest of whom had no background in the issue — was gathered together.

Dick Noyes, who was there, remembers: "Dave Gibney gave each of us a large sheaf of material. Then he read his decision, and said he would give everybody five minutes to comment about this, and would call on us alphabetically. He started polling people without discussion, and without any presentation of our plan. It is fortunate that the last two names in the alphabet were the only citizen members who supported our plan, because by then he had called on us and we had presented it."

Gibney's decision was to run roads into French Pete and clearcut.

"Our next step," says Dick, "was to go to Regional Forester Charles Connaughton, a tough egg but a much smoother one. He was trying to talk us into going directly to the chief of the Forest Service. He was trying to head off a formal appeal."

At this point, Dick and Holly emphasize one thing about dealing with the Forest Service: *you need to know their administrative procedure.* *

ecological and geological systems from the low elevation forests of the Old Cascades, up through and over the typical features of the Young Cascades and across over into the dry pine forests of the east side of the crest.

The total area of the French Pete Valley Drainage is about 19,000 acres, all in the Willamette National Forest. It lies between an elevation of 1,700 feet at the lower end and 5,000 feet at its upper reaches. It is bordered by ridges to the north and south which extend southeastward into the higher areas formed by more recent geologic formations.

A trail system winds through the valley, affording access to choice fishing sites along the creek and its tributaries. A herd of elk is known to exist in the valley, and it affords outstanding opportunities for hunter success because of its relatively isolated nature. The area has long been used for all forms of primitive, backcountry recreation, and because of its low elevation, it is available for recreation use nearly the entire year. This characteristic alone distinguishes it from many other areas in the Oregon Cascades.

The valley of French Pete Creek was once no different than any of the other several hundred in the Oregon Cascades before the white man came. Now, because it still remains undisturbed, it has become unique. It is unique because it is the only major Old Cascades valley which is undisturbed enough for scientific study; it is unique because it offers a variety of high quality backcountry recreation experiences the year around; and the vista of unbroken forest of the valley available from its ridges now makes it unique in all of Oregon.

Editor's Note: As shall be seen, not even Forest Service officials are perfect users of Forest Service administrative procedure. It is a shifting jungle of regulations. If you're contemplating trying to preserve an area in the Forest Service domain, a good way to start is by obtaining a copy of Action for Wilderness, *ed. Elizabeth R. Gillette (San Francisco: Sierra Club, 1972).*

Holly says, "Forest Service procedures call for certain kinds of letters that have to be written to certain officials by certain times. These then become extremely important in laying out your legal case later."

Despite the regional forester's sly urging that they take their case directly to the top, the Committee members knew they had just 90 days to appeal Gibney's decision. "We decided to file our appeal despite Connaughton's advice," says Noyes. "This got their attorney all upset. Then we realized they'd been planning to go ahead with their cutting program all along."

It was the Committee's brilliance in finding the flaws in the Forest Service's administrative handling of the issue, and in exploiting these flaws to the hilt, that saved French Pete from the axe. They beat the Forest Service at its own game.

Although members of the Committee did go directly to the top with their case, and were heard by Assistant Secretary of Agriculture Thomas Cowden, their day at the summit had no apparent effect on the outcome. But the following chronological events did:

June 16, 1969: Brock Evans filed an appeal to Gibney's decision with the regional forester.

June 27, 1969: Supervisor David Gibney signed a *second* management plan, fundamentally changing his first plan, though the Committee to Save French Pete was not told that a new plan had been put forth.

July 7, 1969: Committee members presented their proposal to the assistant secretary of agriculture.

September 1969: Assistant Secretary Cowden and Regional Forester Connaughton denied the Committee's appeal.

Later in September 1969: The Committee discovered the second Gibney plan, and formally appealed it, even though the Forest Service steadfastly maintained that it was only an elaboration of their original plan.

By November 1969 things looked pretty bleak for French Pete. Dick Noyes decided to take a little vacation before going back to Washington to serve on a scientific committee. He threw the *Register-Guard* in the car and drove down the Oregon coast to Gold Beach, where he relaxed and idly opened to the Forest Service timber sales section. To his immense surprise he saw French Pete timber sales announced, at a time when a formal appeal had yet to be answered!

"This was the thing that finally fixed the Forest Service," says Dick. Back in Washington later in November, he had no trouble inducing both Oregon senators and his congressman to ask the assistant secretary of agriculture to withdraw the sales.

"This cost them momentum that they never regained," Dick says. "If they had gone through the motions of the appeal procedure, they probably would have won it. This way, they had to

It was the Committee's brilliance in finding the flaws in the Forest Service's administrative handling of the issue, and in exploiting these flaws to the hilt, that saved French Pete from the axe. They beat the Forest Service at its own game.

cancel sales that they had already advertised in a local paper, giving them a very bad public image.

"They were back to square one. The Forest Service licked its wounds and sat back for about a year and a half. As far as we were concerned, no news was good news. We were willing to let them sit as long as they wanted to."

In July 1971 the Forest Service announced a "cosmetic" logging plan for French Pete. "That closed the door on the administrative route to our objective," says Dick, "but by then it was a very hot issue locally."

Time on Your Side

"If you can find ways to buy time," says Holly Jones, "time is on your side. We were educating the public. We also took part in that general upswing with Earth Day in April 1970. Now there is tremendous interest in wilderness here. We have an Oregon Wilderness Coalition, with a full-time paid coordinator."

Dick and Holly concede that their greatest weakness has been their "ivory tower intellectual" image. Operating without formal (or even informal) organization, they have not reached out vigorously for public support. But they have allies in the students. "Campus groups supply enthusiasm and rally spirit — things we older people can't do without losing credibility," Dick says.

The main French Pete public events were three student rallies, held on about the same November dates in 1969, 1971, and 1973. Though they were rather low-key, non-threatening affairs with speakers and mellow marches, they served to take French Pete into the streets of Eugene.

Dick Noyes thought the first one particularly amusing. "The students marched to the Forest Service headquarters here. Dave Gibney had agreed to speak. He looked out the window, saw 500 students, and refused to come out! As they left, the students picked up every scrap of paper in their wake. The *Register-Guard* did an editorial, saying, 'We don't envy the Forest Service their new enemies.' "

"Late in 1968," says Dick, "Bob Packwood defeated Wayne Morse for the Senate in a very close race. While they were still recounting the votes, Holly and I went up to Portland and talked to him. He later said that this was the first real conservation input

The first phalanx of protestors march down Eugene's 11th Avenue during a day-long community "happening" in 1971. The event was sponsored by a University of Oregon student group, and attracted conservationists and politicians from all over the state. Other events during the day included a debate, and speeches by U.S. Senator Packwood and a member of the 1963 Mt. Everest ascent team. Photo by Matt McCormick from University of Oregon *Daily Emerald.*

he got. Packwood decided this was the issue he could ride and push. Every candidate needs one. It's better still if you can catch them before the election, but they're harder to pin down then."

The French Pete protectors have been quite good lobbyists, both in pushing for protective legislation and in getting elected officials to intervene in the Forest Service administrative process. Senator Packwood introduced the first intermediate recreation proposal for French Pete in the Senate.

In 1970, Congresswoman Edith Green introduced a French Pete protection bill in the House. This resulted, Dick thought, from a two-hour talk he had had with her administrative assistant when she was out of the country. His conclusion: "Get to the administrative assistants," he advises would-be lobbyists.

Senator Mark Hatfield of Oregon was on the Interior Committee. He was not too happy with Senator Packwood's French Pete bill, and he denied the conservationists' request for local hearings on the bill.

This gave the French Pete defenders an opening for good publicity. As Holly Jones recommends to other groups, "If a congressional committee refuses to hold a local hearing, you go ahead and hold your own hearing, and get an official record you can send to them."

The conservationists hired a court stenographer and convened their hearing in the Eugene City Hall. About 125 people gave statements, most of them in favor of saving French Pete. Later, the transcript was printed in the Congressional Record.

In 1975, at the time of this writing, the legislative situation has improved. Jim Weaver, a congressman clearly on record as favoring preservation of French Pete, has been elected from the local district. Senator Packwood has already reintroduced his bill to preserve French Pete. The new governor of Oregon, Robert Straub, opened his campaign by holding a luncheon in favor of saving French Pete.

Senator Mark Hatfield, however, still supports the Forest Service cutting plan, despite the fact that he has visited French Pete. Or perhaps it was his visit that marred his image of the sylvan vale.

During the whole time he was in the wilderness, Holly Jones and Arnold Ewing, a loquacious representative of the loggers, had both been vigorously courting his favor. After returning, ears still ringing, Senator Hatfield offered this solution to the French Pete problem: "Let's put Holly Jones and Arnie Ewing back up on top of Olallie Mountain with one hard-boiled egg between them, and tell them they can't come down until they've worked out their own compromise."

"After six years," Dick Noyes summarizes, "it's back in the lap of the Forest Service supervisor, where it started. We fought French Pete all the way up to the secretary of agriculture and it's back to square one, and this is fine."

After all, what Dick and Holly really want done with French Pete is: nothing.

Now they are preparing for yet another Forest Service plan, due to appear soon. But because of a Sierra Club legal action, an Environmental Impact Statement must be prepared on French Pete (and all other roadless areas) before any development can occur. This means that public hearings will have to be held.

Dick feels that French Pete has become so popular that the Forest Service will be reluctant to log it. However, the Committee to Save French Pete is ready for its final recourse: legal action.

"We have been preparing for a case for years by having people donate money to the Sierra Club Legal Defense Fund," says Holly.

One possible ground for legal action, Dick notes, is the concept of multiple use. The Forest Service often uses "multiple use" to justify logging. "French Pete," says Dick, "is one of only three unroaded and uncut valleys over ten miles long in the whole Oregon Cascades. If they log every valley, that's not multiple use."

To Dick Noyes, who loves French Pete, logging it would be multiple abuse.

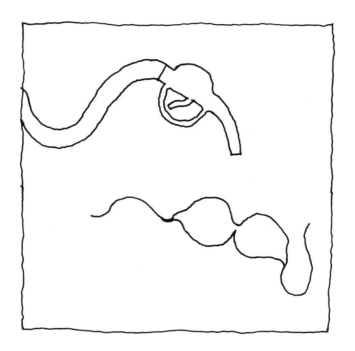

Don't Let Ethyl Strip!

In February 1972, Mr. Joseph D. Ambrose of Fort Worth, Texas, suddenly appeared at the doors of farming families living near Kentucky Lake in Henry County, Tennessee.

Mr. Ambrose was in Henry County for a single purpose: to induce people to lease land (2,000 acres in all) to the Ethyl Corporation at a dollar an acre per year plus mining royalties of indeterminate amounts. Ethyl was actively considering operating a titanium strip mine in the area. Such a mine involves floating a dredge in a 25-acre artificial pond. The dredge eats its way across the landscape 24 hours a day, casting watery slurry in its wake. Two mills — a wet mill and a dry mill — are used in processing the heavy metal, which is to be found in the McNairy Sandbed underlying a large area of western Tennessee. The leases Mr. Ambrose was arranging would allow Ethyl to strip mine to within 150 feet of existing structures, and to build anything that would be needed in the mining operation.

That's what George Bell, an ex-Marine and Vietnam veteran, has to say about his strangely tragic relationship with titanium strip mining. When you learn what has happened recently to this native of Toms River, New Jersey, who married a girl from Henry County, Tennessee, you'll see what he means:

"I fished every creek and brook and river in 20 miles from Toms River, New Jersey," says Bell. "I found good hunting in the woods that were all around that part of Ocean County. Then the chemical plants moved in, the sand mines, the subdivisions, and finally the two big titanium mines. I worked hard as a concrete foreman on all kinds of construction jobs after I got back from Vietnam. Betty and I started paying on a good house. The kids came. But I tried to keep on hunting and fishing, and getting out and walking in the woods, when the season was out. That's what killed me — getting out and seeing nature torn up. Betty and I could have hired sitters and made all the beer joints when I got off from work and we wouldn't even have known what was happening. But see it, and it made me so sick. I had to get out."

The Bells moved with their three children to Henry County. They obtained title to five acres of land, and sank all their savings, and then some, into building a very nice home on it. They built the house themselves.

Then they discovered that the previous owner of the land had signed a mining lease agreement for the land. Ethyl could take their house and run a dredge right through their property if it wanted to.

"They never told the landowner what they were really going to do," George says with obvious anger. "I ran their drillers off with a shotgun. People would pay a million dollars to come to a place like this. I can go to my back yard and see a deer. I can go down to the creek and catch a fish. Can you see turning this country into a strip mine?"

"The picture was that somebody was going to drill, and the titanium would come out like oil from an oil well."

This isn't a very pretty picture. It would be hard to get anybody to let someone do this to his land for a dollar an acre, plus indeterminate royalties. Which is where Mr. Ambrose comes in. He is a professional at getting people to sign away rights to their land, and was retained by the Ethyl Corporation to do just that in Henry County.

Like an Oil Well

Two local residents who took an early interest in Mr. Ambrose's endeavors are Johnny and Jane Gibson. The Gibsons have lived in Henry County all their lives. Johnny is a professional hunting and fishing guide. They live beside Kentucky Lake which, at 180 miles long, is the largest man-made lake in the United States. Outdoor recreation is the lifeblood of the area where they live, near Paris. The family incomes of the Gibsons and many others there, as well as the values which have attracted numerous retired people to the area, depend on the preservation of healthy hardwood forests and clean lake waters.

"The first we heard about this situation," says Jane Gibson, "was when the whole neighborhood began talking about getting rich. The method of testing for titanium is by using a core drill on the back of a truck. A lot of psychology went into this drilling, too. Somebody in the county government gave Ethyl permission to drill on county rights of way. The picture was that somebody was going to drill, and the titanium would come out like oil from an oil well. Nobody actually came out and told people this; but that was the impression created.

"Simultaneously with the test drilling, Mr. Ambrose was going around. He would get people to sign a 'notification of lease agreement.' It didn't have the terms of the lease on it. It didn't even say that Ethyl was in the picture. People never saw the lease until they got it in the mail, later."

Three years later, in February 1975, after the full impact of Ethyl's plans had been widely publicized, the lease signers included people who felt they had been "conned" out of their land, as well as some clinging to the notion that they were on the verge of getting rich. "The first man to sign was our ex-county sheriff," says Jane, "who has since that time put a shotgun to his head and killed himself." Jane believes that the lease with Ethyl was a strong factor in his suicide.

On the other hand, Johnny Gibson says that "the best farmer around," who signed a lease, expects to make a killing. "He said the other day he wished they'd start drilling. He still thinks they're going to pump it out of the ground like oil. He doesn't listen to anybody."

Money and Greed

Ethyl had to lease land in a solid block, or at least obtain corridors large enough for its dredge to eat through in its moving, 25-acre lake. One man with a crucial 325 acres is Early Green; and Early Green won't sell. "They pestered that old man and pestered him," says Johnny, "and finally he ran them off his land with a shotgun. Now his son works for Ethyl. Maybe they figure when the old man dies, the son will cough up the marbles and let them have it."

When Ambrose's wiles proved insufficient, the Ethyl Corporation sent in B. B. Goetzmann, their chief land lease attorney. The Gibsons were in an area where people simply refused to listen to the lease agents at all. However, a farmer had leased land to Ethyl that comes within 200 yards of the Gibsons' house. Also, Johnny Gibson was being so curious about Ethyl's intentions that neighbors were saying he didn't want them to get rich. Mr. Goetzmann dropped in at the Gibsons' fish pond, to see if he could draw out Johnny's thinking.

"Finally I asked him, 'Mr. Goetzmann, why do people sign these leases?' " recalls Jane. " 'Two factors, Jane,' he said. 'Money, and greed. And the greatest of these is greed.' "

One crucial corridor of land lay between the Tennessee National Wildlife Refuge, winter haven for hundreds of thousands of ducks and geese, and the church Jane Gibson attends. Ambrose repeatedly visited the owners of the land, Billy and Frances Crawford, until they rather reluctantly signed. According to Jane, Frances Crawford was particularly reluctant to sign, because her grandmother had once signed away a farm without knowing what she was doing.

When the true nature of titanium strip mining became known locally, the Crawfords sued Joseph Ambrose and Ethyl for fraud. The Crawfords accused Ambrose of falsely saying that no strip mining which would excessively alter the land would happen, and that all of the Crawfords' neighbors had already signed. The suit also alleged that the lease agreement they signed didn't say who the lessee was. Before the case went to court, notes Jane, Ethyl bought the land in question from the Crawfords for a good price.

Truth Dribbles Out

After the 1972 flurry of drilling and leasing, people tended to forget about Ambrose and Ethyl. Speculative oil and gas leasing is common in the area, and usually nothing comes of it.

George Bell began telling his story to the public. On October 10, 1974, M. F. Gautreaux, Senior Vice President of Ethyl Corporation, signed a $4,000 "option to purchase" agreement with George and Betty Bell. This agreement, a public document in Henry County, contains the following interesting clause:

"Section 9: It is further agreed that the first party will make no public or private statements injurious to the operations of the Second Party at any place or location either inside or outside of the State of Tennessee, and if this provision is violated, then the First Party will be required to return one-half of the option payment of $4,000."

In short, George Bell figures he was paid money to try to shut his mouth. He also figures his freedom of speech is guaranteed by the U. S. Constitution. "The city lawyers added that section," he says. "They thought they were dealing with some hick. I fought for this country, and I came back here and I have to fight again. It burns me up."

George and Betty Bell and family pose in front of their fireplace in the new house they built in a forest, which is now surrounded by land slated for strip mining.

Then, in March 1974, Johnny Gibson happened upon Ethyl's pilot plant under construction in the wooded hills he roamed as a hunter.

The plant, a processing facility located next to earthen-diked ponds, was drawing water with a pump set up in Kentucky Lake. Johnny Gibson and others in the resort business didn't like that at all. "Some other people would have cut their pipeline," he says. "But our whole protest has been legal and aboveboard; we were very nice and didn't disturb it."

Instead, Johnny started visiting James Weatherly, the representative of the Tennessee Valley Authority in Paris. The TVA has considerable control over what is done in and around Kentucky Lake, and had issued a permit for the pumping operation. Jane ruefully remarks, "We aren't sure Ethyl didn't give notice in the paper that they were applying for a pumping permit. We've learned to watch for things like that, since then."

"We were trying to get TVA to tell us what was going on," says Johnny, "and they wouldn't. We had an inside contact who was in a position to supply us with information, and he did. We began questioning TVA, and they started giving us a few answers, dribbling out a little bit here, and a little bit there. Then we found out TVA had approved a 50-acre site for the titanium processing plant, and rented it to Ethyl for $175 a month."

On May 14, 1974, Ethyl held a meeting at the Paris Landing Inn — a large hotel on the shore of Kentucky Lake — to explain just what they planned to do in Henry County. Only select officials and community leaders were invited; but the local paper, the

This photograph is reproduced from a KLEAR anti-strip-mine brochure, which in turn is reproduced from a newspaper. It is described as representing the Tom's River area in New Jersey, previously the home of George Bell, which is now a wasteland.

Paris Post-Intelligencer, got wind of the confab, and reported it the next day. At the meeting, the Ethyl representatives distributed a description of a titanium strip mine on Toms River, New Jersey. Johnny and Jane have made a lot of influential friends during their years in the guiding business, and one of these friends passed them a copy of that description.

"It'd make you sick," says Johnny, "the thought of that processing plant sitting out there on a point of land among resorts, boat docks — it's your worst dreams about destruction come true." The giant dredge in New Jersey has left a vast desert in its wake. The proposed mine site in Henry County is hilly, largely forested with hardwoods which shelter the wildlife the Gibsons depend on for their way of life. They, and many others in that area, were confronted with a clear and imminent threat to their livelihoods.

"Immediately at that point," says Jane, "we contacted the president of the *Nashville Tennessean,* the newspaper with the largest circulation in the state."

Perfectly KLEAR

The president of the *Tennessean* has hunted with Johnny Gibson for about 11 years and, in Jane's words, has "a very dear feeling for the Kentucky Lake area." To cover the story he assigned Nat Caldwell, a political reporter of 30 years.

Nat Caldwell's article in the *Tennessean* of June 16, 1974, presented the first true public picture of Ethyl's intentions in Henry County. It described a titanium strip mine, and noted that a mine of the sort Ethyl was contemplating would require about four million gallons of Kentucky Lake water per day. It quoted R. D. Sinner, Ethyl's design director: "We are just starting a six-month exploration and analysis program, and may well drop the whole idea, if both economic and environmental studies should not put us in the clear with relation to both profits and environmental laws. I also mean with the regulatory agencies and the TVA."

Caldwell's article noted that Ethyl's main business is making tetraethyl lead, a gasoline additive which is being phased out because it is considered harmful to human health. Caldwell quoted an unnamed Ethyl spokesman as saying, "The Henry County titanium mine represents a part of a diversification program, but it is not a frantic diversification. We think we're going to keep on making and selling the additive (tetraethyl lead), which we can prove saves gasoline and which the EPA can't prove is dangerous to human health."

This article was followed over the months by features on New Jersey and Florida titanium mines, written by Caldwell. He also became advisor to the Gibsons and others who wanted to

Below you see both Jane Gibson, KLEAR president, and letter-writing Lorraine Campbell in a rare moment of repose. President Jane, whose advice is printed below, is on the left.

QUOTATIONS FROM PRESIDENT JANE

Jane Gibson is a true daughter of Tennessee. Her parents' farm is just up the road from where she lives now, in Henry County. She loves the rolling hills, with their cotton farms surrounded by hardwood forest. She serves fried chicken, soup, beans, and biscuits with red-eye gravy for dinner.

Five years ago Jane was working as an executive secretary. Her family was just about raised. Then a surprise arrived, in the form of a daughter named Julie. Jane quit working, "to come home and work harder," as she puts it.

Like most leaders of grassroots environmental groups, Jane is very rarely at a loss for words. Nat Caldwell, the *Nashville Tennessean* reporter whose advice has been valuable in making KLEAR one of the most effective groups of its type in the country, has been known to interrupt Jane's soliloquies at meetings with a good-natured, "Jane, shut up and sit down!"

Fortunately, many of Jane Gibson's words are valuable, such as these homilies that capture bedrock truths:

"One man's environmental loss is most likely another man's economic gain."

"We were advised to get out of our own area to get an attorney, because of the possibility of hidden conflicts of interest," says Jane.

stop Ethyl in Henry County. "Nat has worked in 15 movements like this over the years," says Jane, "and he has lost only two."

On July 22, 1974, 11 resort owners in Henry County met to form an association. Their immediate purpose was to stop the Ethyl project; but they also wanted to create an enduring group which would protect Kentucky Lake and surrounding areas. They elected temporary officers, and agreed on temporary bylaws.

Forty people showed up at their second meeting, many of whom were retired people living in the area. The group set up temporary committees, and within a short time was incorporated as the Kentucky Lake Environmental and Recreation Association (KLEAR). Jane Gibson was elected president of KLEAR.

Jane notes that their incorporation was necessary to protect personal assets, in case they got into a court battle with Ethyl or other large corporations. The charter stated that the purpose of the organization was to preserve the lake and environs from industrial desecration. "Right now," says Jane, "we feel the most effective thing we can do is fight this Ethyl battle successfully. If we win it, KLEAR will be a household word."

KLEAR retained two attorneys — one corporate, one environmental. "We were advised to get out of our own area to get an attorney, because of the possibility of hidden conflicts of interest," says Jane. "Lawyers won't work for nothing; but ours do cut their rates and don't charge for travel time." KLEAR's objective in the Ethyl fight is perfectly plain, in the words of Jane Gibson: "To stop Ethyl from mining for titanium on the shores of Kentucky Lake today, tomorrow, this year, next year, for all the foreseeable future. We're not willing to compromise. We won't accept a stand-off. We use every legal means available to us to achieve this."

Lorraine's Letters

"KLEAR corresponded initially with 17 regulatory agencies," says Jane, "asking what action if any they had taken on this matter, if there would be public hearings, if they had any information on the strip mining, what action they planned to take. Many of these agencies knew nothing about Ethyl's project before we wrote."

Lorraine Campbell, the wife of a retired military officer, was leading architect of the letter-writing campaign, and her methods are both simple and very effective. Lorraine read Nat Caldwell's article on June 16, 1974. "I whipped out a letter to the Tennessee Department of Fish and Game." It was the first of many.

In July, Lorraine wrote to the federal Fish and Wildlife Service. They replied that they weren't aware of the project before she wrote, but had begun to investigate the situation; and they referred to the possibility that the Environmental Protection Agency would require an impact statement. "This shows how I go about writing letters," explains Lorraine. "I'd get a reply like this, then write to the agencies referred to, asking questions — not their opinions, but pertinent matters of fact I felt needed to be answered. Each letter would incorporate some of the information I had gathered. You'd be surprised at how quickly you can gather information this way, and how quickly you can discover places from which to get information."

After Lorraine had collected information on her own for awhile, she discovered the existence of KLEAR. "One of their petitions asking the TVA to stop Ethyl was hanging in our local grocery store," she recalls. "I took the petition from door to door, and in three days had 106 signatures. Many people near where I live have been around here all their lives, and were displaced when the TVA first created Kentucky Lake and flooded their land in the Tennessee Valley. One typical lady said, 'Anything against TVA, I'm for.' I told her that I was surprised she had carried that grudge for so long, and that she should be better informed on the current issues. I gave her some information. We don't try to influence people, we show them the facts."

After Lorraine Campbell joined forces with KLEAR, the letter writing effort was expanded to include elected officials. "We write letters to U. S. senators and congressmen," notes Jane. "Also we write state legislators — not only those from our district, but all districts. There's a great concern about this strip mining in Memphis, which is quite a ways away from here. It turns out there's a large, clear underground lake in the McNairy Sandbed, which extends that far; and they're worried about a threat to that."

"No public officials can read and digest all information that comes before them," adds Lorraine. "So they rely on the analysis of other people. If you have a group willing to give them serious, pertinent information, they are tickled to death to get it."

Jane believes that often it takes very few letters to influence a legislator. "We have found that only 12 people writing to their senator concerning an issue can change his thinking on it. That shows you how small public participation usually is."

KLEAR people carefully file all letters and replies under personal or agency names. Often the writing of letters to various officials is assigned to other members of KLEAR, in which case copies of the correspondence go into the file. "If it hadn't been for our digging and probing and letter writing," says Lorraine,

"You must win your issue both legally and politically; you can win politically and be overturned legally, or win legally and be overturned politically."

"When you're just a little farmer, and you're trying to deal with big business, you'd better get you an attorney, and you'd better get you a good one. Don't sign your name on anything."

"You want to keep the pot on the fire. I like to hear the other side. If we didn't, what would we fight? We'd be out here batting the air."

"If you're the only person interested in the issue, there's something wrong with you. If you can't get support, forget it."

"Cultivate people, flatter them, and respect them."

"Don't get into name-calling."

"Don't bore people with your cause."

"We're going to have to protect ourselves from ourselves, and we're going to have to protect ourselves from our neighbors."

"America sees what it's doing to itself, and it really doesn't know what to do about it."

"we wouldn't have had so many people come out here to investigate the situation, either as a matter of curiosity or in an official capacity."

A Running Debate

"All the local civic clubs are frantically looking for programs," Jane says. "Ethyl would go to one, and make a presentation; then KLEAR would follow. The paper would report our statements, and we would respond to each other. We weren't together, but we were debating."

During the fall of 1974, this debate went on between KLEAR and Ethyl. KLEAR had committees — secondary impact, zoning, water table, biology, soil, and others — investigating the situation, gathering facts, raising questions. One of KLEAR's lawyers went to Knoxville to get TVA's records on the Ethyl strip mining negotiations; as a government body, the TVA's records are public.

Lorraine Campbell was in charge of studying secondary impact. This is a vital area of concern for any group facing an opponent claiming to be bringing more jobs and tax money into the community. In October, Lorraine sent letters to the county judge and head of the chamber of commerce, with a copy to the *Paris Post-Intelligencer*. The letter, which the paper printed, asked the county court to request a federal environmental impact statement to answer 13 questions:

> 1. *Would jobs created warrant the environmental trade-off? (Lorraine noted that there were not enough unemployed workers in Henry County to fill the jobs which Ethyl would create.)*
> 2. *Is there housing enough for 50 to 100 new families?*
> 3. *How would schooling be provided, and what would it cost?*
> 4. *Are there adequate school buses for the influx?*
> 5. *Is police and fire protection adequate for the new people?*
> 6. *What must be done to provide water and sewage services?*
> 7. *With TVA predicting brownouts and rationing, can the high use of electricity by the strip mine be justified?*
> 8. *Does the federal Environmental Protection Agency require TVA to do an environmental impact statement on the project?*
> 9. *Is a state environmental impact statement required?*
> 10. *The property owners who have leased to Ethyl must pay the property taxes on their leased land, but can't build on that land, according to the leases. What does this do to the tax base of the county?*

"One of their spokesmen actually said that after Ethyl got through reclaiming the land, it would be better than God had done it! That was really a bit too much."

11. How would the strip mine affect sub-surface water?
12. Would Ethyl want to build a railroad spur to the project; and, if so, where?
13. What would be the environmental effects of their processing plant and possible dock facility?

Gradually, inexorably, KLEAR dredged up the inconsistencies and impracticalities of the Ethyl plan. Some of these were easy to spot. For example, Ethyl was claiming that water would be totally recycled and reused in the project, while at the same time saying that it would require 250 to 500 thousand gallons of Kentucky Lake water per day!

"They say they'll level the land off," Jane notes, "and maintain the same contours as it has now. But it's hilly land. They say the lake won't be polluted at all, but if they pump that water uphill it has to go somewhere. We finally got them to admit that 500 rather than 100 acres would initially be stripped. Then one of their spokesmen actually said that after Ethyl got through reclaiming the land, it would be better than God had done it! That was really a bit too much."

A memo discovered in the TVA files, dated February 19, 1974, from R. D. Sinner of Ethyl to a Mr. Birdshaw in TVA's power marketing section, indicated Ethyl was "actively pursuing an extension of our basic project." That would mean, according to figures in that memo, that by 1978 the Ethyl strip mine would be using as much electricity as the total present usage in Henry County. A marginal note confirmed KLEAR's information that only firm contractual commitment to the project from Ethyl was delaying TVA's agreement to supply power (though Sinner of Ethyl denies that the TVA has agreed to supply power to Ethyl). Jane ruefully remarks, "All winter long we heard 'Grayouts, brownouts, blackouts, conserve, conserve, conserve,' from TVA; and they have agreed to sell this electricity to a company."

The weeks ground on, and the debate began to wear. "In going from club to club," says Jane, "it came to a point where the amount of new information coming in was diminishing. Ethyl wrote to KLEAR asking for a public meeting where our differences could be discussed. It was held on December 5. We repeated the same arguments, it was very friendly, and neither side convinced the other. We very wisely decided to take the month of December off. You can get to the point where you're saying the same thing over and over, and it bores the public."

The Dam Bursts

Bob Agee, manager of Ethyl's pilot project, confidently asserted that the ponds used there did not discharge into the lake, and would not overflow during the rainy season. To cause the ponds to discharge their contents, Agee said, "it would have to be some violent act of nature that would do great damage to the entire area."

In late January, 1975, the weather turned so nice that Johnny, Jane, and Jane's brother Franklin went out for a pleasure ride. They dropped in at the pilot project, and while Johnny was talking to the man on duty there, Jane and Franklin took a look around. "That's when we found out they'd cut their dikes," Jane says. "They'd been saying, 'All our water will be recycled and contained,' and there it was pouring out into the bottom land. We came home and reported it to the Nashville newspapers. The next day, Nat Caldwell came down with a photographer. We split up; I went to tell the Kiwanis Club about it, and Johnny went to the Rod and Gun Club."

Ethyl swiftly denied that anything had gone wrong at the project, and told a reporter that the state public health service had cleared them of any charges of permit violation. "Ethyl overreacted," says Jane. "A correction of that statement will appear, by a state public health department official who says the case is still very open."

Jane Gibson believes this incident, in the context of the publicity it got and the agencies KLEAR has alerted over the months, may seal the doom of Ethyl's strip mining plans. "State agencies are now taking a very responsible approach," she says. "Now it will be hard for Ethyl to get water permits."

"Nat Caldwell saw the strip mine as part of the industrialization of the whole Tennessee Valley, due to the opening of the Tennessee-Tombigbee waterway, which will happen in seven years," says Jane.

The Tennessee-Tombigbee waterway, a canal between the two rivers of those names, is expected to cut 13,000 miles off the river journey from Henry County to the Gulf of Mexico. This should take one-third off the cost of transportation. "We have the electrical power and will have the cheap transportation," says Jane. "We can take the cream of the industrial world. We don't have to sell ourselves short. But we'll need a port facility. We want KLEAR to be in on the planning. We're going to be the watchdog that says: you can't ruin our lake."

KLEAR is still in the thick of the fight that began when Joseph D. Ambrose started going around with his notices of lease agreement. But the organization plans to be around for a long time after the Ethyl case is settled, keeping Kentucky Lake and surroundings habitable by fish, fowl, wildlife, and the people.

The Tennessee Valley Authority Blues

Side One: "Entirely Too Negative"

"The Tennessee Valley Authority originally had three purposes," says Lorraine Campbell of KLEAR (see foregoing story, "Don't Let Ethyl Strip"). "One was to furnish electricity to the area, which was pretty much without it. The second was to improve navigation in the Tennessee River. The third was flood control, to be achieved by impounding water."

"Now," adds Jane Gibson, also of KLEAR, "the TVA is a giant bureaucracy in all kinds of businesses, operating like a huge power company. As a branch of the federal government, it has the power to condemn land. However, there are certain procedures they have to go through to operate."

The Tennessee Valley Authority, long lauded as the bringer of wealth and power to the people of a depressed region, is now generating strong opposition among those same people. Forty years ago the TVA started building hydroelectric power generating plants, and has doubled its generating capacity each decade. Now it has a capacity of 24.5 million kilowatts — mostly produced by coal-fired power plants — and plans to go to a capacity of 44 million kilowatts in the next ten years. To achieve this power dream, TVA plans, among other things, to construct seven additional power plants, which will be nuclear-fueled. To assure steady coal supplies, the TVA is negotiating to buy the Peabody Coal Company for $1.2 billion.

The TVA has its own energy expansion plans, made without consulting state and local governments in many cases, and won't put "wet scrubbers," the best devices for removing particles from emissions, on the stacks of its coal burning power plants. KLEAR believes the TVA has agreed to sell electricity to the Ethyl Corporation to run its proposed titanium strip mine in Henry County, Tennessee — enough electricity to *double* Henry County's present power use by 1978.

The TVA also has regulatory powers to halt environmentally unwise development. However, at this time its tendencies seem to be in the opposite direction. Last year R. Lynn Seeber, general manager of TVA, testified in federal court that he had deleted information from a TVA environmental impact statement on the construction of two dams because conclusions reached by staff specialists were "entirely too negative."

Side Two: Upper French Broad Defense

In the mid-1960's, the TVA quietly began planning a project involving 14 dams, 74 miles of stream channelization, and a levee in the Upper French Broad River basin of western North Carolina. The basin divides the Great Smoky Mountains from the Blue Ridge Mountains, and is a beautiful area of small towns surrounded by farms and forests. Asheville, Hendersonville, and Brevard are the main towns in the basin. In the summertime, people flow by the tens of thousands from the lowlands of Florida to the cooler resorts and summer camps of this region.

In 1970, federal funds were appropriated to construct the first of the 14 dams on Mills River, a tributary of the French Broad River. The Upper French Broad Defense Association (UFBDA) came into being at a meeting in the small community of Mills River, some of which was scheduled to be inundated.

With the leadership of Dr. Jere A. Brittain, a plant pathologist residing in Mills River, the group set out to stop the TVA project. They went to all the small towns that TVA wanted to bless with artificial lakes, attacking the TVA's cost-benefit analysis and gaining grassroots support. A speech given by Brittain at the Hooper's Creek Community Club in April, 1971, is typical of the approach used by the Upper French Broad defenders:

In 1933, TVA was created by the Congress to control flooding, generate power, and facilitate navigation along the Tennessee River. The enabling legislation made no provision for comprehensive resource development by TVA. Yet, of a total of $141 million in benefits claimed by TVA for the Upper French Broad Project, only $72 million, or about 50 percent, is attributed to flood control. The remaining $69 million in alleged benefits arise from water supply, water quality control, recreation and shoreline development. It appears that half the purported benefits of the Upper French Broad project may not even be appropriate activities of TVA.

"We all wore neckerchiefs colored in international distress orange with jet black UFBDA letters. The meeting auditorium was a sea of orange color, which came across strongly on color TV."

TVA activities in the Upper French Broad Valley are remarkably analogous to those of Santa Claus. The State of North Carolina has reportedly written a letter to the fairyland at Knoxville, asking TVA to fill the stocking of the Upper French Broad Valley. Santa has arrived with his sleigh full of toys — all with strings attached. Let's reach into the stocking now, and see what the Jolly Elf has left.

Here's a Water Supply — but TVA controls it, and the user pays for it. Here's a game called Water Quality Control — the object is to dilute pollution — another name for this toy is Reservoir Drawdown, or "Where did all the water go?"

Here's an especially clever one called Flood Control — it partially protects one acre of land by flooding another acre. Now, here's a beauty, with flashing lights and ringing bells. It's called Shoreline Development — but TVA decides who gets the shoreline and how it's developed.

By late 1971, the UFBDA had about 1,300 dues-paying members. Retired professionals in the area were contributing their talents, and making publicity, lobbying, and organizational efforts very effective. An interesting technique used was the sending of great numbers of colored postcards to legislators, each with a printed message signed by the sender.

The effort reached a crescendo in August of 1971, when the TVA agreed to hold a public hearing at the University of North Carolina in Asheville. Alex Duris, current director of the UFBDA, recalls that hearing:

"TVA had granted a one-day hearing only, but there was such an outpouring of protest, not only locally but from other states, that TVA was forced to hold a three-day hearing — and even at the stroke of midnight on the third day, there were still people who wanted to testify against their plan.

"The proponents of the project, including a large representation of local area governments, monopolized the opening hours of the hearing for prime TV coverage. UFBDA protested, and we got in on the tail end of prime coverage. At times our members outnumbered others present 10 to 1. We all wore neckerchiefs colored in international distress orange with jet black UFBDA letters. The meeting auditorium was a sea of orange color, which came across strongly on color TV. Some reporters, sensing the ground swell of opposition, came back to record the very large opposition. Little tots barely out of rompers testified why they were opposed to the project, along with elderly citizens in their late eighties.

"We had a hospitality room in which coffee, sandwiches, cakes, pies, fried chicken, and the like were available to those present — newspeople, our supporters as well as our opponents, and TVA personnel."

The hearing broke the back of TVA's plans for the Upper French Broad. In November 1972, the TVA formally abandoned the project, saying: "This type of water resources development plan, involving small units and localized benefits, requires full local support and participation. . . . An assessment today indicates that adequate local support and commitment no longer exist."

The Upper French Broad Defense Association is still very much alive, under the leadership of Alex Duris. Alex, a retired supervisor from a local paper plant, used to be chairman of the chamber of commerce industrial committee. Then he found that one of the TVA dams was going to flood his house, and the guys at the plant began joking about "casting a line down his chimney and catching a bass." That was the beginning of Alex's conversion to the environmental movement.

Now Alex opposes further industrialization of the Upper French Broad Basin, and has led the UFBDA to support a wide range of conservation and alternative energy development efforts. He regularly puts out a newsletter. The latest one noted: "TVA, because of growing pressures, has been forced to open its board meetings to the public and the news media." And, "There is more talk by people in Tennessee who are thinking in terms of a congressional investigation of TVA operations, and the need to revise the charter under which TVA operates."

Thirty Thousand Atomic Bombs Can't Be Wrong

There is a lot of natural gas trapped in the shale under New Mexico, Utah, Colorado, and Wyoming; and there are a lot of idle atomic bombs lying around, doing nothing but deterring foreign enemies. So it is not surprising that the idea of setting off atomic bombs to free natural gas for commercial use should occur to the Atomic Energy Commission (AEC).

Actually, during the 1950s and early 1960s, the AEC was concentrating on its Plowshare Program, which involved investigating ways to use A-bombs for surface excavation. Blasting a bypass to the Suez Canal was studied, among other proposals. High cost, radiation hazard, and the test ban treaty drove thinking on the peacetime use of nuclear explosive devices to subterranean applications.

The essence of the theory behind what the AEC calls "nuclear stimulation" of natural gas is the creation of a cavity surrounded by fissures, by blowing up a nuclear bomb. Theoretically, gas would flow through the fissures into the cavity, where it could be tapped through a well.

The AEC projected that commercial development using this technique could begin by 1977, and could be producing three trillion cubic feet of gas for an energy-thirsty nation by 1995. They suggested that "full field development" — the extraction of all gas recoverable by nuclear stimulation — be undertaken. That, the AEC estimated, would require, between now and the year 2060, fifty-six hundred wells, each stimulated by four to six bombs — for a grand total of about thirty thousand nuclear bombs.

The A-Bomb Sit-in

In 1967 the AEC popped off a 29-kiloton nuclear explosive three-fourths of a mile underground near Farmington, New Mexico (Project Gasbuggy). So far, all gas produced by Gasbuggy has been "flared," or burned away at the well head, because it is radioactive. Nevertheless, the AEC decided to push forward with plans to detonate a 40-kiloton nuclear bomb one mile under the western slope of the Rocky Mountains of Colorado (Project Rulison).

It was 1969, and the antiwar movement was thriving on the campuses of the nation. Morey Wolfson, a student of urban affairs and antiwar activist at the University of Colorado in Denver, saw Project Rulison as "the war come home." Wolfson recalls, "I

*"We're going to blow up your yard . . . interests of science, and all that
. . . don't have time to talk right now . . . congratulations . . . "*

Morey Wolfson, a student of urban affairs and antiwar activist at the University of Colorado in Denver, saw Project Rulison as "the war come home."

was trying to make linkages between the antiwar movement and the environmental movement. This was a good linkage."

Wolfson says a loose group sprang into being to oppose Project Rulison. "The group was primarily women," he says. "The leadership was from wives of medical technicians, who knew the hazards of radiation, and from the antiwar people. We had protests at the state capital, wrote letters like crazy, and had a weak petition campaign.

"Twenty or thirty people staged a sit-in near the blast site. There were helicopters looking for them, but the blast went through anyway. Some of them were thrown into the air."

Rulison resulted in recoverable gas. The AEC announced this gas would be sold to the cities of Glenwood Springs and Aspen in about eight years, after its radioactivity had decreased sufficiently. The city councils of those two cities, facing public concern over the piping of radioactive gas into their homes, voted that no gas from Rulison would be used in their cities without approval of the electorate through a balloting.

The Protest Thing

Despite mounting public opposition, the AEC decided to blow up three 30-kiloton nuclear explosives under western Colorado on May 17, 1973 (Project Rio Blanco). Early that year, Governor John Love announced that he would veto the Rio Blanco blasts. Then Love took a trip to Washington, D.C., and returned to announce the explosions were in the national interest and would go off as scheduled. Dick Lamm, a Denver lawyer, sought unsuccessfully to get a court injunction on the Rio Blanco blasts (Lamm is now governor of Colorado).

"We were still into the protest thing," Morey Wolfson says of the loose but determined group who opposed the explosions from the start. "But it was a better protest than before. We had signs, banners saying 'We refuse to be guinea pigs,' and that sort of thing. Two weeks before the blast we had an unorganized petition campaign against it. We got 8,000 signatures.

"This time we took the protest right to the governor's mansion. I put the petitions on Love's desk myself. He was like a brick wall. We have it all on videotape.

"They blew it off on schedule. They never got any gas out of Rio Blanco. It cost $11 million dollars of public money, which is more than the annual budget for research and development of solar energy."

CONVERTING COLORADO: EAC, PRES, AND WOLFSON

Morey Wolfson still looks a bit like a student antiwar activist. There's the abundance of hair and casual style of dress, the argot of the late sixties "counterculture," the mixture of scholarly mildness and steely determination. The difference between Morey and most student activists is, as he puts it, "There are some of us who just kept going."

Wolfson is a director of Environmental Action of Colorado (EAC), which was formed by himself and other students at the University of Colorado at Denver after Earth Day in 1970. EAC served as a focal point for the evolving group opposing underground nuclear blasting in Colorado — the group which finally became People for Rational Energy Sources (PRES). EAC helped PRES in its successful initiative effort with office space, a telephone, and printing.

Environmental Action of Colorado is mainly funded by student fees from the University of Colorado at Denver. It is one of the best-focused ecology centers in the United States, concentrating almost exclusively on educating people about the hazards of nuclear power and the desirability of solar energy. Among EAC's recent activities are the publishing of a solar energy directory, the holding of a solar energy conference, and the operation of a traveling solar energy exhibition.

"Solar energy works," asserts Morey. "Now the oil companies are buying up rights to the photo cells. The thing to do is to get a public policy on ownership of solar energy production. Otherwise, we'll have vertical integration of industry all the way to the sun."

High on Wolfson's list of priorities is the conversion of Rocky Flats Nuclear Base. "We're 15 miles from a nuclear weapons plant here in Denver," notes Morey. "It has a history of fires, too — in 1969 there was a $50 million fire out there, one of the most costly industrial fires in history. We could get an initiative on the ballot to close the plant, and probably win it. But a 'keep your job' movement could be organized against us. So we're meeting with the union that represents the workers there, to try to work for conversion of the plant to other purposes. If we can get workers to want to do something else at the plant, it will be good."

One of the chief changes in Morey Wolfson's relationship with the "establishment" since his days as a student antiwar leader is that, in 1974, many of his fellow antiwar and environmental activists were elected to Colorado's highest political positions. "I can sit down and talk with these people," says Morey. "Recently, I was discussing how economic conversion of Rocky Flats might be done, with the Secretary of Labor." That helps some.

"After doing some reading, I realized that the federal government has incredible powers; and the citizens, unless they're organized and vociferous, get run over."

Straight to the People

"I'm not a technical person," says Meladee Martin. But I thought, *Really,* this is a bit ludicrous, how could they get so far with this thing?' After doing some reading, I realized that the federal government has incredible powers; and the citizens, unless they're organized and vociferous, get run over."

Meladee Martin, a woman in her mid-20s who had been interested in the environmental movement in general, began going to the meetings of frustrated bomb protestors shortly after Rio Blanco went off. "There was a lot of disillusionment at that time about what people could do," she says. "We hadn't been able to stop the blasts through the courts, through the governor's intervention, through any kind of process. But we had a hard-headed group of people. Many were women; many had been concerned since the first blast. Another Mother For Peace — an antiwar group — had held seminars, debates, and luncheons on the issue. Their leaders were there. It was a very strong group, unwilling to give up. It had been run over for five or six years. They said, 'Let's take it straight to the people. We have that power in Colorado, and they're the ones who count.' "

By "taking the issue straight to the people," they meant getting a statewide initiative petition on the election ballot. An initiative campaign recently had stopped the winter Olympic games from being held in Colorado — an event which would have involved covering a sizable chunk of the Rocky Mountains with asphalt, concrete and cleared ski slopes. "The experience of the anti-Olympic petition was very important," says Meladee. "If you have a history of a successful citizen initiative, that success stays with the people, and they know how to use that tool."

Positive Approach

A crucial phase of any initiative campaign is deciding what the proposed law will say. "We started out in September talking about an initiative petition that would absolutely prohibit underground blasting in Colorado," says Meladee. "From September through December, we hassled out what the petition would say. One of our leaders was Dr. Edward Chaney, who is attached to the University of Colorado Medical School. He said, 'It is my experience that people do not like absolutism. Why not give people the power to vote on the blasts?' We would have had an incredibly hard time trying to convince the people of Colorado that we knew more technologically than the AEC did about their own project. This moderate approach was one of the factors that helped us win by a big margin. People were through with having decisions made for them in some obscure place in a bureaucratic agency."

In January, the group incorporated. "Even getting a name was a process," says Meladee. "It's bad to be negative about something: 'people against the bomb,' or whatever. We finally chose People for Rational Energy Sources (PRES). It sounds like we know what we're doing. And our program *is* positive. We say, 'Look, with energy conservation and solar energy we don't *need* A-bombs.'

"It was about four months into our discussions that we got the idea of developing an alternative to nuclear stimulation of gas. If you take something away from people, it's much, much better if you can give something positive in return. Solar energy is an idea that's been around for a long time, and just hasn't been fully developed. And people have more willingness to conserve energy than the government is willing to give them credit for."

David Engdahl of the University of Colorado finalized the wording of the petition. Wording the petition is another phase at which initiative campaigns are often made or broken. PRES advises that at least three meetings be held between the lawyer who is drafting it and everybody in the core group supporting the campaign, to make sure the petition's intent is legal and clearly stated. Professionals and legislators should also be asked to review the draft petition.

"We got the wording down in mid-March," Meladee recalls. "We went over to the secretary of state's office, where Colorado initiatives have to be read and approved to make sure they are not in conflict with existing laws or the constitution. He gave us a ballot title in three days. I was so excited. The secretary of state, a very old man — he'd been secretary of state for years — said, 'You've got a good petition here. I think the people of Colorado are going to buy it.' "

Signature Freaks

According to Morey Wolfson, the secret of success in getting signatures on petitions is, "You've got to get a together enough group that says, 'Okay, for the next four months of my life I'm a signature freak.' "

On March 27, 1974, PRES set out to qualify their measure for the Colorado ballot of November 5 by getting a number of signatures equal to 8 percent of the registered voters who had voted for secretary of state in the previous election. That meant they needed 50,412 valid signatures, 90 days before the election — or by July 5.

*MELADEE MARTIN'S
SAVING GRACE*

Meladee Martin, a leader of People for Rational Energy Sources and Environmental Action of Colorado, can't think of anything specific in her background which led her to these roles. "I came here from Texas," she says. "I went to a finishing school, and am kind of reserved, really. I'm not a mother, like many of the women in PRES, so I didn't have my own children to worry about."

Like other workers at PRES and EAC, Meladee makes no salary. So how does she make ends meet? "My saving grace is that on the side, at night, I'm a Spanish teacher," she says. "When I first came to Colorado, I did what young women do when they move to Colorado: I worked as a waitress. I made a lot of money at it, and stuffed it away. I kept thinking, 'This is so degrading, I just hate it.' But when I realized I wanted to do nothing but PRES, it was such a good feeling to have that money. I think the initiative campaign was a really rare experience; I'm just 25, and had never been involved in a campaign before."

Meladee Martin at the PRES off-set printing press.

EARTHQUAKE COUNTDOWN

"... it is not impossible in principle that some future explosion, if fired in a region where high natural stress had built up, might trigger an earthquake with greater seismic energy and greater hazard potential than the explosion itself."

Editor's Note: The above was taken from an AEC environmental statement, and was reprinted in a report on the uses of nuclear devices for resource recovery prepared by Environmental Alert Group. The report goes on to state:

"In the process of full field development (of the project) a significant portion of the state of Colorado will be subject to recurring seismic disturbance. As for seismic damage, the AEC estimated that the seismic damage resulting from nuclear completion on the Rio Blanco Unit will amount to about $50,000. Project Rulison involved damage claims, paid thus far, of more than $135,000. The Rulison shock wave also damaged foundations, irrigation lines, mines and an industrial plant."

Meladee says, "We started out with the premise that if 50 people each get 1,000 signatures, then we've got 50,000 names. It doesn't work that way. Instead, it's better to have 20 dedicated people, and tell them to get, say, 3,000 each. Then at the same time, work on people who might get 20, or 5, or 50. You've got to rely on a core group, people who will be at that shopping center every weekend, who will get their friends involved."

Meladee Martin, at first the only full-time PRES staffer, was allotted a desk and telephone in the headquarters of Environmental Action of Colorado, an ecology center funded by the student body of the University of Colorado at Denver. She kept the petitions (8,000 of which were printed in-house) in a drawer, and insisted that everybody who took one sign for it. She had a card catalog of all people who had petitions, with addresses and phone numbers.

"One of the adages of the campaign was, 'Go with your strength,' " she says. "We knew we had strength in Denver, Boulder, and on the western slope of the Rockies, where people were directly involved in the blasts. We didn't really branch out to southern Colorado, but the area we covered had at least two-thirds of the population of the state.

"We sent out petitions only if people requested them — not to any mailing list. On weekdays, we had a campaign of calling people who had petitions. People lose petitions and are afraid to ask for another one, so we'd send them another one. We'd also remind them they had only so many days.

"On weekends, we took out teams of people to stand at the entrances of parks and zoos, in shopping centers, in front of movie theaters. Afterwards, we'd get together and commiserate about what somebody said, like, 'This guy told me I could take my petition and throw it in the trashcan.' Or we'd say, 'Hey, this is a really good spot,' or, 'This place is no good because people are too busy going in and out.' We'd maintain a flow of information that way. You have to experiment. What works one place doesn't work another.

"The fun part of the whole thing is going out and getting signatures. There's a real horror of going out and asking somebody for something. Once people got over that, they'd come back and say, 'This is the greatest thing I've ever done in my life!' We got an incredibly positive response from people. I found people in general were disgusted with the same kinds of things I am disgusted with. They're very much against underground blasting. The people who exasperated me were the few who have given up, who say, 'They've got the money and the power, you don't have a chance, you might as well go to the mountains and have a good time.' I refused to sympathize or empathize with those people.

"Don't badger people, and don't get into arguments. We had people working with us who were so committed they could talk people blue in the face; our instructions emphatically recommended against that. If you blow it in one petition campaign, you've blown it for all petition campaigns. You should not alienate people at all.

"Before setting up in front of a store, we'd usually call ahead to the store manager. It's very important not to obstruct traffic into and out of the store. Sometimes we were run out. We'd call the regional manager of the store; if he still had an unfavorable insight, we felt we shouldn't waste our time with legal action. We had only three months to get signatures. Legal action rarely makes friends. We'd quietly say, 'I think you're violating my right to petition, but I respect your decision and I'll leave.' That made a lot more friends than if we'd said, 'Look, I've got my rights and I'll take you to court.'

"Rock concerts were good places to get signatures. Most of us in the campaign are in our mid-20s. The counterculture thing is to be cool, don't get involved, smooth out in the Rockies. It was kind of neat to see we weren't considered freaks by our own peers; we were able to involve them."

At work on the street. Meladee Martin and Morey Wolfson sign up two more names on the petition to place the PRES initiative on the ballot. They are standing in Denver's Larimer Square, a vintage section of town that attracts many visitors. Meladee is second from left and Morey is standing next to her.

*PARDON ME, YOU'RE STANDING
ON MY NUCLEAR EXPLOSION*

Underground detonation of a
nuclear device creates a cavity in
which rock is vaporized or melted,
and which sends a strong compres-
sional shock wave in all directions.

As cavity enlarges during the explosion, a fracture system occurs
surrounding the cavity, particularly
in a vertical direction, producing a
shear zone.

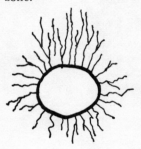

The cavity is structurally unstable, and collapses along the shear
zone fractures, producing the final
"chimney" configuration. The cavity is then "flared," a quick burn-
off of radioactive gas, and then
tapped.

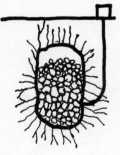

Aside from the hazard of seismic
disturbances, the method incurs the
problems of nuclear contamination

A Timely Exaggeration

"We had twenty thousand signatures in the office by the
first of June," Meladee recalls. "We put them in a bank vault.
There was another group doing three petition campaigns at once.
The director of their campaigns came out in the paper, saying
that all four citizen-sponsored initiatives were in jeopardy (we
were the fourth), that people don't care, we aren't getting a response, it looks bad, and the only one that has the slightest
chance is People for Responsible Energy Sources. I was outraged."

In fact, it was a crucial juncture for PRES. The media were
not giving them much coverage, and getting signatures was proving tougher than they expected. So they decided to sally forth
with a bold and dramatic stroke.

"Dr. Edward Teller, who was in on the Manhattan Project
that developed the first atomic bomb, is a prime mover behind
Project Plowshare and the underground gas blasting," says Meladee. "He scheduled an energy conference in Denver. We scheduled a press conference at the same time and place as his energy
conference, hoping the confrontation would attract reporters.
Some people tried to get us to leave, but we got through that
smoothly.

"A reporter asked me how we were doing. It was my debut.
I said we were sure to get on the ballot, and greatly exaggerated
by saying that we already had forty thousand signatures, and
only needed ten thousand more. My friends were shocked, but
they backed me up.

"If you hear somebody saying there's no hope, you think,
'Why bother?' But if you just need a few more, you really get
out there and try. My exaggeration had the psychological effect
of bringing in even more signatures than we needed. In the next
two weeks we got seventeen thousand signatures, mostly mail-
ins."

PRES did one reminder mailing in the middle of June, to
people who still had petitions out. They capped their signature
campaign on July 4 at an Allman Brothers rock concert. "We all
had tickets and wanted to go anyway," says Meladee. "It was
great." On July 5 they had a total of seventy thousand signatures.

Scare Tactics

"After that, I took off," says Meladee, "and I didn't call
anybody or do anything for at least three weeks. We were physically and emotionally drained. When I got back, there was still
the election to deal with, and it was hard to get the momentum
back up. We established a speakers' bureau, and went through
the phone book, getting names of all service organizations and as-

sociations which might have an interest in the issue. We sent each a packet with information on the initiative. We didn't get much response.

"So we switched tactics. We decided if we couldn't reach the public through speaking engagements, we'd use the only other means available to us — free press. We thought about doing advertising, but no one was fund raising for us. None of us were getting paid, and we were in stiff competition with other campaigns, which had special fund raisers on their staffs. Fortunately, we had a good media person, who knew how to write stories for the press. You need either a good media coordinator or a good fund raiser."

The Atomic Energy Commission did nothing openly to oppose the initiative. "How could they take a position?" notes Meladee. "I mean, if they took the position that the people of Colorado did not have the right to decide, they would incense the entire state of Colorado."

Dr. Edward Teller did actively fight the initiative; and both Meladee Martin and Morey Wolfson believe that Teller's opposition was a great asset to their cause. "Edward Teller debated Senator Floyd Haskell at the University of Colorado Medical Center," says Meladee. "Edward Teller in a debate with Floyd Haskell sounded like a very radical outside scientist trying to tell the people of Colorado what was good for them. You know how the new left and the environmentalists are always accused of using scare tactics? PRES has been accused of using the scare of radiation to frighten people into supporting us. Well, Edward Teller used the most incredible scare tactics at that debate! He said the world is in utter turmoil over the energy crisis, and we have no right to stop any development of new energy resources, and there would be 'economic disaster' — those were the words he used — all over the world if there were not new sources of energy created, and that the only way to get at the gas and oil in Colorado was through the use of bombs.

"Floyd Haskell is very easy-going, mild and rational. His premise was that he was not a scientist, but that he felt the people of Colorado had the right to make the decision on whether or not these bombs would be used."

Threat to Representative Government

In mid-September, PRES got a terrific boost in the form of a secret memo sent out by one of their opponents. Though the memo bore the name of Ray Kimball, president of the Colorado Association for Commerce and Industry, it was, according to Meladee Martin, instigated by the lobbyist for CER Geonuclear Corporation. CER Geonuclear was the AEC's private-industry partner in the Rio Blanco blast, and was to handle commercial exploitation of gas produced by the bombs.

through underground natural water systems, by discharge into the atmosphere during the necessary flaring process, by accidental "venting" of the cavity during detonation, or by consumption of the gas produced which is also apt to be contaminated. Accompanying all of this is the endemic problem of containment of radioactive wastes for periods of from 25 to 4000 years.

The memo, sent to potential sources of funds, said the PRES initiative was "a threat to representative government, and a misuse and abuse of the initiative process." It said the initiative process in Colorado should be "strengthened and improved" — meaning, according to Meladee, that initiatives should be harder to get on the ballot.

"Somebody who got the memo was furious," says Meladee, "and sent it to Dick Lamm, who was running for governor. It was the post-Watergate era of openness; we squashed it in the media. Within a week, we had every major national candidate and many state candidates endorsing the initiative. We went on the tube with our list of endorsers. Only Senator Dominick didn't endorse it, and Gary Hart, who defeated him, played that up in his campaign. People to whom the memo was sent were very embarrassed; as far as I know, it never raised any money to oppose us with."

The last PRES effort was distribution of handbills promoting the initiative. "We didn't start distributing until about three weeks before November 5," notes Meladee. "We didn't want to start too soon. We distributed them through the Lamm gubernatorial campaign, mostly in the Denver-Boulder area, though twenty thousand went to the western slope. They were available at every candidate's and party's headquarters in the state. We coordinated with political campaign staffs to truck them around.

"We won by a 60 percent majority, and celebrated quite extensively. Very soon after the election, CER Geonuclear reported that the ballot had effectively ended underground nuclear blasting in Colorado, because they were not going to pay for the time and effort it would take to bring a ballot measure before the people."

Critical Mass '74

Meladee went to the "Critical Mass '74" conference, held by Ralph Nader in Washington, D.C., on November 17 and 18, 1974. "It was exciting," she says. "There were small environmental group representatives from all over. People were so thrilled to hear about PRES; many were curious about how we did our initiative campaign. Nader brought in brilliant and persuasive speakers from the AEC. But no matter what they say, there's always that flaw: what are you going to do with nuclear wastes?

"We had workshops on petition signing, legal intervention, siting, and other topics. The plan is to work toward passage of a national nuclear moratorium bill. We'll probably ask our people to write to our senators and congressmen in support of the bill. It will be a moratorium on the building of nuclear power plants until safety problems are solved — especially the problem of what they're going to do with nuclear wastes.

"Meanwhile, we hope to put on a state nuclear conference, to study not the technical or the economic aspects of nuclear power, but the *ethical*. I think this is the most important. It's the people of the future who will have to deal with nuclear wastes. We're planning the conference along with the American Friends Service Committee — it's always good to get allies from religious, health, and other groups. There's a procedure of engendering awareness, educating people, before you talk about a nuclear moratorium. If you hit them immediately with action, they fall back and say, 'I'm not informed.' We're informing them not only on nuclear energy, but solar energy and energy conservation."

Meladee Martin, Morey Wolfson, and others at PRES and Environmental Action of Colorado are focusing their attention on finding ways to convert our society into a low-energy-using culture, running as much as possible on the power of the sun. And to them, public enemy number one is nuclear power, whether it is in the form of A-bombs or power plants. "It's American technology that has fostered the growth of nuclear power in the western world," says Meladee. "That's an incredible responsibility. We believe the major problems in the world are caused by the uses of the wrong sources of energy. And there is a dimensional difference in having sulfur dioxide from coal burning in the air for five years and having the radioactive cesium 137 of nuclear wastes floating around for twenty-four thousand years."

"Our representatives depend ultimately on decisions made in the village square. . . . To the village square we must carry the facts of atomic energy. From there must come America's voice."

— Albert Einstein, 1946

No Oil

The modern American's dependence on the automobile and the petroleum which runs it is nowhere more apparent than in the city of Los Angeles. You can't get anywhere in Los Angeles without a car. The many towns and cities which comprise metropolitan Los Angeles are linked together with broad freeways, which day and night are choked with automobiles rushing through the soft smog of southern California.

It is poetically appropriate that Los Angeles is underlain with petroleum — 200 million barrels of it. During the fiscal year 1971-72, 18.73 million barrels of oil were pumped from the Los Angeles urban area, through 1,795 wells, yielding $1.70 million dollars in revenues for the city government.

Nobody ever had trouble getting a permit for an oil well in Los Angeles until 1970, when the Occidental Petroleum Corporation proposed to sink an exploratory core hole in Pacific Palisades. What "Oxy" struck was a solid rock of opposition.

"Nobody was going to be officially notified of the hearing, because nobody lives within 300 feet of the drill site — that's because people live on a cliff *above* the drill site!"

The Killer Slide

"On March 14, 1970 there was an article in the *Los Angeles Times* by Bob Rosenblatt, notifying us of Oxy's intent to drill at the toe of the killer slide," says Shirley Solomon. "On March 16, No Oil was born. It was a matter of how long it took to get in touch with neighbors and find a meeting place."

Shirley Solomon's home is on the rim of a gravel bluff in Pacific Palisades, an expensive residential area of the city of Los Angeles. Before her window sprawls the Pacific — calm, magnificently azure, dissolving all horizons. The island of Santa Catalina is dimly outlined through the light particulate haze. Across the view oil tankers are scattered like toys, constantly reminding Shirley of her five-year obsession.

"In 1958, a state highway engineer stood on top of the cliff over there," Shirley says, pointing south to an area on the bluff's gravelly lip about a half-mile away. "There had been a landslide a week earlier. He pronounced it now safe, and within a matter of minutes he was buried in 600 tons of mud. It slid. He was killed. That was where the name "killer slide" came from. The whole Pacific Palisades area is plagued with slides.

"That slide covered up the Pacific Coast Highway, our main thoroughfare here. Due to the hazardous nature of the slide, there was no way they could clean it up, so they moved the highway out around it. Where Oxy's drill site is now, was previously the Pacific Coast Highway, before the slide. The Via de las Olas, the street on the bluff above, sank eight feet, and is blocked for traffic. Here's where they want to drill for oil! Some of Occidental's geologists have maintained that drilling there would be perfectly safe, that drilling vibrations won't hurt anything. But another of their geologists has said it's a miracle that there's anything standing there anyway, the cliff is all going to fall down one day."

No Oil, which later incorporated, immediately set out to prevent Occidental from drilling for oil in Pacific Palisades. In July of 1970, Occidental was to appear in a hearing before a Los Angeles city zoning officer, to apply for a variance to drill. "They wanted a permit for an exploratory core hole," Shirley explains. "Nobody was going to be officially notified of the hearing, because nobody lives within 300 feet of the drill site — that's because people live on a cliff *above* the drill site! If it hadn't been for Bob Rosenblatt's article, Oxy would have just

SING ALONG WITH "NO"

Shirley Solomon wrote words to some popular songs to keep her troops happy (and noisy) after they had been cleared from the hearing room. She refers to them as "idiot parodies," but the words, and the tactic, are a good deal smarter than that.

To the tune of:
I Get a Kick out of You!

Oil is not like champagne!
When oil bubbles,
    it brings sticky troubles
And doubles the rubble and goo!
Oxy, why don't you skidoo?

Drilling in hills, it is plain —
Hills will start sliding,
    while Oxy's confiding
This sliding cannot happen here!
We fear they are far from sincere!

Their exploitation could lead to change
And rearrange our living.
Values would drop and go kerplop
While they still claim they are giving!

Oxy's determined to rape
Our lovely area —
    what do they care if a
Hair-breadth away there's a spill?
They want to be in on the kill!

To the tune of:
Hello, Dolly!

Goodbye, Oxy! Goodbye, Oxy!
All your tricks and phony claims fell
    through.

You've locked your gate, Oxy —
That's great, Oxy!
Don't forget your derrick and your
    lease-hounds, too!

Here's your hat, Oxy!
Now, scat, Oxy!
You and Hammer put on quite a show —

With all your cheating,
You're gonna take a beating —
It will sure be swell to see you go!

Another chorus:

gotten the zoning variance — nobody would have been notified — and they would have just put the rig in."

"None of us knew anything about fighting city hall," Shirley Solomon says of the small band of Palisadeans who were taking on Occidental Petroleum Corporation. "I went off on my own tangent. I went after very broad political support. I was told two things: one, that I couldn't get it; and two — by some of the people in our group — what do you need it for anyway? I went after what I called "honorary members." We wound up with Senators Cranston and Tunney, Congressman Alphonzo Bell from our district, and several others. I had their statements of support in writing, in letters they'd written me. I didn't know any of these people at that time, so I had to prove myself. I just sent them slews of material; I put together packets, and wrote long, detailed letters.

"I also felt we needed the support of groups — concerned citizens' groups — on a broad basis. Will Rogers State Beach is on the other side of Oxy's proposed drill site, and people from everywhere use it. I eventually got about 125 organizations behind us: the Los Angeles County Federation of Labor, the League of Women Voters, groups from the Chicano neighborhoods in East Los Angeles, and many others. Now it's become almost a pattern for groups to go after endorsements, but at that time I had no idea that was the right thing to do.

"By the July 7 hearing date, I had most of our honorary members. The hearing, before a Mr. Rudser, the zoning officer, was absolutely incredible. Four hundred fifty people showed up at the West Los Angeles City Hall. Firemen cleared the room until only 200 were left in it. Figuring something crazy like that was going to happen, I had talked to the maintenance man, who set up loudspeakers so the overflow crowd could hear. I also got somebody who could more or less lead singing, and wrote some idiot parodies. Oxy spoke from one until six o'clock in the afternoon, so we weren't getting any press coverage at all. Our supporters outside the hearing room sang the parodies of Oxy, which the press enjoyed.

"That hearing was an interesting lesson for me. At later hearings, we'd hold press conferences before the hearing, in the corridors outside of where it was to be held. Usually proponents speak first, so they could dominate the early hours. In our pre-hearing press conference, we'd just use whatever our presentation to the hearing was going to be.

"On July 24, Mr. Rudser came out in favor of Oxy's request for a zoning variance, on the strange theory that if Oxy started drilling right away they'd be done with the core hole before the rains started. At that point we knew that Mayor Sam Yorty and the Los Angeles Planning Department were against us, but we didn't know just why."

Matter of Conscience

No Oil appealed Rudser's decision to the board of zoning appeals, which set September 15 as the date to hear the case. Shirley kept sending materials to various groups, and got support from an unexpected quarter. "I sent a slew of material to the Los Angeles Grand Jury, not asking for their support, just informing them of the situation. In August, the grand jury came out in favor of us, and handed us a letter of support on top of the bluff overlooking the drill site. Local reporters were surprised, and one said that such a thing had never happened before.

In advance of the hearing before the board of zoning appeals, we sent out flyers and had a phone tree* to get people to come to it. At the previous hearing, the first two rows had been reserved for Oxy. So I got down at 11 A. M., two hours early, to the Los Angeles City Hall — which had a much bigger hearing room — and put No Oil buttons and leaflets on the first two rows of seats, reserving them for us.

"Since we were proponents, we spoke first, and Congressman Al Bell was our first speaker. We alleged that Oxy's drilling plan posed a danger to the health, welfare, and safety of the citizens, and that it was very poor planning to put an oil rig at the toe of a dangerous slide. We did have some expert witnesses from UCLA.

"At ten that night, while we were still there, Father Kelley, the head of the board of zoning appeals, said he couldn't find it in his conscience, no matter what way, to allow Occidental to proceed. We won. It was unanimous.

"Then Mayor Yorty came out with long press releases saying, one, that the county grand jury ought to be investigated; and two, that the board of zoning appeals — his own appointees, who we had been assured by local political experts would rule against us — had probably acted illegally. There are still a lot of facts missing about why Yorty supported Oxy so strongly, in spite of the many investigative hearings that have been held.

"After the board of zoning appeals decided in our favor, many in our group scattered, because the threat was no longer there. But the day after the hearing, Congressman Al Bell called me from Washington to congratulate me, and to say that Oxy was probably going to make another try, probably this time for a drilling district."

There are a number of petroleum drilling districts in Los Angeles. Applicants for drilling districts must first get drilling leases on 75 percent of the land in a 40-acre area, then get city government approval. Once a drilling district is approved, permission to drill usually follows as a matter of course.

Editor's Note: A "phone tree" functions much the same as a chain letter: each person called is asked to call two more people, and so forth.

The same to you, Yorty!
You're all through, Yorty!
None of us have liked the Yorty Years.

And when you go, Yorty,
Please know, Yorty,
Only special interests will shed big tears.

You done us wrong, Yorty!
All along, Yorty,
While you've been "the king" at City
*   Hall —*

We're gonna thump you!
It is time to dump you
So we can make our city one for all!

To the tune of:
She'll Be Comin' Round the Mountain

They'll be tearing down our hillsides,
*   if they drill!*
They'll be adding to our landslides,
*   if they drill!*
While Nature weeps and hollers,
They will only think of dollars —
They could trigger nasty landslides,
*   if they drill!*

They'll endanger our fine coastline,
*   if they drill!*
They'll endanger our fine beaches,
*   yes, they will!*
Santa Barb'ra doesn't phase 'em —
And our outcries still amaze 'em —
It could lead to offshore drilling,
*   if they drill!*

They will bring the stench of oil,
*   if they drill!*
Yes, the putrid stench of oil,
*   if they drill!*
Sure, the oil will be smelly,
But to Oxy, what the hell-y?
No, it sure won't be Chanel-y,
*   if they drill!*

They will bring a noisy clatter,
*   if they drill!*
But to them, it doesn't matter
*   what they kill —*
Music of the waves won't greet us,
For the oil rigs will treat us
To a very noisy clatter, if they drill!

We're opposed to drilling in the Palisades!
We'll protect our lovely coastline
*   from their raids!*
And we don't want any core holes
Because those could lead to more holes
And we don't want oil in the Palisades!

"In 1972, in one nine-month period, we had about 33 public hearings. I was going out of my mind."

"In April 1972, Oxy applied for three drilling districts in this area," says Shirley Solomon. "We are in one. Four corporate owners own all the land below the bluff — 112 acres. They got leases on that, which gave them the 75 percent they needed. Hearings started before various agencies and officials of city government.

"At the same time we were trying to get a city ban on inland coastal oil drilling in Los Angeles within a half mile of the ocean, except in existing industrial zones. In 1972, in one nine-month period, we had about 33 public hearings. I was going out of my mind. The public was confused, the media were confused, and *we* were confused. One day I had three public hearings at city hall. You can't do that to people, and keep them interested.

"The city council passed a ban on inland coastal drilling; but Yorty vetoed it. Then we tried to get the city council to put the drilling ban proposal on a referendum ballot. In October 1972 the city council approved Occidental's application for three drilling districts. Then Oxy needed permission to drill. The planning commission, which was backing Oxy, wanted to let Oxy drill two informational *bore* holes. The board of zoning appeals had earlier refused to allow *core* holes, so now they were asking for *bore* holes. There's no such thing as a bore hole in the city codes. All of these things were going on simultaneously."

From an Occidental Petroleum Corporation proposal, we give you this artist's conception of a "Spanish Mission Style Drillsite for Pacific Palisades." (Think the swallows would come back?)

Don't Do Anything Rash

At about this time, two California state environmental protection laws came to the fore in No Oil's battle against Occidental Petroleum. The first was the California Environmental Quality Act (CEQA), as interpreted by the California Supreme Court in *Friends of Mammoth v. Mono County Board of Supervisors,* decided on September 21, 1972. The *Friends of Mammoth* case held that a local government could not approve a private project that had a potentially significant effect on the environment without either preparing an environmental impact report (EIR) on it, or making sure that the project complied with the conservation element of the General Plan. To the Center for Law in the Public Interest, a public-interest law firm working with No Oil, that meant that CEQA required the Los Angeles City Council to do an EIR on Occidental's application for drilling districts.

"The city council said no EIR was necessary," says Shirley, "so the boys from the Center for Law in the Public Interest filed suit in superior court, on our behalf, requiring that an EIR be done. We had trouble getting the right kind of witnesses — geologists — to testify for us in court. They told us that since they are dependent on petroleum companies for contracts, it would have been the kiss of death for them to testify against Oxy. Thanksgiving evening we finally got agreement on Professor Witherspoon of Berkeley to testify for us. The superior court sent the case back to the city council, for a formal vote on whether the drilling districts would have a significant effect on the environment."

The city council voted that the drilling districts would not have a significant effect on the environment, so no EIR under CEQA was required. No Oil appealed this decision in the state courts, and by January 31, 1973 the appeal had reached the California Supreme Court.

Meanwhile, the Los Angeles Planning Department was pushing to give Occidental permission to drill three bore holes in Pacific Palisades. The planning department was racing against a clock that had been set in motion on November 7, 1972, when the California voters approved an initiative proposition called the California Coastal Zone Conservation Act. Under this act, a coastal commission with power to control development on California's coast — inland and offshore — was going to come into being on February 1, 1973.

"Calvin Hamilton, the head of the city planning department, said he wanted to push Occidental's project through before the coastal commission became effective, because he didn't believe in the coastal initiative," says Shirley. "On January 30, 1973 there was a board of zoning appeals hearing on the permit for the three bore holes. On February 1, the coastal commission was going to become effective. We were down at city hall, and a television

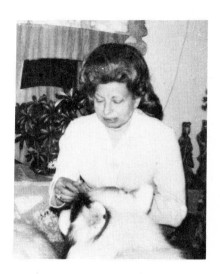

SHIRLEY SOLOMON ON PRESS RELATIONS

Shirley Solomon's background is in public relations for legitimate theater productions, and in writing such things as musical comedies. She believes this didn't prepare her to handle public relations for No Oil, Inc.; but the excellent press relations enjoyed by No Oil are a major factor in its success.

Shirley believes common sense is the best asset in dealing with reporters. "I don't call reporters unless we really have something to put forward," she says, "either something that others have done or something we are doing. Sometimes you stay quiet for a while.

"Credibility rating is the key thing for any group to maintain with the press. I never have given the media anything I couldn't document. If I couldn't document something, I made clear it was a possibility, and not documented.

"In announcing meetings or hearings, I usually send out a notice, and make a brief phone call to make sure they received the notice — *not* to urge them to come. Coverage isn't magic. I sit there and make 40 phone calls, and maybe nobody shows up.

"Whenever we can get a public official to say something we want said, we let him issue the statement.

"One of the difficult things with No Oil has been sitting on people, keeping them from responding to the jibes of Mayor Yorty. We are called radicals, some of our leaders have been accused of making money on our opposition to Oxy — every lie under the sun. In one article, an anonymous Oxy official said we were hysterical, ignorant, liars, and crybabies. They want us to respond. We didn't; but at the proper time, in a hearing, I pulled out the article and used it."

"Occidental Petroleum is one of our biggest donors — a number of their stockholders send their royalty checks in to us!"

newsman came up to me and said, 'Occidental is moving in their equipment.' The hearing hadn't even started yet!

"Then Walter Matthau came tearing in — he's one of our neighbors — and said, 'There's a bunch of kids standing on top of the cliff, threatening to bomb it. You've got to go back and tell them not to do anything rash!' We had all this going on and the hearing hadn't started yet. Naturally Oxy won this time; we weren't even allowed to present testimony.

"On February 1, Occidental started in on their operation. We immediately asked the state supreme court to halt Oxy's operations until our case under CEQA was decided, and asked the state coastal commission to order Oxy to cease operations. On February 7 both the supreme court and the coastal commission ordered Oxy to halt. Now Oxy claims that they have vested rights due to their seven days of work, which they think means they don't need a permit from the coastal commission."

From NO to SEA

In December 1974 the California State Supreme Court held illegal the Los Angeles City Council's approval of Oxy's plans to drill in Pacific Palisades. The opinion, by Justice Mathew Tobriner, added to the *Friends of Mammoth* case by ordering environmental impact reports under CEQA where facts are in dispute and where the project is surrounded by public concern.

When asked if Occidental would begin the lengthy process of reapplying for a city permit to drill, Occidental attorney Edward S. Renwick replied, "I would doubt that Occidental would just want to walk away, particularly when obtaining energy is so important now."

No Oil just celebrated its fifth anniversay, and is ready for Oxy in case it makes another try to drill a hole at the toe of the killer slide. "The coastal commission case is still pending," notes Shirley, "and will be declared moot if the other case handles the situation. Still, I'll be glad when Oxy removes their equipment from the site."

It has been a long, grinding, expensive fight, and Shirley Solomon says she's ready to step aside and let others lead. "We've put a lot of our own money into it," she remarks, "though we were able to raise quite a bit through direct mailings. In fact, Occidental Petroleum is one of our biggest donors — a number of their stockholders send their royalty checks to us!"

Still, Shirley has found the time and energy to head a battle against all the petroleum companies and the United States Department of Interior. More precisely, she is the somewhat reluctant leader of the Seashore Environmental Alliance (SEA), a coalition of citizen groups and concerned individuals opposed to federal leasing of California's outer continental shelf for oil drilling. According to *Sea Log No. 2,* SEA's newsletter, the Interior Department has put 1.56 million acres of California's outer continental shelf up for drilling leases. "SEA believes the California outer continental shelf should be made a national preserve for the people," says the newsletter, "to be used for offshore drilling only if a national emergency is declared by Congress." Though it's just beginning, Shirley has made sure that SEA already has a long list of honorary members and supporting organizations, as well as excellent press relations.

Showdown on the Northern Plains

*PROJECT INDEPENDENCE
COMES TO BULL MOUNTAINS*

This is the Wild West, the West of the Western movie, the Big Sky Country. Montana, Nebraska, Wyoming, and the Dakotas — the Northern Plains, country where a man can still find solitude. This is the site of Custer's last stand, and of present-day Crow and Northern Cheyenne Indian reservations; the sprawling stage for many a confrontation between cattlemen and the farmers and sheepherders constantly encroaching on their range land.

Now a confrontation is joined in the Northern Plains with the very character of the countryside itself at stake. For underlying the entire

"Montana is faced with a choice: We can remain the eighth largest cow-calf producer in the nation and a major food commodity resource, or we can become a major energy-intensive industrial complex. The two are incompatible and the choice is inescapable."

That's the way Bill Mitchell, staff director of the Northern Plains Resource Council (NPRC), sees the showdown between the ranchers of the Northern Plains and the industrial-governmental complex that is attempting to create a titanic coal strip mining and electrical power producing system there. Mitchell, and a lot of the ranchers and farmers in the Northern Plains, believe the power grid's use of land, water, and air resources would cripple the ability of the region to produce food. In other words, the Northern Plains can opt either for short-term, high-energy production, or long-term, low-energy output in the form of cattle and crops. It's a regional problem, but it has implications as large as this fragile planet.

The power grid's use of land, water, and air resources would cripple the ability of the region to produce food.

In the spring of 1972, faced with a regional threat to their way of life, representatives of local ranchers' groups from all over Montana got together and formed the Northern Plains Resource Council. The NPRC is a federation of landowners' groups, with each local group represented on its board. It was initially formed to fight the huge Northern Plains strip mining and power development program.

This group has had considerable impact as an educational, lobbying, and grassroots organizing force. It has evolved over the years, and at present has a full-time staff of nine. Staff members are mostly in their late twenties or early thirties, and make $200 a month — in other words, they're *dedicated* staffers! Some are migrants from urban areas, and some are children of ranchers.

Bill Mitchell of NPRC is usually in the plains somewhere organizing new groups, or in the halls of Helena lobbying. We were able to sit him down recently, however, and got him to talk about the NPRC, and to describe a recent activity which he thought would be particularly illustrative of how this unique federation of grassroots groups works.

The Man from Acorn

Having found the academic study of wildlife management to be irrelevant to the problems of the real world, Bill Mitchell dropped out of graduate school just before getting his master's degree. In 1972 he was working at the San Francisco Ecology Center. In October of 1972 he went to Sheridan, Wyoming for the "Environmental Quality '72" conference, largely to check out the people there, and to find out who was being most effective in fighting the massive power plan for the Northern Plains.

"It was this NPRC group of ranchers, longhairs, and ranch wives who were doing the shaking and moving," he recalls. "They were doing it in a professional way. They weren't paranoid to the point of screening people and ideas out; they were open to me. They were in the process of investigating who was doing the coal leasing. They'd gone through county records to find out how much private and public land had been leased, and put it on a map for the state legislature. Nobody else had done this. They were very high on research, and low on organization and screaming. They wanted to have all their facts together, and knew if they got anything wrong the coal companies would walk all over them."

Bill kept in touch with the NPRC. "I used to live in the intermountain West," he says, "and always wanted to go back

region is the world's largest known coal reserve: an awesome 40 percent of all U. S. reserves, and 20 percent of the world's reserves. But they won't be reserves for long, if the titanic power-generating system envisioned by the North Central Power Study continues to be set up.

This study, issued in 1971 by a coordinating committee composed of the U. S. Bureau of Reclamation and 35 electric power suppliers from many states, envisions a gargantuan grid of coal strip mines, 42 power plants to burn the coal and create steam-generated electricity, and thousands of miles of high-voltage transmission lines to carry the current to urban areas throughout the nation. Even before that study was issued, speculators were hovering around Billings, Montana, trying to bluff, badger, or buy control of blocs of coal leases large enough to be commercially exploitable. They knew that Project Independence — the highly-touted goal of the Nixon (and now the Ford) administration to break free of Arab oil while maintaining a society which uses energy at a high rate — was dependent on the creation of a Northern Plains power grid.

The environmental issues raised by this power grid — threats to surface and underground water, air pollution, land use issues raised by power line rights of way and plant sitings, in addition to the land-mangling effects of coal strip mining — are now being fought on all levels. A federal bill regulating where strip mining can be done, and who will pay for how much land reclamation, is probably the most hotly contested environmental bill of 1975.

Beyond the purely environmental problems of the power grid is the threat it poses to a way of life. Many of the farmers and ranchers in the Northern Plains believe they cannot coexist with coal mines and power plants. It is not simply a matter of losing their clean air and their wide, open spaces, though these are very highly valued. It is a grim economic competition for the land and water they need to keep often-marginal cattle and crop enterprises economically viable.

The first vigorous opposition to coal strip mining in the region arose in the Bull Mountains of Montana, when the Consolidation Coal Company (Consol) came in during 1970 to buy coal leases from ranchers. The ranchers have an emotional attachment to their land and way of life that is rare in this day and age, and incomprehensible to impersonal companies waving fat checks. They formed the Bull Mountain Landowners Association, to keep Consol from cracking their united front of rejecting the leases, and to try to find some way to prevent Consol from stripping in the area.

The Bull Mountain group, ranchers and their wives, wrote letters, lobbied in the state capital of Helena and in Washington, D. C., and in general made coal leasing in Montana a hot, public issue. They also did careful research on coal leasing, and began mapping who was leasing what land in Montana.

In 1973, the Bureau of Land Management, which owns a lot of land in the Northern Plains and leases it to ranchers for grazing, announced that it would not lease land in the Bull Mountains to Consol for strip mining. This decision, probably made because of the pressure and information generated by the Bull Mountain group, ended Consol's hopes of strip mining the area. The only major leasing they'd been able to do in that area had been from the Burlington Northern Railroad, which, because of nineteenth century land grants, owns *every other* section of land along its tracks — and they haven't made steam shovels that can hop one mile like jack rabbits yet!

there. This gave me a good reason. In September '73 I moved up to Billings, and started doing local research for NPRC. Then, that December, Wade Rathke came out for a few days."

Wade Rathke is a professional community organizer. About 26 years old, Rathke began as a welfare rights organizer in Boston, then moved to Arkansas and formed a series of grassroots groups called Arkansas Community Organization for Reform Now (ACORN). ACORN now has some 18 professional community organizers, who organize people at local levels to deal with community problems of all sorts. Rathke has become rather famous where he works, and is now organizing South Dakota farmers to deal with energy and agriculture problems.

"We'd been operating on the idea that it was an all-or-nothing situation," says Bill Mitchell. "We got involved in every issue that walked down the pike. We extended ourselves to the point that we weren't doing anything that was totally effective. Wade conveyed to us that community organizing is a professional activity, and that we should choose achievable objectives that would have a strong effect on the overall situation.

"Wade also got us to be less research oriented, and to start to service the needs of the farmers and ranchers who were members of our group. As he said, 'Let's face it, this will be going on for another 15 to 20 years, you will not get it over with in a year or two. Right now you're interested in coal mining, but in the future you're going to have to get involved in other agricultural issues that your members and board of directors will be interested in, to have a sustaining organization.' "

As a result of Rathke's visit, NPRC made greater efforts to discover and serve the needs of farmers and ranchers in Montana. "We were getting tagged as an environmental organization," says Mitchell, "as only interested in clean air and clean water; whereas we were trying to be recognized as an agricultural organization. I'm defending the economic basis of a way of life."*

The NPRC also decided to focus its efforts in 1974 on one issue: the siting of two power plants called Colstrip Units Three and Four.

Editor's Note: To explain why he feels it is important that the Northern Plains Resource Council not be thought of as an environmental group, Mitchell cites the current "ugly, polarized" relations between ranchers and the Natural Resources Defense Council (NRDC), an environmental group which has fought strip mining for years. About a year ago, according to Mitchell, NRDC sued the Bureau of Land Management, alleging they should file an environmental impact statement on all land leased for grazing. "Surely the BLM is at fault, and has allowed overgrazing in some cases," says Mitchell. "But in resolving the issue, the BLM is going to freeze all leases on some ten million acres in the western states, until they can do environmental impact statements on grazing districts. This threatens the livelihood of ranchers; and offers an entree for BLM to rationalize coal leasing, because the interest of the ranchers has been removed from their land."

Terrence Moore photograph

Setting a Precedent

Colstrip Three and Four, two 750-megawatt power plants
proposed by Montana Power, were to be built near Colstrip, Montana. Two 500-kilovolt transmission lines would carry their juice
westward across Montana, hooking into the Bonneville Power Administration system of the Pacific Northwest. Sixty percent of
the power produced by them would go out of the state.

"They're planning to generate power for export," says Bill
Mitchell. "We believe and contend they want to site here because
of siting considerations: less political hostility, less-complicated
legal situation, less numerical opposition. In an urban area, you
have the social and economic means of absorbing workers — you
probably have unemployed workers available. These plants
would bring two thousand or so workers into the county — Rosebud County — which has a population of six thousand."

$4.60 SHORT

Ann and Boyd Charter of Bull Mountain were among the first to actively oppose coal leasing in the Northern Plains. Their determination stopped Consolidation Coal Company from strip mining their ranch. And Boyd Charter's statements, eminently quotable though sometimes unprintable, have spiced many accounts of opposition to the stripping of the Northern Plains.

"They came down here and wanted to buy my ranch," says Boyd of Consol. "I told them, I said, 'You ain't got enough money to buy that ranch.' I said, 'No matter what you offer me it's going to be $4.60 short. . . . The land is worth more to me for running cattle on than any amount of money I could get out of it. It's my home, and I love my home.'"

The following is excerpted from *The Sun Is Becoming Darker*, by Stan Steiner. We are grateful to him for letting us include this material.

Old Boyd Charter was ornery. He was one of the last of the old-time ranchers, who owned his place on earth and knew his own mind. He was one of those men who was so independent he seemed unreal, but he was real enough. The sort of wiry, resilient, honest, straight-faced, outspoken, tough, boyishly polite, and shy man who had made the West what it once was.

He was the breed of man who always seem to have a four-day-old growth of beard.

Some would say that he was a relic of the impossible past, conservative as hell, his ideas as hard as nails, his face lined as an old leather saddle, the breeder of rodeo horses and American dreams, with vinegar on his tongue and flint in his eyes. And it was true that just a few years ago he was still a "Theodore Roosevelt Republican." Until, he cursed, he found out "The damned — if you forgive my language — Republicans aren't real conservatives. Not really. They believe that ripping up the land and destroying our

The two plants would be the first to come under the Utility Siting Act, passed in 1973 in Montana. This act requires that companies which propose to build large power plants in the state must submit a permit application to the state Department of Natural Resources. They must also finance a study of environmental impact, to be done by the Department of Natural Resources, Division of Energy Planning. The Department has 600 days to complete their study, which must then be submitted — with the Department's recommendations — to a governor-appointed Board of Natural Resources. The seven-member board then decides if the plants will be built at the proposed site.

"Colstrip Units One and Two, which have already been built in the Colstrip area, didn't come under the Act," says Mitchell. "Three and Four would set a precedent for future sitings."

Force along the Line

"Montana Power started out by trying to get part of the right of way for transmission lines to service Colstrip Three and Four on a corridor also servicing Colstrip One and Two. They sent out agents. It was just like coal leasing — they threatened people with condemnation of their land, saying they'd have to sign the right-of-way lease.

"We figured this right-of-way leasing would get their foot in the door for siting Colstrip Three and Four, so we assigned a guy to it right away. We wrote letters of complaint to state officials, got a couple of people to show letters from the company threatening them with condemnation, organized people along the line, and cooled this effort of theirs. They started in January and wanted to have leasing on this little section of the line done by April; we forced them back to September.

"Meanwhile, Steve Charter — the son of Ann and Boyd Charter, two of the first Bull Mountain group members (the Bull Mountain Landowners Association was the first local group to oppose coal strip mining in the Northern Plains region) — was working on the rest of the right of way of the two transmission lines that were going to run from Colstrip Three and Four through western Montana. There was no detailed map of this line available, and leasing hadn't started. Steve went to each county, and got maps showing land ownership. Then we went to the federal government and got the large-scale map of the line — the federal government is involved in the deal. For each county we figured out who owned land that the line was to cross, to figure out who to contact.

"We'd go to the landowners and say, 'We don't know for sure, but there's a good possibility that two 500-kilovolt lines are coming through your property, and we figure you have the right to know. We need a cohesive group all along the line to force this situation into the open. We are also doing research on developing a model easement in case the line does come through.

"It went real well. Landowner groups were formed, and community meetings started being held up and down the line. It drove the utility company nuts. Three of their guys had to come to every one of those meetings. We'd tell our side of the story, they'd tell their side — then they'd answer questions. We'd prime the landowners to ask tough questions. Sometimes the utility team did well, sometimes not so well, and sometimes they wouldn't show up.

"This game went on, and attracted attention. The state Department of Natural Resources started sending a team around to tell people what was going on, in a neutral way. Then Montana Power started holding meetings, and we really got meetinged out! One young lawyer of theirs, John Ross, went to every one of those meetings. When we see each other, we razz the other guy: 'Well, John, whaddya gonna say tonight?'"

Rosebud Ranchers

"At the same time that we were working on the transmission line right of way," says Mitchell, "we were strengthening the Rosebud Ranchers Association. The members lived along Rosebud Creek, in Rosebud County, within nine or twelve miles of where Colstrip Three and Four were to be built.

"About February, there were two guys down there who were outspoken against the plants. They looked on themselves as Lone Rangers, and thought nobody else really cared. We sat them down one night and said, 'Look, forget your past animosities about people who won't do anything. Who along this creek do you think you might trust? Who might commit themselves?' Before that evening was out we had a list of 55 names, and out of that we have a steady group of 35 to 40 people. They changed their name to the Rosebud Protective Association, and the original two active ranchers pulled back from leadership positions.

"Their members go around giving speeches. Each has his own approach: one is technical, one philosophical, and so on. Their main point is local impact: tax coming in from a new plant is always three, four or five years behind the impact of the plant. They've started working on issues such as overcrowded schools, public health, crime, and air pollution control equipment. They don't want the plants to be built at all. One of the state environmental requirements for power plant siting is that it should have minimum impact. They're trying to point out that there's nothing minimum about the impact Colstrip Three and Four would have in Rosebud County."

In making their case, the Rosebud group has the evidence provided by the impact of Colstrip Units One and Two, which
[Continued on page 152]

country by strip mining, is *progress!* Just like everyone else."

If you talked to that old so-and-so, "hope his words were not too salty and if they were that you had an ample supply of water," said Cliff Hansen — Senator Clifford P. Hansen — of Wyoming, who in his youth had ridden the range as a cowhand with his old neighbor, Boyd Charter.

His words were not too salty — they were acid.

This is what he told me:

". . . Some of the coal people say we ranchers are against the strip mines because we don't own the mineral rights to our land. Well, in respect to that, I say they are the biggest liars the United States has ever produced.

"It wouldn't make one hour of difference to me if I had the mineral rights or not. No one is going to tear up my land for the damned dollar. Anyone who thinks otherwise doesn't know how we ranchers think. Lots of ranchers have turned down offers. I, myself, turned down an oil lease, just this year.

"Now, I will admit many ranchers in Montana and Wyoming may be fakes. What they are is big eastern corporations, who bought up the land, and have no regard for it. The one thing they have regard for is money. But, the real dyed-in-the-wool rancher, who makes his living out of the ground, who runs sheep, or cattle, or who is growing wheat, or whatever he does, is anything but a fake. He is trying to save his way of life. He is trying to save his land.

"Always, in the past, when we exploited the land, it had a chance to come back. It may sometimes take centuries to bring the land back, but we could do it. We could have brought the buffalo back, if we had wanted to. If we wanted to we could have got this country back to the way the Indians left it.

"But, I wonder now: If they go through with what they have proposed — the strip mining of the whole eastern plains of the Rockies and the cutting of our timber all

Right: This is the strip mine at Decker, Montana. The mine is owned jointly by Pacific Power and Light, and Peter Kewit Sons, a construction firm based in Omaha, Nebraska. The photograph was taken by Terrence Moore, and appeared in the July 1973 issue of Audubon.

off, for export mostly, and the using up of all our water for power plants and the polluting of all our mountain air — then I say, this is our last chance to preserve America. This land is going to be tore up to such an extent there will not be anything left to preserve.

"For Godsake, why can't we as citizens at least put the brakes on it — before it is too late! Before America is in ruins!

"On my ranch things are just the way they was. Ever see that picture, *Little Big Man*. Well, they made some of it on my ranch. The director told me he was looking all over Montana for a place that was just the way it was one hundred years ago, when Custer came through. Some place where the buffalo grass was waist high, where nothing was fake, where everything was authentic. My ranch was the only place he found. I am proud of that.

"We live in a log cabin. Now, you may think that's pretty primitive. But, I say, we got to learn how to live again, doing for ourselves, controlling our own lives, living on the land and respecting the land.

"Sometimes people ask me: Are you going Indian? I say, what's wrong with that! The Indians had the right ideas, and we had the wrong ideas!

"Listen, give me that pack of cigarettes. I don't know if you're going to want to hear this. When I say what I'm about to say, before I finish up my talk, you may not want to hear this. But I am going to say this: I am as loyal an American as there is anywhere in these United States. But, when anything is ruined and exploited as our coun-

try has been by crooked politicians, I think the government, as it is run today, should be overthrown.

"Now, when you say the word, overthrown, that is a pretty strong word. Well, I am anything but a Communist. I do not say overthrow it and make it Communist, or Socialist, or anything like that. I just say overthrow it as it is today and bring it back to the way the constitution was written.

"I say, the constitution was the greatest document written in the history of our country. But the government of the United States is run every way in the world but according to the constitution of the United States. And so, when I say overthrow the government and the people who are running it, I say let's get people in there to run it the way the constitution says.

"I say, we have to stand still. And fight to preserve America. We have no choice at all. We have our backs against the wall. We are going to be the last generation of Western men, if we lose. There's no place to pioneer anymore. Nowhere to go. Nowhere to run to. Nowhere to hide.

"When we die, America dies."

COLSTRIP PAYS THROUGH THE NOSE

The banner of jobs and prosperity, under which large projects (like strip mining) come to rural areas, often hides a cruel deception for longtime residents, who end up suffering environmental hardships and paying dearly for the privilege through degradation of services and increased taxes. Read this grim account by Duane Bowler, from the Billings Gazette, *of what has happened to Rosebud County, Montana.*

Bill Gillin of Colstrip feels he's been had up to the eyebrows and beyond by all the talk about the wonderful things that coal development is going to do for eastern Montana.

To Gillin and quite a few of the other ranchers, the results have spelled pure disaster.

Gillin is not a boisterous man, one given to highly emotional statements and exaggerations to support his claims. He collects facts and then makes deductions.

"Here's what the impact of the Colstrip development has done to the Colstrip schools, community tax base and to the County of Rosebud. This is not prediction but fact taken from county and school records and my own observation.

"Montana Power's own projection for the Colstrip school is 1,100 students for the 1974-75 school year. This is about six times the average prior to coal development.

"The heavy impact has occurred in the past two years, since beginning construction of the generating facilities.

"Last year it was even necessary to hold classes in the shower rooms. Such important classes as physics and foreign languages had to be dropped long after school started to shift the teacher to other subjects. It became necessary to split classes because of an ever increasing enrollment.

"The irony of all this is that the ranchers of the Colstrip district have not only seen their school, one of the best in Montana, rapidly deteriorate but have seen their tax burden expand with alarming rapidity.

"The actual increase amounts to over 42 percent in just two years.

"The promises of Montana Power's officials concerning the taxable valuation is becoming ever harder to believe when compared with the tax records of Rosebud County.

"Last year the increased valuation of cattle in Rosebud County actually exceeded the increased taxable valuation of all the coal development in the Colstrip area.

"The taxable valuation in Rosebud County increased from $20,-181,496 in 1973 to $26,650,000 for 1974.

"Of this taxable valuation increase of $6.46 million, the Colstrip

[Continued from page 149]

have strained the resources of the county already. "The Rosebud group has forced the company into doing some things better," says Mitchell, "and made them look bad when they didn't. The local chamber of commerce backed the first two plants on a wait-and-see basis; they oppose Colstrip Three and Four."

The Hawk, the Expert, and the Politician

In the fall of 1974, the Montana Department of Natural Resources completed their environmental impact study of Colstrip Three and Four. They then held 19 meetings throughout the state, to tell the public what they had found. NPRC advertised these meetings, and got people to go to them and raise questions about the power plants and transmission lines.

On January 27, 1975, the department issued its final impact statement, and recommended denial of permission to construct Colstrip Three and Four. They arranged for a lawyer to present the state's case against the power plants before the Board of Natural Resources, the seven-member body that will make the decision on siting plants.

"The hearing before the board is quasi-legal," says Bill Mitchell. "There will be factual evidence presented from both sides, and a final determination will be made. We hired a local attorney; it will cost us some money."

The NPRC lost a hearing before the Board in 1974, largely, Mitchell feels, because they tried to do it on their own, without legal counsel. "The Board has seven members," he says. "We talk to them — some support us, and some don't. Our lawyer is good; we searched a long time for him. He's a local man, about 55 years old, who was head of the constitutional convention when they revised the state constitution. He works together with the lawyer for the state Department of Natural Resources, and with the lawyer for the Northern Cheyennes. They make a good team: The Cheyennes' lawyer looks like a hawk, and will go for their throats every time; the state lawyer is very heavy in expertise, and light in political savvy; and ours is very cagey, and savvy in political matters."

Defending the Rural Minority

The Northern Plains Resource Council considers the Colstrip Three and Four case to be a skirmish in what will be a very long, grinding conflict. By keeping close to the needs of the farmers and ranchers of their constituency, the NPRC hopes to generate the staying power needed for the long haul. In addition to their $10 annual memberships, they're creating a "200 Club," in which they hope to get 200 people to pledge $200 per year. The 200 Club now has 60 members.

Among the other activities of NPRC are the maintenance of lobbyists in Washington, D.C., and Helena, Montana, and participation in the formation of the Yellowstone Basin Water Use Association, which is striving to get protection of water resources from industrial exploitation. They have worked with landowners in Wyoming and North Dakota, leading to the formation of the Powder River Basin Resource Council in northeastern Wyoming, and the United Plainsmen of North Dakota. In short, the NPRC is working to create a regional coalition of local farmers' and ranchers' groups, to cope with a regional threat to their way of life.

"You get a lot farther and go a lot longer if you are working with, and representing, local people who are directly affected by the issue you're dealing with," says Bill Mitchell. "Some people think of ranchers as fat cats. We're all so concerned with the problems of minorities. Well, rural people are a minority, and they're being ignored. If we're concerned about the food base and survival, we're going to have to pay some attention to them."

"WHEN YOU SHOW ME THAT COAL IS AS BIO-DEGRADABLE AS A STEAK, I'LL LET YOU DIG."

development contributed only $1.68 million or 26 percent.

"These figures are incredible when one considers that these developments are the largest industrial investments in Montana, two plants under construction and one to be producing in 1975. The investment in these plants is supposed to exceed $180 million yet they have added only $1.68 million to Rosebud County's tax base this year.

"The impact they have caused is devastating to schools, roads, law enforcement and recreational facilities in our county.

"For example, Montana 315 between Colstrip and Interstate 94 carried an average load of 50 vehicles a day before coal development. Last fall it was carrying 1,050 and the Montana Highway Department projected 2,500 a day by this summer.

"We have a four-fold increase in the law enforcement budget in two years. Our area sanitarian has warned of serious health hazards because of the proliferation of trailer courts and inadequate sewage facilities.

"Under the present laws small rural communities, such as Colstrip (was), are going to be destroyed by the impact of coal development.

"Present laws make it possible for coal development companies to shift the tax burdens of their impact onto the farmers and ranchers.

"Not only are these older residents forced to accept a deterioration of roads, schools, law enforcement, recreational facilities, environment and life style, they are subjected to unbearable tax loads to provide social services for the employees of the coal developers.

"This is exactly what happened in the Colstrip area. If the hard lessons to be learned there are not heeded, every small rural community where this type of development occurs will suffer the same fate."

AP wire photo

Damming Up Canada

The North Cascades Mountains offer some of the best scenic and recreational country left on this continent. Glacial action there has created hanging valleys or cirques, ringed by steep-walled mountains. Wide, flat, u-shaped valleys scored by slow ice flow lead to slot canyons containing swift rapids. Coniferous forests shelter a variety of wildlife, and meandering rivers in broad glaciated valleys ripple over gravel beds ideal for spawning trout.

The area straddles the Canada-United States border, and is readily accessible from both Vancouver, British Columbia, and Seattle, Washington.

Also straddling this border is Ross Lake, backed up behind Ross Dam in Washington State. A peculiar, waffle-surfaced structure, Ross Dam is built to be raised by increments, along with the increasing electrical appetite of its owner — Seattle City Light, the public utility which supplies power to the city of Seattle. The initial Ross Dam, construction of which began in 1937, flooded much of the beautiful Skagit River valley in the United States. In 1949, Ross Dam was raised, sending the waters of Ross Lake onto 500 acres owned by Seattle City Light in Canada.

In 1968, Seattle City Light began pushing ahead with plans to raise the dam another 122½ feet — a project called the High Ross Dam plan. That would back the lake up onto 6,300 acres of public land in Canada's Skagit River valley, a flat glacial valley that is one of the very few wide, level recreation wildlands within easy distance of Vancouver, B.C. It would also flood the Big Beaver Creek valley in Washington, another u-shaped glacial valley noted for its large beaver ponds and majestic stands of cedar trees.

Canadian conservation and outdoor groups saw this as a form of liquid imperialism, and organized a coalition called Run Out Skagit Spoilers (ROSS), whose name leaves no doubt as to intention. South of the border, the North Cascades Conservation Council (N3C) of Seattle also is battling against the High Ross Dam project. ROSS and N3C cooperate with each other amiably and vigorously; but they are two very different groups in different situations, as the following discussions of strategy with their respective leaders makes clear.

Part 1:
Farquharson: Getting Them Committed

In 1969, the environmental movement was not very strong in British Columbia. B.C. Hydro, the province's public utility, had dammed virtually every level-bottomed valley near Vancouver except the Skagit. At the same time the population of southern British Columbia was growing, and with it the need for recreation areas.

Ken Farquharson of Vancouver, now president of Run Out Skagit Spoilers (ROSS), was then part of a new Sierra Club group. They were looking for a good issue to fight, one which would help change the political/environmental climate of British Columbia. Provincial fish and wildlife officials told them that the High Ross Dam project was being pushed forward by Seattle City Light.

"We didn't have environmental legislation in Canada," says Farquharson, "like the U.S. has NEPA and the Clean Air Act. In 1969, we had a development-oriented provincial government. We knew that in the Skagit case we had a strong chance of getting the province to press for a good environmental study of the area, because it was Seattle City Light involved. We knew we could use that precedent for other situations in British Columbia. We wanted to establish the principle of requiring detailed environmental studies before hydroelectric development. We also wanted recognition of recreation values."

Since Canada was getting the water without the juice, so to speak, it was a clear-cut ripoff. There *had* been a financial compensation agreement drawn up: in 1967, Seattle City Light

On the opposite page: A small Canadian looks at part of the Upper Skagit Valley in British Columbia destined to be flooded by the raising of Ross Dam in Washington State, a few miles to the south. Meanwhile, in the city of Seattle . . .

"Consumption of power is going up. People seem to desire to raise their standard of living, and the use of electricity seems to be closely related to the standard of living." — *Statement by ("Electric") John Nelson* (above), *superintendent of Seattle City Light.*

Comment on the above by North Cascades Conservation Council, in The Wild Cascades: "AGAHHHHH!!!"

Canadian conservation and outdoor groups saw the High Ross Dam project as a form of liquid imperialism. Since Canada was getting the water without the juice, so to speak, it was a clear-cut ripoff.

agreed to pay the province of British Columbia $34,566 per year for the right to flood 6,300 acres in B.C. That comes out to a rental of $5.50 per acre every year! Seattle City Light's well financed Canadian public relations effort, done by the Vancouver firm of F.F. Slaney & Co., Ltd., focused on the value of a new aquatic recreation area; that was pretty hard to sell to a city surrounded by Georgia Strait, three major natural lakes, and four large reservoirs. In short, it was likely that most Canadians, once they heard of the Skagit case, would agree with Ken Farquharson: "In Vancouver, our domestic power costs twice as much as Seattle residents pay. Why should Canadians subsidize Seattle?"

Eight Canadian conservation and outdoor sports clubs banded together on December 9, 1969 to form ROSS. John Massey, an avid fly fisherman who didn't want to lose one of the very few places near Vancouver he could practice his art, was the first president; and David M. Brousson, an opposition party member of the B.C. Legislative Assembly, was an early supporter.

"We took steps to get our story into the media," says Ken, "and to introduce the issue into the province legislature. The press and television response was very good; we've had consistent coverage, and stories on national television four times. The first reaction of the B. C. government was that it was a bad deal, but a deal is a deal.

"Next, we decided to appeal directly to Seattle City Light, through the Seattle City Council. [The nine-member Seattle City Council directs actions of Seattle City Light.] We wrote up a two-page petition, explaining what would be lost if the Skagit were flooded, and what would be gained, if anything. The petitions were distributed through the groups which made up ROSS. We took the petitions, with 100,000 signatures of Canadians opposed to the High Ross Dam, to Seattle in the spring of 1970. We got an audience with the city council, and explained our case. They said, 'We've got an agreement allowing us to build the dam, and we're going to ride her through.' "

Escalating Political Action

When in Seattle, Ken Farquharson and other Canadian ROSS members got the impression that Seattle City Light considered them a tiny band roused into action by U.S. conservationists. "We decided we had to escalate political action in Canada,"

Ken says, "to force Seattle City Light to see they weren't dealing with a small group."

At the federal level, ROSS enlisted the aid of an opposition Member of Parliament (MP), John Fraser. Fraser did a legal brief which concluded that there were irregularities in the Seattle City Light-British Columbia agreement allowing flooding of the Skagit Valley, and that the agreement was therefore invalid. (The agreement involves the International Joint Commission [IJC], a U.S.-Canada body empowered to judge boundary water questions, which, possibly improperly, delegated its decision-making power over compensation for flooding the Skagit to the provincial government.) "The federal government was not ready to cancel the agreement," says Ken. "They tried informally to persuade the Seattle City Council to cancel it. It didn't work."

At the provincial level, ROSS concentrated on getting as many politicians as possible on record against the High Ross Dam. In October 1970, they also made a dramatic move to increase public awareness of the issue. "Most people had never seen the Skagit Valley," notes Ken. "We got together ten buses, and a great number of private cars, and drove there. It's about a three-hour drive from Vancouver. We had guides, river trips, and speeches. Four thousand people were there."

In 1971, the International Joint Commission held hearings which were limited to considering what the effects of High Ross Dam would be in Canada. ROSS members testified at those hearings, and presented an environmental impact study of the Skagit

NEWS ITEM: PROV. GOVT. WOULD GET $5.50 AN ACRE FOR FLOODED SKAGIT VALLEY.

". . . and in this dream Premier Bennett was multiplying $5.50 by the total acreage of B.C. . . ."

YANKEE AGGRESSOR, GO HOME!

"We spoke earlier of the civilized restraint shown by Canadian witnesses who made the long trip down from British Columbia [to Seattle] to testify at the [Seattle] City Council's hearings last spring. That restraint seems to have given way to a cold fury as City Light stubbornly goes ahead with its plans to flood out the Upper Skagit. The resentment of the Canadians has been intensified by City Light's beginning the contract logging of a square mile of land in the Upper Skagit Valley which the utility bought back in 1929. Our northern neighbors rightfully regard this premature action as the boldest type of American imperialism." —

The Wild Cascades, *October-November 1970*

Canadian resentment described in the paragraph above was apparently directed at their own government as well, which agreed to the City Light deal in the first place and, for a time anyway, seemed reluctant to rock the boat — or rather, the ark. The cartoon to the left is from the British Columbia *Vancouver Sun.*

157

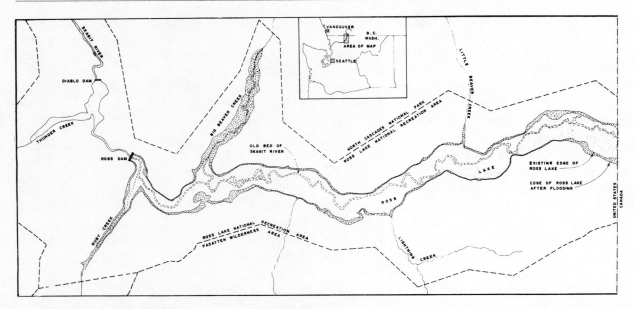

BITING THE HAND THAT FEEDS

Seattle City Hall reporter Mike Conant has expressed with grim eloquence the frustration of many Northwesterners who view Seattle City Light's dogged pursuit of the High Ross Dam project as public servant run amok — at taxpayers' expense. Maybe the feeling isn't limited by geography. The following comes from the February 9, 1970 edition of the Seattle Post-Intelligencer.

"Your City Light," answers the soothing voice on the telephone when a taxpayer dials the city's lighting department.

It is an unusual answer. How strange it would seem, for example, if other switchboard operators answered, "Your City Hall," or "Your Engineering Department," or "Your Corporation Counsel."

"Your City Light," is a friendly, calculated invitation to the taxpayer to identify himself with the utility, to make him feel City Light is actually HIS.

For many years the invitation was accepted gratefully, and City Light's popularity became a source of amazement to other departments struggling in vain to please the taxpayer.

Yet in the past two years City Light has become more a phenom-

Valley done by graduate students at the University of British Columbia. The IJC issued an unexpectedly critical report in December of that year, saying that the Skagit Valley was "an uncommon and non-restorable area and has important social values." In addition to the social values lost, the report estimated that the flooding would cause a $1 million loss in use value of the Skagit Valley.

All this added up to something short of victory for ROSS. "By November 1971," according to Farquharson, "things were dangerously static. All the lobbying possible had been done, Bennett (Premier of British Columbia) wouldn't change his stance (in favor of the dam), the Federal government was sympathetic but appeared to be hung up over the bureaucrats' worries over the status of the IJC. We were all glum as we moved into 1972 without any action. Then elections for both provincial and federal governments were called. This presented a chance for change."

Got to Come Through

On August 30, 1972, the New Democratic Party took power by a landslide in British Columbia. "We had firm statements from their leaders, opposing High Ross Dam," says Farquharson. "So we went to see them, especially Bob Williams, Minister for Lands, Forests, and Water Resources. We'd given them our support based on their statements about the dam. Now we said, 'right, you've got to come through.' "

On November 17 Williams came through, saying that the plan to flood the Skagit Valley was "totally unacceptable to the province of B.C. This land is too valuable to be used as a pawn in a power project of another country." The province government

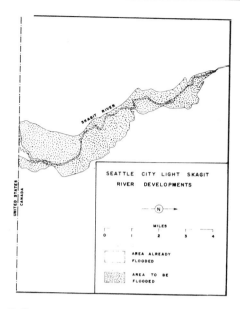

followed up by setting aside 81,000 acres, part of which is the land Seattle City Light wants to flood, as the Skagit Valley Recreation Area. And the province filed an official request with the International Joint Commission to annul the flooding agreement because the procedures used in making that agreement were irregular.

In July 1974 there was a canoe-in at Skagit Valley, to dedicate the new Provincial Recreation Area. "It was then that we knew for certain that the province supported us," says Farquharson. "Three provincial ministers were there. They committed themselves to preserving the area, and sealed the fate of Seattle City Light's program. Our method all the way through has been to get politicians to adopt a position and keep them in that position."

First Green Ban

Seattle City Light prides itself on never having lost a battle, and is not at all ready to concede this one. At this writing it is appearing before a U.S. Federal Power Commission (FPC) judge for approval of the High Ross Dam with plan modifications required by the soaring construction costs since the first dam was raised. The judge's decision is expected in October, 1975.

"We got the FPC to allow ROSS to appear at the hearings," says Ken. "This, of course, is very rare, since we're Canadian. Our operation was low cost until the FPC hearings, which are technical and require large legal fees. We asked the Canadian federal government and the B.C. government to help us financially, but they were reluctant. One month before the hearings I got a call from Ottawa — our national capital — asking us to get in there. I said we wouldn't go unless they paid. Eventually we got

enon of the 60s and 70s, namely, the bigger the governmental unit, the more it frustrates the people.

A letter a few days ago to the *Post-Intelligencer* pointed up the frustration. The writer complained of a City Light advertisement about an environmental problem.

Not only was the advertisement misleading, the writer said, but City Light has used his tax money to circulate it.

Probably never in the country's peace-time history have government and bureaucrats enjoyed a freer hand than during the past 25 years of inflationary economy.

Taxpayers, earning more money than ever before, decided government could take a sizeable paycheck chunk as long as they kept their split-level homes and two-car garages.

Agencies like City Light took advantage of the condition by constructing a fortress of protection with taxpayer dollars.

Today, any citizen or group of citizens who mounts an offensive against the agency's policies are confronted with a formidable obstacle: their own money.

In 1968, for example, City Light spent nearly $1.5 million on "sales promotion." Most went for such "good will" ventures as subsidizing customers, installing air conditioners and switching from flame ranges to electricity.

At a time when the City Council subsidizes the Transit System as much as $300,000 monthly, few would question City Light subsidies to rate-payers. Nevertheless, the danger of the dole is the sell-out of objectivity.

The "sales promotion" budget includes $263,000 for advertising, over which the public has no control. Here is where City Light sells itself and its policies, right or wrong.

In 1968 the agency also budgeted $144,000 on "public relations." This means nine P.R. employees and office expenses.

The public relations staff publishes a monthly magazine called

Seattle City Light NEWS, and a weekly "Newsletter."

Each week 2,500 Newsletters are distributed to City Light employees, City Hall officials and the news media.

In the Newsletter, City Light's public relations staff often goes on the offensive against those opposing the utility publically, or, in a recent case, a taxpayer's letter to the agency merely seeking information.

The newsletter is an advantage that the individual taxpayer does not have to express his frustrations and resentments.

Little known by the public is that City Light also owns and operates an eight-bed home in Newhalem on the Skagit River which features color television, plush rugs, and woodsy privacy.

Here City Light executives give the free red carpet to those worth influencing. The home also is always available for use by mayors and city councilmen and their families, although many shun the obvious temptation.

"If we get the FPC permit, we will build the dam. I don't know what the Canadians can do to stop us."

both federal and provincial money for ROSS to appear before the FPC. Because of protocol they didn't want to appear themselves, so they financed a citizen group."

If the solid bloc of Canadian opposition perturbs Seattle City Light, they aren't letting on. Gordon Vickery, Superintendent of Seattle City Light, was quoted by the December 5, 1973 Everett (Washington) *Herald* as saying: "If we get the FPC permit, we will build the dam. I don't know what the Canadians can do to stop us. If the dam goes up and the water will back into Canadian land, (B.C. Premier) Bennett will be unhappy, but I don't know what he can do to stop the water."

We asked Ken Farquharson what he thought of Vickery's statement. We expected some outrage at what seemed chauvinistic arrogance to us. What we got was a cool, clipped, and quite firmly determined summary of the current situation. "Even if the FPC judge approves the High Ross Dam, the appeal process — to the Federal Power Commission itself, then the U.S. Supreme Court if necessary — will take at least five years. The formal B.C. provincial request to the IJC to annul the flooding agreement because of improper procedure is still pending. And we have found that some of Seattle City Light's actions tend to invalidate the agreement: for example, at one point they raised the dam *without* B.C. agreement, and in two cases violated the provision that only Canadian workers would be hired by bringing U.S. workers into Canada.

"To finish it, the International Woodworkers of America, with the agreement of the B.C. Federation of Labor, have refused to clear the timber for the reservoir if the dam is approved. Under the terms of the B.C.-Seattle City Light agreement, the land can't be flooded without clearing it first, and it must be Canadians doing the clearing. This is the first green ban in Canada."*

Run Out Skagit Spoilers probably will achieve their unequivocal objective. In the process, they've greatly broadened the environmental movement in British Columbia, a fact which will influence purely Canadian conservation battles in years to come.

Editor's Note: A "green ban" is a refusal by a labor union to do work the union considers environmentally destructive. In New South Wales, Australia, green bans have become a potent force for preserving urban open space. The Skagit green ban is the first we've heard of in North America. May there be more!

Part 2:
Goldsworthy: Making a Fuss

While Run Out Skagit Spoilers has been stirring up Canadian opposition to the High Ross Dam, the U.S. effort to stop the dam has been led by the North Cascades Conservation Council (N3C). The N3C is a nonprofit organization with a membership of about 2,000. It was formed in 1957 to protect the natural beauty of the North Cascades Mountains, and to push for creation of a North Cascades National Park.

In October 1968 the North Cascades National Park was declared. Four members of the N3C took a backpack trip into the land they had worked so long and hard to preserve. They decided to walk out through Big Beaver Valley, which adjoins the National Park and was designated a National Recreation Area at the same time the Park was created.

Pat Goldsworthy, now president of N3C, was one of those hikers. He had never seen Big Beaver Valley before, and what he saw was beautiful beyond his expectations. A stream meandered through the broad, flat valley, with large ponds backed up behind

What Pat Goldsworthy saw: the Big Beaver Valley, looking upstream. What you see is the area to be flooded by the High Ross Dam.

Bob and Ira Spring photo

SAGA OF THE KEROSENE (KAOPECTATE) KID

The Wild Cascades ($5/year, edited by Harvey H. Manning, Route 4, Box 6652, Issaquah, Washington 98027) is the liveliest membership organ we've seen for a while. It keeps North Cascades Conservation Council members posted on what's happening in the North Cascades, using nice photos and line drawings to illustrate acid commentary.

For really *deadly work against despoilers, they call in the Kerosene Kid; who, owing to the petroleum crisis, has switched liquids to the equally formidable Kaopectate. Here's a little sample of the K.K.'s fierce but flawlessly factual work:*

"We warned the people of Seattle more than two years ago that High Ross Dam would turn out to be a monstrous bottomless pit down which the taxpayers would find themselves pouring fantastic amounts of money. The City Council, beguiled by the roseate promises of Electric John and his P-R boys, disagreed with us and authorized City Light to spend whatever sums were necessary to perfect its application to the F.P.C. Man, talk about a blank check! No one on the City Council appeared very concerned over what amounts were being spent or who was getting the dough, so the North Cascades Conservation Council took upon itself the task of trying to find out. It's not easy to find out anything that goes on over at 1015 Third Avenue. In fact, the real reason that all previous City Councils have permitted the utility to govern itself is that its affairs are so complex and tangled that no Councilman could figure out how to untie that Gordian Knot.

"By far the most intriguing payments, as well as the largest, were those made to F.F. Slaney & Co., Ltd., a Canadian firm of forestry and recreation consultants. Way back in the Oct.-Nov., 1970, *Wild Cascades* we had very naively stated that City Light had paid Slaney &

beaver dams. The sides of the valley rose to steep peaks, some skirted with glaciers. Hanging valleys spilled cascades into the main glacial trough. A variety of flora and fauna could be seen; most notably, stands of rather rare western red cedar trees were growing in the vale. Only a trail marked the impact of man.

Continuing down the gradually sloping valley to Ross Lake, the four noticed unusual activity around Ross Dam, and soon learned that Seattle City Light was proceeding with plans to raise the dam and flood Big Beaver Valley. Pat Goldsworthy recalls the impact of this experience on the four men: "Before we went there, it was just a valley on a map. You put things on the back burner if you don't know much about them. We saw it with our own two eyes, and that was it. We decided, then, that we just could not let this be flooded."

The Facts

The N3C is an experienced conservation organization, and numbers engineers, botanists, and other technically qualified people among its active members (Goldsworthy is a professor of biochemistry at the University of Washington). "We felt that you can't fight something technical like this on emotion," says Pat Goldsworthy. "Emotion is part of it, and concern for aesthetics and wildlife; but you've got to fight on facts, and find out what your opponents know."

Most of the facts N3C needed were in the files of Seattle City Light, which legally are open to the public, since City Light is a publicly-owned utility. "The people there are obtuse, not co-operative," according to Pat. "Often they'd give the end result of a process of analysis — conclusion — without letting us know what went into making that conclusion."

The N3C researchers persisted, and gradually fleshed out the story of what was going on. "Some of our members spent weeks going through their financial records to find out how much money they'd spent in the U.S. and Canada on the High Ross Dam project, and what they'd spent it for," recalls Pat. "We found out who they were associated with, who their contractors were; otherwise, you don't know who you're dealing with.

"Also, we were looking at cost. What is the cost of this dam in dollars as well as ecologically? A lot of things go into cost. Two N3C members, Joe and Margaret Miller, did an ecological study of Big Beaver Valley for the Park Service; this helped us get a basis for judging ecological cost."

Unlike the Canadians, the U.S. group had to deal with the issue of electrical power, and the N3C faced it squarely. "We asked, 'How much power would raising the dam produce?'" Goldsworthy notes. "Seattle City Light was saying, 'We need more power.' But using their own projections, High Ross Dam would take care of future needs for only three more years, at which time they'd have to find another source of power.

"We also asked, 'Could that same amount of power come from an alternative source?' We found out that Seattle could buy power from the Bonneville Power Administration, and that alternative power sources could be developed. Eventually we suggested some alternative power sources. For example, more generators might be put into existing dams. And in Europe, they use a technique called pump storage: during the peak periods of power use, they let water run down through the generators; then during off periods they pump water back up for re-use.

"We've also researched the possibility of energy conservation. This is not the hardship that it seems. A lot of our power problem centers around providing electricity during peak power periods, when everybody turns his appliance on at once. We could spread energy use throughout the day and night, so there would be no peak power period."

The Hearings

Armed with facts, the N3C set out to generate public support and get some public hearings on the issue. Through their lively, well-illustrated bimonthly publication, *The Wild Cascades,* the group kept their members informed. They got mailing lists from supporting groups, and sent out flyers by bulk postage. They urged individuals to make statements at hearings, and organizations to make resolutions. They had a San Francisco advertising agency prepare a large newspaper advertisement for them, containing coupons to mail to public officials and a coupon for membership and/or donations. Always they were specific about what should be said or written to whom, and when.

The public concern influenced the Seattle City Council to hold nine hearings on the High Ross Dam, each on a different aspect: economic, ecological, wildlife, transmission, and so on. "We would have large turnouts at the hearings," Goldsworthy says. "Sometimes a hundred of our supporters would come. We always had more than did the proponents of the dam. Seattle City Light would appear with some chamber of commerce members, and representatives of other utilities — they're all brothers under the skin. The Seattle City Council let us put on a panel of experts as a bloc. We had four or five experts on our panel; each would speak on a separate topic."

The city council ultimately voted 5 to 4 in favor of the High Ross Dam, and *directed* Seattle City Light to go before the Federal Power Commission to get an amended license (required because a new construction method was to be used on the dam). "Since then," notes Pat, "the balance of power in the city council has changed. Now it's 5 to 4 in our favor. But parliamentary

Co. $15,000 for whipping up a little P.R. effort on the Canadian Skagit. Boy, Were We Dumb! Our auditor found invoices from Slaney totaling $665,268 from May, 1970 through February, 1972. Oh, Slaney & Co. is a talented firm. There just isn't any kind of a study they can't undertake as long as the money's there. For instance, they've been doing fisheries studies in the Canadian Skagit, wildlife studies, soil studies, plant life studies, recreation studies et cetera et cetera. And just to make sure that all these scientific studies are thoroughly unbiased and just as disinterested and objective as possible, they've also been paid $59,981 for public relations programs in Canada! This once again emphasizes what we've been saying all along about City Light's so-called objective studies on High Ross. There's such an incestuous relationship between "scientific" investigation and public relations at City Light that you can't tell who's doing what to whom and for how much."

"Shall we use this area of unique ecological interest for a reservoir, a power station, an overspill, or an airport?"

procedure has allowed proponents of the dam to prevent another vote from being taken. The mayor can't vote on the issue at all; he simply gets an ordinance from the council, and must act."

The N3C, ROSS and other opponents of High Ross Dam had better luck in hearings before the Washington State Department of Ecology. On December 6, 1971, John A. Biggs, director of the Department of Ecology, informed the FPC that the State of Washington was officially opposed to raising the Ross Dam, because of the environmental damage it would do *and* because Seattle City Light "has no planned environmental program but, instead, continues to pursue a program of opportunely selecting and proposing for development new sources of power, with the pursuit of energy being the first objective and environmental concern being decidedly a second one."

Now the N3C is involved in the FPC hearings. Unlike ROSS, they've had to foot the bill for legal and other expenses themselves, and it is a financial burden they never had to face before. "We have had to find people who can qualify, officially, as experts," says Goldsworthy. "Some donated their services; others we had to pay. Our two lawyers get minimal fees; but the hearings are in Washington, D.C., and they have to travel back and forth. The Sierra Club has given some money. When you get into a legal battle, you have to raise lots of money. Seattle City Light, of course, is really paying big money."

The Fuss

"The spin-offs of all these public hearings are very important," remarks Goldsworthy. "The press and TV are there, the story gets kicked around. Pretty soon everybody knew there was a battle going on. The more it gets in newspapers, the better. The worst thing that could happen would be if it never got in the newspapers, and only conservation experts and your opponents knew about it. You would never get the public support. We got people coming out of the woodwork who agreed with us.

"You get chances to give talks, slide shows, and make exhibits. The Millers have a nice three-panel display on the area and the issue. Many times we had a debate situation, where we'd appear along with Seattle City Light. Our story is much more appealing than theirs, because there's more to it than an uninformed layman can understand. City Light's story has a lot of figures on BTUs and kilowatts, which are very dry."

Goldsworthy is not sure exactly how the High Ross Dam controversy will end, but notes that Seattle City Light's plan is now opposed by a wide range of people and governmental institutions in two countries. "If the FPC disapproves the project, it can't be built," he notes. "If they approve it, the Seattle City Council, which now opposes the dam by a narrow margin, will have to appropriate money to build it. A future city council resolution to the effect that the council doesn't want the dam even if the FPC approves it is possible. And the firm Canadian opposition to the project may stop it."

Pat Goldsworthy's formula for grassroots environmental success is: "Just keep making a big fuss." The N3C, following up its efforts to have the North Cascades National Park created, has been raising a long, complicated, expensive fuss indeed. Pat says they're just protecting the fruits of past labors, defending an exquisite valley which adjoins the Park. In the process, they have begun to deal strongly with issues of energy and environment which are crucial not only to the conservation movement, but to our whole future as a society.

Skagit Valley Forever

Words and Music by Malvina Reynolds

There's a fine green valley not far from Vancouver,
The home of the black bear, the marten and the cougar,
It's the tree-rich valley where the Skagit River flows,
A home for God's creatures since Heaven only knows.

Skagit Valley, Skagit Valley,
Ray Williston is selling you away,
Skagit Valley, Skagit Valley,
They would turn you to a mud pond,
To run the Coca Cola coolers in Seattle, U.S.A.

Well, the parks are getting fewer, and the trees are getting thin,
And the cities are spreading out to take the wildwood in,
And the world is getting poorer with every mile they clear,
And they'd sell our Skagit acres for five dollars fifty cents a year.

(Repeat chorus)

Oh my sisters and brothers in this shining Northern land,
It's time to get together, to take each other's hand,
And ring around our wilderness to keep the gangs away
Who would ravage our sweet country for a shameful pocketful of pay.

Skagit Valley, Skagit Valley,
No grabber will have you for a prize.
Skagit Valley, Skagit Valley,
We'll let no vandal drown you,
We'll keep you as we found you,
B.C.'s forest paradise.

John Running photograph

The Mountain That Teaches the People

Just north of Flagstaff, Arizona, is a complex of volcanic cones which white men call the San Francisco Peaks. The Peaks rise abruptly from a high plateau, and are connected to one another with flowing arcs of ridges. One of them is Mt. Humphreys, at 12,670 feet the highest mountain in Arizona.

Since 1969, Summit Properties, a company headed by Flagstaff businessman Bruce Leadbetter, has been seeking county permission to construct a condominium "ski village" on 327 acres, some 8,500 feet up the western slope of the peaks, in an area called Hart Prairie. Summit hoped to use the ski village to rescue its financially troubled Snow Bowl ski area, already in operation on the Peaks. In addition to condominiums, the village was to feature town houses, a shopping area, golf courses, a new ski lift, and a snow-making machine to bolster mother nature's paltry allocation of snow to the Peaks.

Leadbetter's initial applications for county zoning changes and use permits were successful, largely because they were done quietly. Then Richard Wilson, a landowner with property adjoin-

In addition to condominiums, the village was to feature town houses, a shopping area, golf courses, a new ski lift, and a snow-making machine to bolster mother nature's paltry allocation of snow to the Peaks.

ing the proposed development, got wind of what was happening. That was the beginning of an allied effort of Hopis, Navajos and environmentalists to stop Leadbetter from building a ski village on San Francisco Peaks.

Wilson, a professor at the University of Arizona in Tucson, has a summer home on the slope of the Peaks. "Many people in Flagstaff have been opposed to any development on San Francisco Peaks for a long time," he says. "The original zoning granted to Summit was done without adjacent property owners being notified. It was done during the winter. I found out about it the next summer, in 1971. Then Summit came in and proposed a new setup for their development, which meant there would be another county hearing."

In Coconino County, applicants for zoning changes first appear before a planning and zoning commission, then before the three-member county board of supervisors for final decision. Summit needed unanimous approval of the supervisors for the change it wanted. Wilson and others testified against the development at the hearings, and distributed a preliminary environmental statement.

Hopi and Navajo Indians also appeared at the hearings. To them, the San Francisco Peaks are sacred. Hopis believe that spiritual beings called *kachinas* live in them, and fly forth to bring rain and prosperity to all people. Navajos consider the Peaks to mark the western boundary of the Navajo world, and to be a source of all plant and animal life in their world. Both tribes deeply revere the Peaks in ways this brief summary cannot even suggest. They are utterly opposed to any development there, regarding it as desecration of their shrine.

On January 3, 1972 two supervisors voted in favor of Summit's development. Supervisor Tio Tachias dissented, and since the decision was not unanimous the zoning change was not granted. Summit began preparing a new application, and the Indians and environmentalists began studying the law and the environment of San Francisco Peaks.

Did You Ever Sing to a Mountain?

By the next hearing date, Wilson and a small band of supporters — his wife Jean, John Duncklee, lawyer Douglas Wall, and Bill Breed — had put out some bumper stickers bearing the names

Navajos consider the Peaks to mark the western boundary of the Navajo world and to be a source of all plant and animal life in their world.

of the Peaks in Hopi, Navajo and English, and had begun an extensive environmental study of the Peaks. At the planning and zoning commission hearing, opponents of the development were allowed only one minute each to speak. The commission approved Summit's application, and the board of supervisors again voted 2 to 1 for Summit, with Tachias dissenting. This time, however, a majority vote was enough for approval. This gave Summit preliminary plan approval, which was contingent upon their arranging adequate water supply and sewage disposal.

Wilson and some Hopis and Navajos then sued to set aside the zoning actions due to various legal deficiencies. The Indians also claimed that zoning board actions in this case violated their First Amendment rights to freedom of religion. The Arizona Superior Court granted summary judgment in favor of all the plaintiffs, without deciding the religious freedom issue.

John Duncklee, a friend of Wilson's and a geography professor at Northern Arizona University in Flagstaff, found himself becoming more and more committed to saving the Peaks. "I got involved because I did my dissertation on the Peaks," says

Bumper stickers like these — in three languages — helped Arizona environmentalists convey the idea that San Francisco Peaks meant something more than another wilderness to be saved. Top sticker bears the Hopi name for the area, the middle one that of the Navajo people.

Duncklee. He spent about half a year on the Peaks, researching a detailed environmental study. "The mountain did a lot for me personally," he says. "Being up there put a lot of things in focus."

Among the findings of Duncklee's environmental study were that development would pose a serious fire hazard to the forests of the western slope of the Peaks, and that it was very unlikely that adequate ground water for the project could be found. (Summit ultimately spent $900,000 drilling for water through the volcanic rock, with little or no success.) These findings were included in a January 1974 U. S. Forest Service recommendation against Summit's development. The Forest Service, which manages most of the land on the Peaks, said it would have to do a full-scale environmental analysis if the development were approved by Coconino County.

Duncklee quit his teaching job, and in 1973 wrote a number of songs about San Francisco Peaks, the proposed development, and other environmental issues. His recorded song "San Francisco Mountain," sung by Rich Hunt (who also wrote the music for it), skyrocketed to the top of Flagstaff's charts in 1973.* "It did a lot to keep the issue alive in Flagstaff," Duncklee believes. "But it cost close to $5,000 to produce, not counting my time. Environmental records are just not top pop sellers. That's why I'm selling steel buildings right now!"

A Groundswell of Opposition

On January 29, 1974 Bruce Leadbetter took another crack at getting his development approved by the Coconino County Planning and Zoning Commission. Ray Berman, a professor of management and computer sciences at Northern Arizona University who was concerned about the religious freedom of the Hopis and Navajos, attended.

"The meeting was to have taken place at the courthouse," Berman recalls, "but was shifted at the last minute to the high school gymnasium. There were fifteen hundred or two thousand people there, many of whom were Indians. The Indians spoke of the religious significance of the Peaks, an issue the commission did not deal with. Summit's application for rezoning was denied on a technicality. We had won the hearing for the wrong reasons — not the Indian rights or the conservation issue. If it won on a technicality, it could have lost on a technicality." Out of that meeting emerged the Coconino Citizens Association (CCA), a group formed to oppose the Summit development and to seek long-term protection for the San Francisco Peaks.

Bruce Leadbetter, whose uncle owns the local newspaper, ran a couple of full-page ads promoting his development and de-

"We had won the hearing for the wrong reasons — not the Indian rights or the conservation issue. If it won on a technicality, it could have lost on a technicality."

nouncing Dick Wilson, Wilson's lawyer Doug Wall, and his other opponents. The confrontation was escalating.

On March 26, Summit made yet another bid for planning and zoning commission approval. "The Coconino Citizens Association split up the issue," says Berman. "Some of us talked about water, some about roads, some about fire hazard, and so on. I was concerned, then as now, with basic human rights of the Indians. Again the medicine men spoke, and again the rezoning was denied on a technical point.

"Summit appealed to the board of supervisors. The board hearing, on April 26, took all day. It was beginning to look like a ground swell of opposition to the project. Near midnight, the board made a Solomonic judgment: the famous moratorium."

That "famous moratorium" was a one-year freeze on all development above 8,000 feet on the Peaks, during which time the CCA was to attempt to make "substantial progress" in getting private land up there into public ownership.

Drunk with Joy

"We were drunk with joy," says Berman of the CCA. "We philosophized all summer. In August we applied for incorporation, and by September we were incorporated. On September 11, the board of directors and officers were elected. We spent most of our time then planning for a benefit rock concert, to raise funds."

Summit Properties, on the other hand, was quite sober. It filed a conspiracy suit against a large number of people, asking for damages. Among the alleged co-conspirators were Richard Wilson, Wilson's hydrologist, lawyer Doug Wall, the Navajo reservation school district (which allegedly provided buses to take people to hearings), the United States Forest Service, and Don Seaman, Supervisor of Coconino National Forest (which manages most of San Francisco Peaks land). Summit named a long list of "John Does" as co-conspirators.

Then, early in January 1975, Bruce Leadbetter dropped a bombshell: he told the Coconino County Board of Supervisors that he would be willing to trade his land on the Peaks for other forest service or Arizona state land on a "fair market value" basis to be determined by a disinterested third party.

"Early in February," says Berman, "the Forest Service was saying, 'We won't trade land unless you drop your conspiracy suit against the Forest Service.' Summit was replying, 'Well, you're just saying that.' It occurred to me that there was a place for a middleman between Bruce Leadbetter and the Forest Service."

So Ray Berman of the Coconino Citizens Association approached the two parties, offering his services as a negotiating agent. "I promised to be an honest broker," he says, "and to expose any party which might break a commitment. Eventually I was able to get a letter from the Forest Service, saying they would trade land if Summit's suit against them was dropped. I forwarded that letter to Leadbetter, listing his options as I saw them.

"In February, just before our benefit rock concert, Bruce Leadbetter consented to drop the Forest Service from his conspiracy suit. I got up and told the students during the concert. It was delirious."

"Then things started to go wrong," says Berman. "The U. S. Attorney in Phoenix refused to accept the dismissal of the Forest Service from Summit's suit. It took five weeks to get it dismissed.

"Then the Forest Service said Don Seaman, the forest supervisor, had to be dropped from the suit before they would negotiate a land swap. That had been implied, but not spelled out, in their letter to me. That showed Bruce what they were really like. Items began to appear in his uncle's paper here, the *Arizona Daily Sun,* that Summit would reopen its zoning application. The items implied that names would be given to more Does in his suit, which might include a good portion of all county officials.

"The next two weeks were pretty frantic. Probably the most effective thing we did was talk with Congressman Sam Steiger, asking him to unjam the silence the Forest Service and U. S. Attorney's offices were maintaining. The regional supervisor of the Forest Service came to see us, along with Don Seaman — probably because of Steiger's intervention. They indicated that if Leadbetter dropped Seaman from the suit, they would negotiate a land swap with him based on his Peaks property's value appraised at its highest use. I asked what the highest use of the property was. Seaman said, 'development.'

"Leadbetter thought the appraisal as development property was a breakthrough. He now sounds agreeable. He instructed his attorneys to dismiss the suit against Don Seaman, and to enter negotiations for the land swap.

"Now a meeting between officials and Leadbetter has been arranged. There will be batteries of attorneys. It's very complex: there are four ways that the Forest Service might have acquired land to be traded, and each way calls for a different law. Both groups asked myself and Ben Huffert, an attorney for us and the Indians, to be there, to keep everybody honest.

"Credibility is all we've really got. Because we are sincere, and honest, we got this action."

"The next thing to do is to get everybody else who owns land there off the mountain."

A Danger to Itself

"The real issue is not the Summit development," Ray Berman believes. "The real issue is the development of the western slope of the San Francisco Peaks. If one area is developed, the rest of the privately-held area will follow.

"The next thing to do is to get everybody else who owns land there off the mountain. The major landowner up there is Dick Wilson. He is a gentleman in every sense of the word, and will trade his land after Leadbetter gets out."

Berman notes that Joyce Griffen of the CCA has been exploring various means of getting San Francisco Peaks permanently protected from development. "This will take a long time, and we need to act fast to protect it now," he says. "I'm not totally at peace with putting it in Forest Service hands, but it's the best we can do now. Times change, economics change, and we can't count on indefinite protection from the Forest Service. San Francisco Peaks is so indescribably beautiful. It's like a beautiful girl — it's a danger to itself."

Ray Berman believes the CCA will be involved in the effort to preserve San Francisco Peaks long after the Summit case is settled. "If we keep our momentum, and keep getting funds, we'll succeed," he believes. "A hundred members at $2 a year isn't going to support us. We have a grant from Defenders of Wildlife, and had that rock concert benefit, and these are needed. We're going to work on our public image as soon as we have time."

Many of the people who have been involved with San Francisco Peaks believe the issue has taught the people of Flagstaff to respect their natural heritage and the Hopi and Navajo cultures. "The issue has caused Flagstaff to mature," says John Duncklee. "Before, Indians were treated scornfully there; now, there's a new respect."

"There have been new zoning regulations developed as a result of this issue," says Berman. "Coconino County is getting to be known as a place that's tough on developers. We're just trying to get them to let it be."

Perspectives on the Sacredness of a Mountain

The struggle over whether to allow the building of a condominium resort on San Francisco Peaks is different from other developer-versus-conservationist battles because the Peaks themselves play a central role in the conflict. Both the Hopis and Navajos of the Southwest hold the Peaks sacred. They regard themselves not precisely as protectors of the Peaks, but rather as the voices of the Peaks in the councils of the white man. In those voices — sometimes bitter, sometimes humorous, prophetic, or matter-of-fact — is the realization that, for reasons not clear, "Anglo" culture appears bent upon destroying nature and, thus, itself.

To Hopi and Navajo, it is obvious that they as people are one and the same with the Peaks. "You are killing me," they say to those who kill the land. Very few white men can even comprehend this organic sense of oneness with nature, let alone experience it.

The white men who do listen to the words of the Hopis and Navajos, and who encounter the Peaks themselves, are often deeply affected. Sometimes the light shines deep into their souls, and their lives are changed. Sometimes the desire to destroy, or to exploit, is firmed.

The Peaks, like anything truly sacred, defy classification. The Hopis and Navajos see them as much more than a "threatened environment," or "fragile ecosystem." To them, the mountains hold sacred powers which lie at the roots of their beliefs and values, and from which they derive a sense of well-being. Hear them:

Hopi Testimony Before the Coconino County Planning and Zoning Commission, January 29, 1974.

MR. HAROLD ALBERT: Mr. Forest Kaye, who is approximately seventy-five years old, asked me to read this letter for him.

"My name is Forest Kaye, I am a member of the Kachina clan. It is our belief that the Kachina clan originated from the San Francisco Peaks area.

"It has been told by my elders that the deity of Kachinas resides in the San Francisco Peaks area. Since time immemorial, shrines have been erected among and around these peaks, these shrines are used for offerings of prayers.

"Since beginning of time, Hopis have made pilgrimages to these peaks for evergreen and religious offerings — evergreens which are essential for all ceremonies, offering of prayer feathers in the hopes of creating harmony for all mankind.

"Your regulations have forbidden us from utilizing these shrines, and we have respected your wishes with grief. Now I and the Hopi people are asking you to respect our humble wishes by refraining from desecrating the San Francisco Peaks area. Your continued infringement on the peaks for monetary gains, will not only destroy the sacredness of the peaks, but also the reason why the Hopis exist.

"I ask you not to destroy the San Francisco Peaks area, so that we may continue to practice our beliefs in furthering the welfare of all mankind."

MR. ALTON HONAHNI, SR.: Planning and Zoning Commission of Coconino County, Flagstaff. My name is Alton Honahni, I was born in the Village of Moenkopi and I am a member of the Fox clan.

Ever since my childhood days, I have been an active participant in the Kachina society. I have been instructed by my elders to respect and preserve the sacredness of the Kachina. It has been prophesied that we will encounter hardship, if

we desecrate the kingdom of the Kachina.

Since beginning of time, God has instructed us to heed and live in accordance to His instructions. One such instruction is that all prayers are to be sent through the Kachinas.

The practice of Kachinas is the last of all religious practices, we therefore consider it to be the ultimate, in the lives of all Hopis.

It is well known that God created all living things regardless of their characteristics; we must respect and appreciate them as such.

Respect is important in the lives of Hopis, for it has created a foundation upon which religion, moral values, and culture are established. Religion is supreme, and it is necessary to have respect for it to have value and understanding.

This must be one of the reasons why my elders have instructed me to be an active participant in the Kachina society. I have humbly participated, praying for all mankind for peace and harmony. I have been convinced that the devil has instructed you to desecrate the San Francisco Peaks area in pursuit of monetary satisfaction. You seem to have lost direction as to why God created nature. Put your greed aside, and respect Mother nature.

I prefer to promote harmony for all mankind. The Hopi have such intentions, through the usage of corn. The yellow corn represented by the north, all prayers are delivered north to Tokonave, 'Navajo Mountain'; blue corn, west to the land of water, 'Pacific Ocean'; however we have used the powers of San Francisco Peaks to reach both of these areas. Red corn south to Neuvatikyao, 'San Francisco Peaks'; and white corn to the east, where our father emerges. We have made offerings through the use of these corns, ground into corn meal, asking for peace and brotherhood among all mankind.

So these are some of the reasons why we respect the San Francisco Peaks area, and another reason for

[Continued on page 176]

Mr. Robert Fulton, *right,* Navajo medicine man:

"This pouch has within itself four more pouches. In each of these four pouches are soils from each of the four sacred mountains of the Navajos — each pouch represents a sacred mountain and each pouch is identified by the cuts made on the lip of the pouch.

"The stone in the middle of the four pouches is representative of the inside of the sacred mountain. Among these pouches are also carved images of a horse, a sheep, and a cow. These are representative of the importance of the horse, sheep, and cow to the existence of the Navajos.

"Tied around the pouch is a string of turquoise — for the sacredness of the mountain soil deserves only the turquoise. Every medicine man has a pouch like this. This allows us to have within reach the soils of the four sacred mountains, wherever we may be. This is important to us for the well-being of ourselves and to our medicine.

"If we allow the white man to dig away at our sacred mountain he is also tearing at this pouch and destroying its sacredness. He is, in essence, destroying our very soul. We must not allow the white man to desecrate our religion and thereby our soul.

"Doko'o-sliid begins with a single cloud to bring us rain, it brings us the snow in the winter and it also brings the wind. We go up to Doko'o-sliid for our medicine and we go there to pray and when we see it from our home, it tells us things are well and good. If we destroy this mountain, we will also destroy the rain, the snow, the wind and we will also destroy the serene life we have now under Doko'o-sliid's eyes.

"We will no longer be able to see the clouds as they drift forth from Doko'o-sliid, bringing us rain, nor will we be able to seek comfort by the sight of our sacred mountain, for we will have violated her and we will not be worthy of her powers."

John Running photograph

Mr. Alton Honahni, Sr., member of the Kachina society, Hopi.

John Running photograph

[Continued from page 174]

our quest for survival. The white men have established laws with the intentions of satisfying their greed. God has presented the Hopi with Kachinas, and it appears now that they can remedy your ideals. However you must believe and respect them. I must add that you people do not believe as shown by your intentions, and if you continue in your actions you as individuals will be held accountable to God, and subject to punishment in accordance to His wishes. He has given you a warning last year, by moving the ground upon which you walk.

I am only telling you a small portion of what I know. The important thing is, you must heed and respect what I have tried to convey to you, in the hopes that we may all become Hopis and live in harmony.

The four colors of corn I have mentioned, the white corn is the purest, and I ask you to use it in promoting harmony for all mankind.

Corruption and turmoil have been seen in the White House at Washington, D. C., because they lack respect for all mankind.

Members of the Kachina clan are my elders, and it is they who are the actual owners of the San Francisco Peaks area. The Tobacco clan and Corn clan are my fathers, I respect them; so on this basis I oppose the development of San Francisco Peaks. To the Hopi, it is our mother; we nurse from these Peaks for religious survival. If you are set on destroying the existences of Hopis, then don't listen to us. God reigns over all man. Ask for His guidance before you make your final decision.

I thank you. (Applause)

Navajo Testimony Before the Coconino County Planning and Zoning Commission, January 29, 1974.

MR. FRED KAYE: I am a Navajo medicine man. I live outside Tuba City in Coconino County, Arizona, Navajo Nation. I have been informed of the plans of the whites to desecrate our Sacred Mountain, Doko'-o-sliid, or the San Francisco Peaks. I would like to explain why the mountain is sacred. Six sacred mountains have been placed under the care of the Navajo people. The San Francisco Peaks, and the area surrounding them, have been placed under our care, and under the care of our ancestors and of their ancestors before them. One reason that the mountain is sacred and I object to development of it, is that the mountain brings rain to the people. We use its forests, trees, and plants for medicine. The mountain is there for the benefit of the people.

It is known that the sacred mountains speak to each other. Tsisnajini speaks to Tsodzil', Doko'-o-sliid (the San Francisco Peaks) speaks to Dibentsa. These sacred mountains are endowed with plants, food, and medicine. They bring harmony and balance to the people. People live according to the mountains.

The mountain also is a teacher. It teaches people the way of life. If the white man desecrates, ruins, or develops the mountain, its teaching will be lost to the people. The gods have ordained that these mountains are the bodies and lives of the people. The Pueblos also know this. The mountain teaches our young their responsibilities as Navajo and Indian people. It keeps our traditions, prayers, and songs intact for future generations. We cannot and will not allow the mountain to be ruined for the benefit of a few.

The white man does not know the mountain. He does not know its benefits. He does not know how to treat it. He does not know how to live with the mountain. For example, a road has been built from the eastern side of the mountain.

This past Christmas white people have cut many trees from the mountain. As soon as Christmas is over, these trees are thrown out in the trash and hauled to dumps. This glaring fact shows the white man's misuse of the mountain. Navajos view the mountain as sacred and would not do this to its trees. Navajos use the trees for their benefit, for shelter, medicine, and food. The white man uses the trees for ornaments, with no respect for the trees of the mountain. The result of the white man's attitude is that the trees end up in trash and in dumps.

The white man is supposed to have an organization, the Forest Service, to protect the trees. What has become of them? What is their philosophy which allows the destruction of the trees? These people are supposed to be trained concerning the effects of destruction of the trees. But if this destruction of the trees continues, the mountain will be left bare as a result of the white man's thinking.

In the east is the sacred mountain, Sisnajini, to the south the sacred mountain is Tsodzil'. And to the north the sacred mountain is Dibentsa. The people who live in these areas protect those mountains. They will not allow their destruction. Likewise, the people who live in the west, by Doko'-o-sliid, are its protectors. We look up to the mountain. The mountain is the mother of our people. We Navajos living in the west do not want any kind of destruction or desecration of our mountain to take place. Our ancestors and their medicine men have always protected the mountain. That is why it remains whole. The mountain has been protected in the past and it is our responsibility to protect it in the present day.

Doko'-o-sliid was set in the west and adorned with abalone shells. Doko'-o-sliid was made to speak to Dibentsa, the sacred mountain of the north. And Dibentsa looks and speaks to Doko'-o-sliid. The sacred mountains were made to speak and to look at each other and to remain as a whole together. The destruction of one mountain affects all of the other sacred mountains. They are interrelated and speak to and look at each other.

The six sacred mountains provide life. The white man has never learned this. He has learned some things, like water will provide power. He has learned some of the benefits that can be derived from the mountains, but often what the white man thinks of as benefits from the mountains are taken at the cost of the destruction of the mountains. The basis of life is derived from the mountains.

The benefits of the mountains known to Navajos and other Indian people are different from the white man's benefits and are in harmony with the mountain itself. These benefits have been known for a long time. For example, we make a mixture of plants called mountain tobacco, which is used for medicinal purposes. It heals people and animals.

The plans for these mountains have been derived from the gods. According to their plans the sacred mountains have been made. First Man and First Woman, First Girl and First Boy knew of the mountains' existence and of the plans that were made. Just as white missionaries and Christians have their gods and their Jesus, we have our ways and our religion. Many of the ways that we respect and practice our religion, are similar to the ways of the white man.

Doko'-o-sliid is used as a place of prayer, and offerings are made to the gods that live there. At the mountain we make prayers for Navajo young people who go overseas and fight for the American people in the wars of the Americans. We ask the mountain to help our children so that they may be safe and return home to our lands. We look to the mountain to help us and our children who are helping the white people fight their wars.

Leave the sacred mountains alone. If white people want to develop and destroy, there are other mountains and other places which are not sacred to the People. Take your development, destruction, and desecration elsewhere if this is what will benefit you white people as human beings. If these are your values take them some place else. We have our values, and we know what is right. We have been here for centuries and we know what is sacred and of benefit to us.

According to the ancestral laws of our people, although those laws are not written, the holy mountains have names. They are not to be desecrated. They are the names of the gods. The mountains are prototypical beings. Stop this development. We know now that the white man does not know what is sacred.

I have learned the uses of plants in administering my medicines. When doctors are unable to heal, often I do. I know the Yei-Bi-Chai healing rites and chants. I know the Night Way and Blessing Way and other related songs and prayers. I know other songs and prayers such as the Mountain Way, the Enemy Way, and the Shooting Way. Many times when all else fails, medicine from these mountains has healed the sick and wounded and restored balance and harmony among the people. The mountains have protected us from destructive forces.

Who are these white men who are making plans regarding the mountains? Do these men have pollen? Do these men have an offering to give to the mountains? Do these men know the prayers, legends, and songs from the feet of the mountain to its head? Do these men have the necessary things to allow them to approach the mountain and ask for its benefits, instead of just taking from the mountain? Does the white man feel that he can take what does not belong to him? Perhaps I can give the white man an offering to take to the mountain. Then he will learn to do things the right way, and will no longer wish to develop the sacred mountains.

Ms. Miriam Hufford and Mr. Tsinnijinnie Singer, *above,* Navajo medicine man. Mr. Singer:

"My name is Tsinnijinnie Singer. I am a Navajo medicine man. I live in Tuba City, Arizona, Coconino County, Navajo Nation. A long time ago four Peaks were created and they were our first leaders. These four Peaks were placed here. We pray to them. Our prayers are to those Peaks. Both Navajo and Hopi have prayers and ways that lead to and pertain to the San Francisco Peaks. The four Peaks are for the Navajo and Hopi people and the Indians who are surrounded by the Peaks.

"The San Francisco Peaks is a woman. As you look at it closely, she is facing the east. She has her knees in front of her and you can see her shoulders. You can see the water draining down the eastern part. So she is a woman.

"I am objecting to the development of the Hart Prairie area of the Peaks. Developing the Peaks would be like walking on your home and not having respect for your own home. Some white people may not believe this way, but I am representing myself and my Navajo people. For these people who believe in the mountain, development would be like walking on your own home.

"The Peaks are sitting there and protecting us from evil. When there is something wrong among the Navajo people, when there is sickness or maybe somebody is not thinking right or is not feeling right, we always pray to the mountain to protect us from evil.

"We use the Peaks in our ceremonial as happiness. It is happiness. We have sand paintings of the San Francisco Peaks and we have prayers and songs to it and from it. Also we use part of the Peaks in our medicine bundle which we hold and pray with.

"Those of us who believe in the Peaks still go there to worship to them. I do not go to one special place on the Peaks. I go from either side and I go there and pray. I go to pray to the mountain. Whoever that man is that says that he owns part of the property around the Peaks, is saying that he can do what he wants to, regardless of my beliefs. That is not so."

John Running photograph

179

RESOLUTION PASSED BY THE NAVAJO TRIBAL COUNCIL

1. From time immemorial the Navajo people have lived within the bounds of the Four Sacred Mountains; that these mountains were originally brought to this world by the Holy people to delineate the boundary for all time of the land of the Navajo, and

2. The Navajo people worship through natural objects, and in natural surroundings, just as white men worship in churches; these Sacred Mountains are holy places fundamental in the religious beliefs of the Navajo people; they are the sacred religious worshipping places, and

3. The Navajo Nation has now learned with sadness that there are encroachments upon our Four Sacred Mountains, destroying, defacing, and degrading in a disrespectful manner our religious, cultural, and ceremonial beliefs, and

4. Further, these encroachments destroy the natural state and are against the beliefs of the Navajo people.

Now Therefore Be It Resolved That:

1. The Navajo Tribal Council of the Navajo Nation hereby opposes any commercial development of the Four Sacred Mountains; the Tsisnajini *or Blanca Peak (East), the* Tsodzil *or Mount Taylor (South), the* Doko'-o-sliid *or San Francisco Peaks (West), and the* Dibentsa, *or Mt. Hesperus of the La Plata Mountains (North), which will lead to the degradation of their holiness and sacredness. Any violation of them is deemed a sacrilegious and profane act to the Navajo religion.*

2. It is further directed that the chairman of the Navajo Tribal Council and the vice-chairman of the Navajo Tribal Council do any and all things necessary to carry out the intent of this resolution in protecting the Four Sacred Mountains.

Certification:

I hereby certify that the foregoing resolution was duly considered by the Navajo Tribal Council at a duly called meeting at Window Rock, Navajo Nation (Arizona), at which a quorum was present and that the same was passed by a vote of 52 in favor and 0 opposed, this 29th day of January, 1974.

Signed by Wilson C. Skeet, Vice-Chairman, Navajo Tribal Council.

RAY BERMAN

"I am in this principally because of the Indians," says Ray Berman, President of the Coconino Citizens Association.

Ray is a professor of management science and computer science at Northern Arizona University in Flagstaff. His background is in engineering. "I minored in economics," he says. "I developed ideas rather uncommon in business school. There, the usual question was: How far can a corporation go in the name of profits? To me, the question is not how the buck is spent, but how the buck is made."

A German Jew, Berman fled Nazi Germany in 1933. From 1938 to 1950, he was in Israel, "fighting for another mountain there." Last year he read *Bury My Heart at Wounded Knee.* "It made my blood boil," says Ray Berman. "The county planning and zoning com-

mission can listen to 25 hours of Navajo and Hopi testimony — I've watched them do it — then say that the religious issue is not significant."

How does Berman himself view the sacredness of the mountain? "I'm an agnostic, really. When I look at that mountain in the moonlight, snow-covered, I ask myself, 'How can anybody prove that kachinas don't live up there? Is that any more incredible than the story of Moses and Mount Sinai? If the Hopis believe that, we have no right to take that belief or that shrine away."

Submitted to the Coconino County Board of Supervisors at its public hearing on April 29, 1974, by: Ray R. Berman, 3605 N. Paradise Road, Flagstaff.

Chairman Tachias, Members of the Coconino Board of Supervisors:

I speak in opposition to the specific rezoning appeal by Summit

Properties and to the general opening up for commercial development of the western slopes of the San Francisco Peaks. Other speakers will address themselves to legal and technical problems. My concern is with the moral aspects of this proposal.

Our Navajo and Hopi neighbors have addressed themselves often and eloquently to the religious significance of all the San Francisco Peaks. I want to go on record that many of their white neighbors and friends support their demands and ancient claims. Even though we may be talking about Indian rights, this is not merely an Indian issue to be treated as Indian rights have been treated for generations. Not to speak of the many cruel injustices perpetrated on the Indians and documented to the everlasting shame of the White Man and the Judeo-Christian ethic in *Bury My Heart at Wounded Knee*, it is a fact

that even in our times public authorities too often decide that the most economical highway, dam, or reservoir is the one that is sliced out of an Indian reservation. Too often our actions are reminiscent of Erskine Caldwell's novel *God's Little Acre.* We keep moving the Indian's Little Acre until we are sure the land contains nothing of value. It should be clear by now to any person of reason and reasonable intelligence, that the quality of the proposed usage of Hart Prairie is not what concerns the Indians, but the taking it out of its natural state. For those of us who believe that we should not do unto others what we would not have done unto ourselves this creates an insurmountable obstacle of conscience, and we are and shall remain unequivocally opposed to the commercial use of the western slopes of the San Francisco Peaks.

Notwithstanding the shaky legal foundations of this appeal for rezoning and the technical deficiencies of the proposed development, we know that with the expenditure of large sums of money and much effort some of the shortcomings could be rectified. The real issue is that we want to preserve the entire peaks area at least in its present state, and that we will fight this through the courts, by referenda, and through the ballot boxes until we prevail.

Free enterprise gave Summit Properties the right to own the land and to propose this project, but it does not give it the right to force it on us. Risk taking is an essential ingredient of free enterprise. Summit Enterprise took a bad risk and found its own "Edsel". Ford could not force Americans to buy his Edsel. Why should the people of Coconino County have to accept even the best planned development on the western slopes, if we wish to keep them just the way they are now?

The persistence of Summit Properties in its never-ending appeals manifests a galling arrogance many people in this country deeply resent. By now, there is no doubt in our minds as to what Summit Properties' objectives are, nor that we do not wish to be the unwilling beneficiaries of their alleged contribution to our welfare. This is a clear manifestation of the often unreasonable power of money and profits, which is also a national problem which manifested itself by the political events of the past year. Such persistence rallies our own determination, but it also draws battle lines that need not be there, and antagonisms that profit no one. It is clear that unless we the voters, through our elected representatives, call a halt to this practice, this display of corporate power and insolence will not end until the last socially indifferent corporate executive has developed the last of our scenic and environmental treasures and religious shrines. If this appeal is not denied, what is there to stop this corporation or others like it from ravishing the peaks, until nothing is left to be ravished?

There have been sufficient legal precedents in recent years to indicate a nationwide trend towards curbing untrammeled exercise of so-called property rights. A mere Assistant County Attorney ruled that the Forest Service has no voice in these proceedings. This decision disenfranchised all the people of this nation who jointly through the Forest Service own this land. In an era of ever increasing personal rights, and one-man-one-vote legislation and court rulings, such an arbitrary and partial decision can, and probably will be challenged and overturned. We will not be satisfied until the San Francisco Peaks region reverts to public ownership and strict controls by the people for the people.

It is difficult to comprehend why the Coconino County Board of Supervisors should not sustain the decisions reached twice so torturously by its own planning and zoning commission. I sense no groundswell of public sentiment in favor of Mr. Leadbetter. The issue is one of personal gain versus the public welfare and beliefs and convictions we all profess to share. Next Tuesday has been declared a Day of Prayer, and some of you Commissioners will be attending a public prayer breakfast. Let us not forget that we all, Indian and White Man, pray to the same God, and that even today our cherished dollar bills bear the imprint: *In God We Trust.* I urge you in the name of an already ravished environment, and in the name of conscience, religious tolerance, and political wisdom to deny this request.

I thank you.

JOHN DUNCKLEE

It is not enough to say that San Francisco Mountain is unique, for every mountain has a particular personality. The beauty of this mountain dominates the surrounding landscape for miles and miles in every direction, but a scarlet primrose blooming in a patch of soil between two summit boulders, or a commune of columbine dancing in the summer sun are no less beautiful than her magnificent profile. An avalanche track adds to mountain beauty, a demonstration of the power of nature, but the scars of roads and ski lifts subtract from that beauty, a demonstration of man's apathy toward nature.

Not only is the mountain a living system — a system of systems — but a source and influence to land, water and life far beyond the horizon. The snows which blanket her peaks in winter and the rains which drench her slopes in summer sustain her immediate life. Surplus water, that not remaining in her porous soil or finding its way back to the air, finds its way down her streams to join rivers, and finally — if left alone — spills into the Gulf of California. But man has changed all that. . . .

Should a man doubt the power of San Francisco Mountain, he can witness it as I have. When the would-be developers attempted to drill a well, the mountain caved in their efforts and buried their machines. Man, with his notions of good and evil, has sought to eliminate a natural environmental factor, fire, from the mountain habitat. The mountain retaliated by growing her pine so close together that the trees are worthless for timber and constitute far greater potential for obliterating fire than nature ever conceived on her own. Perhaps casting off the chains of science leads toward an understanding and feeling of the power of San Francisco Mountain.

There is solitude on San Francisco Mountain — not silence, for there is too much life for silence; but silence is not necessary for solitude. Alone on the mountain I was able to recycle my own time, putting together the puzzle of my own life into a perspective which led to my own inner peace.

I now live far to the south of San Francisco Mountain. I can no longer look up and see her sparkling in the morning sun or turning to gold through a summer storm at sunset. Far away are the deer and elk refreshing themselves with the cold, clear water of Snowslide Spring, and the venerable bristlecone pine, bent, twisted and grizzled from a thousand years of living near her summit. But the distance away that I find myself matters not, because the mountain is part of me — and I am part of San Francisco Mountain.

John Duncklee
Tumacacori, Arizona 1975

Putting Some Shine on the Apple

To lovers of wilderness, New York City is an unholy place. A patchwork raft of telephone cables, sewers, subway tunnels, and concrete towers, permanently anchored in a polluted body of water and occupied by eight million people who want to do whatever you want to do at precisely the same moment. The city's problems often seem as dense as its population — all interconnected, often manifesting themselves in such numbers that the place seems unmanageable, and unnatural — somehow unreal. It is odd, this reluctance to assign the modifier "natural" to the works of man as though he were capable only of unnatural acts. Fortunately for New York City, and probably for the rest of us as well, there are numbers of resident environmentalists who fervently believe that "natural" or not, New York is worth saving — or at least that it is necessary to try.

Guy Billout

It isn't easy. Aside from its bewildering array of problems, the political machinery of the place is formidable. Each of the five boroughs has its own administration over which is superimposed the municipal government. In addition, there are networks of metropolitan authorities and commissions with overlapping jurisdictions and sometimes conflicting objectives. Beyond all of that, there are state and federal regulatory agencies operating in the same territory. Taken as a whole, it is impenetrable. As the following sampler of New York stories will demonstrate, the only manageable way to approach environmental problems in that city is to start somewhere — anywhere — with one problem. That's what Marcy Benstock did.

Soot on My Windowsill

Marcy Benstock sits at her desk in a midtown office building, holds a huge yellow and red Chock-Full-O-Nuts paper coffee cup with both hands and peers through the steam. She speaks softly and chooses her words carefully, pausing often to consider, but seldom backtracking. An academic background — a private college degree in English lit. and New School M.A. in economics — is not hard to guess at. But it is only after a time that one becomes aware of the glint of residual anger that must accumulate in anyone who takes on the power structure of a big city. Marcy Benstock is a professional environmentalist. She is good at it. That does not mean she is 100 percent effective. Victories in New York City are always tentative.

Marcy talks about how it is difficult for her to limit her activities in the NYC Clean Air Campaign, of which she is director, to identifying and dealing with the sources of air pollution in Manhattan. Though the grant under which she operates charges her with that task, she has found that the problems of clean air in any urban setting are inextricably linked with other problems, particularly those of energy and transportation. She must do two or three jobs at once. There is little relief. One gets the impression it is not exactly what a girl from Buffalo dreams of as life in the big city.

"I became an environmentalist only this winter" she says gently. "Before that I wanted to attack specific things, like the soot on my windowsill."

Near the end of 1969, Marcy Benstock left a New York City job and went to Washington to work at Ralph Nader's Center for the Study of Responsive Law. While she was there, she kept her apartment on the upper West Side and when her work permitted (which wasn't often) she'd come back for a day or two. She spent all her time off vacuuming the soot out of her digs. "It was awful," she says.

About the same time she decided to return to Manhattan and do something about the soot in her apartment, John Lindsay signed into law a municipal air pollution control code for New York City that he described as "the toughest and most comprehensive in the nation." One of its principal features was intended to encourage citizen participation in pollution control for the first time. It provided that if the city's Department of Air Resources did not act on a legitimate citizen's complaint within 45 days, the citizen himself could initiate action that would be prosecuted in something called the Environmental Control Board, specially installed in order to bypass New York's clogged judicial system. And best of all, citizens who filed action against a polluter were to receive 50 percent of any fines collected. Not a bad scheme.

In January 1972, Marcy Benstock opened a tiny office above the Olympic Theater on upper Broadway. She had convinced the Fund for the City of New York to give her money to do something about the direct sources of air pollution in her neighborhood, on the upper West Side, between 72nd and 110th streets from Central Park to the Hudson — 200 city blocks. What her Upper West Side Air Pollution Campaign provided was a mechanism for putting New Yorkers outraged by dirty air into action in compliance with their new pollution control ordinance. What she did was to make heroes out of apartment building superintendents. Or some of them, anyway.

Super Heroes

This man is an upper West Side building super. The piece of paper he's holding attests to his having completed a course in the proper maintenance and operation of a boiler or incinerator which uses no. 6 residual fuel oil, a major source of air pollution in New York City.

The upper West Side is a district of large apartment buildings. Each one has a superintendent whose duties are the maintenance of building services — including heat and sometimes incineration. Rather than tracking down landlords, Benstock's volunteers poked around basements looking for incinerators and heating equipment which used heavy residual no. 6 oil as fuel, already identified as a principal source of sulfur dioxide and particulate matter. According to the city's ordinances, these burners were to have been upgraded by landlords, and licensed, and their operators were supposed to take a city-sponsored course in proper operation and maintenance of the equipment, steps that would reduce pollution from that source by as much as 50 percent. In many cases, neither the modification nor the training had taken place.

Volunteers were organized block by block. If a super had taken the city course, or signed up to do so, a great fuss was made and his name went on the Super Honor Roll with appropriate publicity. If the landlord had not complied with the law requiring upgrading, volunteers filed a citizen's complaint with the Air Resources Department. Campaign organizers awarded prizes to the volunteers who signed up the most supers. By April of that year (1972) 103 of the 200 blocks in the district had been organized, 70 supers had been enrolled to take the

Marcy Benstock, *right*, on the street. It was at streetside tables such as this that her Clean Air Campaign was brought to the attention of New Yorkers on the upper West Side. The signs on the wall name the names — of polluters, and also of those who made the effort to comply with N.Y.'s stringent air pollution control code. Her tactic was to make no bones about who was causing pollution, then applaud like crazy as soon as the polluters changed their ways.

city course, and more than 100 formal complaints were filed with the Air Resources Board.

By the end of 1972, the campaign had been expanded to a city-wide effort, the name changed to the Clean Air Campaign of NYC Inc., and Marcy Benstock got herself a paid assistant. Her job was to organize neighborhood campaigns like the one on the upper West Side all over Manhattan. By all accounts, Marcy Benstock's efforts were successful. What doesn't show on the record is that Marcy Benstock and her supporters had not only to take on the enforcement of the city's ordinances in the first place, they also had to cope with enormous red tape and sloth in dealing with city agencies. Though the city had promised neighborhood instruction in boiler operation as soon as 25 supers signed up, it was fifteen weeks (and over 70 additional names) before the city came through with a neighborhood precinct house to give the course in. And only then after Marcy Benstock placed 89 telephone calls chasing the matter from one civil servant to another. When it came time for citizens to take advantage of the famous "you enforce it if we don't" provision in the new ordinance, harassed officials found there were no forms on which citizens could file their complaints. Another 15 week delay.

Now, though Marcy Benstock still works at the neighborhood level on a city-wide basis (to the extent possible with limited help), her optimism is tempered. She knows too well that decisions made in Albany and in air-conditioned limousines and Manhattan penthouses about the management of real estate fortunes and large corporations have much more to do with the environmental ills of New York City than does Jose Salgado's boiler at 666 West End Avenue. She also knows it is impossible to tug at one environmental ailment without raising a tangle that includes them all.

Grass in the Cracks

What gives Marcy Benstock the gumption she needs to persevere despite incredible odds may be the energy she encoun-
ters down on the street. New Yorkers are anything but trod-
den masses. Present them with any threat, and they'll snap into action like folks possessed. It seems as though at least one
response to a hostile environment is some indomitable instinct
for survival. In New York it shows up everywhere, like grass in
sidewalk cracks, and is just as resilient. If that city is to be in
any way saved as a habitat for humankind, it must be thanks
to this dogged will to persist.

Its aggregate form is the Block Association — looking
something like a vigilante group (defense posture), town meeting (working posture), and grange picnic (at rest), these small
groups are fraught with political portent far beyond their size.
They function as the guardians of a way of life, are used to
flog New York's sagging bureaucracy into something resembling
attention to local problems, and are social organisms which
seem to be the focus for positive energy, something that can be
regarded as a luxury in most cities. This last, the matter of
constructive enjoyment, should not be underrated. It is probably the fact that neighborhood folks gather periodically to enjoy themselves that makes them a consistently effective political force. The tie that binds may be not so much a pang of
fear as an embrace. Some sense of sharing good as well as bad
seems to have given the most active of these neighborhood
groups a tribe-like sense of kinship.

Neighborhood is not a particularly apt word to describe a
block association's zone of influence, since it is usually rather
smaller than what is commonly thought of as a neighborhood.
Actually the boundaries vary, ranging from both sides of a
street in a single block between two cross streets to several
times that, often defined by major arteries or other landmarks.
Though these groups tend to be somewhat insular, they readily
combine forces, particularly when responding to some general-
ized threat. Normally such alliances are temporary, and con-
fined to district or neighborhood issues. There is little evidence
that block associations are effective in dealing with city-wide
affairs, which is probably more an omen for city hall than an
indictment of the block associations.

The block association, as practiced in New York, is one of
that city's most encouraging features, and may well be the only
political device that can ultimately save it from environmental
exhaustion — since it seems to be one of the few political formations that works on a day-to-day and issue-to-issue basis.
There is a lesson here for other cities. It may be that the environmental health of any urban center depends to a large degree
on the political effectiveness of its smallest subunits. It's get-

ting things down to a manageable size, tinkering with the very specific problems of too much dog poo and not enough street greenery, and taking matters into one's own hands that has made these little enclaves seem so much like home. They are working. And in New York City, anything that works is worth looking at. Hard.

Chauvinism by the Block

Joan McClure lives on Bethune Street in New York's West Village. She is the president of the Bank/Bethune Block Association. She is also its founder. Ms. McClure used to work for *Vogue* magazine's fashion department. She is also one of New York City's most outspoken advocates, and one of its most relentless critics. The two go hand in hand. Here is her story of how her block association came to be, and how it works. It's all changing now, but that's the nature of such things.

"If you really respect people, you know that no two are alike. It's the same with block associations — and that's their virtue. Ours started as a means for neighborhood government. I'm very excited about that idea and went to England to study it there. I got a lot of old-timer people together first, here at

Joan McClure, and some kids on the block. They all have Bank/Bethune balloons. The picture was probably taken at one of their annual block parties.

189

my house. It grew to include first Bank Street, then Westbeth (a nearby artists' cooperative housing project), and then it reached its natural boundaries of the two streets (Bethune and Bank) between Hudson Street and the river. Funny, it's chauvinism by the block. The other end (across Hudson) calls itself the Upper Bank Street Block Association.

"We made a big mistake. We should have gotten better organized. You must take the trouble to search out leadership. We said, 'We're going to learn from our mistakes. We'll have committees for 6 months only as a try-out.' We wasted a lot of time over a constitution, bylaws, and Robert's Rules, which can prevent people from saying what they want, except for the smart-asses who call for point of order. You have to know your neighbors and pull them out to participate.

"Side issues can divide a block association. We have all sorts of people on all political sides interested in all sorts of things: prison conditions, the women's movement — you name it. We decided that we would concern ourselves only with things that apply directly to our area. We have no shortage of those issues: street crime, trees, recycling, traffic, dog behavior, the West Side Highway, locks, street lighting, broken sidewalks. Just getting the Sixth Precinct police to do what they are hired for is a big job."

On the following pages you will find a collection of photographs and stories that show how block associations work in New York's West Village, and the kinds of things they do. Leila Mustachi, who is a Bank Street resident and New York City advocate who takes a back seat to no one, has served as our reporter. Except for editing required by limited space, the words are hers or those of other residents she interviewed. We are deeply grateful to Ms. Mustachi for her help, and to her West Village neighbors for their cooperation.

"It's a tree son . . . a tree."

THE KISS OF THE SUN FOR PARDON
THE SONG OF THE BIRDS FOR MIRTH
ONE IS NEARER GODS HEART
IN A GARDEN
THAN ANYWHERE ELSE ON EARTH

*THE JANE STREET
COMMUNITY GARDEN*

Her name is Ms. Phyllis Katz. She lives on Jane Street and is the co-chairperson of the Jane Street Block Association which made this garden on a vacant lot, with the owner's permission. You asked me to ask her who owns the lot and how long they can use it. She didn't want to say too much about this but hopes that soon they will be able to use it permanently. Everyone is welcome to use the garden. Just come right in whenever the gate is open. She says: "We have given away about 70 keys to the gate. We gave them away free, but now we charge 50 cents. That's how much it costs

us to make them. Forty or fifty people worked on the garden at various times. A lot of thoughtful people had something to do with it."

The first thing she showed me was a book made by 22 fifth and sixth graders who visited the garden with their teachers. Mrs. Katz showed them around. The garden is organized around an herb garden in the center. She showed them how to smell the mint, spearmint, sage, chamomile, strawberries, and other fragrances. (These are city kids, remember!) The children were especially enchanted by the Halloween witch scarecrow.

I asked her about the sculpture. She said that some anonymous donor had left two of them out-

side the fence. "In the Village, you can always be a scavenger because people throw out extraordinary things. This sculpture of a woman is my favorite. She has no face, but she's still so beautiful. We fished her out of a garbage can and put her there near the wall. We call her Gladys."

[Editor's Note: There is a sad postscript to this story. As this book is being readied for the printer, we have received word from Leila Mustachi that the owners of the lot have destroyed the garden. Apparently the destruction came without warning (though gardeners had been promised a chance to remove plants) after months of maneuvering by the owners for a commercial development opposed by residents. In a statement to the press, Gregory Aurre Jr., one of two owners, justified his action by claiming that residents had used unethical tactics in dealing with the Landmarks Preservation Commission, whose approval is required for any new building in the Greenwich Village Historic District. The same day, notices like the one reproduced here were posted on the garden fence by the Jane Street Association.]

NOTICE

This garden was built by the contributions and love of the residents of the entire West Village. It was a meeting place, an open green environment, a sense of wonder for children and, most of all, expressed the community's ability to create something of beauty out of what was once rubble. We all enjoyed many hours in planting, watching it grow and the appreciation of everyone who passed.

The new owners promised the Jane Street Block Association that they would give us 24 hours prior notice in order to evacuate our plants. On Monday, May 12 at 1:30 p.m., they sent in a workman, locked the garden and viciously destroyed the plants and flowers despite our pleas to take them out. Only after the interception of the 6th Precinct were two members allowed in to save what was left.

The Jane Street Block Association has offered to purchase the property from the owners in order to maintain it as a garden for the entire community. Thus far they have refused.

We have opposed the pending building on the basis of its "appropriateness" in an historic Landmark district and we have expressed our concern about what the one-room studio apartments above and the commerical space on the main floor will do to the character of the neighborhood and the quality of life in the West Village in general.

At all times we have tried to express our concern with dignity. We wish to maintain this position. Although you undoubtedly share our grief at the loss of the garden and the savage way it was destroyed, we ask that no threats or invectives be posted on the garden fence. They are not our tactics.

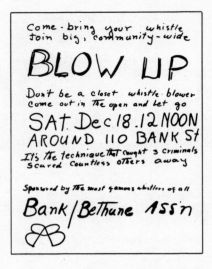

Come - bring your whistle
join big, community - wide

BLOW UP

Don't be a closet whistle blower
come out in the open and let go

SAT. Dec 18. 12 NOON
AROUND 110 BANK St

It's the technique that caught 3 criminals
Scared countless others away

Sponsored by the most famous whistlers of all

Bank/Bethune Ass'n

THE VILLAGE WHISTLERS

I hope you will find room for this story in the book because it is one about conserving *people* — a non-violent way of dealing with street crime. The Bank/Bethune Block Association whistle story has made TV and newspapers all over the country. Here it is from Joan McClure:

"In 1971 we had a situation here where people, especially old people, were afraid to go out at night. There had been two murders within two months right in this neighborhood. We put up flyers on Bank and Bethune Streets calling for a 10-minute emergency meeting right out on the street. We didn't say what it was about, and people came out of curiosity. I told them about the murders, the robberies, and rapes that had been going on and said, 'But we can do something about it!' Then I showed them the whistle and blew it. It was very dramatic. We worked out procedures for what to do in case of trouble, educated the neighbors and now it's working."

[Editor's Note: The procedure is simple. On hearing any calls for help, neighbors are to first telephone Sixth Precinct Station or the emergency police number, give the location, and then run to the street or nearest window and blow like hell. The din, apparently, is frightening.]

"We've never had a false alarm, though once a rookie cop answered the call, saw all those people in nightclothes on the street blowing whistles, and thought it was a riot. Within minutes, we had everything the police have on wheels down here.

"One very important point: When a suspect is apprehended in the neighborhood, our block association always pays the cab fare for witnesses to go to the arraignment. If you are not there when the suspect is booked and are not in court to testify, a criminal could be back on the street right away."

THE VILLAGE RECYCLING CENTER

This story comes from Lyda McKenzie who started the Center. "One night I got up at our Bank/Bethune Block Association meeting and said, 'I'd like to start a recycling center but I can't do it alone. Would anyone like to help?' I was put in touch with Allinson Tupper. We did a little research with help from the Environmental Action Coalition. We put up notices on Bank, Bethune, Jane, Horatio and West 12th Streets asking for volunteers, and on May 1, 1971 we had our first recycling day. We've been doing it ever since. Now two other block associations have joined us.

"We have depots around the neighborhood. Every second Saturday we rent a truck and pick up at all of them. Some people bring their stuff directly to our collection site at Jane and Washington Streets. We take the glass to a manufacturer in New Jersey (1¢ a pound), the aluminum to Reynolds in Brooklyn (10¢ a pound) and the tin cans to the Environmental Action Coalition (½¢ a pound). The city sanitation people take the paper to a dealer for us.

"We've already bought 49 trees for the neighborhood with the proceeds. We donated $75 for planting that triangle at Horatio Street, and we're giving them another $25 for rose bushes. We contributed to the Jane Street Garden too. We donated $75 toward guards for street trees and we give money to all the Block Associations who participate. We are completely nonprofit. All our money goes back to beautification of the neighborhood."

Trees and guards like these have been installed by residents all over the West Village.

BLOCK PARTIES: GETTING THE PEOPLE TOGETHER

I love block parties. In the spring and fall there is at least one, and sometimes three or four, going on every Saturday. We inform the Department of Sanitation, get the "no parking" signs put up, get the street closed off, washed down and then get it set up. Ours is held the first Saturday in May. We have banners, balloons, and flowers all over. There are tables selling all kinds of food, domestic and ethnic (we have a very varied population), second-hand stuff, arts and crafts (the local painters, potters, weavers and other craftspeople sell their stuff and give 10 percent of their money to the block association), used clothing, and much more. Ecology groups set up their information tables as do people representing every other cause. We have more causes in Greenwich Village than anyone

could count. Maybe it's the Cause Capital of the World. There are all sorts of booths for children — face painting, knock-over-the-bottles, shave-a-balloon, fortune-telling, etc. — also music, dancing, and entertainment. We've had belly dancers, Scottish bagpipers in full regalia, English morris dancers, dancers from India complete with toe bells, and square dancing, all on one block on one day. We're very eclectic! Of course we sell plants and window boxes to beautify the street. We make about $1000 each time and use the money to buy trees for our streets. We lean on the city to make them match us tree for tree, but we do all the measuring for the best planting sites ourselves. All the City has to do is put them in.

Usually the Off-Center Theater performs too, from the back of a truck. They put a big old rug down right in the middle of the pavement so all the kids (big and little) can sit

193

down. Once they did a wild, rag-baggy version of *Little Red Riding Hood* wherein the wolf tried to seduce Red into giving up her police whistle so she couldn't summon the woodsman (dressed in a Boy Scout outfit). One ploy he used was to offer her a huge cone "with no added preservatives." She asked the children if she should make the deal and we all screamed "No! No!" Granny was an old dear swigging "heart medicine" from a Vat 69 jug. At the end, the wolf came out and made a speech about how wolves are really good animals, misunderstood and unjustly persecuted and creatures to be cherished. I wish I could remember it all — it was such fun! Then they'd pass the hat.

This is the Horatio Street Triangle — built and lovingly cared for by block association members in the West Village.

THE JANE WEST HOTEL

I want to make a pitch for putting this story in the book because one of the charges levelled against environmentalists is that they care more about trees, animals, and landmark buildings than they do about people.

I got this story from Jo Ann Fluke. She is secretary of the Jane Street Block Association and chairperson of the Jane West Hotel Committee.

"The Jane West Hotel is all single-room occupancy — men only. About three-quarters of them are on welfare and the rest are old seamen and people on social security. It used to be a nightmare.

"The reaction of the people on Jane Street was, understandably, fear. There was constant panhandling, derelicts passing out in doorways, garbage can rummaging — all kinds of stuff. One of the main reasons the Jane Street Block Association was formed was to deal with this problem.

"At first everyone was in favor of organizing all the neighbors to march down to the hotel and demand that it be shut down. Then Ann Shrank had the idea that we could do something positive instead. St. Vincent's Hospital had a part-time case worker in the hotel. Through her we finally got a doctor and nurse from the Visiting Nurse Service, who came on a regular basis. Then we approached the City and demanded that they put a resident case worker in there. If they didn't, we would take action! It was a threat that worked. The Department of Social Services gave us someone who was there four days a week and he was just wonderful.

"The block association collected clothes for the men because welfare and social security barely cover rent and food. The men decided to pay for the clothing and they do — a nominal amount.

"We had other meetings with other city agencies. The Department of Parks, for instance, sent someone to teach crafts. At one of the block parties, the men got themselves together, set up a table, and sold their craft items. The fear in the neighborhood started to diminish. Now if people see a drunk zonked out, they know how to help. The men don't need to panhandle.

"This year we had our Fifth Annual Christmas Party at the hotel. All the food was donated by the local stores and the neighbors. We had decorations and entertainment.

"The men want to be more active and more a part of the street. They've been very helpful at the Jane Street Garden. They want to attend block association meetings. They are coming to us now. People have so much to give. It's amazing the resources you have."

One of the World's Great Ruins

Sometime during December of 1973, a section of New York City's elevated West Side Highway, built in the 1930's and long neglected, collapsed near West 12th Street, depositing two vehicles on the street below. Facts surrounding the incident are vague. There are several versions, the most bizarre of which has it that the two vehicles were city public work trucks loaded with blacktop sent aloft to do another cosmetic patch job on the road surface. However vague the cause, the response of city officials was quick and decisive — most of the highway was immediately closed to all traffic. The southern section, between 46th Street and the Battery is still closed.

There was an immediate public uproar, particularly from residents living on the West Side in the vicinity of the closed portion of the road, who feared that traffic diverted from the tottering highway would glut the streets. Simultaneously, there began a city-wide controversy, which rages unabated, over what to do about the problem. In the months since the collapse, virtually everyone who is anyone in New York City has gotten into the act — studies have been made, reports have been written, preliminary road plans have been proposed, violent opposition has been mounted. Already the business has taken on epic proportions. No less than five major proposals for re-working the West Side's major north-south artery have been proposed. Each has its own set of proponents, each attracts an equally vocal array of detractors. Two of the proposals are for interstate highways — both of them schemes that would funnel hundreds of millions of dollars of federal money into the project — a glittering prospect considering the City's impoverished condition and its present level of unemployment. Powerful downtown groups such as the Chamber of Commerce, the Downtown-Lower Manhattan Association, business and building trades are solidly in favor of these plans — by far the most radical of the lot. One of them, referred to as the Outboard version, calls for as many as twelve lanes, including access roads, massive fill along the Hudson River and the creation of new real estate. Residents on the West Side are opposed. This response from a local newspaper, *The Villager,* is explicit:

Although planners have dangled the plum of parkland as a possible use for the landfill, battle-scarred Villagers who have been through similar wars before, see the landfill as a real estate deal that will affect the zoning of Greenwich Village and Chelsea and make our low rise buildings financially unfeasible. Some proponents of the interstate admit to envisioning a wall of high rise office space and apartments along the Hudson River, and call it progress. These are people who see "growth as the end-all of economic activity," according to Wade Greene writing in the New York Times Sunday Magazine. *The impact of thinking by environmentalists has tended to alter such theorizing across a broad front so that some American cities are attempting to reclaim existing slum areas and clean up and improve existing mass transit facilities.*

When confronted with the specter of massive doses of air pollution from such a monster highway, planners' response has been to propose sealing off bordering buildings and venting them with filtered air.

Environmental groups, though unable to agree on an alternative, are uniformly opposed to both interstate proposals. Activists representing these groups, among them Marcy Benstock, are trying to use the controversy as a way of focusing attention on the city's rattletrap subway and surface transit systems, claiming that any highway expansion will make current traffic and air and noise pollution problems even worse and that pumping a half a billion dollars into the city to further complicate its already serious problems is sheer madness. Federal Interstate funds *may* be used instead for mass transit projects, though the amount of money available for that use is somewhat less.

Heard from a distance, the hue and cry from Manhattan Island takes on a melancholy timbre that is at once desperate and somehow madcap. With its own life-support systems functioning hit or miss, and an uncertain future hanging over all petroleum-hungry cities, huge road-building schemes, fantastic even in the best of times, have surfaced and are supported with an eerie logic that mesmerizes. Snakes in a basket.

Strangely enough, the huge traffic jams anticipated on West Side streets after the close of the highway never materialized. The traffic that used to course the length of the city on the West Side Highway has simply melted away. No one is quite sure how, though environmental advocates would dearly like to know. Local traffic counts in the West Village have shown some increase in truck traffic, but trucks were never permitted on the West Side Highway in the first place; so that increase must be due to other factors.

Which brings us to a darkhorse highway proposal. In September 1974, *The New Yorker* ran a piece which issued a clarion call for sanity. In it, the writer proposes that the highway be left alone. Just that. The idea may lie too close to the heart of the problem to be explorable. As far as we are able to determine, it has attracted little serious attention. Perhaps coming from a layman (and a writer at that!), it doesn't stand a chance in a field dominated by politicians, engineers, and other experts. But because the proposal makes a kind of quiet good sense amid the clamor of great sounds and alarms, and because it is eloquently stated, we reprint it here. We have another reason. We suspect that it may have much meaning for those of us who live in other cities. There is something ominously archetypal about New York City's problems. As Manhattan goes . . .

Last December, when that section of the West Side Highway collapsed, a miraculous transformation occurred. The highway was closed to automobile traffic between Forty-sixth Street and the Battery. Overnight, a bumpy, dilapidated, inadequate highway, a highway that had degraded the waterfront of the lower West Side with noise and poisonous gases, became the broadest, most magnificent, most beautiful elevated bikeway in the world. We've ridden our bicycle on it regularly ever since. We've ridden on Sundays, when the highway is a promenade for the self-propelled, both on wheels and on foot. Once, we rode at midnight, and a rogue car, its headlights doused, careered at us down the wrong side of the road and scared us out of our wits. Last week, the sun came out after four days of monsoonlike rains, and we went for another ride.

We'll get to the ride in a minute. First, a proposal. All five plans of the West Side Highway Project, ranging from a simple repair job to the grandiose one-and-a-half-billion-dollar scheme for an Interstate Highway, share that ever-receding goal of modern transportation alchemy known as "easing the traffic flow." Our proposal is simple. Forget about "solutions," and leave the highway exactly as it is. The traffic has been "flowing" — not altogether smoothly, perhaps, but without undue suffering — on West Street, under the highway. And as a ruin — as a crumbling monument to the age of automotive optimism — the highway has a dignity and a beauty it utterly lacked when it was a mere conveyance for cars.

We got on the highway at Twenty-third Street, and immediately entered a region of stillness and peace. Without cars, the highway is not in constant vibration, and riding on it is like skimming over the city in a bubble of silence. The sounds of horns and trucks can still be heard, of course, but on that empty, bleached highway we felt detached from them. We rode up to Forty-sixth Street — where, appropriately, the crumpled, wheelless wreck of a Buick marks the spot where downtown car traffic must exit — and then down to the Battery.

We stopped here and there to examine details. The metalwork of the highway's railing, its gray paint now flaking away, creates a frieze dotted with municipal seals. Each crosstown street is marked by a metal bas-relief along the railing. The basic motif is gears: gears within gears, sun rays shooting out from gears, gears with powerful wings, eagles surmounting gears, helmets crowning gears, and, right in the middle of each relief, a universal joint. Between Twenty-seventh and Fourteenth Streets, the road surface is of cobblestones instead of asphalt, and there are fine Art Deco lampposts in the middle. Elsewhere, the lampposts are of the modern, arching, mercury-vapor variety. They look hideous at the moment, but in fifty years, when the ghastly vision of the future their designers were trying to express is only a historical curiosity, they, too, will be beautiful.

The highway is now a good spot for automotive archeology and urban botany. In every cranny are little pieces of hubcap, shards of headlight and taillight, and scraps of chrome trim. We found a perfectly preserved inch-high chrome "R," probably from an ancient Rambler. Along the edges of the road, where grit has accumulated in the metal gratings, and in the middle dividing strip, where the concrete has started to crumble into something like soil, plant life is flourishing. We noticed a dozen varieties of weeds and wild flowers, and some plants were four feet tall. In the stretches of cobblestone, the vegetation has begun to creep into the roadway itself.

During our ride, we saw about a dozen cyclists, mostly of the ten-speed backpacker type. We chatted with a gray-bearded painter and a handsome woman, who were out for a stroll together, and who told us that their favorite time for walking on the highway is in the winter, just after a fresh fall of snow. We talked with Eric Romanelli, who has short brown hair and a trim beard, and was wearing a tiny gold ring in his left earlobe. He had on purple jeans, a white tank top, Argyle socks, and a pair of over-the-ankle roller skates with rubber stoppers on the toes. He told us he prefers to skate south, because it's slightly downhill and the wind is at his back. We talked with a couple of transit cops in a battered police station wagon — the only motor vehicle we saw on the highway — who said that, as far as they knew, there is no crime on the highway.

And we saw the sights. To our right, as we rode downtown, was the Hudson, with, successively, the cruise ship Raffaello, the liner France, and the ruined piers of the Erie-Lackawanna and Lehigh Valley railroads. To our left was the city: the midtown skyline in the background, and, in the foreground, the huge, shuttered brick warehouses of the late Industrial Revolution. The pall that the West Side Highway casts over West Street has kept much of it as it was two generations ago. In the Gansevoort wholesale meat district, we peered down at trucks backed up to covered sidewalks, animal carcasses hanging from hooks, and a topless bar that opens at eleven in the morning, just as the men are knocking off work. We saw a half-dozen true diners — that is, diners that make a serious effort to resemble railroad cars — and one or two of them were still in business. We saw fine, brawling old waterfront lodging houses, such as the Christopher Hotel.

Downtown, as we came out behind Pier 25, we suddenly saw the Statue of Liberty, surprisingly large and surprisingly close. A little farther down, the north tower of the World Trade Center rose some thirty yards from the edge of the road. As we coasted down the ramp to Rector Street, we thought gratefully of the decades of neglect that have brought the highway to its present happy pass. With such a ruin, New York is truly a civilized city.

Steps to Power

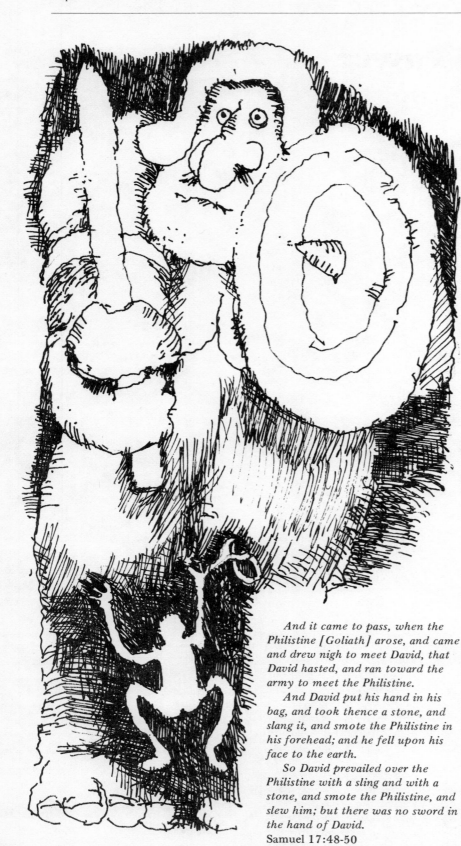

And it came to pass, when the Philistine [Goliath] arose, and came and drew nigh to meet David, that David hasted, and ran toward the army to meet the Philistine.

And David put his hand in his bag, and took thence a stone, and slang it, and smote the Philistine in his forehead; and he fell upon his face to the earth.

So David prevailed over the Philistine with a sling and with a stone, and smote the Philistine, and slew him; but there was no sword in the hand of David.
Samuel 17:48-50

The forces arrayed against you in your environmental battle probably will at first look as invincible as Goliath did to the Israelite army. Most likely, the opposition will have professionals of all sorts working for them. They have money, and they have power. Often they have staying power too — they can try again next month, or next year.

And, unlike a few years ago, when the grassroots environmental movement was just emerging, your opponents will not be caught totally surprised by your appearance on the scene. In fact, they may be spending great sums of time and money in preparation for your onslaught.

For example, the U.S. Brewers Association spends millions of dollars every year, promoting "pitch in" anti-litter campaigns and recycling of wastes. What the U.S. Brewers Association *doesn't* want is laws that do away with throwaway cans and bottles — laws such as the returnable container bills now in effect in Oregon, Vermont, and South Dakota.

The Kiawah Beach Company, which is developing Kiawah Island in South Carolina for the Kuwait Investment Company, has a team of environmental consultants planning what they bill as an environmentally sound development. They say they will engage in "cluster development" — the grouping of housing units together, leaving open space undeveloped — a concept which is fast becoming the first item in the developer's bag of tricks to fight environmentalists.

And, of course, your opponents will usually say that their plans will bring the twin blessings without which America is doomed: *more taxes and more jobs.* (The thing is, they're usually wrong. If there's one message that comes through loud and clear in the grassroots accounts in this book, it is: *debunk the economic claims of the opposition.* Ask the question considered fundamental by Ted Radke, environmentalist and city councilman in Martinez, California: *"Who bene-fits, and who pays?"* More on this later.)

Nobody would set out to slay a giant, build a dam, log a forest, or even take a vacation trip without having a plan. So why do so many grassroots environmental groups go off "halfcocked?" The answer, of course, is that they've never done what they're doing before. They learn the hard way, if they learn at all.

In this section are broad cate-gories, steps that we believe every grassroots environmental group should consider as early as possible in their efforts. These categories emerge from the experience of nu-merous grassroots campaigns. Un-der each category are presented some of the more interesting and/or effective means various groups have used to respond to the problem posed. We hope their ideas will stimulate you in devising your own strategies.

Please don't get bogged down in planning. Sooner or later, if you're going to nail Goliath, you're going to have to get out there and take him on. So we're also presenting a number of skills, techniques, and tactics which might be useful to you as your enterprise progresses.

The main advantage that David had over Goliath was not that David's planning was superior. It was, quite simply, that God was on David's side. Or, to put a more mo-dern light on the story, it was that David *knew* God was on his side, and that therefore he couldn't lose.

There is no substitute for faith in your ability to win. The most successful grassroots groups know that their objectives are good for people; they have faith in the ability of the people to understand that, and in their own ability to com-municate it. This is the main ad-vantage grassroots environmental groups have over exploiters of the environment, who often must rely on concealing, deluding, and plain lying to the public in order to get what they want.

We hope the following Steps to Power may help you find that soft spot between the giant's eyes. You're going to have to think for yourself, and act boldly. Remember the stakes, and know that you can succeed.

1.

The Core Group

Find a few other people who are as dedicated as you are to achieving your goal.

Two people working on a grass-roots environmental problem do not double the effectiveness of one per-son — they *create* the effectiveness of that person.

For nine long, frustrating years, Aurora Gareiss of Douglaston, New York, tried to save the Udalls Cove marsh on her own. She wrote let-ters to every authority she could think of. No one acted to preserve the marsh until Mrs. Gareiss got to-gether with her neighbors and formed the Udalls Cove Preserva-tion Committee. This organization was able to get New York City and the Village of Great Neck Estates to preserve the cove as a wilderness park.

"Volunteer office workers were sporadic and not persistent," says Mrs. Gareiss, "with, as usual, a few dedicated and persistent workers — and even these had to be called and tactfully asked, and many times were not available. In a crisis the response was terrific."

Richard Marx, whose effort to form an environmental commission in Jamesburg, New Jersey, ran out of steam when he went to summer camp, wishes he had found some-body to keep things going while he was gone.

How and where will you find that small group of eager beavers, without whom you'll probably be a lonely voice crying in the wilderness? Use your imagination. Think: What sort of people *should* be as interested in this issue as I am? Then get in touch with them — write, phone, walk over and ring their bell, ask them to see you after the Birdwatchers Anonymous meeting. Do what feels appropriate and comfortable to you.

"Who along This Creek Could You Trust?"

"About February, there were two guys down there in Rosebud County, Montana, who were outspoken against the power plants. They looked on themselves as the Lone Rangers, and thought nobody else really cared. We sat them down one night and said, 'Look, forget your past animosities about people who won't do anything. Who along this creek do you think you might trust? Who might commit themselves?' Before that evening was out we had a list of 55 names, and out of that we have a steady group of 35 to 40 people."

— *Bill Mitchell, staff director of the Northern Plains Resource Council in Rosebud County, Montana, talking about organizing ranchers to oppose strip mining and power development in the state.*

Signature Freaks

According to Morey Wolfson, the secret of success in getting signatures on initiative petitions is, "You've got to get a together enough group that says: 'Okay, for the next four months of my life I'm a signature freak!'"

Meladee Martin adds, "We started out with the premise that if 50 people each get 1,000 signatures, then we've got 50,000 names. It doesn't work that way. Instead, it's better to have 20 dedicated people, and tell them to get, say, 3,000 each. Then at the same time, work on people who might get 20, or 5, or 50. You've got to rely on a core group, people who will be

at that shopping center every weekend, who will get their friends involved."

Getting the Ball Rolling

Editor's Note: The following is excerpted from People Power, *a 1972 booklet put out by the League of Women Voters of Nevada, 2432 Natalie, Las Vegas, Nev. 89109. At 25¢ a copy, it gives plenty of good grassroots advice per penny, more of which will appear in later sections of "Steps to Power."*

The biggest problem novices in citizen action face is not knowing how to get the ball rolling.

1. The first step is to contact the basic leadership in a community about the formation of a broadly-based group — perhaps the newspapers, religious leaders, political party leaders, heads of organizations — in order to find the names of citizens who are interested in a given issue.

2. Talk to the people suggested about what you are trying to do and what would be expected of them.

3. An organizational meeting is usually necessary, sometimes with press coverage. Ask for names of others to involve. Provide the group with basic information.

4. With a small steering committee of others interested, plan the next steps.

2.

The Goal

Decide exactly what you want to achieve, and exactly what you will settle for; then forget what you will settle for, and go after what you want.

In the initial flush of rage, many grassroots environmental groups are thinking on the level of a football crowd: "Stop the Bulldozers!" "Save the Trees!" The sooner you sit down with your core group and figure out exactly what your goal or goals are, the more likely you are to achieve them.

The participation of everyone in the core group in identifying goals is vital. The choice of goals will also determine the core group. Agreement, not always easy to come by, will then provide the force that leads to coordinated involvement.

In some cases, though by no means all, it is appropriate to choose a "minimum acceptable solution." This could be crucial in the final stages of your battle, when the opposition is ready to settle the issue. Is the "compromise" they offer a victory for you; or is it, in the words of Claire Dedrick, "changing the upholstery on the electric chair?" If everyone in your core group agrees on what is the least you will settle for, you can maintain cohesion while settling the issue — a time when dissension in your ranks could lose everything.

"People Do Not Like Absolutism"

A crucial phase of any initiative campaign is deciding what the proposed law will say. "We started out in September 1973 talking about an initiative petition that would absolutely prohibit underground nuclear blasting in Colorado," says Meladee Martin. "From September through December, we hassled out what the petition would say. One of our leaders was Dr. Edward Chaney, who is attached to the University of Colorado medical school. He said, 'It is my experience that people do not like absolutism. Why not give people the power to vote on the blasts?' We would have had an incredibly hard time trying to convince the people of Colorado that we knew more technologically than the AEC did about their own project. This moderate approach was one of the factors that helped us

win by a big margin. People were through with having decisions made for them in some obscure place in a bureaucratic agency."

The Atomic Energy Commission did nothing openly to oppose the initiative. "How could they take a position?" notes Meladee. "I mean, if they took the position that the people of Colorado did not have the right to decide, they would incense the entire state of Colorado." — *Meladee Martin of People for Rational Energy Sources in Denver, Colorado.*

Stop That!

Sometimes an environmental group springs into existence in order to stop something. In a sense, the goal picks the group. Choosing the overall goal is no problem; finding out how to reach it *is*. Two examples: the objective of the Kentucky Lake Environmental and Recreational Association in the words of Jane Gibson: "To stop the Ethyl Corporation from mining for titanium on the shores of Kentucky Lake today, tomorrow, this year, next year, for all the foreseeable future. We're not willing to compromise. We won't accept a stand off. We use every legal means available to us to achieve this."

The goal of Citizens Against Wildlife Wonderland, in the words of Elizabeth Dunbar: "What we wanted to accomplish was to stop Wildlife Wonderland. We thought we'd all be directly affected by it, adversely."

Want What You Can Get

Perhaps a short definition of happiness is: Want what you can get. There's no point in choosing an impossible goal; but there's also no point in choosing a goal that doesn't give you what you *really* want.

One group that took what they could get and got what they wanted is the Eugene Future Power Committee. They were lucky. Most of its members wanted to stop a nuclear power plant from being built, by getting an initiative measure passed by the voters of Eugene, Oregon. Instead of asking that the plant not be built, the committee wrote a measure calling for a four-year moratorium on nuclear plants while their effect on the environment and economy could be studied. The measure squeaked through, winning by 850 votes out of 22,000 cast. Four years later, the cost of building the nuclear plant had risen so astronomically that plans to construct it were scrapped.

The Committee to Save French Pete, another Eugene group, was faced with the task of keeping the French Pete Valley from being logged. "We decided that, given the climate of public opinion at that time, we wouldn't go for wilderness designation," recalls Dick Noyes. "We had a wilderness, we had logging roads and clearcuts, but there was no classification in between. French Pete is at a low elevation; you can get to it almost every day of the year. It's near Eugene. We decided to ask for an intermediate status, a roadless recreation area where scout troops could go in and find some campsites and the like." Noyes believes this choice of goal has helped keep French Pete from being logged to this day. Though the fate of this beautiful valley in the Oregon Cascades is not yet settled, public support for preserving it has grown so great that the committee may now push for wilderness status for part or all of the area.

People Power, Rule Number 1

Have well-defined goals for what you want to accomplish. Many a good idea goes floundering for lack of the ability to see it as a part of the whole or to articulate it to laymen. People do not like to waste their time in meetings where the nature of the problem and the aims of the group are never set forth in explicit terms.

To say, for example, that you want Nevada citizens to take action in developing the state's water resources for the greatest benefit of its citizens, while entirely praiseworthy, is too diffuse, too subjective, to motivate people in large numbers to rally to your cause. We all want clean water, properly managed and with qualities which will permit multiple use wherever we live. But we see these things with different priorities and therefore give different definition to the words we use. To be effective, we must set forth various levels of goals, from the specific and immediate to the ultimate.

The well-defined goals should be accomplished by a timetable of priorities. Set your aims high enough to attract the dreamer and the idealist, but provide for various levels of achievement, for the citizen needs to know he is making progress toward a well-defined goal in order to maintain a high level of interest and activity. — *People Power, League of Women Voters of Nevada*

3.
Who's in Charge?

Find out just which individuals and institutions have the power to grant you what you want.

It is a rare situation in which only one public body — a board of supervisors, city council, commission, or whatever — has all power over an issue. We live in a great web of rights and obligations, becoming more complex every day. Victory goes to those who are most diligent in tracing all the strands of power, and learning how to tug them.

Lorraine's Letters to Regulators

There are now a multitude of regulatory agencies charged with watching over the environment. An excellent way to discover which ones have power over what concerns you, while at the same time informing them of your situation, is by writing letters.

Lorraine Campbell of the Kentucky Lake Environmental and Recreation Association (KLEAR) has demonstrated the simplicity and effectiveness of this method. On June 16, 1974 Lorraine read a newspaper article about a titanium strip mine that the Ethyl Corporation was thinking of putting in her neighborhood in Henry County, Tennessee. "I was furious about the implications of it," she says. "I whipped out a letter to the Tennessee Department of Fish and Game." It was the first of many.

In July, Lorraine wrote to the Federal Fish and Wildlife Service. They replied that they weren't aware of the project before she wrote, but had begun to investigate the situation; and they referred to the possibility that the Environmental Protection Agency would require an impact statement. "This shows how I go about writing letters," explains Lorraine. "I'd get a reply like this, then write to the agencies referred to, asking questions — not their opinions, but pertinent matters of fact I felt needed to be answered. Each letter would incorporate some of the information I had gathered. You'd be surprised at how quickly you can gather information this way, and how quickly you can discover places from which to get information."

By the time Lorraine got together with KLEAR, she had refined her technique. "KLEAR corresponded initially with 17 regulatory agencies," says KLEAR president Jane Gibson, "asking what action if any they had taken on this matter, if there would be public hearings, if they had any information on the strip mining, what action they planned to take. Many of these agencies knew nothing about Ethyl's project before we wrote."

KLEAR carefully files all this correspondence, creating a record

very useful in future hearings or possible court cases.

"He Doesn't Like Zoos"

The following vignette illustrates how crucial support for your cause may be found in a totally unexpected place —— indeed, that the locus of power may not be where you think it is. Careful analysis may turn up unusual allies.

Peter Smith, of Citizens Against Wildlife Wonderland (CAWW), had been endeavoring for months to stop Dr. James Kinsey from building a game farm in rural Vermont, through processes provided by Vermont's environmental protection law, Act 250. Suddenly Edward F. Kehoe, Vermont's fish and game commissioner, called the game farm "a farce." Peter says, "It turned out that, personally, he doesn't like zoos." The Vermont legislature gave the fish and game board authority to regulate the importation and management of non-native animals into Vermont. The fish and game board scheduled a hearing in Manchester, Vermont, on the content of the regulations.

"I went to the fish and game board hearing with proposals drawn up with the idea of stopping Wildlife Wonderland," says Peter Smith. "Kinsey and his lawyer were there. They presented their case, then left, saying, 'We've heard enough from this guy in the past 15 months.' That was a bad, *bad* mistake on their part.

"I proposed that all animals in captivity be kept in buildings as well as cages to reduce the likelihood of escape. That would rule out any open-air game farms. Mostly as a public relations thing, I proposed that all imported animals be inspected by a veterinarian who is neither the person selling them nor the person keeping them. The third thing I proposed was that there should be no contact areas — that is, areas where animals and people mingle. Kinsey wanted to bring in European deer that you could put your kid on the back of. I argued that this was the wrong attitude toward wildlife to encourage.

"The fish and game board bought all three of my recommendations, incorporating them into law. The result is that the game farm has had the course."

4.

Access to Process

Find out at what points you can influence decisions important to your goal.

This is where you get into the "nitty-gritty" of your effort. You have your core group, your goal, and some idea of the structure of power you're dealing with. Now, how are *you* going to become part of that power structure?

Many of the groups appearing in this book took years to find an effective entry point into the decision-making process. And the point of power for each was unique, as unique as differences in time, place, personality, and issue. Some, such as No Oil, Inc. of Pacific Palisades, California, used a recently-passed state environmental quality act and the state court system. Others, such as the Committee to Save French Pete in Eugene, Oregon, have relied heavily on the administrative processes of a government agency — in this case, the U.S. Forest Service. Anne Taylor of Raleigh, North Carolina, finding there was no existing institution that could effectively create a greenway linear park system for the city, worked toward the establishment of a new institution — the quasi-official Raleigh Greenway Commission. In Denver, Colorado, people who for years had been frustrated in all attempts to get govern-

mental or court action to stop underground nuclear blasting finally won by going to the ultimate source of power in a democracy: the people, who in many states can vote initiative propositions into law.

As you begin the fascinating process of discovering how to influence decisions in a democracy, it is well to note that most organizations have both a *formal* and an *informal* power structure. It is essential that you understand the formal power structure relevant to your goal, the letter of the law regarding hearing rights, appeal dates, decision review powers of various officials, and so on. It is equally vital that you master the many informal factors, the public and private pressures, that influence government officials to act as they do.

As you probe for access to the political processes that influence your life, you may well run the gamut of emotions: frustration, rage, elation, weariness, and others. Like many people presented in this book, you may begin as a total political innocent, utterly ignorant of how our government works, and soon be an expert and powerful environmentalist, sought after for citizen commissions or public office. Surely you'll find that our government is run by the people who take the time to do it; and, to a very large extent, we live in the environments we deserve.

"Eighteen Steps to Glory"

Editor's Note: Here's some useful advice for anyone who wants to cope with the U.S. Army Corps of Engineers or another large public bureaucracy. From a Sierra Club Publication, Engineering a Victory for our Environment *by Thomas M. Clement, Jr., Glen Lopez, and Pamela T. Mountain. (San Francisco: Sierra Club, 1973), p. 39.*

There are 18 primary steps — from initial planning to completion of construction — which the Corps follows for all its projects. The

"God Would Have Done It In The First Place If He'd Had The Money."

Corps and the Public Works Committees of Congress have often called them the "18 steps to glory." They are set forth in Corps Pamphlet 1120-2-1, and if thoroughly understood by citizen groups seeking to influence Corps planning they can be a most valuable tool. . . . The greatest opportunity for effective citizen action is in the first phase of planning, from Step 1 through Step 6. The completion of these six steps may take up to five years, sometimes longer. This is ample time for groups to collect facts and present them in a concise and organized manner. It is important, too, for citizen groups to understand all the steps well enough to know which ones afford good opportunities for action, and which ones are conducive chiefly to waiting and watching. A sense of timing is important; nothing is more counter-productive than for citizens to demand a public meeting with the Corps when the project plans are being reviewed by another agency, for example. An early entry into the planning and review process will allow citizens to use their time judiciously.

To put it another way, it is far better for citizens to be involved in initial planning than to have to resort at a late hour to such tactics as court injunctions to stop a project which has already been funded and contracted for. Litigation can be costly and should be viewed as a last resort.

Three Routes

In many grassroots environmental efforts, a citizen group can follow three routes in seeking to influence governmental decisions: *the administrative, the legislative, and the judicial.* One group which has a carefully planned strategy of following all three routes is the Committee to Save French Pete. Their goal is to keep the U.S. Forest Service from allowing logging in the French Pete Valley, one of a very few uncut valleys in the Oregon Cas-

cades, and to have the valley permanently preserved in a near-wilderness state as an "intermediate recreation area."

Administratively, the Committee has carefully followed Forest Service administrative procedure, filing appeals of adverse official decisions before deadline dates, and so on. In November 1969, Committee head Dick Noyes caught the Forest Service announcing timber sales at a time the Committee had an unsettled appeal pending with the Forest Service. The furor caused by that stopped the threat of logging at a crucial point.

Legislatively, French Pete's defenders have been pushing for passage of a U.S. Congress bill to protect the area. The lobbying and rallying of public support for the bill has, in turn, put pressure on Forest Service administrators to leave the valley alone.

And, as a last resort, the Committee to Save French Pete has been collecting donations in case they have to fight a legal battle for the valley. One possible ground for legal action, notes Dick Noyes, is the concept of multiple use. The Forest Service often uses "multiple use" to justify logging. "French Pete," says Dick, "is one of only three unroaded and uncut valleys over ten miles long in the whole Oregon Cascades. If they log every valley, that's not multiple use."

5.

Your Group's Form

Organize your group in a form appropriate to the people and issues involved.

Ask yourselves: How are we going to make decisions in this group? With groups as with life forms, different structures are appropriate for different situations. In this book we have seen grassroots groups in many different shapes, from the lone-wolf style of container deposit legislation advocate Forest Golden in Cayuga County, New York, to the carefully structured corporation of the Kentucky Lake Environmental and Recreation Association in Henry County, Tennessee.

Usually, if you're out to save or stop or create something specific, it gives your cause a great boost to formally announce an organization. Peter Smith of Vermont feels he was getting nowhere in efforts to stop the construction of a game farm until he and a few friends formed Citizens Against Wildlife Wonderland. "We had to have a group to share the load," says Peter. "Forming an organization also gave us the appearance of having more strength than we otherwise would have appeared to have. We could type up letterheads, and have an address. And, along with the Mount Holly Planning Commission, it meant that two groups were against the game farm."

The Hindus believe that name and form, *nama-rupa*, are inseparable, and this is certainly true for grassroots environmental groups. "Even getting a name was a process," says Meladee Martin of the Denver group opposed to underground nuclear blasting to free natural gas. "It's bad to be negative about something: 'People against the bomb,' or whatever. We finally chose the name, People for Rational Energy Sources (PRES). It sounds like we know what we're doing. And our program *is* positive. We said: 'Look, with energy conservation and solar energy we don't *need* A-bombs.'"

The name gives a group a public image, but it does much more. It shapes the character of the organization. The Eugene Future Power Committee is still active in planning Oregon's future energy system, though the nuclear power plant they

organized to stop will not be built; but the Citizens Against Wildlife Wonderland probably will become extinct as a group once plans for Wildlife Wonderland in Vermont are scrapped for good.

The ideally structured organization strikes a fine balance between giving a sense of involvement to all its members, and vesting enough authority in leaders so that their word carries weight in the world at large.

Should Your Group Incorporate?

There's no easy answer to this question. You should get good legal advice before deciding whether or not to incorporate.

Grassroots groups often incorporate if they expect to get into legal battles, and want to protect the personal assets of individual members. Jane Gibson of Kentucky Lake Environmental and Recreation Association notes that Tennessee rural people simply won't join an environmental organization that isn't incorporated, because they have a healthy respect for the power of big corporations to use the courts against them.

We heard from one group that regrets having incorporated. The Amherst Growth Study Committee, Inc. of Amherst, Massachusetts, incorporated on January 10, 1972. The next day it appealed a zoning board of appeals permit granted to a developer who wanted to construct a whole community, complete with golf course and commercial area, in east Amherst. The appeal, filed in superior court, alleged various procedural improprieties and said that impact on local resources such as sewage and water had not been dealt with properly.

The developer moved to dismiss the suit, and on February 17, 1972 the superior court ruled in favor of the developer. The judge held that the Amherst Growth Study Study Committee, Inc. had no legal standing to sue, because it was not an "aggrieved person." The decision was based on the fact that the Committee had not been incorporated until after the decision by the zoning board of appeals and that it did not own any "real property" in Amherst.

"The state court of appeals ruled during the summer of 1973 that the superior court had been correct in denying legal standing to the Amherst Growth Study Committee," notes Ellsworth Barnard of the Committee. "There remained no legal basis on which the AGSC could challenge Papparazzo [the developer], and the Committee ended its efforts. . . . In this case we probably made a mistake in becoming incorporated; we might have fared better in the courts if we had acted as individuals."

The Environmental Commission

In New England and the states of New York and New Jersey, the State government provides for establishment of local environmental commissions. These environmental commissions in effect can give environmentalists a semi-official standing with the town, city, or county government. The Cayuga County Environmental Council, for example, made it possible for Forest Golden to get a container deposit law passed in that New York county. Richard Marx has been striving to have a similar environmental commission set up in his town of Jamesburg, New Jersey.

Ideally, a special-purpose commission established by some unit of government can unite the authority and persistence of government with the creativity and independence of citizen action.

The Neighborhood Association

Neighborhood associations lend themselves to a hierarchical form of organization, with a council or board of directors at the top, sub-neighborhood groups in the middle, and block workers at the grass-

roots. Such organization often can mobilize crowds of hearing attenders or letter writers on short notice. It is also often possible for the association to levy a set sum per household, making fund-raising an orderly matter; of course such a levy goes over best if the association is dealing with issues of direct concern to the neighborhood.

A good example of neighborhood association organization is the Rockridge Community Planning Council (RCPC) of Oakland, California. Formed to develop a rezoning plan for its neighborhood, the RCPC has won that issue and gone on to others. (For an account of the RCPC's rezoning effort, see "How to Rezone Your Neighborhood," in Step 9, "Your Alternative.")

Louise Burton of the RCPC outlined the organization for us:

The Rockridge Community Planning Council started as an ad hoc group of about 15 people. At first it was devoted to the single purpose of getting a plan developed for the Rockridge neighborhood. The organization evolved as it confronted new issues. Its structure became more complex and "grassroots" as RCPC developed into a multi-purpose community organization.

Presently RCPC has a board of directors, which includes two representatives from each of six sub-neighborhoods. In many cases, couples share the responsibility of being board members. The board schedules meetings and decides which issues RCPC should be working on. The board also prepares recommendations on some issues and coordinates the flow of information to and from the sub-neighborhoods. All policy decisions, however, are made at monthly meetings of the general assembly. These meetings are open to the entire community. About 50 people are active in the general assembly at any one time. There is no "official" membership *per se*. Anyone who participates is a "member."

All major policy decisions are referred to well-publicized, district-wide, mass meetings for ratification. Attendance at these meetings has averaged about 400 persons.

In addition, some of the "sub-neighborhoods" have active neighborhood associations. RCPC has worked with them to organize and improve communications and to enable them to carry out smaller projects, such as street tree planting and crime prevention. The sub-neighborhood groups have frequently sponsored their own meetings on issues like zoning. They then report to or seek the assistance of RCPC in implementing proposals.

We are actively working towards the eventual goal of establishing RCPC as a full-fledged district council, representing a number of neighborhood groups. The merchants in our district work with us on a regular basis. Decisions on matters affecting both groups are handled through close liaison. RCPC has established several working committees as needed to deal with specific items, such as zoning and traffic planning.

The organization has a chairman, vice-chairman, and treasurer.

6.

Your Constituency

Decide which people are most likely to support you, communicate with them, and get them to join your cause.

Just like a legislator, you have a class of people you're representing. If you don't, you'd better go back to Step 2, "The Goal," and have an agonizing reappraisal session! But don't give up on your potential constituency too soon, because they may not know they're constituents until you communicate properly with them — a process that often takes much time.

Environmental groups often fall victim to the "voice in the wilderness" syndrome. They think they're the only ones who care about the marsh, forest or whatever, and that the rest of the world considers them a lonely gang of bird-watchers. In the first stages of a grassroots effort, this is often a true picture! **The successful groups are those who reach out to people, put themselves in others' shoes, and show others how their self-interest is served by the environmentalists' goal.**

Your constituents are your life-blood. They finance you, and respond to your requests for letter campaigns, attendance at hearings, and other vital support activities. Unlike the core group, the constituents rest mute and inactive most of the time, awakening to action only when you can convince them that a crucial hour has arrived. You have to keep them posted as to what's going on, and give them a sense of intimate involvement. They're your true believers, and you have to give them something to believe in.

Who Wants What You Want?

When you've answered this question, you know who your potential constituents are. The thing is, people might want what you want for different reasons.

The core group interested in stopping the Butler Valley Dam in Humboldt County, California was concerned with the aesthetic and recreational values of a delightful valley. When the issue was put on the county ballot, that group had to broaden its appeal. "Judging by Humboldt County voter preference on other environmental ballot issues," says Wesley Chesbro of the anti-dam forces, "it was fairly obvious that only about one-third of the voters could be said to be environmentalists. On the other end were one-third of the voters who are extremely against environmental issues. That leaves a nebulous one-third in the middle that had to be reached in order to win."

By emphasizing the tremendous tax burden the dam would place on the county, the dam foes got much support from people who simply wanted low taxes. Potential destruction of salmon spawning grounds gained the support of commercial fisherman. The clincher, believes County Supervisor Don Peterson, was that people felt the "dam would basically alter lifestyle in the county — lifestyle in its broadest sense. People don't live here to get rich." The Butler Valley Dam was rejected by a solid 70 percent of the voters in a lumber-industry county where conservationists are widely believed to be enemies of the public welfare.

Getting in Touch

June Viavant, who for years has been striving to preserve the Escalante wildlands in Utah, has built up a rock-solid constituency by communicating directly with backpackers in the area. She has put flyers at trail heads and under windshield wipers, and buttonholes people by their campfires.

The Citizens Against Wildlife Wonderland (CAWW) drummed up support by going door to door in Mount Holly, Vermont. "We got into some arguments with people, but we tried to keep it short," says Elizabeth Dunbar of CAWW. "We regularly talk to people, old people who can't get out, and keep them up-to-date. Also, we can hear rumors that are going around, and raise money."

Each situation calls for a different approach to communicating with constituents. But once you do get in touch, *keep* in touch. (For more advice on communication techniques, see Step 20, "Publicity.") We ran across one group that had no card file for recording name, address, phone number, and skills of people who wanted to help. Get it together!

What's Going On?

Keep the channels of communication open. Once you have enlisted individuals or organizations in your efforts, it is important to keep in contact in order to maintain their interest. People easily become discouraged if they feel they do not know what is going on.

Even if the news is discouraging or downright bad, it is better to tell your cohorts regularly what is happening — what others are doing, what works and what doesn't, what the outlook is — than it is to paint a rosy picture and leave people to operate in a vacuum. If you have recruited citizens to back a certain proposal in your legislature or city council, let them know: Did the letters have an impact? Was the hearing well attended? What's going on, behind the scenes, about compromises? People react much more effectively and consistently if they feel they are part of the "inner circle" where decisions are made. They will stay with you for a longer period if they feel they are trusted participants in a common cause.
— People Power, *League of Women Voters of Nevada*

7.

Your Allies

Get as many respected groups and individuals as possible to endorse your cause.

When members of No Oil, Inc. of Pacific Palisades, California, first set out to prevent the Occidental Petroleum Corporation from drilling for oil below the landslide-prone bluff on which they reside, they were all neophyte citizen activists. "None of us knew anything about fighting city hall," says Shirley Solomon. "I went off on my own tangent. I went after very broad political support. I was told two things: one, that I couldn't get it; and two — by some of the people in our group — what do you need it for?

"I went after what I call honorary members. We wound up with Senators Cranston and Tunney, Congressman Alphonzo Bell from our district, and several others. I had their statements of support in writing, in letters they'd written me. I didn't know any of these people at that time, so I had to prove myself. I just sent them slews of material; I put together packets, and wrote long, detailed letters.

"I also felt we needed the support of groups — concerned citizens' groups — on a broad basis. I eventually got about 125 organizations behind us: the Los Angeles County Federation of Labor, the League of Women Voters, groups from the Chicano neighborhoods in East Los Angeles, and many others. Now it's almost a pattern for groups to go after the same sort of thing, but at that time I had no idea that was the right thing to do."

Like Shirley Solomon, you need allies to broaden your base of support outside of your more intimately involved group of constituents. You also need them to give you good advice, and to back you up during the "crunch."

Perhaps most important of all, the endorsement of highly reputed groups and individuals helps in getting your point of view recognized as a valid, important opinion on a public issue. Acting alone, you may seem to be nipping at the heels of an inevitable development or a foregone conclusion. But with a couple of senators and a labor federation — or some local service clubs — on your side of the ring, suddenly you're a real contender, slugging it out with your opponent.

Allies Are Where You Find Them

Some groups which frequently support grassroots environmental causes are national conservation organizations and their local chapters, the League of Women Voters, neighborhood associations, outdoor sports associations, and labor organizations. But cast your net wide, and you may catch some support from surprising quarters.

For example, two groups in California — No Oil in Los Angeles and the Concerned Citizens Committee in Eureka, opposed to an oil drilling plan and a dam, respectively — were surprised when their county grand juries came out against the projects.

Anne Taylor of Raleigh, North Carolina, takes the diplomacy award for enlisting seemingly unlikely allies. In her efforts to create a linear greenway park system in Raleigh, she got a substantial contribution from a creekside housing developer, organized a joint Sierra Club/U.S. Army Reserve creek cleanup, and now is working to advance the greenway in concert with state highway engineers!

It's a Worker's World Too

Of all people, workers and their families most need public land and beaches, and a pleasant urban environment, in which to derive some joy from life. Yet laborers and conservationists are all too often pitted against each other in phoney "jobs-versus-ecology" confrontations encouraged by those who would exploit both worker and land.

An increasing number of labor organizations are joining with environmentalists, and many environmentalists are workers as well. The Builders Labourers' Federation of Sydney, Australia has gone so far as to impose "green bans," strikes to halt developers from destroying urban natural areas.

Editor's Note: Here's an excerpt from an article by Jack Mundey, Honorary Treasurer of the New

South Wales branch of the Builders Labourers' Federation of Australia. The article appeared in the June 19, 1974 issue of Habitat, *published by the Australian Conservation Foundation.*

The First Ban — Kelly's Bush

Many people here said ironically that the B.L.F.'s first green ban made bed-fellows of people from widely different social classes. Yet by acting in concert, these people, who normally have little interest in each other, saved the last piece of natural bushland on the Parramatta River close to the heart of Sydney.

The "Battlers for Kelly's Bush" were mainly middle-class women from Hunters Hill, Sydney, who took up the cudgels against the New South Wales Government and a millionaire developer, hell-bent on building luxury houses and apartments for the fortunate few at the expense of the many who would lose a natural outdoor space of beauty and recreational value. Just one more instance of a nice business deal taking precedence over any other consideration. But it became one too many.

After the women's formal protests to save the bush were unavailing, they simply went down in front of the bulldozers. And they stopped them. In the respite and in desperation, they requested the N.S.W. Builders Labourers' Federation to ban further work proposed for Kelly's Bush.

At a very large meeting of the residents of Hunters Hill, the Federation acceded to the request, and the first of the green bans came into force, much to the delight of the local people. But our action provoked vitriolic threats by the developers and some leaders of the N.S.W. Government.

The developer particularly concerned announced that he was going to ignore the ban, but he soon sobered up when work stopped immediately on a high-rise office block that he happened to be building down town. The workers at this site expressed their unanimous support for the green ban and declared that if one blade of grass or a single tree was destroyed in Kelly's Bush, the half-finished office block would stand incomplete forever as a monument to Kelly's Bush. So the bush remains intact to this day.

This extraordinary success brought a torrent of letters to the B.L.F. from various resident action groups requesting green bans to correct the myopic attitudes of State and local governments on conservation and preservation matters.

As in the case of the ban on Kelly's Bush, all 40 green bans imposed subsequently have been decided upon only after large public meetings.

8.
Your Opposition

Study your opposition: Know its strengths and weaknesses, and try to find out what it is going to do and when it will act.

You may have no opposition to what you are attempting to achieve, and may need only overcome apathy, or raise money. But resources on this finite planet are getting scarce, and the appetites of their users are ravenous. So, most likely, you're going to run up against somebody who wants to turn a buck with the piece of planet you're protecting; or else you're going to encounter one of those supra-organic governmental bureaucracies which, with its multi-brain, believes that its survival depends on building dams, laying freeways, or harvesting trees.

The main thing is: don't be afraid. Simply going against a trend of events can be frightening. In some cases, opponents of grassroots environmental groups supplement this fear with economic threats (such as loss of contracts or a job) or lawsuits of various types. What you are doing is exercising your right to participate in the democratic political process. In fact, it is lawful citizen action which keeps our democratic system vitally alive. If defenders of a good cause are frightened into silence, then we should all fear.

In studying the opposition, you should be ever alert for the sympathetic ear which may be attached to a sympathetic voice as well — in short, the source of valuable "leaks." More and more people in all walks of life are becoming outraged at the human abuse of this planet; you may find friends anywhere. But keep in mind that you'll get most of your information from doing hard research with publicly-available sources.

Keep cool, and maintain at least the veneer of courtesy and friendliness to all. Pure evil is a very rare phenomenon, and so is pure righteousness. Remember what Ben Gibbs of the Kiawah Defense Fund in Charleston, South Carolina, said of a couple of young development company employees: "Their backgrounds are different from mine; they have families to feed. I can understand their attitude."

Smoking Them Out in the Black Hills

Editor's Note: A very nice example of how to get "leaks" and what to do with them comes from Tom McKiernan, Chairman of the Citizens' Committee to Save the Black Hills (CCSBH). McKiernan, a Keystone, South Dakota, businessman, got wind in 1972 of a plan to build a 3,000-car parking lot for nearby Mount Rushmore, coordinated with a state highway plan that would bypass Keystone. That touched off a confrontation between the National Park Service and Black Hills residents who, for a variety of reasons, *opposed the "secret" parking lot-highway plan. In August 1973, the National Park Service agreed to postpone their parking lot plan until a study of transportation needs for the whole Black Hills could be done. Tom McKiernan wrote us the following letter, giving us insight into how the CCSBH works.*

Dear Editors,

The businessmen in Keystone had been having a running battle with the highway department for years about plans (or lack of them) regarding a new highway through town. After our disastrous flood in June 1972 I pressed for a decision so our businessmen would know how to rebuild. I was civil defense coordinator for Keystone, and had been President of the Better Businessmen's Association.

I made a few trips to the state capital, and during one of my talks with Jack Allmon, highway director, he inadvertently let it slip that the National Park Service had a plan that would bypass Keystone. I tried to get information about the plan, but everyone denied any knowledge of *any* plan. I did get a *leak* from a friend who was an engineer on the project, and from surveyors.

In an attempt to flush it out into the open, I had the chairman of our town council send a letter to Mr. Hartzog, director of the National Park Service, and sent a copy to the newspaper. We picked up immediate support from local residents, and from as far away as Sioux Falls.

During this time, residents in the area where the proposed parking lot was to go were getting disturbed about the surveyors running over their property, coupled with the denials of a plan. They retained an attorney.

We finally brought the plan into the open when they tried to get the county commissioners to support their plan. We asked our senators to help, and they both put pressure on to get public hearings.

The Keystone group and the Hill City group joined forces, along with other ecology-minded people in the Hills, and formed the Citizens' Committee to Save the Black Hills. Dave Miller had been fighting for ecology and was from Deadwood, in the northern Hills. He was elected president because he was a good man and because he was not a purely "local" man. This gave greater range, credibility, and an unbiased approach to our Committee.

Our Committee was made up of businessmen who had business interests in Keystone and Hill City, homeowners in the parking lot "target" area, ecologists, people concerned with our tax base, and people who just loved the beauty of the Hills.

We pressed hard through public meetings, ads in the paper, letters to the editor, calls to radio talk shows, speeches to civic and service clubs, and political pressure, to have the plan fully exposed and to have a public hearing. We played up the fact that the bureaucrats were working in secret and were trying to *force* a plan down the public's throat. This brought in a lot of people who may not have become involved on a strictly ecology problem, or a problem that involved Keystone or Hill City businesses or homes.

I think this is the *biggest* factor in pulling such a strong cross-section together. People resent having "big brother" force things upon them. It is just a matter of making the public aware of the problem and giving them a course of action — and they will rise to the occasion.

We have since picked up other areas that required work. We are opposing the unnecessary destruction of our "pig-tail" bridges, slurry coal mining, and excessive road building in the Hills. We are still pushing for a master transportation study for the Hills area. We use the same tactics: public involvement. We keep people informed through press releases and, when interest is aroused, through public meetings. We also apply political pressure.

Our group is respected now, and many agencies call us in during their planning stages to discuss plans with us. We also get good support from our senators. We try to study the problems and take a sensible, logical stand. We don't want to get a reputation for being extreme, or irrational.

I hope this will help you.
                    Sincerely,
                    Tom McKiernan

Taking the Heat

"If you can't stand the heat, get out of the kitchen," said Harry Truman. That's easy to say, but actually to stand firm under the pressures sometimes encountered by grassroots environmental groups is difficult indeed. In fact, a certain stubborn courage is probably a quality shared by all leaders of such groups, though more timid souls often do vital behind-the-scenes work.

Thanks to God and a vigilant public, we have a general cultural consensus and a legal system which at least tolerates citizen action on vital community issues, and often encourages responsible public input into the process of making environmental policy. In short, America is on your side. So if you keep your facts straight, and speak and act responsibly, you have a very strong position.

But what if you get veiled threats that you might be killed if you persist, as happened to people in two of the stories in this book? That, of course, is uncommonly heavy heat. More common are threats of lawsuits and countersuits, crank mail and calls, and threats of economic reprisal (which are rarely carried out), and (especially in the early stages) peer group community pressure to get you to "go along with the crowd."

Probably the best preparation for the counter-pressure you may get from the opposition (remember — *you're* putting heat on *them*), is

to expect it. The piece of planet you're trying to save may be priceless to you, but to the opposition it often bears a very specific (and very large) price tag. As Ben Gibbs of the Kiawah Defense Fund in Charleston, South Carolina, put it, "Some people think the ecology movement is all good vibes, green flags, and nice nature walks. Well, it can get pretty tough if you're threatening the power structure and economic interests." He should know!

Keeping Cool

"One of the difficult things with No Oil has been sitting on people, keeping them from responding in kind to the jibes of Mayor Yorty," says Shirley Solomon of Pacific Palisades, California, setting for the story "No Oil." "We have been called radicals, some of our leaders have been accused of making money on our opposition to Oxy [the Occidental Petroleum Corporation] — every lie under the sun. In one article, an anonymous Oxy official said we were hysterical, ignorant, liars, and crybabies. They wanted us to respond. We didn't; but at the proper time, in a hearing, I pulled out the article and used it."

The importance of keeping cool in the face of your opposition's heat cannot be overstated. Then, if your opposition cracks and starts yelling at you, the contrast is often enough to win the issue for you. Our lead story in this book, "Get Back in Your Kitchen, Lady, and Let Me Build My Road!" draws its title from the splenetic statement which galvanized a grassroots group into forming.

For sheer flailing vituperation our favorite is this utterance by James D. Kinsey, reprinted to great advantage in fund raising brochures by opponents of his proposed Wildlife Wonderland in Vermont: "We will carry this project through, we won't be done in by a group of bigoted people and rich people who don't want their property changed

when it isn't their property. I won't be harassed by people like that, and I won't be out-talked by them, and I won't be out-spent by them. I've always told them that they're doddering old people and I'll outlive them if I don't do anything else. If I can't out-talk them and I can't out-spend them, then I'll still be here when they're not." When your opposition puts its foot in its mouth, get ready to take advantage. It *always* works.

9.
Your Alternative

If you are opposed to a project, you should consider proposing an alternative to that project.

"If you take something away from people," says Meladee Martin of People for Rational Energy Sources (PRES), in Denver, Colorado, "it's much, much better if you can give something positive in return." PRES wanted to do away with the use of nuclear explosives to stimulate underground natural gas; in return they offered to the people of Colorado the alternatives of solar energy development and energy conservation. It worked.

Negativity is a frequent, and sometimes justified, criticism of environmental groups. Often a grassroots group is entering a planning process that has been grinding on for years, with heavy financing and elaborate studies and reports and phases. Suddenly the neighbors (you) hear the bulldozers warming up, and begin throwing sand in the gears. Well, ask the developers, what's *your* plan?

Keep in mind that this is the oldest trick in the developer's bag, designed to befuddle, divert attention from real issues, pin you to a fixed plan, and get you to concede a need for some development. Sometimes the last thing you should do is propose an alternative which would divert attention from the evils of their plan.

At other times you may be well advised to come up with an alternative. For example, the Kiawah Defense Fund of Charleston, South Carolina, wants to stop a resort development project from being built on Kiawah Island. The island had been owned by one family for many years before the potential developer bought it, and the public has never had access to its beautiful beach. So to gain public support (among other reasons), the Defense Fund proposes that the island be designated a National Seashore, which would open its beach to the public.

As developers increasingly allege that their projects are needed to create jobs, broaden the tax base, and solve the energy crisis, environmentalists must confront nothing less than the great economic issues of our times with viable alternatives to dead-end resource exploitation.

How to Rezone Your Neighborhood

Zoning ordinances of local governments restrict what can be done on land in specific zones. They are designed to set the character of certain areas — industrial, commercial, residential, or other. In many cases, a developer must get a variance in a zoning law in order to do what he wants, and an environmental group opposed to that development must defend existing zoning regulations before local officials. In some cases, however, a change in zoning laws is a means that can be used by a grassroots group to create an alternative future for a neighborhood threatened with destructive development.

One use of zoning ordinances as an alternative to destructive development occurred in the Rockridge neighborhood of Oakland, Califor-

nia, which has suffered the fate of many a nice urban community. Rockridge is characterized by well-built old homes, with a commercial area along College Avenue, its main thoroughfare. In the mid-60s a freeway was rammed through the heart of Rockridge, over the vigorous protests of its residents. "As a result," says Rockridge resident Louise Burton, "the neighborhood experienced a sharp decline, and residents became extremely discouraged and cynical about the possibility of working effectively with the city. Many families deserted Rockridge for the suburbs."

The next dose of "progress" came to Rockridge early in 1970, when a Bay Area Rapid Transit (BART) station was placed in the middle of the neighborhood. The new BART system was designed to be an artery for rushing commuters to and from San Francisco, across the bay from Oakland. A proposal was made to rezone large areas adjacent to the BART station to permit construction of high-rise apartment buildings for commuters to live in.

This time Rockridge residents organized the Rockridge Community Planning Council (RCPC) to fight back. After lengthy efforts, the RCPC finally concluded that the City of Oakland was not going to prepare a plan which would save their neighborhood from being overwhelmed by "development." They decided their only alternative was to create their own alternative. Louise Burton of the RCPC wrote this account of their efforts:

Having realized that the city was not going to do a plan for us, we began efforts to put together an effective organization which would be able to communicate with all sectors of the community. We defined six major sub-neighborhoods, gave them names, and helped them select board members and organize a communications network. People were enthusiastic, and the work proceeded rapidly. We began to print newsletters to inform the

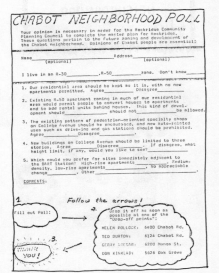

community of the important issues we were dealing with and to give people a chance to share information on smaller neighborhood improvement projects, like street tree planting. We distributed 5,000 newsletters door-to-door to all residences in the neighborhood on a regular basis.

Early in 1974, we got wind of a proposal to build a drive-in food concession on College Avenue in the middle of our commercial area. People were outraged. The drive-in represented the epitome of all that threatened Rockridge (plastic America versus the preservation of our heritage). Because we were well organized and in the process of planning a major neighborhood meeting, we were able to act quickly. A massive outpouring of people combined with some excellent work by volunteer attorneys resulted in the city adopting a building moratorium for Rockridge just two weeks after the controversy started.

Inspired by our first major victory, we mobilized a total community effort to develop an effective zoning plan. We sponsored workshops in the sub-neighborhoods, conducted polls, and utilized a variety of other techniques to get people involved. Through the spring of 1974 we coordinated the preparation of our zoning plan. Merchants started working with us seriously, and we worked hard to get all of the diverse groups in Rockridge to accept compromises and agree on a single, unified plan. The widest possible range of issues was explored. People considered the problems of traffic noise, open space, and many others.

The final result of our efforts, which involved direct participation of many hundreds of residents and merchants, was a plan with some very sophisticated new zoning proposals. The residential zones provided for some new apartments, while preserving good single family areas. Flexibility was sought through design review and use permit procedures. The new commercial zoning mandated a

pedestrian-oriented commercial district, with specialty shops on the ground floors of all buildings. Auto-oriented businesses were banned and parking was severly restricted. Design review, landscaping, and other important items were included.

Through a massive campaign, involving coordinated letter-writing campaigns, organized public presentations, and very large, overflow turnouts at important meetings, we succeeded in getting our plan adopted despite strong opposition. Our last battle before the Oakland City Council even resulted in the adoption of legislation to remove all billboards from our area, a battle we thought we could not win.

Our project created a real sense of community in an urban neighborhood that had begun to fall apart.

The Big Alternative

Our Earth has only so many resources, yet our economy exploits resources as though they were endless. The alternative to this is an economy in harmony with nature, a steady-state economy which would neither deplete non-renewable resources nor befoul the environment with wastes. The creation of a steady-state economy before huge environmental/resource crises occur is probably the chief social problem of our era. While grassroots environmental groups cannot be expected to take on this task alone, they can be guiding lights to involve the rest of our society in this monumental, urgent task.

Many groups featured in *The Grass Roots Primer* are pushing for energy conservation, alternative energy sources, and preservation of stable economic/ecological systems. The Northern Plains Resource Council in Billings, Montana, is striving to preserve a low-energy, stable economic system (farming and ranching) from being destroyed by a high-energy, unstable, short-term energy system (strip mining coal and burning it to generate electricity). Environmental Action of

Colorado (EAC) in Denver, an environmental center supported by student fees from the University of Colorado, concentrates its attention on opposing nuclear energy and promoting solar energy. EAC has begun to explore ways to have Rocky Flats Nuclear Arsenal near Denver converted from a plutonium plant to some other type of enterprise which would employ the same workers.

The problem of providing jobs is very acute and becoming more so, and environmentalists are often unfairly blamed for taking jobs away from loggers, construction workers, miners, and so on. The truth is that our natural world is sorely depleted, and if we allow a final rush for our last resources we'll have neither an environment nor jobs when the dust settles. The employment problem is one that grassroots environmental groups will probably have to begin facing more strongly, as will many other groups in our society.

The grassroots environmental movement itself is a strong force working toward "the big alternative" of a society living in harmony with nature. Every time you stop an environmental abuse, you contribute to the building of a steady-state economy.

10.

What Do You Need to Win?

Determine exactly what you need to win, and what resources are available to meet your needs.

By the time the North Cascades Conservation Council (N3C) set out to stop the High Ross Dam from being built, they had over a decade of experience behind them, and had seen through the creation of the North Cascades National Park. They knew what sorts of people they needed to win: researchers, experts to testify at hearings, a professional advertising agency, volunteers to give speeches and publish their bimonthly magazine and do office work. They also had a good idea of the material resources they would need, from office supplies to money to pay travel expenses and the like. But even the N3C was caught a bit short by the tremendous legal expenses of involvement in lengthy Federal Power Commission hearings. (See "Damming Up Canada," part 2.)

Determining needs and resources goes hand in hand with Step 11, "Your Action Plan." The best groups have detailed plans early in the game, and know what they will need as they go along. Plans and estimates of needs should be constantly revised as the situation evolves.

The Indispensable Secretary

It is well known that sergeants run the army and secretaries keep the rest of the world going. This is certainly true of grassroots environmental groups. At the center of many a successful group is someone who knows how to keep an office with orderly files, someone who answers letters, keeps membership lists up-to-date, and generally keeps tabs on what's going on. Often those efforts don't get anywhere until that vital person comes along. You can get along fine without political geniuses and brilliant tacticians, but you'd better have a good secretary.

Lawyers and Experts

Lawyers and expert witnesses are the two professional types most commonly needed by grassroots groups. You need a lawyer if you're going into a regulatory hearing or into court, or if you're thinking about incorporating your group. Lawyers are, of course, useful in many other situations, since some of them are familiar with the ropes of power you're tugging at. Experts with certification or professional licenses in various fields can be indispensable in presenting testimony at hearings. (For more on the need for lawyers and expert witnesses in hearings, see Step 14, "Handling Hearings.")

When looking for the right professionals, ask your allies for advice. Capable lawyers willing to work hard for low pay are often found in public-interest law firms, though they may be found anywhere. Experts with the proper technical knowledge, sympathy for your cause, and (very important!) economic independence of the industry you're opposing are almost always found in colleges and universities.

Try to anticipate your needs for expertise well in advance. And if you're paying for professional help, be sure to get the terms down clearly in writing.

11.

Your Action Plan

Develop an action plan that will carry you through to victory.

Be sure you plan to *win*! Too many groups put all their time and money on one "crucial" decision — for example, the decision of a hearing board — and have no idea what to do if the decision goes against them. Remember the "three routes" to victory outlined by the Committee to Save French Pete: the administrative, the legislative, and the legal. If you can't win through executive or regulatory agency decision, and you can't get a law passed, then you should consider legal action.

Often your opposition is frozen into an inflexible strategy: they have to plod with their plan from review step to permit application, on a channel tightly prescribed by law. You, however, have a nearly endless range of tactics to draw upon, limited only by proscriptive laws, good taste, and your vital need to attract rather than repel public support. Next to righteousness, flexibility is the main natural advantage a grassroots environmental group has over its opposition. Use it!

Seize the Initiative!

Make every effort to go on the offensive, force the opposition to respond to your moves, and in general get control of the forum and the timetable. This, of course, is exactly what the opposition will be trying to do to you. The side which has most control over the sequence of events and arenas of action has an advantage.

There are many ways to get the initiative. You may challenge the opposition to debate, make strong (but true) public charges to which they must respond, call for hearings before friendly or neutral public bodies, launch a legislative campaign, or simply carry out a campaign to inform and arouse the public.

At a symposium on the Mad River in Humboldt County, California, a Corps of Engineers colonel let slip that the Corps would be glad to have workshops on a dam they proposed to build in Butler Valley, *if* the environmentalists there would organize the workshops. The dam opponents leapt at the chance; and the seven workshops held on various aspects of the dam, during which much expert testimony against the dam was presented, caused the Corps much embarrassment. The Corps could not control the proceedings, and in the end agreed to totally revamp their environmental statement. It was a far cry from the typical Corps hearing as described by Harold Silverstein of John

Dewey High School in Brooklyn: "They're very polite, they listen, they tape everything, and they never respond."

Flow Chart

Flow charts simply show in graphic form how your campaign will unfold in the months (years?) ahead, with predictable events marked, along with what you should have done by then. Such a chart can help you get people and resources together when they're needed. A flow chart can prevent you from being surprised by the predictable — there will be enough unpredictable surprises to handle!

12.

Who Does What?

Match people with tasks that suit their abilities and desires.

Once people hear about your grassroots effort, they're going to get in touch with you and ask: "What can I do to help?" By all means you should have something for them to do! It may be anything from writing a letter or coming to the marsh clean-up, to researching and writing an environmental study. It is people *doing* things that makes a grassroots organization. A person's commitment is increased dramatically when that person actually does something for the cause.

The most subtle and difficult tasks facing leaders of grassroots groups are matching the right person with the right task. If the leader is too bossy and insistent, the workers rebel — you just can't force anybody to go out and save the world. If the leader is too easygoing, as is very often the case, then the leader ends up doing all the work

— while dutifully praising the tremendous popular movement that made it all possible and the many persons who gave selflessly!

13.

Elan Vital

Maintain high spirits in the group, and confidence in ultimate victory.

Leo Tolstoy called it "the spirit of the army." If you have it, never mind that you don't have anything else; you'll get what you need to win as you go along. If you don't have it, you might have the world's greatest army and still lose a war against a band of determined peasants.

Spirit simply can't be bought, or hired, though you can hire a lawyer or expert who *shares* your enthusiasm. That's why those who would use our natural resources for personal profit must spend incredible amounts of money on advertising — it takes a lot of gaudy imagery to disguise that hollow motive at the core.

A formula for spirit also is not something to be prescribed in a grassroots action manual. There are a few things you might keep in mind, however, as you endeavor to spark and keep alive that necessary *elan vital*.

To win a tough environmental battle, you have to *really* want what you're fighting for — badly enough to sacrifice considerable chunks of your personal time, resources, and emotional stamina. The best fighters for wilderness preservation are intimately concerned with the area they're trying to preserve, and would feel a personal loss if that area were destroyed. If you don't *feel* your commitment, think twice before you take up the standard of an issue.

Ego tripping kills! The cancer of the grassroots environmental movement is use of the cause to advance personal aims. If people think they're being exploited not by their opponents but by their cohorts, the group can come apart in an exceedingly nasty manner. The best way to to evade this situation is by really believing in what you're doing, so much so that your goal naturally comes first.

Take a positive attitude; be *for* something, even if your *raison d'etre* is to stop something. Be for beautiful river valleys, rather than simply against dams; for clean air, land, and water, not just against coal-burning power plants. The eagerness of people to rally around causes which merely decry environmental destruction has diminished greatly since Earth Day 1970. Nearly everybody knows what is going down now. What people gather around are creative efforts, rays of light which lead to a better world.

And don't forget the nice little touches — the get-togethers to celebrate victory, commiserate over defeat, or keep spirits up as the fight grinds into its fifth year. Give credit where credit is due, and sometimes where it isn't due. Many people find a sense of warmth and community in the common effort to preserve and improve our planet's environment; keeping this neighborly attitude alive makes what could be just a tough grind into a rare pleasure.

"Never Entertain the Thought"

A striking case of persistence in the face of adversity is the effort to prevent Interstate 40, a freeway, from being run through Overton Park in Memphis, Tennessee. From 1956, when the route was first proposed, to the time of this writing, a doughty band of Memphis citizens has been able to prevent the Memphis city government, downtown business interests, and the state highway department from pushing through plans to bifurcate one of

America's greatest urban parks with a six-lane expressway.

The main galvanizing force which has kept the preservation effort alive so long is the tremendous beauty and value of that which would be lost. The 340-acre Overton Park offers a wide array of recreational facilities: a nine-hole golf course, a baseball field, a zoo, an outdoor theatre, nature trails, a bridle path, an art gallery, an art academy, playgrounds, a small lake, formal gardens, and picnic areas. In addition, it has a majestic near-virgin hardwood forest of a type which is quite rare. Some two million people visit Overton every year. The effect a freeway would have on the ambiance of the park, as well as on the health of people, plants, and animals there, would be catastrophic.

To highway promoters, the catastrophe is that the Citizens to Preserve Overton Park, Inc. (incorporated in 1969) has been able to prevent a traffic mainline from being run through the park to downtown Memphis. Opposition to to park preservationists has been quite vituperative, and has included numerous threats (and some acts) of physical and economic intimidation. Many times the effort to save the park has seemed hopeless. Two expressway-wide strips of land cleared of all structures run up to the east and west sides of Overton Park, and land for the highway through the park is already owned by the state.

Since December 1969, the efforts to stop the freeway from going through Overton Park have centered around legal action based on Section 4(f) of the Transportation Act of 1966. In March 1971, the United States Supreme Court ruled that Section 4(f) did indeed bar the freeway, as proposed, from being run through Overton Park (for details on this decision, see "A Plain and Explicit Bar" in Step 16, "Your Day in Court"). The legal action has called for tremendous effort on the part of the Citizens to

Dr. Arlo Smith, president of Citizens to Preserve Overton Park, Inc., in the park's magnificent hardwood stand.

Mrs. Anona Stoner, secretary of Citizens to Preserve Overton Park, Inc., in her home-based office.

Preserve Overton Park, as over the years they have raised money and kept up enthusiasm through appeal after appeal. Despite the Supreme Court decision, advocates of the freeway continue to try every means they can think of to get the expressway run through the park, and at this writing are pushing for federal legislation to get the job done.

When asked what had kept the Citizens group inspired for so long, long-time member Mrs. Sara N. Hines replied, "By faith in God, in what we're doing, and in each other. When we've had to raise large sums of money over the past five years of litigation, it has taken the courage and belief that it could be done. Some of us might falter sometimes at a new challenge, but when the decision to go on was made, everyone would work to do his part."

These are simple truths, simple and powerful. Another expression of the secret of the spirit to persevere comes from Mrs. Anona Stoner, secretary of the Citizens to Preserve Overton Park, who has been active in the group since 1964. Mrs. Stoner, who says she is now "at the edge of my 70's," looks deceptively tiny and frail. The impression that she might be weak vanishes once one looks into her steady, determined eyes, and hears the amazing command of detail she has as she recalls the long, tortuous story of the freeway and the park. When asked if she believes the preserva- · tionists will ultimately win, she briskly replies, "I have never entertained any other thought. Never lose sight of your goal. Do not deviate, and you cannot compromise."

14.

Handling Hearings

Know the different types of public hearings, how best to testify in them, and how to use them to further your cause.

Anyone who has glanced through the stories in this book knows that public hearings are central to the grassroots environmental movement. Often the first public thing a group does is demand a hearing on their issue. This demand publicizes the issue. If the hearing is not granted, then the institution in question is "insensitive, secretive." If the hearing is held, then an event worthy of news coverage is created, and the group's point of view becomes one of two sides of a public question.

There are three types of public hearings: legislative, administrative, and regulatory. Legislative hearings, before congressional committees, boards of supervisors, city councils, and the like, are generally less technical and more philosophical in nature than the other types. Administrative hearings — Forest Service, planning commission, state board hearings, and so on — generally are more technical, with expert testimony playing an important role. Hearings before regulatory agencies with quasi-judicial authority often resemble courtroom procedure, with strictly defined issues, attorneys for both sides, and cross-examination of witnesses.

Common errors made by grassroots groups are not preparing expert testimony for administrative hearings, and not retaining legal counsel for regulatory agency hearings. Peter Smith of Citizens Against Wildlife Wonderland lost the first administrative hearings on the issue, because he was trying to handle all the testifying himself. The Northern Plains Resource Council, trying to save some money, appeared before a state regulatory agency without legal counsel, and lost a power line right-of-way case.

If a hearing on your issue is scheduled, you should choose a hearing coordinator. Psych out the whole situation. Why is the public body holding the hearing — to improve its image, to get a balanced view, because it legally has to, because you (with public pressure) forced it to? How big is the hearing room? Will there be seating for your supporters? What is the order of testimony, and time allotted to each speaker; and how does one get to testify? Should you concentrate on colorful statements that the press will eat up, strong expert testimony, a large number of brief statements showing broad support for your side, or a combination of these?

At the first hearing on Occidental Petroleum's bid to drill for oil in Los Angeles, Shirley Solomon of No Oil learned an important lesson: proponents of measures normally speak first at hearings, and often are prepared to monopolize enough time to wear out reporters and carry through afternoon press deadlines. Shirley had written parodies of Occidental's plans; they were sung outside the hearing to gain the attention of the press. At other hearings, Shirley held press conferences in the corridors. But, it is important to devise releases so that the lead statements are presented immediately. Then, a reporter with an early deadline can leave and yet report your position accurately.

All hearings should be seen as opportunities to advance your cause. Even the most hostile hearing board gives you a forum to which you can bring throngs of supporters, and where you can quotably declaim against your enemies and in favor of righteousness (your side). However, it is rarely, if ever, advisable to antagonize the hearing officers themselves. Environmental groups often labor under the illusion that all government officials are insensitive bureaucrats at best, and are surprised when decisions in their favor come down. If your testimony is strong and presented respectfully, you may well be favorably surprised.

CYA (Certainly You Appeal!)

If you are not satisfied with the formal decision handed down by a public body which has held hearings in your case, file a formal appeal of that decision before legal time limitations expire. **At first glance this seems obvious, but be careful: it is not uncommon for a public agency to formally decide against you, while its officials make informal assurances or give advice that might lull you into overlooking your legal appeal rights.**

After the supervisor of Willamette National Forest in Oregon decided to allow clearcutting in the French Pete Valley in 1969, Dick Noyes of the Committee to Save French Pete went to see Regional Forester Charles Connaughton to see what might be done to stop the logging. Connaughton tried to talk Noyes into going directly to the head of the Forest Service with his appeal.

"He was trying to head off a formal appeal," Noyes says. "We had just 90 days to formally appeal the supervisor's decision. We decided to file our appeal despite Connaughton's advice. This got their attorney all upset. Then we realized they'd been planning to go ahead with their cutting program all along." Noyes went ahead with a direct informal appeal to the chief of the Forest Service, which got him nowhere; but the formal appeal, filed in accordance with Forest Service regulations, set a process in motion which ultimately stymied logging of that beautiful valley in the Oregon Cascades. (For details, see "In Love with French Pete.")

Something similar happened to the Committee for the Improvement of the Alameda in its effort to keep a street in Menlo Park, California from being widened. At a crucial meeting of the board of supervisors, the board reached an informal compromise on the street plans with the Committee. The board then explained that parliamentary procedure required them to formally override the Committee's protest to their street-widening plans, so the compromise could be implemented. Everybody on the Committee went home happy, thinking that their front yards had been saved.

Everybody, that is, except Committee lawyer Ted Carlstrom. He realized that, as Claire Dedrick puts it, "what was binding on the board was not their agreement with us. What was binding was their resolution to override our protest."

The Committee had 30 days in which to file a lawsuit contesting the formal board decision, after which time the statute of limitations would close their avenue of appeal. They agonized about the possibility that a lawsuit would muck up their compromise with the board, finally deciding, as Claire says, "We are the public. Our only legal recourse was to file that lawsuit. We weren't assuming the board would be dishonest, but we'd have been irresponsible if we didn't protect our people every way possible."

The Committee filed the lawsuit, which infuriated the county attorney. "They would have gone ahead with their original road design and every bloody thing we had done all year would have been lost," Claire recalls.

Mobilizing Your Forces

Even the most technical public hearing is influenced by the throngs that pack the hall (or by the hollow emptiness which resounds through the chambers). Make sure your hearings are well attended by your supporters, that your supporters are polite at the hearings, and that the hearing officers know that the well-behaved mob is backing your side.

Sometimes it is obvious that the crowd is with you. If it isn't obvious, have your people wear something that will identify them. When the Tennessee Valley Authority held a hearing on their proposed 14-dam complex near Hendersonville, North Carolina, opponents of

the dam showed up wearing international orange kerchiefs with the initials of their group (Upper French Broad Defense Association) on them. On color television the hearing looked like a sea of orange. Public opposition at the hearing was so overwhelming that the TVA dropped their dam plans. (For the whole story, see "Tennessee Valley Authority Blues.")

The Rockridge Community Planning Council (RCPC) of Oakland, California could turn out upwards of 400 Rockridge residents at hearings which led to the rezoning of their neighborhood. The RCPC has the support of a local newspaper, which would prominently announce the hearings. They would also distribute mimeographed leaflets door-to-door, and post notices on utility poles. Free transportation via bus was provided to distant hearings.

Shortly before major hearings, RCPC block workers would visit people on their blocks and urge them to attend. "There is nothing like personal contact to make people feel needed, and that their presence at a hearing can affect the future of their neighborhood" says block worker Eleanor Lewallen of the RCPC. "Besides, it's nice to visit your neighbors."

Pedigreed Expertise

"One of the problems citizens encounter in public hearings or in court cases is that expert testimony is required, and 'expert' means possessing some sort of certification or a professional engineer's license."

So writes the Poricy Park Citizens Committee, a group in Middletown, New Jersey, which is devoted to protecting 300 undeveloped acres of land along Poricy Brook there. They sent us an excellent write-up of the lessons they had learned in their years of conservation effort. Their report contained the following experience they had, which taught them something about hearings and pedigreed expertise:

Here's a good example of how to use newspaper advertising to help get people to attend hearings. It was prepared by the Friends of Santa Paula Creek of Santa Paula, California, in an effort to prevent the U. S. Army Corps of Engineers from channelizing that creek. Though they generated a lot of support, the Friends failed to convince either the Corps or the county board of supervisors that they were right. So they hired a creative attorney, one "who was able to put together a viable legal case and marshal the supportive services he needed for such," as Laurie Chisler of the Friends puts it. They sued the Corps, challenging its environmental impact statement (EIS) on the proposed project. At this stage the Friends' suit is successful, though an appeal by the Corps is possible and preparation of the new Corps EIS will have to be monitored by the Friends.

Note the elements of this advertisement. It's striking but factual, and presents the main issues briefly. An appeal for funds is included. Should the hearing announcement be more prominent?

This sort of thing reached an absurd level when the Colts Glen developer brought in a (paid) professional engineer to testify at the Township Committee review of his plans. Our committee's attorney showed the engineer the photo of the gully included with this brochure [submitted by the developer], one of several gullies created by preliminary grading. The engineer claimed that the gullies were there prior to construction. At this point, we triumphantly produced a detailed aerial photograph of the area taken for the Monmouth County Planning Board. The certified date of the photograph established that it was taken just prior to grading. It clearly showed that no gullies existed. The engineer was able to evade this by stating that he was not expert at aerial photo interpretation.

For a number of reasons, the township denied the builder's subdivision, and the builder sued the township. At that trial, the issue of the gullies came up. The judge ruled that the builder could not be held responsible for the damage, since the citizens had failed to supply expert proof that the gullies did not exist before construction began. In other words, we had failed to pay $200 to have a professional aerial photograph reader state what was obvious to anyone looking at the picture.

If this sounds cynical, it is because we have repeatedly seen intelligent lay testimony swept aside because professional credentials were lacking. We have no objection to professional testimony; our complaint is that it is necessary to hire professionals to state the obvious. But until the rules change, *conservationists need to be sure that they secure their own professionals to neutralize the testimony from the other side.*

One brief statement of fact from a pedigreed expert is often worth a thousand impassioned words extolling the beauties of nature. Hearing officers *need* those certified statements in order to justify and defend their decisions.

Unfortunately, there are precious few sources of expertise like the marine biology classes of John Dewey High School in Brooklyn, New York. The John Dewey classes make ecological studies of marshlands in their area, providing data which has led to conservation victories in many hearings. (For the full story, see "John Dewey's Giant-Killers.") It seems that more high school and college biology instructors could work with their students to provide much-needed field data for conservationists. Right?

15.

Getting a Law Passed

If there ought to be a law and isn't one, you should consider getting one passed.

It is in the hurly-burly world of legislative politics that the fate of many a river, forest, and mountain is settled. Do not be awed by lawmakers, nor dismayed by their practices; an ordinary citizen can master the techniques of getting a law passed. Legislators, especially the ones that represent your area, are eminently approachable. What's more, they *need* people like you. "No public officials can read and digest all information that comes before them," notes Lorraine Campbell of Kentucky Lake Environmental and Recreation Association. "So they rely on the analysis of other people. If you have a group willing to give them serious, pertinent information, they are tickled to death to get it."

Winners of environmental legislative battles often couple dogged persistence with the ability to strike a favorable compromise. The unyielding, uncompromising approach which is useful or even vital in other situations usually leaves one uncorrupted but empty-handed in the halls of legislatures. If you can get your *principle* enacted, you can come back next session and work on the details that might get lost in the crush of log-rolling.

A central fact about lawmakers is that votes are their lifeblood. None can afford to push far ahead of public opinion. Your job is only partly to convince legislators that your law is good policy. You must also convince legislators that their constituents are at least neutral about your proposal, and preferably that those constituents are clamoring for passage of the law.

Steps to Legislative Power

Editor's Note: The following steps to legislative power are based on an article by Robert Satter in People Power, *put out by the League of Women Voters of Nevada. Mr. Satter is a lawyer and former member of the Connecticut legislature. Although we've digested and rewritten it, direct quotations are from Mr. Satter.*

Step 1: Distill from your notions of good legislation a proposal that is both feasible and specific.

"Occasionally, you must limit your proposal to less than your conception of the perfect law.... The important thing is to get the principle, the essence of the idea enacted. You can come back in succeeding sessions to improve the details in the direction of your long-range goal."

Step 2: Try to commit both political parties to your specific measure at the time they are making up their campaign platforms.

"The parties are never more amenable than at the start of a political campaign. Their platform committees will seriously consider almost any proposal which has the support of a substantial group of voters. The wise approach is to draft the specific measure your or-ganization favors and then try to get the precise operative language into the party platform. Moreover, get it into the platforms of *both* parties."

Step 3: Have your bill drafted clearly and accurately.

"Draftsmanship is so important that even if your group is operating on a limited budget, it is worth hiring an experienced craftsman to do the job right."

Step 4: Get proper sponsorship for your measure.

You want an active sponsor who will fight for your bill all the way through. A wide range of co-sponsors is desirable, including if possible the leader of the majority party. If your bill has reference to a specific area within a legislator's district (such as a wilderness preservation bill), the sponsorship of the legislator from that district is invaluable; legislative courtesy often gives legislators great (or even absolute) power over many bills specifically affecting their districts.

Step 5: Early in the session endeavor to commit individual legislators to your measure.

"At the outset, before tensions mount, legislators are easy to approach. They are flattered to have constituents discuss matters with them and enlist their support. Moreover, they are more likely to have an open mind and to consider the bill on its merits than they might later in the session when party pressures may build up around your measure. A firm commitment obtained early from a legislator generally will be honored when the vote is taken."

Step 6: Be fully prepared for the public hearing on your bill.

"The first rule is to make your presentation relevant to the standards a committee applies in deciding a bill. *These are: What is the public interest? Who will benefit? Who will be hurt? What other states have similar laws and how have they worked out? Which politically significant groups favor and which oppose the bill? How much will it cost?*"

These appeals for letters were distributed door-to-door by the Rockridge Community Planning Council of Oakland, California, and got excellent response.

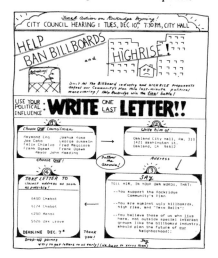

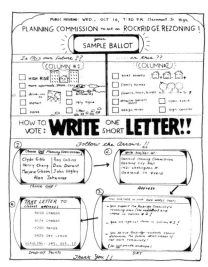

Step 7: Work with a legislator on the committee deciding your bill, and respect his advice.

A friendly legislator on the committee which is deciding your bill is your best advisor on the total political situation within which your measure exists, and on how you should respond to that situation.

Step 8: Keep in touch with the status of your bill right up until the time of the vote. Take nothing for granted.

'The most common hazard a bill faces is that it will be bartered away for a vote on a major party matter. . . . The most tortuous thing that can happen to a bill is for it to be amended. This is the method of flank attack used by the opposition when it cannot frontally defeat your measure. Often, it is done with unctuous solicitude. The amendment may be the disembowelling type, which leaves only the meaningless form of the bill. Or it may be the pie-in-the-sky type which purports to improve the bill beyond your fondest hopes, but utterly destroys its chances of passage. . . .

"It is helpful if your legislative friends can arrange to have the vote on your measure come up late, but not too late, in the session. . . . Later in the session, as the number of bills ready to be voted on mounts and the leaders become concerned whether the legislature will complete its work before adjournment, the consideration of bills becomes more casual and the recommendations of committees are more readily accepted; many measures are put on a non-controversial calendar and passed without debate. Obviously, this is the time you want your bill to come up. . . .

"At the time your measure comes up for debate, have a delegation of your group in the gallery. Their presence will not only give your legislator friends the audience they love to play to, but will also give them the moral encouragement to fight even harder for your bill."

Step 9: After your bill has passed one branch of the legislature, follow it through the other and into the governor's office.

"If a veto is in the wind, you can let the governor know of the strong sentiments of your group by letter, by a delegation to his office, and by newspaper publicity. . . .

"After your bill has triumphed over the legislative snares and perils and miraculously has been enacted into law, there is one more thing to do: send letters of thanks to all those who were responsible for its passage. You would be surprised to know how pleased politicians are to receive letters of thanks. They get far more abuse than praise."

How to Approach a Legislator

The best approach is direct personal contact with the legislators; but letters, telephone calls, and newspaper publicity can be effective.

A buttonholed legislator is like a fish on the hook. He may get away, but he is going to have to do some wriggling. A legislator should be approached by the citizens of the town or district from which he has been elected. Although legislators will listen politely to anyone, they give eager attention to voters from their own area.

If your group cannot talk to the legislators personally, then you have to get your message to them by mail or telephone or through the newspaper. The most telling letter campaign in the 1959 session of the Connecticut legislature was of billboards on limited access highways. Every legislator received a blizzard of letters on the issue. It was the massiveness of the attack, the sheer weight of numbers, that won.

However, a few well-written and sincere letters can be just as effective. Since a legislator receives a great deal of mail each day, his attention span is short. Letters should be brief, relevant, and factual. They should also be original. The same form letter sent by members of an organization is resented as an insult to the intelligence of the legislator. The first few telegrams sent to legislators are impressive but later in the session they are not worth the cost.

Direct telephone calls to legislators can also be persuasive. I remember with amusement a telephone campaign organized by the members of a large cemetery association in opposition to a bill which would have prohibited cemeteries from selling tombstones. The barrage started suddenly one afternoon, and for two days the phones of legislators didn't stop ringing. The calls were made by local voters, who were sincerely outraged at the bill. The Connecticut House of Representatives buried the measure — without a tombstone.

Favorable newspaper publicity on your bill is always helpful. Legislators regularly read newspapers, first, to look for their names, and, secondly, to find out what's going on in the legislature. This type of publicity should never be left to chance. The best approach is to seek out the capital reporter covering your type of study and educate him on the merits of your bill. *Above all, if one of your group makes a public statement, get it in writing and hand it to the reporters.* [italics added] The mangled newspaper quote is a despairing experience, and almost never reparable. — *Robert Satter, former member of the Connecticut legislature, in* People Power, *published by the League of Women Voters of Nevada.*

16.

Your Day in Court

If you believe an action you oppose would break a law, and no administrative remedies can be obtained, you should consider legal action.

Is anybody breaking a law? Recent federal and state environmental protection laws have greatly extended legal protection of our natural resources. (See "Putting Teeth in the Law.") There are also a host of other state and local laws — zoning ordinances, health codes, and many others — which often apply to environmental cases. Natural areas have been preserved because they contain endangered species which are legally protected, historic sites, or Indian graves. "If you look long enough," says Jane Gibson of the Kentucky Lake Environmental and Recreation Association, "you can find a law that protects any piece of land," and she's not exaggerating very much.

Naturally, if you're considering legal action *the first thing to get is a good lawyer.* The ideal lawyer is philosophically in tune with you, doesn't charge much, and is creative. Such a lawyer doesn't need to be spoon-fed his case by you (though you should support him or her with research); he or she can take what you have and *make* a winning case. You may have to try a few before settling on the right legal counsel, so don't commit yourself too early.

In many cases, you must exhaust all attempts at administrative remedies before going to court. Otherwise, the judge will toss your case out until you do so, and you'll have a court loss on your record.

As early as possible, you should start collecting a legal defense fund. The Committee to Save French Pete in Eugene, Oregon, has been putting aside money for years (held for them by the Sierra Club Legal Defense Fund), to pay for a lawsuit which may never have to be filed. You should also consider incorporating (with the advice of your good lawyer), to protect your personal assets. And if you're suing a private party, prepare your psyche for getting sued yourself, as sometimes happens.

It is said that "everybody gets his day in court." Anyone, whether on your side or the opposition's, who can't get any public official to listen to him can file a lawsuit and get initial consideration of his case. But, you won't do yourself or the environmental movement any good if you file suit merely to harass, or delay. But if you have a genuine cause of action, don't be shy — sue!

Occasionally the belief that a law is on their side leads environmentalists to ignore seeking public support for their cause. This is a dead-end attitude: there are a thousand ways to evade or weaken a law or court judgment that citizens oppose, and legislatures can make new laws. You should make every effort to convince people that what you want is good for them, and not get cast as part of a system that imposes its will from on high.

"A Plain and Explicit Bar"

Often a law doesn't mean anything until someone asserts his rights under it by becoming a plaintiff in a court case. Grassroots environmental activists often play this role. It's generally a fairly expensive role, and often the "day in court" drags on for years. If the legal principle at stake is precedent-setting, legal assistance often can be had from national conservation organizations. At the end of the process, the grassroots group may not only win its case, but will contribute to making the law of the land

a little tougher on environmental abusers.

A case in point is the story of Citizens to Preserve Overton Park, Inc. of Memphis, Tennessee. In December 1969, having exhausted every out-of-court legal means of preventing a federal freeway from being run through Overton Park in Memphis, the Citizens group sued Secretary of Transportation John Volpe in U. S. District Court. The Citizens case alleged that the freeway project was in violation of Section 4(f) of the Transportation Act of 1966, which reads in part: "The Secretary [of Transportation] shall not approve any program or project which requires the use of any publicly owned land from a public park . . . unless (1) there is no feasible and prudent alternative to the use of such land and (2) such program includes all possible planning to minimize harm to such park. . . ."

The Citizens group kept losing and appealing their case as bulldozers literally gnawed at the borders of the park. The case reached the U.S. Supreme Court, which granted a certiorari hearing. By that time a number of national conservation groups were supporting the redoubtable Citizens to Preserve Overton Park.

On March 2, 1971, the Supreme Court overthrew the decision of the lower courts. The decision by Justice Thurgood Marshall interpreted Section 4(f) for the first time. "This language is a plain and explicit bar to the use of federal funds for construction of highways through parks — only the most unusual situations are exempted," Justice Marshall wrote for the Court. Justice Marshall noted that parks are obviously the easiest pieces of land to put highways through. "But the very existence of the statutes," he wrote, "indicates that protection of parkland was to be given paramount importance."

At this writing the Citizens group is still legally battling efforts to run the freeway through Overton Park. Thus far, proponents of the freeway have not been able to get around the Supreme Court's "plain and explicit" decision about how to read Section 4(f). And that decision has protected a lot of other parks throughout the country. (For another perspective on the Overton Park story, see "Never Entertain the Thought," in Step 14, "Elan Vital.")

17.

Taking It to the People

If administrative, legislative, and legal processes are of no avail, you should consider taking your issue directly to the public through an initiative or referendum.

On the worthy theory that in a democracy power resides directly in the people, a number of states and localities provide that citizens can initiate and vote on a law (an initiative), and that they can — under certain circumstances — vote on a legislative proposal referred to them by the government (a referendum). Initiative and referendum campaigns are true last resorts, giving voice to the majority (and saying something about the responsiveness of the government in power). They are generally difficult, and consume a lot of time, energy, and often money. They are also becoming an increasingly potent tool of the grassroots environmental movement.

In *The Grass Roots Primer* are accounts of a referendum campaign ("How Are You Going to Fight Blackberry Jam?"), a local initiative campaign ("Second Thoughts on Future Power"), and a statewide initiative campaign ("Thirty Thousand Atomic Bombs Can't Be Wrong"). All three of these campaigns were very well done, and if you're thinking of taking your case to the people you might get some tips from these stories.

Both initiative and referendum campaigns focus on getting votes, so your best advice is likely to come from people with experience as campaign managers, precinct organizers, and the like. As in all ballot campaigns, timing is very important. Note also that an initiative effort is really *two* campaigns: first there's the push to get the measure written, and to get enough signatures on petitions to put it on the ballot; then there's the problem of getting a majority of voters to approve it in the election.

Initiative and referendum campaigns are quite exhilarating, according to those who have been through them. There's the excitement of an election campaign, and the thrill of taking what you consider a great social issue directly to people in the street. "The fun part of the whole thing is going out and getting signatures," notes Meladee Martin of People for Responsible Energy Sources, which managed a successful statewide initiative campaign in Colorado. "There's a real horror of going out and asking somebody for something. Once people got over that, they'd come back and say, 'this is the greatest thing I've ever done in my life!' We got an incredibly positive response from people."

Initiative Petition Campaign Checklist

Editor's Note: Here's a checklist for initiative petition campaigns developed by People for Rational Energy Sources (PRES) of Denver, Colorado. PRES got a measure on the Colorado ballot to prohibit underground nuclear blasts unless they had prior voter approval. This measure was approved by Colorado voters on November 5, 1974.

I. The Initiative

1. Study your state's initiative or referendum process as outlined in the State Constitution. (Not all states have such processes provided for.)

2. Know your legal boundaries of action. Consult with a lawyer or lawyers to help you interpret your state's provisions.

3. Find out from the Secretary of State's office the number of signatures needed to place the initiative on the ballot and also the amount of time allowed to obtain the signatures.

4. Begin to set up a budget and raise funds.

5. The wording of the initiative is very important. Arrange at least three meetings with your lawyer and everyone in the core group to make sure the intent is legal and clearly stated.

6. Ask knowledgeable legislators and professionals for their review of the initiative.

7. Route the final wording of the initiative through all appropriate state offices. (In Colorado there is a legislative drafting office; approval by this office means the wording of the initiative is not in conflict with existing laws or the constitution and can't be challenged.)

8. Apply for the ballot title for your initiative with the Secretary of State.

9. Review *carefully* the wording of the ballot title. This is what the voters will read when they vote, and it should represent the meaning of the initiative as succinctly and clearly as possible. If you are not satisfied with the ballot title, go to the Secretary of State and ask for the appropriate changes. Be prepared to state *why* these changes must be made.

10. Be prepared to print the petitions as soon as the ballot title is approved.

11. Each petition should have a cover sheet which has instructions for circulators of the petitions. In addition to *complete instructions,* the cover sheet should also contain (1) the address where the petitions should be returned; (2) the date (at *least* 5 days before the actual deadline); and (3) the phone number of the headquarters. These three items should be in bold print and in a very conspicuous place.

II. Signature Gathering

1. Concurrent with planning the initiative and printing the petitions, there should be an ongoing effort to contact every kind of organization to inquire *how* to make the petition available to their membership.

2. Arrange to leave petitions at various organization offices (schools, churches, environmental groups, etc.). Find a person to be in charge of answering questions about the initiative and to record who takes petitions for circulation.

3. Arrange with individual store managers to gather signatures at designated places and times in front of their stores. *Every* effort must be made to make these personal contacts as it is increasingly hard to get permission to petition. *Do not* go to a store without asking permission; store managers will often harass you even if you are within the limits of the law.

4. Arrange for booths in shopping centers.

5. Keep a card file on every person who has a petition, with that person's address, phone, and date (s)he took petition. Have volunteers call these people regularly (at *least* once a month) to give them encouragement, to supply ideas for places to circulate petitions, and to ask about their progress. This is a *very important* way of keeping in touch with the people who can help you the most in this phase and who will become your staunch person-to-person campaigners. This process is also very good for estimating how the signature gathering is progressing and how much last minute effort there must be.

6. Make "sandwich boards" that state the purpose of the petition and which have a shelf on which people can sign. This is effectively used at busy downtown street corners, fairs, and in front of fast-food restaurants, concerts, museums, libraries, bars, sports events, and churches. (For petitioning at museums, permission must be obtained from city departments.)

7. Approach every person as positively as possible. Be sure to allow people to read the entire text of the initiative if they wish, and be prepared to answer any questions. Avoid getting into extended arguments with people.

8. Send mail notices of a potluck, rally, or some other function about halfway through the signature gathering campaign so people can bring completed petitions and meet you personally.

9. One week before the deadline stated on the cover sheet, call everyone who has a petition to ask them to send it in, no matter how few signatures.

18.

Turning a Buck

Draw up a budget for your effort, and determine where you will raise that much money.

If a grassroots group has little or no fund-raising capacity, the core group members must constantly pay for things out of their own pockets. This puts a millstone around the neck of the whole effort. Yet too many groups tend to ignore budgeting and finances until the bills start piling up.

Financial requirements vary widely. Some groups need little more than postage, office supplies, minimal printing, and telephone payments. Others must hire professional advertising agencies, experts, lawyers, or staff. The main thing is to figure out what you need as soon as possible.

Fund-raising methods also differ greatly. To start, you should appeal for donations in every leaflet you put out and speech you give. This is often done as part of an appeal for membership. Most groups don't charge too much for membership — two to five dollars per year, generally — but have categories for "sustaining members" and the like for more substantial donors. **Members are worth more than money, so membership dues should be kept down.**

The most no-nonsense method of raising money is direct assessment, which is often appropriate if a neighborhood or community is facing an environmental threat. The Committee for the Improvement of the Alameda, formed in Menlo Park, California to prevent the widening of a street, levied such an assessment the night it was formed. "We assessed each household $20 and everyone paid right up," says Claire Dedrick of the Committee. "We must have walked out of there with $1,800 in cash. And except for a couple of big gifts later on, that's how we raised all our money. A few of us went around door to door later and collected from the ones who couldn't come to the meeting. We covered the whole length of the project — almost three miles — and for two blocks in either direction."

For donations of substance the personal touch is required. The Concerned Citizens Committee of Humboldt County, California raised $8,000 for its referendum campaign against a Corps of Engineers dam by first sending out solicitations through the mail, then following up with personal phone calls from Roberta Allen. Members of Citizens Against Wildlife Wonderland collected $4,000 by going door-to-door in their small Vermont town and explaining who they were and what they were doing.

Foundations, wealthy individuals, and national conservation organizations will be more likely to favor your cause with their cash if you have attracted a large number of smaller contributors.

Fund-raising events of all sorts may be planned for their spirit-raising as well as money-raising qualities. The main concern with such events is to plan so you don't expend more in time and money than you take in. A delightful potluck or crafts festival that breaks even financially may be a winner in terms of *elan vital*.

Don't let initial absence of funds prevent you from launching your grassroots effort. Some great victories have been won on a shoestring. It costs a lot less to defend truth than it does to insult it, and if you're right you'll get by.

19.

Who Benefits and Who Pays?

In developing the issues in your campaign, focus on costs and benefits, with the goal of proving the social good of what you advocate.

Frank Ragsdale, a Memphis, Tennessee, traffic engineer, once said that advocating any expressway plan because of its benefits to the construction trades was like advocating a tornado for Memphis because it would create jobs. Again and again, we hear the argument that we have to destroy our environment in order to create jobs. If that premise is accepted, then issues are drawn in terms of "trade-offs" between "economy" and "ecology." It is as if we can't make a living

without destroying the household of life.

It is vital that you analyze *all* of the costs of what you are opposing, and all the benefits of what you favor. Proponents of dams, power plants, strip mines, development projects, and the like always claim that their programs will bring more taxes and more jobs to a locality. What they ignore is the impact their program will have on the community in areas such as schools, roads, water and sewage, housing, and transportation. You should carefully research these areas of "secondary impact," and sharply question your opponents about just how many jobs they'll create, how much tax they'll pay, and what they plan to do to help the community provide needed services.

Public bodies are showing more willingness lately to put money values on wildlife, recreation, and other environmental values formerly without price tags. For example, the International Joint Commission estimated that the recreational use value of Canada's Skagit Valley would drop $1 million if it was flooded by a proposed dam in the United States (see "Damming Up Canada" for details on this, and for an account of some very good issue research). Many of the values that environmentalists fight for — spiritual, aesthetic, preservation of complex ecosystems and endangered species, among others — have no money value now, and perhaps never should. But, our milieu of economic struggle being what it is, official money valuations of "intangibles" can be useful in gaining public support.

Take the offensive on the economic issues. If it is true, as it often is, that your opponent's project means that a special interest will benefit while the public (present and future) pays, make this clear in no uncertain terms. Keep your opponent busy trying to explain why society should give him something of inestimable value — a part of our natural environment.

One Hundred Years of Jobs

As this section was being written, the news announced that President Gerald Ford had vetoed the bill which would regulate strip mining because he said it would cause loss of jobs. That bill has involved one of the greatest efforts of environmental legislative action in U.S. history. It would simply ensure that our land would be restored to something similar to its original state after the shovels had chewed it up, and that valuable areas that cannot be restored would not be stripped.

We wonder what unregulated strip mining now will mean in terms of jobs a hundred years hence. If the Northern Plains continues to be stripped, for example, the area's ability to produce food will be permanently damaged. Would it be possible to do a hundred year job impact statement of this gargantuan mauling of a region? Should future jobs be traded off for present jobs; and if so, at what ratio?

We believe that the whole concept of what a job is should be challenged by grassroots environmental groups. At present, a job is simply something legal that a person is paid to do — period. Why not demand that present jobs not destroy future jobs, and insist that we should plan for (at least) one hundred years of jobs which would create more jobs a hundred years hence — for example, why not pay people more to restore environments than to destroy them?

20.
Publicity

You should publicize your cause in ways that will help you achieve your goal.

The easiest way to get lots of publicity is by committing an infamous crime. Thank goodness no one has done *that* in the name of ecology; but autos have been sledgehammered and buried, factories sabotaged, and many other inane or violent things done to grab the attention of the mass media. The point is that there is all kinds of publicity, and the kind you want is that which moves you toward your goal.

Many grassroots groups mesmerize themselves with the volume of publicity they get, and consider network television coverage the epitome of good public relations. Walter Cronkite can't give you what you want, but sometimes the editor of your local paper can give you crucial support. The best grassroots campaigns concentrate their attention on grassroots media — community newspapers, radio and television stations — and strive for quality rather than quantity of coverage. "Quality coverage" to a grassroots group means publicity which helps it get that support, those dollars, or those votes it needs for victory.

Before seeking publicity you absolutely must have your goal clearly defined, and should have your effort well along in its planning stages. In terms of this manual, you should have dealt with or be dealing with Steps 1 through 9 before scheduling your first media event.

You also should have your "impact issues" clearly formulated. The impact issues are simplified but accurate statements of the main problems and solutions involved in your campaign. Impact issues must have strong public appeal, and sometimes are not the issues which most deeply concern your core group members. They are the rare or unique features which could be lost, not the intricate ecosystem which stands in danger; the great cost of the particular dam or freeway, not the global implications of the concrete engineering mentality.

We are like fish in a mass media ocean, so most of us have a pretty good idea of what goes into an advertisement, news story, flyer, or radio or television interview. Don't get hung up because you aren't a public relations professional. Often slick, professional public relations work backfires on grassroots groups. People often expect plain folks to be amateur and impecunious, and if you come on like an oil company advertiser they turn off right away.

When talking with a journalist, be neither paranoid nor gullible. If you sound secretive and suspicious to a reporter, his attention will focus on what you seem to have to hide. If you tell more than you want known, he may inadvertently publish something that will harm your cause. Especially avoid criticizing your friends and allies around newsmen. Reporters are trained to dig up all the facts, and even the most friendly ones will instinctively try to nose out things you don't want to be made public.

You can't go far wrong if you know and respect your audience. You'll take a different tack when addressing a student rally than you would before the garden club. Every chance you get, give your publicity a power kicker by asking for endorsements, contributions, letters to vital officials, and other specific forms of support. Publicity is a means of finding and cultivating constituents for your cause; use it as such.

Editor's Note: The following article by Dorothy Gray on how to write a good press release also contains good advice about how to relate with the mass media in general.

Dorothy is a veteran of many local environmental and political campaigns.

Press Release Power

by Dorothy Gray

To the overworked and badgered newsman fighting off myriads of people who want free newspaper space, a press release is too often just another hustle. To the overworked editor of a small community paper (I was one once), a press release is too often another rewrite job for a short-handed staff. To a radio newsman, most press releases are too diffuse and too lacking in punchy word pictures that are vital to verbal copy. For the T.V. newsman, a press release is virtually useless without film.

To the grassroots environmental campaign, however, the press release is the staple of the publicity campaign. It's the free way to get your issue in the news and reach the public, to formulate the issue, to build support and understanding in the minds of the public and the minds of the press.

Given the resistance of newsmen to the bulk of flak directed at them, an environmental campaign has to be sure that it has the best chance of getting favorable attention to its press releases. Three elements are crucial to a good news release: format, content, and timing. Goof on one and your press release is probably dead.

I. Format

A press release has a definite, utilitarian format. If you follow the format you not only give the impression that your organization knows what it's doing, but you also convey information to the journalists in the clearest way possible. If your press release is well done, you also save a newsman a considerable amount of rewrite work. This indicates that you respect him and the pressures he's under. In turn, he'll likely respect you. The press release thus becomes more than an instrument for conveying information; through proper format, it becomes an important element of good press relations.

A press release is always typed on an 8½-by-11-inch piece of paper. The paper should be *white* and nothing else.

The print on the paper should be dark and clear. Don't use a worn typewriter ribbon, and don't fool around with a marginal mimeograph operation. Never use ditto. Never send a newsman a carbon. If you don't live near a photocopying machine, then you'll have to type an original for each newsman.

On the other hand, if you live in a major urban area and have a hot issue, you could conceivably be putting out fifty or more copies of a release. In bulk quantities like these you might get a cheaper price than with photocopying by using photo printing. Quick print centers can be found in the yellow pages under "Copying."

In recent years campaigns — whether political or environmental — have tended to get a bit fancy with paper. One current fad is sepia-colored paper, for example, typed with brown ribbon. This isn't as bad as pink mimeographed paper, but it has drawbacks. Somehow the punchiness of black and white is lost. Also, you're locked into typing each copy of the release.

Another new gismo in campaigning is the campaign paper with an eye-catching logo (a logo is the artwork and type that identifies the organization on each piece of stationery). If done with blue or red ink for greater visibility, such a logo can be helpful in making your press release jump out of the pack, but keep in mind three things:

1. The logo must be tasteful.
2. It shouldn't take up too much room or you'll be running over two pages unnecessarily.

3. The colors won't show on a black and white photocopy, so unless you type each copy of the release or have them quick-printed on your paper, the colors of the logo will be lost.

Your organization may come up with campaign stationery on which a list of supporters is printed down one side. This destroys one margin of the press release and consequently (for reasons discussed below) should never be used for press releases.

With the correct paper in the typewriter you're ready to go. In the middle of the top of the paper goes the name of your group. You can use all capitals, if you want. Single spaced below the name goes the address. Next comes the main phone number for your campaign.

The Contact

Below the identification of your group and on the right hand side, goes the word "Contact," followed on the same line by the name of the person issuing the press release. It is understood that this person knows all about the subject of the press release and is authorized to speak for the organization. If the person issuing the press release doesn't know the subject matter, then whoever does should be listed. Generally, however, the person putting out the press release should be knowledgeable and competent to talk to the press. This person should also be readily available. It's bad form to list a contact who can't be reached. Sometimes an organization lists two people to maximize availability.

All phone numbers that might lead to the contact person should be listed: organization, office, work phones, and home phones. (There's nothing like a radio station waking you at 6:30 a.m. for a comment for the morning news.)

All persons listed as contacts on the press release have to be reliable, stable people with good judgment. They have to know what to say and what not to say. They have to understand that anything may be quoted and that verbal statements can seem a lot different when set down in cold print. The flippant remark with the light laugh can be deadly in print, because the tone of the voice is missing.

Once you've issued a press release and put your name on it, you're open to the press. They can call you any time of day, under any circumstances, and you are obliged to be available. In effect you've invited the press into your life.

Most of the working press will treat the relationship responsibly, but you have to keep in mind that the role of the press is to ascertain the *whole* story. The ethics of journalism include objectivity, and no one — not even a grassroots environmentalist — is automatically a "a good guy." It's the job of the press to dig out any ulterior motives, any internal strife, and future tactics. Some press people will probe. Anyone who can't stand pressure or who has a short fuse shouldn't be listed as a contact on a press release.

The Slug and Dateline

Opposite the contact person's name goes what is known as the "slug," (left hand side of the page). The slug is so-called because it functions as does a slug of type on news copy. It is a label or a mini-headline. It can be one, two, or three lines long, whatever is necessary to label the story:

100 CITIZENS
TO COUNT CONDORS

RECYCLING CENTER OPENS

COUNTY LAUNCHES EFFORT
TO HALT SNOWMOBILE
DAMAGE IN MOUNTAINS

COUNCIL STUDYING
MARSH PURCHASE

Note that the words of the slug are all in capitals ("all caps" in the jargon). The lines should be single-spaced and run about equal in length.

Following the conventions of headline writing, the slug uses the present tense of the verb for past action and future tense is expressed by the infinitive. Continuing action is in the present progressive ("Council Studying. . ."), and always omits the words "is" or "are."

About an inch and a half below the slug comes the release dateline. If the press release is to be published after a certain date, the line should read: FOR RELEASE APRIL 2. The reasons for a time-dated release can vary. Maybe your group will be presenting petitions to a city council on a certain night and you don't want publicity until the day of the happening. Most of the time, however, your release dateline will probably read: FOR IMMEDIATE RELEASE. The line is written in all caps and underlined.

The Text

Next, you drop about an inch and a half on the page to begin the text. The space between release dateline and text is for a copy editor to pencil in a headline. If your slug is good, he may use it as the headline.

The text must be typed double-spaced. This allows room for copy editing marks. Similarly, margins should be generous on both sides: an inch and a half on the left and an inch on the right are minimums. If you don't leave enough room on the press release for changes and corrections by a copy editor or reporter, then the story will have to be retyped and this extra chore may result in its rejection.

The body of the text should always be in upper and lower case, capitalizing only where you normally would. I've actually seen press releases typed all caps, perhaps as an attempt at getting attention. This means a retype for the newsman and, again, may kill the story.

The first line of each paragraph is indented ten spaces. Sometimes, if you're really struggling to keep a press release down to two pages, you can cheat and indent eight spaces instead of ten.

Keep your paragraphs short. Think of how a news story looks (and don't think of the *New York Times*, the beloved "grey lady" of the trade). Readability in a newspaper depends on plenty of white space, and frequent paragraphing helps.

At the bottom of the page, you leave enough room to sign off in one of two ways, depending on which is appropriate. If you'll be continuing on to a second page, drop below the last line of the text, center the typewriter carriage and type: -*MORE* - . To mark the end of a story use: - *30* - . This is the time-honored sign-off in journalism, its origins lost in the mists of tradition.

As implied earlier, you should try never to go beyond two pages. If your issue is very complex, attach back-up material to explain the fine points rather than running the story long.

II. Content

The best way to write a good press release is to write a good news story. The essential quality of a good news story is that it conveys information in a clear and concise manner. Every high school journalism student learns a little jingle that begins, "I have five friends, they serve me well. . ." I can't remember the rest of the jingle except for the friends: Who, What, Where, When, and Why. The jingle only mentioned the five W's, but "How" is also essential.

No matter how beautifully written otherwise, a news story or press release that omits one of the above elements is a failure. A good press release must also have a strong lead.

The Lead

In seeking the lead, you're looking for the most significant, interesting, controversial or exciting element of the story. The evaluation must be made not in the terms of your group's point of view, but through an objective sense of what the news media will consider most newsworthy in terms of the general public.

Probably no other aspect of developing a press release or news story requires as much good judgment as does finding the lead. It is here, more than anywhere else, that the power of the press to define reality lies. In a complex situation, the newsman picks out what seems most significant. If he's bent on equating significance with sensationalism, his reporting of your issue may not convey to the public what you feel is essential. It's important, therefore, to keep the issues clearly defined in your press releases and to make those issues dramatic.

Sometimes drama is found in the small aspects of the big picture. There may be very significant reasons of a broad ecological nature for opposing the vast destructiveness of a freeway project, but the public may not sit still for the complex and academic argument; you may have to peg the larger issue on noise and air pollution, or loss of property from the tax rolls, or people being forced from their homes, or destruction of a prized landmark. You may have many hot fights within your organization over the tactics and strategy in choosing such specific issues; but once you have settled on them, then the press releases should build those issues to the point where the media can't be sidetracked into issues that deter from your campaign.

The best way to build strategically valuable issues is to present them in an action context. An event is always better than a statement. If you are consistently building your news releases around who *did* what or what *happened*, then you're doing an effective job.

All through this primer are examples of how campaigners translated a point of view into specific actions. Press releases should be strongly action-oriented. The publicity chairman who is aware of this need will be doing the group a great service by constantly saying, "What are we *doing* for use in my next press release?" And keep in mind that the press release that is event-oriented will attract television coverage. Your lead, then, is the element that most strongly presents your position. The lead depends on "the angle" you're playing in that particular story. Keep asking yourself what's the most grabby element that *also* relates to your central point.

Who

In most cases your organization or its leadership is the subject of the story. Most of the press releases you'll be initiating arise out of the actions your group is initiating: organizing, fund-raising, petitioning, filing suit, etc. Reporting on what the planning commission, the court, or the property owner does ordinarily will rest with the news media. Sometimes, however, the news media miss the actions of these others, actions that you want the public to know about. In this case, you develop a reactive news release: Your group publicizes the actions of others by publicizing the group's reaction to those actions.

The following slugs illustrate:

ENVIRONMENTALISTS
APPLAUD COMMISSION
DECISION

SWAMP SUPPORTERS TO
APPEAL COURT RULING

In putting together your news release, there will be other times when "Who" is not so clearly your group. Suppose that a United States Senator comes out in support of your goals (or the mayor, fire chief, or the town's banker). If you make your group the principle "Who," you may lose your strongest story angle. The significant element of the story is the VIP who is now backing you. It is much better to write, "Senator Thurston Throttlebottom today pledged his support for the campaign to halt the construction of Interstate F . . ." than to write, "The foes of Interstate F today received the support of Senator Thurston Throttlebottom in their fight to halt construction of Interstate F."

(The best thing of all might be to get Senator Throttlebottom to put out his own news release saying that he supports you. In this case, be certain you lay out clearly for his staff what should be in the news release.)

In those cases where the "Who" is other than your group, be certain you have back-up material for your press release. You should have a telegram or letter in hand from Senator Throttlebottom before you announce what he has said or done. Similarly, you should have a written offer of compromise from a property owner before accepting or rejecting it in a reactive news release. This back-up material can keep you and your group out of the embarrassing situations that arise when a property owner isn't really offering a compromise but instead running up a trial balloon, or a Senator is offering his support, but may change his mind when he learns that your foe is his wife's cousin. In getting back-up material you not only protect the integrity of your press release, but you also insist that supporters and opponents deal with you in a responsible way.

Ordinarily, the "Who" is the lead-off element in writing your press release:

"*Friends of the Swamp* today filed suit in superior court. . . ."

"*Foes of Feckless Freeways* yesterday elected officers for the newly organized group. . . ."

*"Phineas Philpot, president of
Rich People's Bank,* today donated
$500 million to the Society for the
Yellow Breasted Tail-Waver for the
purchase of Manhattan Island, the
last nesting ground of the rare
species."

In the cases cited above the
action is being done by some person or persons. Since people make
the news in these cases, the "Who"
is the strongest element.

What

In the examples cited above, the
action of people is the "What":

"Friends of the Swamp today
filed suit in Superior Court. . . ."

In other words, these press statements answer the question, "Who
did What?" There is, however, another kind of question: "What happened?" In this case, an action
occurred virtually of itself or was
more important than any "Who,"
as, for example, in the following:

"Last month's flood on Dry
Creek destroyed the habitat of the
red-bellied swamp mouse. . . ."

"Donation of land to Open Space
Advocates of Alabama qualified as
tax deductible under a new court
ruling. . . ."

"A report was issued today by
Stop Gruesome Growth proving
that development costs to the city
will exceed tax revenues. . . ."

Any release is better if action
verbs are used. Try to stay out of
the passive mode. Someone releas-
ing a survey is better than a survey
being released. Similarly, punchy
words should be used instead of
"said" wherever reasonable: challenged, argued, vowed, etc.

Where and When

These two elements are so obvious as to need little discussion.
The important thing is that they
never be forgotten, but always included in the lead paragraph or
close to it.

With respect to When, a good
practice is always to use a date instead of the day of the week. This
saves a lot of confusion. Always
write out the month fully and never
include the year.

It's "November 23 at 4 p.m."
and never "Nov. 23rd at 4 o'clock."

Occasionally, "When" or "Where"
may be your lead element:

"On Arbor Day five thousand
residents of Hooperville will plant
trees. . . ."

"A Munoo Indian 'magic place'
will be the site of a rally against
strip mining. . . ."

Again, it's a question of what
angle best introduces your issue.

Why

This fifth friend also belongs in
the lead paragraph or close to it.
It completes the thought, making
clear the purpose of the action or
event.

"Antiques will be auctioned by
the Friends of the Fish on June 3
*to raise money for a suit against
industrial pollutors. . . ."*

The most important thing about
"Why" is that it should be clearly
defined and succinctly stated.
"Why" should never be a long dissertation or an involved recapitu-
lation of complex events. Having
to express "why" concisely will
help you and your group to focus
on the rationale of the action behind the press release.

How

This element is most ususally developed in the text following the
lead paragraph.

"The Citizens Committee for a
County Archives today announced
plans for restoring the historic
Murphy Building, now threatened
by the wrecker's ball.

*Funds for the restoration will be
obtained through a federal grant
program under the Historic Preservation Act of 1966."*

Supporting Material

A press release or news story is
an inverted pyramid, with almost

all of the essential information packed into the lead paragraph.

The supporting material consists of details amplifying the lead elements: what kinds of antiques will be auctioned; how much dance tickets will cost; names of attorneys carrying the lawsuit; specifics of the animals whose habitat is threatened; locations where petitions may be signed; statements by leaders of your group. Always keep in mind that the good press release or news story can be cut from the bottom up without impairing the sense of the story. This is not to say you should pad your story with closing paragraphs of trivia. What is meant is that none of your five or six essential elements should be buried far down in your story.

Just the News Please

As mentioned above, your supporting paragraphs may include statements by your group's spokesman. This brings up the question of attribution and editorializing. The term "attribution" in its narrow sense means that you always assign an opinion or assertion or statement to someone through a direct or indirect quote. In the broader sense, "attribution" also relates to "editorializing" in that a skillful use of attribution can keep you from the sin of editorializing.

Why is editorializing a sin? The basic traditional premise of journalism is objectivity. Some younger newsmen question whether true objectivity is possible, but the standard goal of journalism is to present only facts as news and to present opinions and assertions as being offered by an identifiable source. Thus, if you want to say that the mountain you're trying to protect is beautiful, you have to treat that as an assertion or opinion and put it in the form of a quote. The mountain is a fact; its beauty is a matter of opinion and "beautiful Mt. Mossback" is a form of editorializing. Always remember that editorializing belongs on the editorial page.

A press release can get the same point across by using a quote:

" 'Beautiful Mt. Mossback is a prime tourist attraction and if it is logged we will lose more tourist dollars than the timber will produce,' argued Mary Jones, president of Spare that Tree Society."

It pays to carry objectivity even a step further than attribution: give newsmen the straight story on your opposition. This means, at the very least, identifying the opposition fully and accurately whenever mentioned. You should even go a step further and routinely recap the conflict dispassionately. Thus, Ms. Jones' statement on beautiful Mt. Mossback might be followed by:

"A proposal for timbering on Mt. Mossback was announced last March by Paul Bunyon, president of Buzz Saw Company of Slash, California."

This places Ms. Jones' statement in context, identifies the opposition objectively, and saves the newsman searching his pockets for his note on when Bunyon announced his plan. A good newsman will double check your data anyway, but in time he'll find that you're always accurate. At that point you'll cease to be a writer of flak and become a newsman's most valued associate, "a source."

Avoid florid language, jargon, slang, and unusual words. Avoid wordiness. Write simply and clearly. You've been reading newspaper stories almost all of your life and should have a feeling for how they are written. The good news story or press release lets the facts convey the excitement or carry the action. "Colorful" phrases can, however, enliven quotes if the phrases are apt and in good taste.

Quotes

As implied above, you may have to assist spokesmen in your group in developing quotes for press releases. Always be sure you check the exact wording with the person to whom you are attributing a statement. To prevent any misunderstandings, you may want that person to initial a draft copy to show approval of the quote attributed to him or her.

Similarly, you should take seriously the responsibility to review quotes which members of your organization may want to include in a press release. An obvious concern is that nothing libelous or slanderous be stated in a press release. Name calling is always to be avoided. Further, you should give great care to substantiating any allegations you make concerning the opposition. One misstatement of fact can damage your group's credibility. In fact, it's a good idea to attach documentation to a press release. This not only substantiates your assertion, but can save a newsman a lot of work.

Journalists frequently use "alleged" or "reportedly" to guard against libel or slander. If a strip-mining company has paid off your city councilman and you have documentation, remember it's not fact until proven in court. It "appears" to have happened, or "serious questions are raised by certain documents," etc.

Deadlines

You should ascertain what deadlines there are for various kinds of news. Commonly the front page has a later deadline than inside pages. Ask reporters or the city desk by what time they prefer to have copy. You have to give a newsman a chance to work over your press release, so your deadline will be earlier than his.

If something really important happens and one of your local papers is close to deadline, phone in your story instead of waiting to do a press release. This is much better than allowing a paper to miss an important story that the other papers with later deadlines will have. Competitiveness among news media is very high and you must avoid even the appearance of playing favorites. The way to do so is to release your news simultaneously to all media as close to the time the news item occurred as possible. Leaking news to a favorite reporter is a dangerous game and can cost you more in the long run than you gain from any apparent advantages.

Radio is the medium that has a built-in edge in the competition for news beats, particularly all-news radio stations that can schedule an item for airtime at will. But even "instant news" radio stations need some time to work up air copy from your press release. Knowing how much lead time a station needs will give you a fair idea of when your item will be aired so you can monitor what is actually said.

Television deadlines are perhaps the most cumbersome. Generally speaking your press releases will not be used by television unless the station shoots some film. If you have any control over the timing of an event to be filmed, schedule it early enough in the day to allow television stations time to process and edit their film. Mid-morning is a a good time for events.

Timeliness

The subject of timing also involves what newsmen call "timeliness." The term is hard to define, but boils down to a simple question. In terms of reader interest, is this the right time for this story? Complex judgments are involved whenever a reporter or editor makes a decision on a story with respect to timeliness. Is it too much like a lot of earlier stories? Has the peak of the action passed? Is the other news competing for space right now more interesting? Has public awareness evolved to a point where the story has an audience? Is there anything really new in this? These are some of the elements involved in the determination. Keeping them in mind may help you maximize the timeliness of your press releases.

Rhythm

A third aspect of timing involves maximizing the potential readership (or listening audience) for your story. One rule of thumb is to time your releases so that they stay out of the weekend papers. People just aren't much interested in news on the weekend.

There are limits to how closely you can play the timing game in terms of picking your days. Never hold a "hot" story for a better day because then you risk its timeliness. Never try for Monday morning's paper with a Sunday press conference because news staffs are too thin on Sundays to cover anything much less newsworthy than a disaster or a triple murder. Never obviously stall a newsman because that's trying to "manage" the news and will be resented.

Experience is a great teacher and the experience of doing press work is rewarding in itself. Be accurate, be clear, be timely. And may all your press releases make page one. As we say in the business, that's -30-.

Publicity Planning Checklist

Publicity planning is a major part of Step 11, "Your Action Plan." Publicity coordinated with major hearings, committee votes, and the like is the hallmark of good grassroots action. Below is a partial checklist of modes of publicity you might consider in making your plan:

Free Mass Media (press, television, and radio coverage). See "Press Release Power" by Dorothy Gray in this Step for a discussion of how to relate with the mass media.

Press Conference. A special case of using the free mass media. Press conferences should be called for only really major news breaks, and press packets should be prepared with written statements and supporting material. For television coverage, hold them in mid-morning and offer something to photograph (for example, hold them on the site you're concerned with).

Paid Advertisements. Especially useful if the local paper is editorially hostile to you, and in the last stages of a campaign (especially a ballot campaign). Make it brief, direct and punchy. Professional advice is useful, but too "slick" ads can turn people off. Always ask people to do something (write a letter, send a coupon, attend a hearing, vote for your side, etc.), and always tell them where to contact you to join or send money.

Newsletters, Flyers, Handbills, and the Like. Staples of grassroots communication with constituents. Everybody knows how these look: light and folksy. Just don't get bogged down in cranking out newsletters at the expense of pursuing victory.

Gimmicks, Stunts, Street Events. Use with extreme caution. Never do anything which threatens the lifestyle or values of your supporters. A good, orderly placard-bearing rally has gotten many a grassroots campaign off the ground; if you plan one, make sure police know what you're doing, have a well-organized monitor system, and clean up after yourselves. The light, humorous touch is indispensable.

Visiting People Door-to-Door. One of the most effective publicity techniques, used far too little.

Letterheads. Stationery with a letterhead, and a list of notable supporters running down the left margin, can have quite an impact.

Letters to the Editor. Keep a steady stream of letters flowing, on different aspects of the issue, signed by different people.

Speakers' Bureau. Most civic clubs have program chairpeople who are eager to find speakers. Help them out!

Exhibits and Posters. A good way to get across the beauty of what you're concerned with.

Nature Walks, Clean-ups, and the Like. Good events all around: good focal points for publicity, ways to get people committed, to educate people, and to raise spirits.

The Letter That Launched a Movement

In the spring of 1960 Earth Day was ten years in the future, and it looked as though the Pacific Gas & Electric Company (PG&E) would be able to build a nuclear plant on Bodega Head — a lovely promontory jutting into the ocean north of San Francisco — without much of a public squawk being raised. PG&E's proposal sailed easily through a California Public Utilities Commission (PUC) hearing in March of that year. Then Karl Kortum of San Francisco wrote a letter to the editor of the *San Francisco Chronicle*. Kortum's letter brought a flood of letters and petitions to the PUC, causing them to set aside PG&E's application and schedule more hearings.

This gave David Pesonen of San Francisco a chance to gather support for a full-scale citizen effort to stop the nuclear plant. A high point of the campaign's publicity was the release of balloons on a windy day at Bodega Head. Many of the balloons, intended to show where the winds would carry emissions from the plant, drifted to the Golden Gate.

Eventually PG&E withdrew its application to build the nuclear plant on Bodega Head, ending the movement launched by a letter to the editor. Here's the essence of Karl Kortum's powerful letter:

. . . Conservationists from the State Park Commission and the National Park Service came in the last decade to walk among the lupine and decided that this [Bodega Head] should be a public preserve. But about the same time came men of a different type. They too walked out on the point and gave it the triumphant glance of demigods. . . .

The scene shifts to the home office:

"Our engineering boys think we ought to grab Bodega Head."

"They do? (low whistle) That might be a little rough."

"Why? Why more than Moss Landing or Humboldt Bay?"

"Well, it's more scenic. There will be more protest. The state park people and the national park people are already on record for public acquisition."

"Our engineers say we need it. We'll just buy, fast. Get in ahead of them. It's legal."

"Well . . ."

"What we can't buy we'll condemn."

"What about public protest? This one could get a little noisy."

"Keep it at the county level. Or try to. Every service club in every town has got our people in it rubbing shoulders. In the country, opinion is made at the weekly luncheon . . ."

"How about the newspapers?"

"It's the local businessmen who buy the space. Oh, I don't say we haven't got some work to do. But these guys have got other things on their minds — they're scratching out a living."

"Have you got an angle? I mean apart from the fact that we want it."

"Oh, sure. We'll get out some speeches on how the country will be improved. We might even try calling it a tourist attraction."

"And the county officials?"

"They're O.K. We'll set the tone up there and they'll respond to it. Just as elected representatives should. Oh, you might get some idealists . . ."

Karl Kortum continues. If everyone would take five minutes to write a letter PG&E would be licked. But a licking is not what to ask for; regulation is sufficient — regulation in the full breadth of the public interest. We have a Public Utilities Commission charged with doing just that.

Not many of us, perhaps, are able to concoct a fictional scene such as Karl Kortum did, but letter-writing does work — in two ways.

One, in getting the issue to the public's attention through publication; two, in eliciting other letters to the locus of power.

21.

Acquiring Land

If you want to preserve a natural area, explore every public means of preserving it; if public means don't work, raise money and buy it.

If you want to preserve land, you should first try to do it through federal, state, or local governments. These governments provide for creating parks, nature preserves, wilderness areas, and so on. If a public body creates the park, you won't have to raise the money to buy it, and you'll help set precedents for public preservation of natural areas.

The Raleigh Greenway Commission of Raleigh, North Carolina, is proving to be effective in acquiring land for a linear park system (greenway) in that city. Created by the city council, the commission is composed of private citizens. This gives the commission the permanence and some of the prestige of a government body, while allowing its members to negotiate for land sales and donations as citizens. "We point out the tax advantages of making a donation," notes Raleigh Greenway Commission Chairman Bill Ross, "and mention the zoning benefits that might accrue to the donor. Density trade-offs can be arranged, where the city will allow high-density development for land donors on the land that they retain. Developers sometimes get involved in a terrible row with the city; if you approach them as citizens not in the employ of the city,

you have a better chance of working something out with them. And we publicize the names of land donors."

Preservation of natural areas is the tangible sort of thing which often attracts large financial contributors. In raising money to buy land, note that a broad appeal for small contributions can be effective, and if successful will attract larger donors.

After you've gotten the land into some sort of protected status, remember that no piece of land is permanently locked up. John Muir formed the Sierra Club to save the Yosemite Valley, as well as Yosemite Park, and the fate of that valley is still a hotly contested issue today.

Assess Yourselves

Residents of the Mission Hills area of San Diego, California, found a unique way to preserve a canyon in their neighborhood: they brought about the formation of an assessment district for the purpose of buying the land for open space.

"It started when we saw a notice posted for a resolution of intent to develop the canyon," says Sally Hamburg of Mission Hills. That meant that the city of San Diego was planning to run roads into the 40-acre canyon. A nucleus of six families living near the canyon circulated a petition door-to-door, calling for it to be preserved.

With the backing of about 50 families, the group went to city hall. "Some young engineers in urban planning told us the city had a new Park Procedural Ordinance that might be implemented in this case," recalls Mrs. Hamburg. That innovative ordinance enables the creation of assessment districts to buy open space.

The city of San Diego drew up assessment district maps for the proposed district. Then the *ad hoc* citizens' group went to the property owners in the district with kits explaining the situation. Owners of 62 percent of the property in the district signed their agreement with the proposal. The Citizens' group went to the San Diego City Council with this strong vote of approval, and in the winter of 1971 the assessment district was created.

"The money to buy the property was put up by a bonding company," notes Mrs. Hamburg. "Now we're paying our assessments in the form of property taxes. Assessment rates are based on proximity to the canyon; people farther away pay lesser amounts."

The City of San Diego is still involved in litigation to acquire some privately held parcels of land in the canyon, and just what sort of park it will be has yet to be determined. "The City of San Diego told me this was the first assessment district formed in California to buy open space," notes Mrs. Hamburg. Let's hope others follow!

Buying the Cotton Tract

Editor's Note: The Poricy Park Citizens Committee of Middletown, New Jersey, exists to preserve about 300 acres of undeveloped land in their town. They have used a wide range of preservation techniques, and have produced a mimeographed description of their practical conservation experiences. If more groups would analyze and write up their strategic and tactical experiences as well as the Poricy group has, the grassroots movement would greatly benefit. Here's their section on "acquisition of land through fund raising":

We will state here and now, for reasons that will become apparent later, that *the most secure means of preserving the natural integrity of an area is to own it.* In terms of controlling land use, one old yellowed deed is worth 10 reams of easements and restrictive clauses.

The best way to acquire land is to have it donated, but since we have not been so fortunate, we had to resort to other means. For one year, beginning in September 1969, we had pleaded with township and county officials to rescue the Poricy

area. We distributed thousands of brochures, packed town meetings, and had petitions signed, but all we received was polite interest. Land is not secured with polite interest.

Then, in August 1970, we went to see Mr. E. Leigh Cotton, whose old horse farm (now a housing development) bordered Poricy Brook. We asked if he would sell us a 14-acre tract of virgin forest which he had saved for his retirement house. He replied that at 73 he was "too old to retire," and said we could have the *entire* tract for its assessed value of $5,000 *total.* (Undeveloped land in Middletown in 1970 was selling for $4,500 per acre.)

At this point we enlisted the aid of the Nature Conservancy, a national land conservation group based in Arlington, Virginia. The Conservancy served three important functions: (1) It held the option and later took title to the land, thus relieving our committee of the burdens of real estate ownership. (2) It served as a repository for and kept an accounting of the funds we collected. (3) By being both prestigious and tax-deductible, it increased the number and amount of contributions.

Getting these contributions was hard work. At first we thought that by appealing to prominent people of means, we could easily raise the $7,000 we had set as our goal. (This money was to cover not only the price of the land, but also legal fees, title searches, property improvements, and our own expenses.) People were willing to give, but they were also good at mental arithmetic, especially division. They each gave what they calculated to be their share of the $7,000, no doubt influenced to some degree by the shaky condition of the stock market at that time. As a result, about halfway through the ninety day option period we had collected only $2,500.

We then appealed to the general public with circulars, asking for contributions in categories of $5,

Failing to interest Township officials in the idea of Poricy Park, a citizens committee purchased a 14-acre forest with money raised in a public campaign. The purchase of this forest, called "The Cotton Tract" persuaded the Township to seek additional land. The Park now contains about 250 acres.

$10, $25, and $50. To our surprise, previously indifferent township officials openly began to support our cause and asked the public to help. The local newspapers gave us their editorial support. The checks began to pour in, and we actually exceeded our goal.

Two points should be made. First, *raising money requires a great deal of effort, even for amounts that appear to be small.* Second, *it is possible to attain a goal with small contributions if you reach enough people.* Hundreds of contributions in the $5 and $10 category *do* add up.

The Making of an Urban State Park

Editor's Note: The following article appeared under the title "Tryon Creek State Park: A Place for All People" in the April 1972 issue of The Journal *of Lewis & Clark College in Portland, Oregon. It's an excellent account of how private fund-raising and public acquisition can work together to create a park. Without the vigorous citizen group action it is clear that no Tryon Creek State Park would have been established. It is equally clear that the active cooperation of public officials was crucial to making the park.*

The Friends of Tryon Creek Park, Inc. is still alive and well. Jean Siddall of Friends reports that $168,000 has been raised for a nature center in the park. "In our initial fund-raising drive in 1970," she says, "340 volunteers went door-to-door asking for contributions. We kept names and addresses of everybody who contributed, because we thought we might not raise enough money to save the park, and would have to return it. Now those 1,500 families on the list are the basis of our mailing list, and most of the money for the nature center came from small contributions."

Can two housewives, "who never thought they couldn't," save 600 wilderness acres in the center of a metropolitan residential area?

Entrance to the Nature Center Shelter, Tryon Creek State Park.

The Nature Center trail at Tryon Creek State Park, Lake Oswego, Oregon

The answer is yes, and Oregon's new State Park, Tryon Creek, is living proof — its establishment due to the efforts of a grassroots task force headed by Mrs. Borden Beck and Mrs. A. Clair Siddall.

The Tryon Creek area, which now runs from Lake Oswego's State Street to the edge of the Northwestern School of Law campus, first appeared on park planning maps in the 1920's. Subsequently the area received the official blessings of Multnomah County, the City of Portland, the City of Lake Oswego and the Columbia Region of Commerce appointed a committee which studied Tryon Creek for several years.

But through the years the problems were always the same: lack of coordination between county and city government agencies, shortage of funds, and that old excuse for heel-dragging — "there's still plenty of space."

The first sure-footed step in acquiring the park came in spring 1969, when at the urging of Commissioner David Eccles, Multnomah County purchased 45 acres on the west side of the canyon which borders Boones Ferry Road.

Mr. Eccles then requested citizen support, and a public meeting was called in June by local citizens. As a result of this, a steering committee was created, which worked with the Multnomah County Planning Commission. At this time Lucille Beck and Jean Siddall conferred, concurred, and coordinated their efforts to save "the last natural area of any size in the southwest sector of the metropolitan community."

Out of this partnership came the Friends of Tryon Creek Park, Inc., a non-profit citizens organization. Its first board meeting was in January 1970. Goals included soliciting private donations and coordinating efforts between the local governments.

"Only a few weeks later," Mrs. Siddall recalls, "we learned that one of the landowners had optioned his 200 acres to a developer from Seattle. As a matter of fact, the developer had a master plan for the entire canyon. We knew the best use for the land was as a park and not as a housing development; if we were ever to have a park, we would have to act now. We threw away the rule book and pushed the first of many panic buttons."

"We scheduled meetings in Lake Oswego, Dunthorpe, and Collinsview during March and April and, spurred by the success of these," says Mrs. Beck, "we formulated a neighborhood fund drive in three weeks, with the immediate goal of raising money for options."

"One of our male board members," Mrs. Siddall remembers, "threw up his hands in horror and claimed such an undertaking required three months, not three weeks."

Board member Barbara Eamon of Lake Oswego was named chairman of the fund drive. Within a week, 340 persons had volunteered to solicit their neighborhoods. Fourteen days later, during Earth Week 1970, the drive began.

Each ten dollar donor was given a certificate for one foot of trail. "You'd be surprised," comments Mrs. Siddall, "how many grandparents gave these to grandchildren."

A spaghetti feed at Forest Hills School in Lake Oswego, which was cooked by the teachers and served by the students, was sold out two weeks in advance and raised $1,024. Scout troops and civic organizations gave money, and grade and high schools sponsored innumerable projects on behalf of the Park, including marches, sock hops, and book sales.

Bright yellow buttons which declared in black letters "I am a friend of Tryon Creek" were awarded those who donated 25 cents. In this way, schools contributed more than $1,000.

"Within three weeks we had collected $27,000 — and at a time," Mrs. Beck points out, "when school bond issues were going down."

Mrs. Siddall and Mrs. Beck logged some 68 talks before various groups, and the Beck dining room became a depository of literature and campaign material.

"The ball that was so difficult to get rolling gathered such speed that we had to run to keep up with it."

Although $27,000 was far short of the estimated $2 million needed, the drive indicated tremendous citizen response. Through discussions with landowners and with the help of an attorney, the Friends began their work by taking an option on the most threatened parcel.

Another "panic button" crisis occurred one spring morning when Mrs. Beck phoned Mrs. Siddall.

"Jean, we have to have $25,000 in four hours. One of the canyon landowners is about to sell, and we need this as a deposit."

"At 1 p.m. she called again," Mrs. Siddall recalls. "Jean, I got the $25,000 from a man in New Hampshire," was the excited message from Mrs. Beck. Just another incident in the amazing story of Tryon Creek.

During the summer the group arranged options on 28 acres and had a contract on 13 — these in addition to the 45 the County had purchased. (Earlier, in March, the Department of Housing and Urban Development had matched the funds laid out in the County's original purchase.) With the Nature Conservancy in San Francisco having agreed to "a standby understanding" for a loan, the outlook was encouraging.

In autumn events began to occur rapidly. The Friends gained the approval of the Multnomah County Commissioners on new boundaries, which included all the available land in the canyon. Also Board members conferred with a professional fund-raiser about launching a city-wide drive in spring 1971.

"We were in the process of putting this together when we talked with Glenn Jackson, chairman of the State Highway Department." The women remember Mr. Jackson leaning back in his chair, smoking his pipe and listening quietly to their proposal. "If the State could

Sword fern and maples in Tryon Creek State Park.

participate on a 25 percent basis," they pleaded, "it would be of immense value to the Park."

"No, we can't participate on a sharing basis," Mr. Jackson replied, "but I will look into the Park."

That was on a Tuesday in October. Eight days later Mr. Jackson and the State Parks Department had obtained matching funds from the Parks for People Program, which had just been introduced by the U.S. Department of the Interior. On Thursday, October 29, newspapers reported on Governor Tom McCall's announcement that the Tryon Creek area was to become a 600-acre state park. This was the first state park ever created in an urban area. It was indeed a victory for the people.

Both Mrs. Beck and Mrs. Siddall agree that Mr. Jackson accomplished in one week what it would have taken them five years to do.

Mr. Jackson also has a comment about the women and their presentation. "I knew by the determined look in their eyes when they came into my office that it was a matter of run or cave in; I caved in."

Today, markers on Terwilliger Boulevard proclaim Tryon Creek State Park. The Friends have asked that the State agree to three stipulations: that the Park be kept natural and that management objectives carry this out; that citizen participation and involvement be continued, and that the State work with Friends of Tryon Park and the County in planning.

Perhaps for the first time in State history, citizens had laid the groundwork for the State in procuring a park. The State looked with curiosity, then affection, on this kind of "people-involvement."

Hiking, bike, and equestrian trails definitely are in the plans. A Nature Center, where groups of children and adults can gather for nature learning, also is being discussed. Development in the park will be held to an absolute minimum; only those changes will be made that are compatible with the natural environment.

Picnic tables are in question. "If we have them at all," Mrs. Siddall explains, "they will be designed to fit in with, not intrude upon, the surroundings."

Both women are quick to remind that there are few cities in the country that have 600 acres of wild area in the center of urban development. Fifty-eight species of birds, 14 trees, 19 shrubs and small trees, 10 ferns and fern allies, 5 vines, 58 birds, 8 animals, and 77 flowers (and no poison oak) have been recorded within park confines, plus four of the five types of geological formations found within the Portland area.

"Perhaps the total silence is the park's greatest resource," they add.

This effort brought together the citizens of Lake Oswego and its surrounding area, Multnomah County, the State of Oregon, the Federal Government, in addition to the press — *The Oswego Review, The Oregon Journal,* and *The Oregonian* — "all rooting for the same team."

"How could two persons enter so many situations backwards," the pair reminisces, "and have things turn out right? Perhaps it proves that if you have a job that cannot be done, give it to someone who doesn't know it can't be done, and he will go ahead and do it."

Or, consider a statement by Winston Churchill which has become the motto of the Friends of Tryon Creek Park: "We shape our cities, and they shape us. Shaping them properly should be our most important space program."

22.

The Existential Moment

In every campaign there are moments of crisis when only grace under pressure saves the day.

The Chinese write the word "crisis" with two characters, one of which means "danger," and the other "opportunity." Crises, sudden and out of your control, often from unexpected quarters, are virtually sure to strike during your campaign. The better prepared you are, the better able you will be to cope deftly with these shocks. You may find, as others have, that crises bring up hidden resources and elicit unorthodox responses.

The Rockridge Community Planning Council (RCPC) of Oakland, California, was in the doldrums. No one seemed very interested in their efforts to rezone their neighborhood to prevent development. Then a drive-in chain made a move to set up a fast food concession in the community. This threat gave RCPC something on which to focus opposition. They stopped the drive-in by arousing the neighborhood against it, using flyers, utility pole posters, and meetings. This gave them the momentum to carry through their rezoning plan.

In the previous section (Step 21, "Acquiring Land") is the story of Friends of Tryon Creek Park, Inc. of Lake Oswego, Oregon. In 1970 the Friends were slowly and cautiously organizing an effort to save a natural area in their metropolitan residential area. Then they learned that a Seattle developer had an option on 200 acres in the natural area, and a master plan for the whole tract. "We threw away the rule book," says Jean Siddall of the Friends, "and pushed the first of many panic buttons." Though some members of their board thought the effort premature, the Friends organized meetings, had a spaghetti feed, sold buttons, organized a door-to-door canvass, and generally did everything they could think of to raise money right away. They came up with $27,000 and gained the impetus to carry through creation of a Tryon Creek State Park.

On February 6, 1970 dozens of dump trucks suddenly appeared at Udalls Cove near Douglaston, New York, laden with fill to convert part of the marsh there into a parking lot. The Udalls Cove Preservation Committee, an upper middle-class group not at all given to lawbreaking, swiftly alerted Douglaston supporters. By noon, a small band of women were standing, arms linked, between trucks and Cove. Then the men of the community came, leaving their jobs and putting their reputations on the line for Udalls Cove.

"We confronted police from two counties," notes Aurora Gareiss of the Preservation Committee, "and almost were arrested." Most of the trucks were stopped, the Committee got a court injunction to stop further dumping, and resulting publicity increased support for saving Udalls Cove. Now the Cove is a Wildlife Preserve within New York City.

Your opening is presented when your opponent strikes. Ponder the lesson of the judo teacher as presented by Vietnamese writer Nguyen Khac Vien: "Your opponent is movement. It is in that same movement, not in your own strength, that you must find the force to defeat your opponent. Grab his moves at the end of their thrust, prolong them, and you will lure your adversary into a fall which he himself has precipitated."

23.

Eternal Vigilance

After you have won your battle, establish a means to guard your victory.

"You can lose conclusively," notes Claire Dedrick of the Committee for the Improvement of the Alameda in Menlo Park, California, "but no victory is ever final." Your opponents are often large organizations which can lick their wounds, bide their time, and try again in future years. Once the great crises have passed, grassroots environmental groups tend to dissolve like the morning mist, leaving what they "saved" open to future attack.

Follow-through if a battle appears to be won, is important. This usually takes the form of a watchdog operation, directed at the agency or institution responsible for enforcing a decision.

A number of the successful groups featured in *The Grass Roots Primer* have found ways to grow beyond the settling of the issues which caused their formation. For example, the Upper French Broad Defense Association, which in 1972 stopped the Tennessee Valley Authority from building 14 dams in the Hendersonville, North Carolina area, is now concerned with the conservation and energy policy in their area. Executive Director Alex Duris puts out a newsletter, and there are still many dues-paying members. Though the Association is not as large and active as it was at the height of its fight against TVA, it is ready to mobilize again in case, as Alex puts it, "the bureaucrats, like camels, try again to get their noses under the tent."

Many groups gain expertise and prestige in the areas they're dealing with. After the initial battle is won, core group members are called upon for advice, and to serve on boards and commissions of various sorts. This has happened to the Eugene Future Power Committee, which ran a successful local initiative campaign against a nuclear power plant. Committee members are now active in Oregon state efforts to plan environmentally sound and safe energy programs. Though the Committee as such has not been actively involved in an issue lately, they keep their file of members' names and addresses current, and are ready to act if the situation demands.

The best way to secure your victory is by creating a society in which environmental values are strong. This is best done from the bottom up. The grassroots level is the place to start, and the time to do something is now.

Putting Teeth in the Law

by Steven M. Bundy

Editor's Note: Steven Bundy is a student of environmental law, a veteran of a number of political campaigns, and has been involved in environmental politics — particularly issues relating to land use — for the past several years. His review of environmental law is intended to serve as a guide to readers who are entering environmental politics for the first time and need a general orientation. For readers who wish additional information, Mr. Bundy has supplied a bibliography, which follows. (See also "Grass Roots Review," on page 271.)

"Putting Teeth in the Law" introduces one of the most powerful tools available to grassroots activists — the law itself. It presents the chief actors at the Federal level, along with the most important Federal environmental laws, and discusses some of the innovative legislation that has been adopted at the state level. Its intent is to orient those unfamiliar with environmental law to some of the avenues that are available to activists.

Ten years ago it wouldn't have been possible to write this part of the book. In 1965 only one of the laws discussed in this chapter was on the books. Environmentalists who sought help from the statutes rarely found it. In fact, the important environmental laws were usually written with loopholes to exempt more damaging developments.

Today that situation has been dramatically altered. Air and water quality are governed by stringent Federal statutes that apply nationwide. The Federal government and more than half of the states have adopted laws requiring that all government projects be subject to a publicly conducted, judicially reviewable analysis of their environmental effects. And many states have acted on their own to create agencies specifically empowered to halt or limit destructive development in important resource areas.

The Problem of Enforcement

These new laws have been a real help to environmentalists, but not a panacea, for it turns out that new environmental laws are almost invariably ineffective without careful citizen monitoring and enforcement. Insofar as they are valuable, the new laws have a profound and sometimes wrenching impact on those whom they regulate. All of a sudden, what has passed for business as usual in this country is being declared illegal. A local land developer suddenly finds that his carefully planned shopping center is in the middle of a wetland, and that he will be lucky if he can get a permit to build a few vacation bungalows on the site. A Forest Service official is told by the courts that he has to prepare a full environmental analysis of his decision to log a valuable *de facto* wilderness area, and then explain that analysis to the public. A man who commutes 70 miles a day to work reads in the papers that in order to bring air pollution down to the levels required for preservation of public health, automobile use in the Los Angeles basin may have to be reduced 40 percent. These are big changes and, while they may work to the benefit of society and the natural environment, to the individuals involved they seem like tremendous and unwarranted hardships, to be avoided whenever possible.

Another problem is that the agencies entrusted with enforcement authority are almost always given a fraction of the funding needed to do the job. The Maine Environmental Improvement Commission, for example, had two staff members to administer a law which regulated every new development over 20 acres in size in the entire state. New York City's air pollution control authorities have 16 inspectors to police a city of eight million people. A dozen other examples could be cited. With no staffing, no enforcement is possible.

These understaffed, underfunded agencies, conscious of the public distaste for rapid change and of their own vulnerability, often seek to follow a "reasonable" course, especially when the economy is stagnant and energy prices are high. This eagerness to be "reasonable" can lead agencies not merely to ex-

ercise their discretion to favor harmful development, but to do things that the law gives them no right to do.

Enforcement of the new environmental laws must begin at the grassroots level. Unless those involved in the pollution and destruction of our environment are made to accept their legal responsibilities by an aroused citizenry — with the weight of the courts behind it — these laws will be ignored.

Knowing the Players

At the Federal level, major environmental decisions are made by a handful of key agencies. Like football players, the Federal agencies often appear to be the same, hidden as they are behind masks of bureaucratic language. But each agency has a special character and style, as you will discover when you get involved with them. The players described here are the major agencies of concern to environmental activists.

The Council on Environmental Quality

Created under the National Environmental Policy Act, the Council on Environmental Quality (CEQ) is predominantly oriented toward research and policy making. CEQ publishes an annual report which reviews the "State of the Environment" and sponsors analyses of other important issues relating to the environment. Its only enforcement function is to oversee the implementation of the Environmental Policy Act itself, and specifically the preparation of environmental impact statements (EIS). Its guidelines for EIS preparation are closely observed by Federal agencies. A negative comment from the Council on a Federal EIS carries substantial weight with the courts and the public. The CEQ has a relatively small staff, and operates exclusively out of Washington.

The Environmental Protection Agency

The Environmental Protection Agency (EPA) is responsible for the implementation of regulations regarding the national air and water pollution control programs — including permissible levels of radiation and, in the near future, toxic substances and solid wastes — and has authority to intervene when states fail to take action. It is required to set emission standards for virtually every type of air and water polluter, and therefore has enormous power to effect the economic course of the nation as well. Many of EPA's actions are unpopular and, although many people support its goals, the agency draws much opposition from people who stand to suffer a real inconvenience from a new regulation.

In addition to clean air and water control, EPA has other responsibilities. Under the Federal Insecticide, Fungicide, and Rodenticide Act of 1972 (FIFRA), the Agency is required to certify all pesticides marketed in the United States. It was under this authority, for example, that the use of DDT has been halted. The Noise Control Act of 1972 gives the EPA further authority to set standards for a wide variety of products sold in interstate commerce, including motorcycles, skimobiles and lawnmowers.

EPA is a much larger organization than CEQ. Generally, its staffers are younger and more idealistic than those in older bureaucracies. The Agency has regional offices in each of the ten Federal regions, and — a minor but useful point — maintains a library in each region which is open to the public and contains a fine selection of materials on the environment.

The United States Forest Service

The Forest Service, under the Department of Agriculture, is responsible for the management of the entire national forest system. On that land, its environmental responsibilities are defined by NEPA, and by three more general statutes, the Organic Act of 1897, the Multiple Use and Sustained Yield Act of 1960, and the Wilderness Act of 1964. The Forest Service has traditionally been oriented strongly toward the lumber industry, and has therefore been hit hard by NEPA. Even today the agency is heavily weighted toward foresters, with forestry being regarded as involved more with the cutting, rather than

the growing of trees. But there are signs of change. Years too late, the Forest Service is beginning to take the first small steps toward more responsible timber management. At the same time, because legal action by environmental groups is forcing a reassessment of the way decisions have been made in the past, the Forest Service planning process is becoming more accessible to the public. In many areas the change is only on the surface, but it is a change. Finally, some Forest Service personnel are becoming more sensitive to environmental values and more willing to express environmental concerns in the face of angry loggers. But since the timber industry provides the National Forest Service's chief source of revenue, more effective land management will depend on a better balance of Federal funding between other programs and sale planning and road building.

The Bureau of Land Management

The Bureau of Land Management (BLM) is a relatively small Federal agency under the Department of the Interior that is responsible for the management of vast tracts of range and desert land and tundra throughout the Far West, Alaska, and the outer continental shelf. Until recently, "land management" was a gross overstatement of the BLM's relationship to its holdings, which with the single exception of some very valuable timber in southwestern Oregon, rarely received any but the most cursory attention. The growing concern for the environment and the energy crisis have changed that. Today the BLM is responsible for most of the major off-shore drilling programs, as well as the large western oil shale, geothermal, and coal leases. In addition, some of the resources under the BLM's control, such as the entire California desert have been discovered to be important resources requiring careful management.

The bureau, which has traditionally been mostly a grazing management and forestry operation, has found itself unprepared for the new scope of its responsibilities. Underfunded, understaffed, and short of needed new expertise, the BLM has often appeared ludicrous. When a use plan was adopted to control off-road vehicles on the 10 million acres of the California desert, the BLM was able to supply only a handful of men to police the area, none of whom had any statutory authority to tell anybody to do anything. Enforcement of the plan has been a farce. But the BLM, like the Forest Service, is changing in the same ways and for the same reasons.

The Department of Transportation

Through its administration of the Highway Trust Fund, the Department of Transportation (DOT) pays for most of the major road construction in the country. The Department does not take a lead role; most of the planning of highways is done at the state level. DOT's programs are supposed to support a wide range of transportation alternatives, but the political preference for highways and the massive bulk of the Trust Fund itself provide an impetus to continue the emphasis in that area.

The Nuclear Regulatory Commission

The Nuclear Regulatory Commission was created in 1974 in response to strong public criticism of the Atomic Energy Commission's dual role as the promoter and regulator of nuclear power. The Regulatory Commission has no research and development responsibilities. But it is responsible for setting safety standards for the design of nuclear reactors, the transfer of nuclear fuels, the movement and storage of nuclear waste, and the amount of radiation in cooling water discharge (although EPA also claims jurisdiction and has gone to court to obtain a definitive ruling.) The Commission also must rule on applications for nuclear reactor licensing. It remains to be seen whether the Commission will do a better job than its predecessor.

The Army Corps of Engineers

The Corps of Engineers is responsible for the maintenance of river navigation and harbors, and for flood control. In fulfillment of their first responsibility they have filled thousands of acres of marshland. Their flood control duties have provided the justification for hundreds of dams — most of which have served to benefit developers on downstream flood plains. The corps is perhaps the least environmentally aware of the Federal agencies, and almost certainly the most difficult to communicate with.

The Bureau of Reclamation

The Bureau of Reclamation builds dams and canals in the West. Its goal is to bring water to the land, and in pursuit of that goal it has provided a heavy subsidy to most of the water users in the region. Like the Corps of Engineers, the Bureau tends to think in very straight lines, as witness their proposal to build a dam that would have backed water into the Grand Canyon National Monument. There is increasing pressure within the Congress for requiring that those who benefit from Bureau projects pay the full cost of construction (including interest). Since the Bureau's future already is clouded by lack of appropriation, declining constituency, and ineffective leadership, the probable result of such a policy would be a drastic curtailment of the Bureau's activities.

The Department of Housing and Urban Development

The Department of Housing and Urban Development (HUD), despite its name, is not one of the Federal

government's master builders. It is, however, charged with the administration of an innovative law that is of importance to environmentalists, the National Flood Insurance Act of 1968. Under the Act, HUD subsidizes low cost flood insurance in communities where flooding is a major problem in return for the community's commitment to regulate new uses in the flood plain according to Federal standards.

In 1973, new amendments strengthened the program. Today the Act provides that unless communities subject to flooding join the Federal insurance program and adopt the new flood plain zoning standards, they will lose not only the flood insurance benefits, but also all Federal disaster benefits of any kind. Moreover, all Federally insured banks and savings and loan firms will be forbidden to issue any loans on property in those areas, essentially freezing all property sales and development. Because of this law, it is likely that by the end of 1975 nearly every flood-prone area in the country will have the beginnings of a flood plain zoning ordinance.

The National Park Service

Most of the natural wonders of the country are administered by the National Park Service. Beginning with Yellowstone National Park in 1872, the nation has put together a magnificent system of national parks and similar areas which this agency administers. The system embraces 300 units of three different types: natural areas, historic areas, and recreational areas. Classic natural scenery usually is protected under various designations within the natural area category; e.g. national parks, national monuments, and preserves. Historic monuments and sites memorialize both recent and archeological history, while recreational units vary from National Recreation Areas, and parkways, to National Seashores and Lakeshores.

While the National Park Service is entrusted with preserving some of

the most sensitive parts of America's environment, it is not exempt from controversy. Conservationists often object to plans for excessive development in places such as Yosemite Valley and there is a long history of controversy over proposals for new roads, tramways, and lodges in existing parks. This has led to efforts by conservationists to have the wilderness within most park units designated by act of Congress to specifically exempt it from development. Moreoever, conservationists continue their efforts to have additional fragile and superlative natural areas set aside for protection within this system, particularly now in Alaska.

Fish and Wildlife Service

This agency within the Interior Department both operates a system of National Wildlife Refuges and Ranges and a number of grant-in-aid programs to the states. More than 350 units exist in the refuge system it administers, encompassing more than 30 million acres. Most of them exist to protect migratory waterfowl, but there are also a limited number of major ranges designed to protect the habitat for such large mammals as bighorn sheep and grizzly bears. The service has recently had administration of some of these ranges taken away from it over the protest of conservationists; the Bureau of Land Management was given administration instead, ostensibly as an economic measure. The Service also administers over 100 fish hatcheries and 35 wildlife and fishery research stations and laboratories. It also administers the Endangered Species Act which bans taking endangered species and sets up a habitat acquisition program for them. The service rebates portions of excise taxes on sporting equipment to states for restoration of wildlife habitat.

Unfortunately, the service has historically been forced to undertake the task of controlling predators, such as coyotes, as well as protecting wildlife. As a result of a recent Executive Order, however, it has largely stopped using poisons to do this, but the agency has not altogether gotten out of this unhappy business. The service is indirectly involved in many environmental disputes over Corps of Engineers' water projects because it is required to comment on the impact these projects have on fish and wildlife; it also comments on many other federal environmental impact statements. The service is the center of field biological studies in the federal government.

The Bureau of Outdoor Recreation

A relatively new agency, the Bureau of Outdoor Recreation in the Interior Department administers no land, but it does play a key role in helping to protect more land. It administers the crucial Land and Water Fund from which hundreds of millions of dollars are granted to the states to acquire land for state and local parks. The adequacy of plans for new parks are to be judged according to the National Outdoor Recreation Plan, which it must prepare (though it has been hamstrung in its efforts to accomplish this task by federal economizing). It also oversees the Federal system of Wild and Scenic Rivers, and conducts most studies to determine whether additional rivers qualify for protection from dams. This agency also plays an important role in reviewing many environmental impact statements by other agencies, and particularly is charged with reviewing whether "feasible and prudent" alternative routes exist for proposed freeways that would cross parks, refuges, and recreation areas.

Energy Agencies

With the breakup of the old Atomic Energy Commission, its research laboratories were transferred to a new agency — the Energy Research and Development Administration (ERDA). ERDA is not supposed to be preoccupied with promoting nuclear power in the single-minded fashion of the AEC; it is also supposed to look impartially at the future for other fuels, from coal to such new alternative sources as solar and geothermal power. Moreover, it is supposed to stress the need for energy conservation as much as energy development. One of its six major divisions is devoted to conservation; another is devoted to assessing environmental impacts of various energy development strategies. However, it is all too likely that ERDA will absorb a developmental bias from the various agencies which were merged into it, but hopes continue that it will institutionalize some strong pockets of environmental thinking within it.

The Federal Energy Administration recently created is charged with developing a coherent national policy for the country, but so far its recommendations have been colored strongly by high-level political considerations in the current administration, and Congress has been wary. It also is supposed to maintain a balance in its thinking between energy development and conservation, but after a partly promising beginning, its emphases tilted with "Project Independence" toward heavy development. However, a few of its divisions do focus primarily on conservation and environmental concerns.

Federal Laws

The National Environmental Policy Act

The National Environmental Policy Act of 1969 (NEPA) and the state laws modeled upon it are in many situations the most important legal tools available to grassroots activists. Their provisions are binding on a wide variety of Federal and state government actions and have, at least at the Federal level, been strictly interpreted and enforced by the courts. When applicable, they provide for a full public review of the environmental effects of a proposed action and of available alternatives, and require the government to provide a formal answer to public comments on the proposal.

This section reviews the central provisions of NEPA, lists the basic steps involved in a proceeding under the act, and suggests how the law can be of use to environmentalists. Much of this material also applies to the state environmental policy (or environmental quality) acts, but each state act has slightly different legal provisions and administrative procedures, and each one has been interpreted by a different set of judges.

What's in the Law

NEPA has two titles, the second of which establishes the formation of the President's Council on Environmental Quality and is of no concern here. Title I, Section 101, sets the framework for the act by outlining a broad national policy toward the environment and then goes on to state that it is "the continuing responsibility of the Federal government to use all practicable means, consistent with other essential considerations of national policy" to plan and coordinate its activities in order to attain a series of environmental goals relating to: preservation of long- and short-term environmental health, attainment of a wide range of beneficial uses, preservation of our cultural and natural heritage and of an environment that encourages diversity, limitation of resource use, and improved management of renewable and non-renewable resources.

To assure that these goals be met in practice, Congress decided to include a set of "action-forcing" procedures, of which the most important is contained in Section 102(C) of the act. This section requires that *all* agencies of the Federal government shall:

(C) Include in every recommendation or report on proposals for legislation and other major Federal actions significantly affecting the human environment, a detailed statement by the responsible official on —

(i) The environmental impact of the proposed action,

(ii) Any adverse environmental effects which cannot be avoided should the proposal be implemented,

(iii) Alternatives to the proposed action,

(iv) The relationship between local short-term uses of man's environment and the maintenance and enhancement of long-term productivity, and

(v) Any irreversible and irretrievable commitments of resources which would be involved in the proposed action should it be implemented.

Section 102 further requires that the official preparing this environmental impact statement (EIS) must consult fully with all relevant Federal agencies before issuing the statement; and that copies of the statement must be made available to the public.

What the Act Means

At first glance, Section 102(C) may appear innocuous. Certainly it appeared that way to members of Congress, who passed it virtually without dissent, and to President Nixon, who signed it into law. The required content of the EIS was not spelled out in detail, and the preparation of the statement appeared, at that time, to be merely a procedural formality, the conclusions of which were not binding on the preparing agency. Therefore, most politicians apparently believed that the action-forcing procedures would have little effect on the workings of government. The Federal agencies agreed, and when the act became law in 1970 it was treated casually. Statements were seldom prepared; and if they were, their analyses were perfunctory and often inaccurate. But despite the expectations of the politicians and the bureaucrats, within two years after its passage NEPA had brought to a halt a large number of major Federal projects, and had begun a slow but visible transformation of bureaucratic attitudes toward the environment and environmentalists.

The reason for the dramatic effect of the act is simple: using the courts, environmental activists have forced the issue. Faced with a statute of "almost constitutional" breadth, and a reluctant bureaucracy, they have brought literally hundreds of suits alleging noncompliance with NEPA, and specifically with Section 102(C), forcing the courts to refine the broad language of the law and to clarify its application. As a result of these suits it is possible to give a fairly clear idea of when you can expect an Environmental Impact Statement to be prepared, what the statement must contain, and what will happen if the statement is taken into the courts.

When Must a Statement Be Prepared?

Section 102(C) requires a statement for "major Federal actions significantly affecting the human environment." "Federal actions" have been judged to include a wide variety of agency projects and programs, Federal leases and licensing of private industrial facilities (e.g. nuclear power plants), adminis-trative actions of regulatory agencies, and state and local projects funded through Federal agencies (but not through general revenue sharing money).

The authority of NEPA has been challenged by the Defense Department, which contends that when a project is essential to national security, the public decision-making process required by the act must be forgone. The problem has been raised with special force by the Navy's decision to locate its huge new Trident submarine base in a rural, lightly populated area along the Hood Channel in the state of Washington. Local environmentalists contend that the Navy made the decision to locate on the channel 16 months before preparing the statement, and a coalition of local citizens and national environmental groups have brought suit to force reconsideration of alternatives. Since a quarter of the national budget is allocated to defense, the issue is clearly of great importance to environmentalists. Agencies operating in the area of foreign policy also have been resisting the notion that NEPA applies to them, but gradually the State Department is giving way.

When is a Federal action "major," and what is a "significant effect?" The Council for Environmental Quality, which is NEPA's overseeing authority in the matter of environmental impact statements, has prepared its own guidelines, which reflect the court decisions of the first three years following the passage of the act. These guidelines stress several factors, in addition to the direct impact of the action, that must weigh in the decision to prepare or not to prepare a statement, including: secondary impacts, potential for cumulative impacts, the nature of the area in which the action is proposed and public concern over the action. This final point is of real importance. The CEQ guidelines say: "Proposed major actions, the environmental impact of which is likely to be highly controversial, should be covered in all cases." The practical implication is, *if you can organize some real opposition to a project, a statement will probably have to be prepared.*

What Should You Expect an EIS to Contain?

The quality standards for the content of an EIS are high. The courts have generally agreed that NEPA imposes a "strict standard of compliance for government agencies." They have based this interpretation on the language of Section 102, which states that the EIS requirements are to be complied with to the fullest extent possible.

Building on this interpretation, the courts have established specific requirements for both the tone and content of impact statements. The basic standard is "full disclosure." The statement must discuss "all known possible" environmental effects, including those brought to the agency's attention by the public. It must fully discuss the unavoidable adverse environmental impacts that would result from proceeding with the action. It must present its findings in an objective rather than a conclusive manner. And it must be written in clear, nontechnical language that can be understood by laymen. A full range of alternatives must also be discussed, including the alternative of "no action" and alternatives which may be beyond the current power of the agency to perform. Alternatives must be treated in sufficient depth to enable the non-expert to judge them. Not every possible alternative need be discussed, nor need the agency consider alternatives that are "speculative and remote."

The view of NEPA held by the courts is revolutionary in its implications, for what they have said is that citizens are entitled to a fully documented, unbiased, and honest assessment of the Federal decision-making process as it effects the environment, and that no action which qualifies under NEPA can proceed

until that full public accounting has been given. The EIS is therefore the perfect tool for all those who believe that if only the full facts were available then the public would rise up and halt the project. Under NEPA, unless the facts are out, there is no project.

Bringing Suit for Enforcement

Needless to say, not every government agency can meet this standard every time. An agency may not want to put up with the expense and delay involved in preparing a statement, or it may fear that if all impacts of the project are candidly discussed that public support will evaporate. The result can be a conspicuous reluctance to prepare any statement, although this trend has diminished as the courts have clarified the meaning of the law. More frequently now the problem is in the content. In either case, the solution lies in the courts.

Here, too, the legal trends have been favorable to environmentalists. Under NEPA, it is relatively easy for citizens to gain standing to sue. Generally the courts have held that suits for enforcement of the act can be brought by individuals or organizations who can show that the action would cause an "injury in fact" to their interests. Specifically included in the list of defensible interests are recreation, conservation, and aesthetics. Organizations are not required to show that they will suffer direct financial injury, nor are they required to show that all of their members would suffer the "injury in fact" that they allege.

In some instances, it now appears that individuals and organizations may bring an NEPA suit as members of the general public, in a type of environmental class action. This conclusion results from a suit brought by a group of George Washington University law students against the Interstate Commerce Commission demanding preparation

of an EIS for a proposed railroad rate increase which, the students contended, exacerbated a rate bias against scrap metal. They claimed standing as members of the public whose interests were damaged by the tendency of the rates to discourage recycling, and the Supreme Court upheld their claim of standing.

If a statement does get to the courts, the current standard of review is extremely strict. In pursuit of the full disclosure standard, many judges conduct what amounts to a complete reexamination of the technical evidence in the case. Theoretically, that review is limited to the question of whether the statement does in fact meet the conditions which the courts have established, and whether the facts and analyses advanced in the document are complete and accurate. But in practical terms, the effect of an extensive review of the evidence, complete with expert witnesses on both sides, is to raise with great explicitness the problems of conflicting values that led to the legal dispute. Almost inevitably the merits of the decision itself lie close to the surface in a court review. In situations where the outcome of a dispute depends on a value like safety, and the courts rule that an adequate statement must include a full discussion of the dangers of the proposal, the effect may be to kill the project forever.

Will a bad environmental impact statement provide a legal rationale for halting a project? Probably not. But the judicial trend is in that direction. The issue is whether the Federal agency is bound to honor the substantive policies of Section 101 of the act as well as the procedural requirements of Section 102. An adverse statement on an action would indicate that the agency was not honoring those policies. But courts are wary of intruding into areas that are left by law to the discretion of the responsible agency. And much here is left to their discretion, as long as an agency is not arbitrary or capricious.

The EIS Procedure

Based on what the law says and the way the courts have interpreted it, there are several practical conclusions that can be drawn. First, if you want to force a statement to be prepared for a proposed action, make some noise. More important, make sure that your allies, including local and state government, also request that a statement be prepared. The legal precedents for an area may be important, and you will probably want to do some research to see what kind of projects have been held to require impact statements in your region, but your best handle is almost certainly the fact that most agencies are required by their own regulations to prepare an EIS whenever the potential for serious controversy exists.

Second, you can influence preparation of the statement. The standards of analysis set by NEPA are often beyond the reach of the preparing agency, particularly when the planning work is being done at the district office level, as it often is. It is not uncommon to have a single planner trying to cope with four or five statements simultaneously. Under these conditions it isn't surprising that a lot of statements read as though they were concocted from form-books and boiler plate. They were.

Under the act the preparing agency is required to respond to information submitted by the public. If a local group can supply technical assistance and/or detailed knowledge of the region that will be affected by the project, it can often improve the quality of the statement markedly. You benefit both ways. If the information is accepted, the rationale for halting the action is strengthened, while a rebuff from the agency reflects poorly on them.

Third, when the government prepares and circulates its draft statement for comments, make sure that it gets ample publicity and that all interested agencies provide comments. If you are considering a court challenge, you should keep in mind that the courts will give much more weight to negative comments from other government agencies. Most agencies are asked to comment on many more statements than they can do justice to. The best way to assure that the statement with which you are concerned is not passed over, is to contact the agencies yourself, either in person or by letter. The individual preparing the comments will do a much better job if he can leaven the bureaucratic language of the statement with first-hand knowledge of the situation.

You should consider legal action only as a last resort. In doing so, you should keep in mind that the threat of a suit may be all that you need to achieve your goal. A full-dress court action, complete with expert witnesses, can cost an awful lot. Moreover, unless the agency's proposed action is clearly outrageous, a favorable decision will probably do no more than force further revisions in the statement.

A more effective course is to master the judicial interpretation of NEPA (see Bibliography), and to use that knowledge to put the preparing agency on the spot by pointing out the statement's failure to meet the criteria set by those interpretations. The fact that you know the law may in itself tend to sway the agency. If you have a lawyer, have him write letters on his stationery — that too will have an effect. If you know of a public interest law firm that will write your letters for you, your impact will increase. The goal: Get them to back off before they begin going in the wrong direction.

What the EIS Can Do for You

A bad EIS cannot in itself stop a project. But that does not mean that statements have no effect. Often "full disclosure" of a proposal's impact will by itself arouse public opinion enough to stop the project or force major modifications. The delay required for the preparation of a statement can in itself be an important weapon, particularly in these uncertain times. During a one to two year delay, new technology or the collapse of expected demand can make a project unnecessary, cost-inflation can make it uneconomic, or changes in the laws or the dominant political regime can halt it forever. These effects of the EIS are substantial and not to be scorned.

A Note on the States

Statutes modeled on NEPA and governing the actions of state governments now exist in about half of the fifty states. Although they differ in detail, many of these acts are alike in requiring the preparation of an environmental impact statement or report for state actions with significant effect on the environment. Some require that local governments also prepare statements. In a few states — including California, Washington, and Minnesota — the law requires that the granting of local zoning and construction permits for major projects also be subject to an EIS. Usually, local agency procedures for preparation and review are less structured than at the Federal level, and the standard of review in the courts will also be lower; but for local conservationists, the EIS is still a valuable tool.

The Clean Air Act and Amendments

The Clean Air Amendments of 1970 provide the governing air quality legislation for the entire United States. For years before their passage, air pollution control had been largely delegated to the individual states. But the competition between states to attract new industry prevented any single state from enacting a meaningful pollution control bill, despite the growing severity of the pollution problem. The Federal government assumed a limited, and ineffective, role with the passage of the Clean Air Act in 1965. In 1970, at the height of the Earth Day fervor, the Congress passed the amendments, which substantially modified existing Federal legislation and put the national government in charge of assuring clean air for the entire country.

Basic Provisions of the Amendments

There are five key features of the amendments. First, the Environmental Protection Agency is empowered to set national ambient air quality standards, specifying the maximum allowable concentrations of the major air pollutants (particulates, sulfur dioxide, carbon monoxide, nitrogen dioxide, and photochemical oxidants) that shall be allowed. Two standards are established: primary standards are those required to protect public health; secondary standards are those required to protect property, wildlife, and other aspects of public welfare. (Section 109)

In order to assure that primary standards are achieved as rapidly as possible, the amendments require that individual states must submit implementation plans for EPA review and approval. Plans were required to provide for the attainment of national primary standards by 1975. In order to win EPA approval a state had to be able to demonstrate that it had the legal authority, the funding, and the manpower:

—to adopt and enforce emission standards or limitations necessary to meet the national standards, including land-use and transportation controls,

—to enforce its own regulations,

—to abate polluting emissions when they threatened public health,

—to prevent construction, modification, or operation of buildings or other facilities that would prevent attainment or maintenance of a national air quality standard, and

—to require operators of stationary sources to install monitoring devices and to make regular re-

ports to the state on the type and amount of their emissions, and to make those reports available to the public. (Section 110)

If EPA judges that a state implementation plan does not meet the requirements of the law, or if a state fails to submit a plan, then EPA is authorized to step in and prepare a plan which does meet those requirements. Moreover, if a state should become derelict in enforcing its plan after EPA has already granted its approval, then — after giving the state notice of noncompliance — the Agency is authorized (but not required) to assume enforcement of the law until such time as the state has satisfied them that it is again able and willing to meet the standards of the amendments. (Sections 110, 113)

Under the act, EPA is required to set: standards of performance for emissions from stationary sources (e.g. blast furnaces, power plants, incinerators); standards for emissions of hazardous pollutants; and standards for truck, automobile, motorcycle and aircraft engine emissions. These standards are all established nationwide.

Finally, the act provides that any citizen or citizens' organization may bring suit against private individuals or public agencies allegedly in violation of any stationary source or hazardous emission standard established under a state implementation plan. Suits may also be brought against EPA for failing to perform any of the duties required of it under the amendments — including the promulgation of standards and the drafting of implementation plans for states or regions where they are defective.

How the Law Has Worked

The act gives the states five years to meet the primary standards for the major pollutants, five years that ended in mid-1975. As the deadline passed, it was estimated that about three quarters of the country's population still lives

in an area where at least one of the common pollutants regularly exceeds the levels set in the act. Los Angeles, Chicago, and Philadelphia exceeded the standards for all five pollutants. The New York metropolitan region exceeded the standard for three. Some experts projected that Los Angeles would not reach the primary standards by the year 2000.

The reasons for this failure are complex. One problem has been that advances in control technologies have been slow to occur and are costly. Energy and economic problems have also led to strong political pressure for easing of standards by big business.

But far and away the most important reason for the limited success of the amendments is our national dependence on the automobile as our major mode of transportation. In the most heavily polluted urban regions, the only way to meet the primary standards is to reduce the use of the automobile. This is political dynamite for both local and state politicians. Los Angeles, the most car-ridden American city and probably the most polluted as well, illustrates the problem. The state of California was initially charged with seeing that an implementation plan for the Los Angeles basin was prepared. They refused to include any transportation controls in their plan or indeed to produce any plan at all by the statutory deadline. EPA in turn did not begin to prepare a plan until forced to do so by a lawsuit brought by San Bernardino and Riverside, both of which are in the direct path of the smog generated in Los Angeles. EPA's first plan stated that gasoline rationing would be necessary to achieve clean air on schedule. Public reaction was immediate and hostile. Seeking to palliate public opinion, EPA then proposed a downtown parking tax, but got an equally negative response. That plan was also withdrawn. Similar plans in other major cities met with equally stiff opposition.

Citizen Involvement

The list of problems above discloses two areas where citizen involvement is badly needed. The first is enforcement. A citizen monitoring group of twenty or thirty people could sharply increase the effectiveness of a local air pollution control authority. The second is participation in the development of workable implementation plans, including transportation and land-use control strategies. This second task will require more time, effort, and political sophistication than the first, but the potential for air quality improvement is far greater than with any other approach.

The Federal Water Pollution Control Act and Amendments

The Federal Water Pollution Control Act Amendments of 1972 (FWPCA) are modeled on the Clean Air Amendments. Like the air quality legislation, they place the ultimate responsibility for setting and enforcement of pollution standards at the Federal level, while at the same time establishing a procedure for turning day-to-day enforcement over to the states. It contains strict penalties for violation of the law and provisions for citizen enforcement.

The amendments are based on the supposition that no one really has the right to pollute and that a strict timetable must be set to force the pace of reform. By 1977, those who would discharge pollutants from an identifiable outlet (or point source) must install the "best practicable technology" to abate pollution. By 1981, they must replace that with the "best available technology." By 1983, the goal is to improve all water quality to a level which is suitable for recreational use, including swimming. And by 1983, the goal is to eliminate discharges into navigable waters entirely. However, the Congress did appoint a National Commission on Water Quality to review the feasibility of trying to meet the schedule.

The amendments are long and complex, dealing with water-related subjects as diverse as small boat plumbing and the cost-benefit ratios of dams. But the broad outline of the act is fairly clear. Titles I and II of the act provide respectively for Federal financial assistance to states for water quality planning and for 75 percent Federal support in the construction of new treatment facilities. Their essential purpose is to enable states and local governments to meet the strong regulations set in Titles III and IV of the act.

The act also requires that states must adopt receiving water standards (statements of the maximum pollution load that will be tolerated in any body of water) for all waters in the state. All must be submitted for Federal review, and if they are weaker than those under the act itself, they must be amended to meet the EPA's objections. Thereafter, any changes in a state's receiving water standards must be approved by EPA.

EPA is authorized to set "standards of performance" for almost all of the major industrial and agricultural polluters — from paper mills to feedlots. These standards are required to be based on the EPA's judgment of what is "achievable through application of the best available demonstrated control technology, processes, operating networks, or other alternatives."

The act also requires EPA to set standards for the discharge of industrial waste — particularly waste containing heavy metals — into municipal sewer systems, for the discharge of toxic materials, and for any discharge into the ocean.

The mechanism for achieving these goals is the National Pollution Discharge Elimination System, a nationwide permit program. Under the act it becomes a Federal crime carrying a fine of up to $10,000 per day to discharge wastes to the nation's waters without a permit issued under the authority of the act. No permit can be issued unless the discharge is found to meet all of the standards established under Title III. EPA is granted overall responsibility for the administration of the program, and initial authority to issue permits. Permit authority passes to a state only after it has satisfied EPA that its own program includes: discharge standards at least as stringent as those set by the act; adequate implementation authority, including the power to conduct inspections of private facilities, their records, and their monitoring equipment; and a priority ranking for new waste-water facilities.

The act also provides for Federal enforcement in the event that a state should cease to enforce its plan. If such a failure is brought to the attention of EPA, the agency must intervene and take over the administration of the plan. In the event that EPA fails to act when a state is clearly in violation of its approved plan, any citizen may bring suit against the agency to require that the Agency do its duty. Similar suits may be brought against any private or public discharger who is alleged to be in violation of Federal discharge standards or of a cease and desist order issued pursuant to those standards.

Citizen Involvement

It is possible for citizens to become involved in implementation of the Water Pollution Control Amendments to achieve short-term goals. Two examples would be intervention in a state agency hearing to protest the issuance of a permit to a large polluter in an area where it can be shown that progress is not being made toward "swimmable water," or a legal action to halt an obvious violation of the act. However, effective involvement in water pollution control requires a more serious commitment. Because of the heavy costs of compliance and chronic foot-dragging by many industries, the issue is often moved back into the political arena.

How clean is clean enough, given the technological and financial limitations? If your area is heavily dependent on pollution generating industry, you will find that the major employers in the area think they know the answer: "Not very much." They will probably have a host of water quality technicians and hired biologists to back them up, and they may have support from other local business interests and perhaps the newspaper as well. On the other side will be the law — and the law, to a disheartening degree, will be you.

If you expect to be taken seriously by government officials who often operate under intense political pressure, you must know the law as well as they do. The only preparation for this kind of participation is to immerse yourself thoroughly in the law itself and the regulations issued under it. Conservation organizations have put out handbooks for participation in FWPCA proceedings, two of which are listed in the bibliography on page 269.

State Land-Use Laws

State air and water pollution control laws are closely modeled on the requirements of the governing Federal legislation. Most state efforts have therefore focused heavily on the different aspects of land use. State land-use laws fall into four general categories: resource conservation, industrial siting, regional development, and statewide planning.

Resource Conservation

The most common type of resource conservation law is aimed at protecting wetlands, which are extremely important biologically and which cannot be developed without being destroyed. One example of such legislation is the Delaware Wetlands Act. The act establishes a planning process in State government for the designation of wetland areas. A public hearing is required for designation.

In an area that has been identified as a wetland, no development, including dredge and fill, can proceed without a permit from the state. New York's Wetlands Law takes a similar approach, but with the added provision that during the period when designations are being established a moratorium is placed on all development in tidal wetland areas.

States have also taken action to preserve specific wetland areas. California has established a Conservation and Development Commission to regulate development around the edges of San Francisco Bay. The commission has permit authority over all development within 100 feet of high water line, as well as over any project to fill or dredge the bay itself.

Such legislation illustrates the trend toward regulation of both fresh and saltwater shorelines. Wisconsin's Shoreline Protection Program requires that counties enact shoreline protection ordinances for all unincorporated land within their

jurisdiction within 1,000 feet of a lake, pond, or flowage and within 300 feet of a navigable river or stream or the landward side of the flood plain, whichever distance is greater. Within that area, counties are required to regulate the subdivision of land, creation of single lots, building location, logging, landfill and sewage disposal according to minimum standards established by the state. In the event that a county fails to adopt such regulations, the State Department of Natural Resources is authorized to impose them. The act has been successful in forcing counties to prepare ordinances, but the effectiveness of the program has suffered from the unwillingness of local government to enforce the law against disgruntled property owners, and from the fact that the ordinances cover only the unincorporated areas of the county.

Other shoreline protection efforts range from Delaware's law regulating all heavy industrial development in its coastal zone to California's ambitious coastal planning effort. The California law, which passed as a citizen sponsored initiative after coastal legislation had twice been killed by pro-development interests in the legislature, establishes a State Coastal Commission and six Regional Commissions to regulate development along the 1,000-mile California coast. The law provides a three-year period during which the commissions are to prepare a comprehensive conservation plan for the entire coast. During those three years no development of more than $7,500 in value can take place anywhere within the three-mile limit offshore, or within 1,000 yards of the mean high water line without a permit from the regional commission stating that the development meets the goals of the act and would not result in any "substantial adverse environmental impact" on coastal zone resources. Regional permit decisions can be appealed to the state level by applicants whose permits have been denied or by local activists who meet the loose definition of "aggrieved person," and State Coastal Commission decisions may be appealed in the state court system. At the close of the three-year period the commissions are required to submit their plan to the legislature for approval or modification.

To date, state and regional commission decisions have substantially altered the size and quality of coastal development, but it is agreed that the strong conservation plan which they have prepared will have a difficult time in the legislature. The trend marked by Delaware, California, and other states has been encouraged by the Federal Coastal Zone Management Act of 1972, which provides financial assistance to states which implement coastal zone planning programs which meet the requirements set in the law.

Still another type of resource conservation law provides preferential tax assessment for open space lands, particularly those used for agriculture. These laws are intended to reduce the economic pressure on farmers to convert their land to a "higher and better use" that results when development of neighboring lands raises the value of their property, and hence their tax bill. Typically, under these laws land is assessed on the basis of its potential income from farming, as capitalized at prevailing interest rates, and is taxed according to that value. Almost every state has one of these laws, but they have generally been failures for the reason that many programs offer the tax concession without making any demands on the farmer — the farmer simply takes the tax break and continues to farm until someone makes him an offer that he can't refuse. Many states have tried to deal with this problem by requiring that the farmer make a legal commitment to keep his land in agricultural use in return for his reduced assessment, but even in these areas, participation in the program is voluntary. This is a real flaw, since it means that farmers generally stay out of

the contract arrangement if their land has substantial value as real estate. The problems with these laws suggest that some kind of state zoning may be the only way to protect agricultural lands.

Industrial Siting

If there is an archetype of the grassroots environmental battle, it is the outraged citizens of a small town struggling to stop a major utility from putting a power plant in the middle of their community. So many of these struggles have been waged, and at such great cost both to the utilities and to the public, that many states have now acted to speed up the power plant siting process. In some cases that action has been token — creating, for example, an advisory committee for siting problems. But in other states, major changes have been made.

Maryland's Power Plant Siting Act is a good example. The act authorizes the state secretary of natural resources, working with the Public Service Commission (PSC), to conduct a detailed environmental review of all possible and proposed sites for new electric power plants, based on the PSC's ten-year forecast of electricity demands. After that review has been completed, the secretary may disbar any sites which he thinks justify an "unsuitable classification." After further study of environment impacts, the state is required to designate sites suitable for construction, and to purchase at least one such site for each of the major utilities operating in the state, which shall be available to the utilities for lease or purchase. Sites may be acquired by eminent domain. The planning program, and an accompanying program of research into means of minimizing plant impacts, are both funded from a 0.1 mill tax per kilowatt hour of electricity that is sold in the state.

A close relative of power plant siting legislation (which, ironically, excludes power plants from its proceedings) is the Maine Site Location Law. Under the law, all industrial

or commercial developments which require a permit from the state pollution control authority, or which occupy more than 20 acres, or which contemplate drilling for or excavating natural resources, or which would occupy more than 60,000 square feet of floor space, are required to obtain a permit from the state Environmental Improvement Commission. A permit can be granted with conditions to mitigate the impact on the environment, or it can be denied if the commission finds that the impact on the site would be excessive. Subdivisions of land for residential use of over 20 acres in area are judged to be commercial uses. Significantly, the act is regarded as having been successful in dealing with new development, despite the fact that for most of its history it has not had the staff to police its own jurisdiction. The reason: environmental activists have acted as an informal alliance to assure that the commission was informed of all development that fell under its rules. Of further significance, unfortunately, enforcement of commission decisions has usually been poor, emphasizing the need for citizen monitoring of new environmental programs.

Regional Development

In heavily developed urban areas, city and town boundaries rarely make sense environmentally. A shopping center next to the border between two communities may have more effect on the neighboring town than it does on the town in which it is located. Yet the voters in the neighboring town have nothing to say about the decision and receive none of the tax benefits. On the other hand, if the town where the shopping center is to be located rises up in anger to protect a favorite patch of open space, there is no guarantee that the center won't relocate in the middle of a priceless wetland that happens to be located in a town that is less concerned about environmental quality. Problems like this have given rise to an interest in more regional government, and that interest has been spurred by Federal requirements that air and water pollution management be conducted on a regional basis.

The most well-known of these regional approaches is the Metropolitan Council of the Twin Cities in Minnesota. The council has authority to develop its own Comprehensive Development Guide to the region, and to review the plans of independent commissions, boards, and agencies for conformance to that guide. If the council finds that the regional plan is not in conformance or is detrimental to the orderly and economic development of the metropolitan area, it can suspend the plan indefinitely, thus halting the operations of the agency involved. The council also has authority to review local plans or other local matters "which have a substantial effect on metropolitan area development" and may mediate disputes between local governments. It does not, however, have the authority to modify local plans.

In addition the council retains substantial authority over local development through its control of all sewer construction in the metropolitan area and of airport construction (and the zoning of the surrounding land as well). A final, important aspect of the council is its authority, under the so-called Fiscal Disparities law, to collect 40 percent of each community's growth in commercial-industrial assessed valuation, with the intent of equalizing the tax benefits of development to those communities who are paying the school and service bills to house the workers at the new facilities.

Statewide Planning

An increasing number of states are now combining resource conservation and development policies on a statewide basis. Initially, this trend was strongest in rural areas which were suddenly threatened by rapid population growth and heavy speculative land development, and where local governments were often unprepared for development pressure.

But today more urban states are considering statewide land-use management efforts. The Federal government is partially responsible for the trend. Air and water pollution control requirements are forcing governments to consider land use on a regional basis. In addition, it is likely that in the near future, Federal financial assistance will be made available to states with land-use planning programs, under the so-called Jackson-Udall bill. This legislation narrowly failed to pass the House of Representatives in 1974, and is expected to be enacted in 1975.

The Hawaii Land Use Law

In 1961, soon after achieving statehood, Hawaii enacted the first statewide land-use law in the nation. The law was prompted by urban encroachment into the fertile agricultural lands north of Honolulu, and passage was simplified by the support of the large landholders who control most of the agricultural land in the state. Another factor making for relatively easy passage was Hawaii's small size. With only four counties in the state it was difficult to excite the public with the specter of being controlled from a distant and hostile state capital, which has stymied land-use reform in many states.

The law provides for the zoning of the state into four land-use categories: urban, rural, agriculture, and conservation. Within each zone, permitted uses are clearly spelled out. Urban districts comprise the areas of the state that have already been built up, as well as a reserve for future urban growth. Within areas that have received this designation, control passes to the county or city involved. Agriculture districts comprise most of the prime land in the state (about 10 percent of the state's area) as well as large areas devoted exclusively to grazing. Conservation districts include most of the publicly owned land, land along natural corridors like stream beds and ravines, and a forty-foot strip of land along the ocean front. Rural land is a mixed classification providing for scattered large lot development and small scale agriculture.

Land in the rural and agricultural districts is under the jurisdiction of the State Land Use Commission, which is made up of seven private citizens, as well as the director of the Department of Land and Natural Resources, and the director of the Department of Planning and Economic Development. The commission establishes the boundaries of the different districts, promulgates development regulations for each district, and rules on requests for rezonings — usually from agriculture to urban. Every five years, the commission is required to conduct a review of all district boundaries and to alter them where appropriate. Land in the conservation district is administered by the Department of Land and Natural Resources.

Citizen access is limited to public hearings on zoning changes and to the five-year review. Despite this, one study of the act states that public pressure for sound conservation policies has been a major cause of the Land Use Commission's willingness to take a strong stand against the rapid development of the state's agricultural land.

The Vermont Environmental Control Law

The Vermont Environmental Control Law (Act 250) passed the State legislature in 1970 in response to a wave of shoddy, quick-buck developments in the southern part of the state. The act created the State Environmental Board, and empowered it to issue development and subdivision permits through seven district commissions and to prepare a three-part statewide land-use plan. The Environmental Board was to consist of nine members appointed by the governor; the district commissions, of three members from each region, appointed in the same way.

The permit authority of the state board governs all development down to one acre in towns without a zoning or subdivision ordinance, and down to ten acres in areas with such ordinances. It also governs housing projects of ten units or more within a radius of five miles; state and municipal government developments; and all development at altitudes over 2500 feet. The act exempts farming, forestry, and electric utilities from its coverage.

Every application for a permit must go before the district commission with jurisdiction, and if it is challenged by any public or private person the district must hold a hearing. All applications are reviewed by a committee of environmental specialists from the State government, who prepare an advisory technical report. In order to grant a permit, the district commission must find that the development conforms to standards set in the law for water and air quality, soil erosion potential, traffic, the effect upon and availability of public services, and natural and historic values. Permits may be denied, or granted with conditions. In some cases the conditions attached to a project may in themselves be enough to halt it.

If the applicant, or a state or local agency that was party to the hearing, is dissatisfied with the district commission's decision, he may appeal to the Environmental Board. In theory, private groups or individuals in opposition to the project may not appeal, but that rule is sometimes bent in practice. Further recourse is available in the Vermont Supreme Court.

The three plans provided for under the law are: (1) an interim capability plan, (2) a capability and development plan, and (3) a land use plan. The interim plan went out of effect as soon as the final two plans were completed in 1973. All permit applicants must now show that their proposed development is in conformance with the two statewide plans in order to receive a permit.

Florida Environmental Land and Water Act

The Florida Environmental Land and Water Act illustrates the "areas of critical concern" approach to state land-use planning, which has also been adopted in Minnesota. The act allows the state to designate areas of "critical state concern" within which all development must conform to standards for the area. Local governments in the affected region must revise their plans to meet the state's requirements or else face imposition of standards from above. Areas of critical concern can be chosen because they contain "environmental, historical, natural, or archaeological resources of regional or statewide importance," because they surround major public facilities or areas of major public investment, or because they are an area of major development potential. Recommendations are solicited from the regional planning agency, and ultimately receive formal consideration from the Administration Commission (the Governor and his cabinet sitting in another role).

The act also empowers the state to set standards for "developments of regional impact." Such development is not defined in the act, but the state is required to prepare guidelines for identifying such development based on the potential for pollution, traffic generation, population increase, total area, growth-inducing impacts, and irreversible and irretrievable commitments of resources. Developments of regional impact are still subject to local government approval, but only after the local government has received a formal advisory review from the regional planning agency. If the development is located in an area of critical state concern then it is subject to the regulations for development in that area.

Any local government decision regarding development of regional impact or development in areas of critical state concern may be appealed by the owner, the developer, the regional planning agency, or the Division of State Planning. Such appeals are heard by the State Land and Water Adjudicatory Commission (the Governor and his cabinet again). The Adjudicatory Commission has 120 days in which to render a decision, pursuant to the standards of the act. Decisions of the commission are subject to judicial review.

Bibliography

Federal Laws

In addition to the laws themselves, which may be obtained from the Government Printing Office, EPA, or in the case of the air and water laws from your state pollution control agencies, there are several basic tools.

One is the *Code of Federal Regulations* (CFR), especially Chapter 40, which contains the regulations issued under the laws discussed in this chapter. The second is the *Federal Register.* Published daily by the Federal government, the *Register* reports on all agency decisions and on proposed amendments and additions to the existing regulations. Chapter 40 of the *Code* and back issues of the *Register* can be obtained through the Government Printing Office in Washington, D.C.

Since 1970, the Council on Environmental Quality has published an annual report, *Environmental Quality;* the first five reports are available from the Government Printing Office. These provide a good introduction to the history of Federal environmental laws — the rationale behind them, and the specifics of their implementation.

The Bureau of National Affairs, a private research organization in Washington, D.C., publishes the *Environment Reporter,* an extremely informative and useful publication that reports on the environmental activities of both state and Federal governments every week. Unfortunately, the *Reporter* is expensive — several hundred dollars per year — but local libraries can be persuaded to subscribe. Federal and state environmental agencies with offices in your region may also maintain a subscription.

A good technical guide to the entire field of Federal law dealing with the environment is:

Dolgin, Erica and Guilbert, Thomas, eds. *Federal Environmental Law.* St. Paul: West Publishing Co., 1974. This is a law textbook and is not easy reading, but the content is of very high quality. Each area of Federal concern is treated by an expert in the field.

The National Environmental Policy Act

Anderson, Frederick R. *NEPA in the Courts: A Legal Analysis of the National Environmental Policy Act.* Baltimore: Johns Hopkins University Press, 1973. Everything you could conceivably want to know about NEPA unless you plan to take legal action. If you're involved in a statement proceeding, this will tell you where you stand.

Yarrington, Hugh J. "The National Environmental Policy Act." *Environment Reporter*, vol. 4, no. 36 (Jan. 4, 1974). Bureau of National Affairs. This is a shorter, but still very useful, analysis of NEPA and its interpretation in the courts. If you read this, you'll know more than almost any of the bureaucrats.

The Clean Air Amendments

Natural Resources Defense Council. *Action for Clean Air: A Manual for Citizen Participation in State Implementation Plan Proceedings under the Clean Air Act Amendments of 1970.* Washington, D.C.: Natural Resources Defense Council, 1971.

Natural Resources Defense Council. *Transportation Controls for Clean Air: A Manual for Citizen Participation in State Implementation Plan Proceedings under the Clean Air Act Amendments of 1970.* Washington, D.C.: Natural Resources Defense Council.

The Federal Water Pollution Control Act Amendments

Izaak Walton League of America. *A Citizen's Guide to Clean Water.* Arlington, Va: Izaak Walton League, June, 1973.

Natural Resources Defense Council. *Water Pollution Control Handbook: A Citizen's Guide to the Federal Water Pollution Control Act Amendments of 1972.* 3 vols. Washington, D.C.: Natural Resources Defense Council.

State Laws

Babcock, Richard F. *The Zoning Game: Municipal Practices and Policies.* Madison: University of Wisconsin Press, 1966. Although this book is highly critical of zoning, and of the ability of government to make better land-use decisions than the free market, it provides numerous practical insights into the way local land-use decisions are made.

Bosselman, Fred, and Callies, David. *The Quiet Revolution in Land Use Control.* Prepared for the Council on Environmental Quality. Washington, D.C.: Government Printing Office, 1972. A great study of the new state land-use laws, including sections on Hawaii, Vermont, San Francisco Bay, the Minnesota Metropolitan Commission and others. Careful analyses of the political and environmental background of each law, its statutory provisions, and its practical effects. Stylistically bland and heavily footnoted, the book is not easy reading, but careful study is very rewarding.

Bosselman, Fred; Callies, David; and Banta, John. *The Taking Issue.* Prepared for the Council on Environmental Quality. Washington, D.C.: Government Printing Office, 1974. What happens when your city council downzones the half-acre that was supposed to become highrise apartments, and has been taxed accordingly? Is it a denial of property rights or a proper exercise of the police power? This book explains the historical view of property rights in America and shows how the courts are reinterpreting those rights in the light of new environmental awareness.

Haskell, Elizabeth H. "Land Use and the Environment: Public Policy Issues." *Environment Reporter*, vol. 5, no. 28 (November 8, 1974). Washington, D.C.: The Bureau of National Affairs. A thorough review of the basic issues in land-use policy. Short and well worth reading.

Reilly, William K., ed. *The Use of Land: A Citizen's Policy Guide to Urban Growth.* New York: Thomas Y. Crowell Company, 1973. Prepared by Lawrence Rockefeller's Task Force on Urban Growth, this report reviews most of the important strategies for assuring better land use. A good section at the end on the Role of the Citizen.

Whyte, William H. *The Last Landscape.* New York: Doubleday & Co., 1968. A very well written and interesting book on the problems of open space preservation.

State Land-Use Laws

California

McAteer-Petris Act of 1969 (San Francisco Bay): California Government Code, sec. 66600-653.

Odell, Rice B. *The Saving of San Francisco Bay.* Washington, D.C.: The Conservation Foundation, 1972.

Coastal Zone Conservation Act: California Resources Code, sec. 27000 et seq.

Delaware

Coastal Zone Act: Delaware Code, chap. 70, title 7, sec. 7001 et seq. (1971).

Florida

Environmental Land and Water Management Act of 1972: Laws of Florida, chap. 72-317.

Myers, Phyllis. *Slow Start in Paradise: An Account of the Development, Passage, and Implementation of State Land-Use Legislation in Florida.* Washington, D.C.: The Conservation Foundation, 1974.

Hawaii

Hawaii Land Use Law: Hawaii Rev. Stat., chap. 205 (1968) as Amended (Supp. 1969).

Maine

Maine Site Location of Development Law: Maine Rev. Stat. Ann., title 38, sec. 481-88 (Supp. 1970).

Maryland

Maryland Power Plant Siting Act: Annotated Code of Maryland, Natural Resources Article; title 3, Environmental Programs; subtitle 3, Power Plant Siting and Research Program.

Minnesota

Minnesota Metropolitan Council: Minnesota Stat. Ann. chap. 473B (Supp. 1971).

Vermont

Vermont Environmental Control Law (Act 250): 10 V.S.A., sec. 6001-6091 (Supp. 1970).

Myers, Phyllis. *So Goes Vermont: An Account of the Development, Passage, and Implementation of State Land-Use Legislation in Vermont.* Washington, D.C.: The Conservation Foundation, 1974.

A Grass Roots Review

Editor's Note: In order to make this book as complete as possible, we asked a particularly well-informed environmental journalist friend who calls herself "Blackbird" to assemble a source list for our readers. On the following pages her selection of books and other information sources appears together with her commentary. With a few exceptions, sources listed here were published within the past two or three years.

Energy

Energy for Survival: The Alternative to Extinction by Wilson Clark. Anchor/ Doubleday Books. $12.50. This is the most talked-about book on energy, period, and with much good reason. Wilson Clark, who began this work when he was in his early twenties — he is only a few years older than that now — has presented a finished statement that could pass for the work of a person decades older. *Energy for Survival* is extremely lucid and well-researched. It presents an uncompromising overview of our culture, beginning with a history of energy use for the past fifty or one hundred years and moving through how energy is used in industry by monopolies and transportation, agriculture, in homes and other buildings. After having described the situation: "The advertising industry has grown exponentially with development of high-energy American civilization," Clark presents a look at the future, discusses the tremendous dangers of nuclear energy, and views possibilities of natural energy use within a changed culture. Not an easy book, certainly, because of its accurate honesty, but one excellent tool for informed action.

Senator Mike Gravel's Energy Newsletter, U.S. Senate, Washington, D.C. 20510. Free. A terse, friendly, periodic report on current trends and developments relating to nuclear power, solar power, and other energy-related issues.

Rodale's Environment Action Bulletin. Rodale Press. Emmaus, Pa. 18049. $10.00/yr (biweekly). Two special issues, dated March 30 and April 6, 1974, discuss the dangers of nuclear energy, and tell about ongoing individual and group efforts to halt nuclear power plants, including information about the energetic work of Pennsylvania housewife Pat Hoffman (who is a wonderful example of citizen-turned-activist).

Information about nuclear and solar energy, including films, books, pamphlets, articles, bumper stickers, glossaries and charts is available from Environmental Action of Colorado, 1100-14th St., Denver, Colorado 80202. Ask them to send you their brochure. A rich anthology of resource and public education materials.

Sixteen energy briefs of one page each are available from the League of Women Voters, 1730 M St., NW, Washington, D.C. 20036 for $.15 each. They provide a solid background in current cultural energetics patterns in many aspects of energy use — fuel, architecture, fertilizer, waste, etc.

A number of good energy-related booklets are put out by the Environmental Action Foundation, 724 Dupont Circle Bldg., Washington, D.C. 20036. *How to Challenge Your Local Electrical Utility: A Citizen's Guide to the Power Industry* ($1.50) talks about public power, limiting growth of utilities, and dealing with power industry rates. *The Case for a Nuclear Moratorium* ($.50) describes the dangers of nuclear power and suggests alternatives. You can get a complete list of the Foundation's publications by writing and asking for it.

A Shopper's Guide to the Public Utility Law, by Herbert S. Denenberg. Consumers News Inc., Washington, D.C. 20045. $1.00. Herbert Denenberg is counsel to the Pennsylvania Public Utility Commission, and he originally wrote this book for use in his region. The version here is adapted to national use, and you will find it very helpful in dealing with the maze of public utilities in your area.

Hidden Waste: Potentials for Energy Conservation edited by David B. Large. The Conservation Foundation, 1717 Massachusetts Ave. NW, Washington, D.C. 20036. Out of print. The premise of this report is that "there exists a variety of practical ways to reduce energy consumption without reducing our material standard of living or demanding significant changes in lifestyle." Working from where we stand now in the midst of industrial culture, *Hidden Waste* points out practical ways to use less industrial energy, by such methods as turning down the corporate air-conditioning. (There are some people who are saying that industrial lifestyle itself *does* need to be significantly changed. One group, the Center for Applied Energetics, Governor's Office, Salem, Oregon, has issued a vanguard report on the uses of both psychic and physical energy in our culture, and how we can re-align our society to be more truly energetic. The report is titled *Cosmic Economics.* Another group, the Cultural Paradigms Project, Advanced Concepts Centre, Department of Environment, Ottawa, Canada, posits that the lifeways of Western industrial culture *are* the environmental problem, and they are collecting research to support this thesis and to create models for change.)

Energy Primer. Portola Institute, 558 Santa Cruz Avenue, Menlo Park, Ca. 94025. $4.50. This outsized tome assembled in the eclectic scrapbook manner of the *Whole Earth Catalog* was put together by some of the most inventive experimenters in the country, including people from the Whole Earth Truck Store, New Alchemy West, Palo Alto's Ecology Action, and the *Alternative Sources of Energy Newsletter.* An excellent resource covering many categories, the book lists materials and tools available to help change our lives into regionally oriented and self-sufficient ones. Besides listing and describing materials and tools in areas like agriculture, aquaculture, natural pest control, wind, solar, methane, composting, and water systems, the book has some excellent articles on specific visions and projects. The best compendium on how to get back over into using natural energy cycles and methods, well-written, richly and compactly presented.

Producing Your Own Power edited by Carol Hupping Stoner. Rodale Press, Emmaus, Pa. 18049. $8.95. A good anthology of articles on the use of renewable resources. The book contains material on ready-made and do-it-yourself wind generators, small water power sites and constructing a hydraulic ram, heating and cooking with wood, space and water heating with solar energy and building methane units. A primer that is substantial and clear.

Alternative Sources of Energy: Practical Technology and Philosophy for a Decentralized Society edited by Sandy Eccli and others. Seabury Press, 815 Second Ave., New York, N.Y. 10017. $6.95. Another outsized book crammed with practical help on the use of energy systems, this one is largely collected from articles which appeared in the *Alternative Sources of Energy Newsletter*. It is divided into three parts: one on technology, which includes descriptions of communities using alternative energy, some good words on inventive use of transportation, agriculture and architecture; one on building a social network in the field; and one on philosophy. A very good book, perhaps a little too loosely edited, but very resource-full.

The Elements. The Institute for Policy Studies, 1901 Q St. NW, Washington, D.C. 20009. For individuals $5.00/yr, for institutions $10.00/yr, (monthly except August). This fascinating newsletter takes a wide-lens look at the elements. It talks about weather changes on the planet, what may be causing them and what their effect is; it reports on use of natural elements like bauxite and iron and tin as commodities on the world market, and tells us about human elements as waves of migrant labor are moved from place to place to accommodate changing conditions. A recent issue had a very good article on seed monopolies and the world grain situation — an informative view of the planet from an interesting position.

Land Use

Who Owns the Land? by Peter Barnes and Larry Casalino. Center for Rural Studies, 1095 Market St., San Francisco, Ca. 94103. $.40. A brilliant little miniprimer on corporate control, this booklet details how the railroads, corporate farms, timber plantations, energy companies, and land developers have gained control of land in the U.S. since the country's inception. The precis also tells about the exodus of small farmers, and discusses the economic and social ramifications of massive land reform.

The Quiet Revolution in Land Use Control by Fred Bosselman and David Callies. Superintendent of Documents, U.S. Government Printing Office, Washington, D.C. 20402. $2.75. This report, commissioned by the Council on Environmental Quality, reports on "innovative land use" in a number of states, including Hawaii, Massachusetts, Maine, Vermont, and California. These innovations are the result of an underlying change in attitude, "treating land as a resource *and* a commodity" rather than simply as a commodity. It is not totally inspiring reading because it presumes a minimum of cultural change in its approach to land development, planning, tourism, and preservation of wildlife, but it contains useful information on key state government projects, and thereby gives a view of the subject which may help accelerate positive action.

✓ *The People's Land, A Reader on Land Reform in the United States* edited by Peter Barnes for the National Coalition on Land Reform. Rodale Press, Emmaus, Pa. 18049. $6.95. This is the best document on land reform available, a working partnership of thoughtful, innovative text and wonderful photographs. Peter Barnes, a leading figure in the movement for land reform, has done an excellent job of collecting prime materials for this book. The sections on regional depredation, from Appalachia to New England, are bedrock commentaries on industrial regress at the expense of both the biosphere and ordinary folks. The book also includes vivid outlines of the industrialization of agriculture, a sound case for the family farm as the most efficient way to raise food; the story of the destruction of small towns and its effect; unjust land taxes; and movements for change in all those areas, in the form of community

land cooperatives and trusts, a return to small farming and regional, watershed living.

People and Land, Newspaper of the Land Reform Movement. Center for Rural Studies, 1095 Market Street, San Francisco, Ca. 94103. Free to land reformers; additional copies $.60 each ($.25 postage). *People and Land* is a good-looking, readable, and very energetic newspaper working from the interface of small farming, cooperative ownership of land, and regional self-sufficiency. It reports well on these areas, and gives a clear picture too of what large energy combines, corporate agriculture, subdivision of land, deforestation and unfair taxation have done to the quality and structure of our lives as individuals, with particular attention to effects on urban and rural poor.

Southern Exposure, P.O. Box 230, Chapel Hill, N.C. 27514. $8.00/yr (quarterly). Focusing on land use and reform in the South, this fine newspaper is really heartening to read. From front page to back, its voice is strong and committed, its vision rich with local color described through a journalism both accurate and anecdotal. *Southern Exposure* talks about black people, red people, small farmers, sharecroppers, corporations on the make, and communities on the mend. Special issues include *No More Moanin': Voices of Southern Struggle* ($2.75), and *Our Promised Land* ($3.50).

Nebraska's New Land Review. Center for Rural Affairs, P.O. Box 405, Walthill, Nebr. 68067. $.35 copy. The *New Land Review* is yet another regional newspaper on land use and reform — at the time of this writing, it is nearly newborn, in its second issue. It is not so polished visually as *Southern Exposure,* but it is every bit as regionally valuable a publication in terms of content. The cover story on the second issue featured Nebraska's farm women: "Doing a Man's Job in a Man's World." Another piece described kicking the chemical fertilizer habit — "we cannot continue to treat our soil like dirt" the paper said. The *Review* also talks about water, wildlife, and community, in ways that make one see that there is some substantial change afoot in the land. Besides the *Review,* the Center for Rural Affairs puts out *An Introduction to Family Farm Legislation at a State Level,* a good brief describing efforts ongoing in various states to ban corporate farming and bring back the family farm, and *Land Tenure Research Guide,* a learning guide which can be adapted for use in other regions. The Center doesn't list a price on either, but would certainly appreciate your donation. For any of this material, and to keep in touch with regional progress in banning agribiz, contact this Nebraska group.

√*The Community Land Trust: A Guide to a New Model for Land Tenure in America.* International Independence Institute, West Road, Box 183, Ashby, Mass. 01431. $4.00. A comprehensive manual detailing how to go about selecting, financing and acquiring land to be held in community trust, this book is a coherent working tool for anyone who wants direct and accurate information on land trusts. Besides describing various options of group ownership and the legalities involved, the book offers views of a number of successful, ongoing community land trusts, including foreign, religious, and homesteading groups. Because of its wide vision and clear detail, this book is the current authority on the subject, and well worth reading.

√*A Bibliography on Land Reform in Rural America* by Charles L. Smith. Center for Rural Studies, 1095 Market Street, San Francisco, Ca. 94103. $1.00 ($.25 postage). A great bibliography that spans five decades — it covers a wide range of interrelated subjects, including natural resources, agriculture both corporate and family-run, real estate speculation, development, and soil impoverishment.

Clean Air and Water

Your Right to Clean Air. The Conservation Foundation, 1717 Massachusetts Ave. NW, Washington, D.C. 20036 Free. An informative look at air pollution around the country, with effective suggestions on how to organize clean air efforts locally, how to talk to industrial polluters, both legally and in community blocs. Samples of clean air programs and a bibliography of publications and films for public education are also provided.

A Citizen's Guide to Clean Air. The Conservation Foundation, 1717 Massachusetts Ave. NW, Washington, D.C. 20036. Free. This booklet began as an update of the aforementioned one, but as work progressed on it, it developed into a separate thing entirely. Basically, it is comple-

mentary to the first booklet, and deals in more detail with complexities of governmental regulations concerning clean air, and with the process of governmental policy-making on this issue.

The Campaign for Cleaner Air, by Marvin Zeldin, Public Affairs Pamphlet No. 494. Public Affairs Pamphlets, 381 Park Ave. So., New York, N.Y. 10016. $.35. Another good background booklet on pollution and how to organize to clean it up — more information than action-oriented in focus than the other booklets already mentioned. It has a good list of relevant organizations.

A Resource Guide on Pollution Control. American Association of University Women, 2401 Virginia Ave. NW, Washington, D.C. 20852. $.75. A very helpful guide in the effort to clear the air.

So You'd Like to Do Something About Water Pollution. League of Women Voters, 1730 M St. NW, Washington, D.C. 20036. $.15. A simple but powerful fold-out pamphlet which can serve as a good public education tool. The League also publishes *Safe Drinking Water for All: What You Can Do* ($.25) which outlines clean water standards and suggests ways to clean up. Another League booklet, *Where Rivers Meet the Sea* ($.50), discusses problems of river and marine pollution and what citizens can do.

Clean Water: It's Up to You. Izaak Walton League of America, 1326 Waukegan Road, Glenview, Ill. 60025. Free. A good, basic booklet on what communities must begin to do in order to clean the water. It gives background on pollution laws, how to enforce them locally, using media communications, waste treatment plants and how to get them built in your area; and it includes a directory of anti-pollution organizations and officials. A very useful book.

Transportation

Energy and Equity by Ivan Illich. New York: Perennial Library. $.95. Here is Illich's statement on the nature of transportation by automobile in our society: "The typical American male devotes more than 1600 hours a year to his car. He sits in it while it goes and while it stands idling. He parks it and searches for it. He spends four of his sixteen waking hours on the road or gathering resources for it... puts in 1600 hours to get 7500

miles; less than five miles per hour. In countries deprived of a transportation industry, people manage to do the same, walking wherever they want to go." Bicycles, which travel at an average rate of 15 m.p.h., are the most satisfying resolution to this cultural conundrum. They *are* actually faster, more efficient, and less polluting than cars!

Dead End by Ronald A. Buel. Penguin Books. $1.45. A cogent look at automobile culture and some proposals for change, including ongoing and projected mass transit and individual transportation alternatives. A thoroughly researched and readable job.

The Immoral Machine by Alvin L. Spivack. Mileu Information Service, 33 E. Fernando St., San Jose, Ca. 95113. $3.75. This book is a very personal statement about automobiles, which the author calls "fierce toys." It is well-researched and exemplary because it takes a position of responsibility and acts it out, rather than merely reporting objectively on the condition of the patient. Spivack talks about death, loss of human contact and community, pollution, and other negative impact that the automobile has been demonstrating to our culture for decades, and includes an interesting section on alternative vehicles, both for mass-transit and individual traveling. A heartful, straightforward book.

A Handbook for Bicycle Activists. Stanford Environmental Law Society, Stanford Law School, Stanford, Ca. 94305. $3.95. A basic guide for transportation activists, this book details the legal status of bicycles, state and local regulations regarding their use, and how bicycle paths can be integrated into national transportation networks.

Recycling: Industrial and Organic Waste

How to Start a Recycling Center. The Ecology Center Bookstore, 2179 Allston Way, Berkeley, Ca. 94704. $.50. The Berkeley recycling group was one of the first in the country, and is still going strong, recycling urban solid wastes with a contract from the city. This good booklet is a revised and enriched version which includes both the early energetic vision and later pragmatic experience of organizing, funding, staffing and publicizing the recycling effort.

Compost Science. Rodale Press, Emmaus, Pa. 18049. Single issue, $1.00; subscription, $6.00/yr (bimonthly). There's goodness in garbage, as folks from Rodale would have told anyone ten years ago when the subject was not nearly such juicy news as it is today. *Compost Science* has been enjoying a rapid rise in circulation, as have all of Rodale's visionary publications. The magazine covers all manner of maneuvers intended to use garbage and sewage sludge in a more natural and wholesome agriculture. In its January-February 1975 issue, *Compost Science* covered the ORE Plan, a comprehensive collection and recycling plan for household organic wastes which has been successfully used for several years in Portland, Oregon. The article is very worthwhile reading — regenerating a sadly depleted soil with household garbage is such an obvious idea that we wonder how it could have been neglected for the past fifty years. Another idea whose time is long overdue is covered in that same issue. The article details how the city of Denver is using sewage sludge to fertilize the earth. Chicago's use of sewage is covered in an article in the Summer 1974 issue of the magazine.

Energy Primer by the Portola Institute (reviewed here under "Energy") provides information on chemical toilets and composting privies. (One member of a small-town California water board shocked folks last year by predicting that the flush toilet would be outlawed in ten years, but by the look of developments in large urban areas, he may yet be vindicated in his view of the flush as "public enemy number one.")

Methane Digesters for Fuel Gas and Fertilizer. New Alchemy West, Box 376, Pescadero, Ca. 94060. $3.00. In this third newsletter of the New Alchemy Institute, the background and biology of methane digestion is described; designs for working models and an extensive bibliography are included too.

Magazines and Bulletins

Rodale's Environment Action Bulletin. Rodale Press, Emmaus, Pa. 18049. $10.00/yr (biweekly). This is the liveliest, plainest-talking and most positively-oriented periodical in the field of environmental action. It enjoys a healthy juxtaposition of subjects, gives brief, accurate reviews of helpful action materials, and is always clear and quick to tell what is actually happening across the country with food, energy, population, recycling, you-name-it. In addition to all that, EAB has both a sense of humor and a certain fearlessness, backed by the conscientious Rodale stance. A really valuable human resource — keeps spirits up, informed, and on the right track.

The Co-Evolution Quarterly, Box 428, Sausalito, Ca. 94965. $2.00/issue. This updated version of the old *Whole Earth Catalog* is published by the same folks, and is a valuable resource of information and access in the fields of planetary systems, land use, shelter, communications, community, craft, business, learning and technologies, natural science and spiritual/psychic developments. Articles and essays by specialists like Gregory Bateson, Hazel Henderson, and Carl Sagan have been providing *Co-Evolution's* readers with wide-lens visions of the present and future, and the Sears-Roebuck aspect of the magazine is wonderful for keeping in touch with current tools, movements, media, rumors and effects of change.

Briarpatch Review, 330 Ellis St., San Francisco, Ca. 94102. $1.00. A new, homey magazine of irregular (so far) publication schedule, the *Briarpatch* emanates from a circle of social change artists in the Bay area. It is concerned with creating right livelihood and sharing-based economics, humanistic management, country and city survival, simpler living and better work traditions. Some very innovative thinkers contribute to this cheerful, useful magazine.

Environmental Action Magazine. 1346 Connecticut Avenue, Washington, D.C. 20036. $10.00/yr; for profit-making corporations, $30.00/yr (biweekly). A solid and lively magazine which gives strong emphasis to change through legislative efforts, this publication reports on the current state of the earth in a compact and clear way. One special issue worth obtaining deals with access to the government — it's called *Make Yourself Heard in Washington,* dated March 29, 1975 ($.50). *Make Yourself Heard* contains a good listing of national environmental action and lobbying groups, and a useful documentation of federal agencies dealing with the environment, plus a partial listing of Congressional committees and members concerned with environmental legislation.

Rain. ECO-NET, Environmental Education Center, Portland State University, P.O. Box 751, Portland, Ore. 97207. Free (monthly). This newsletter, which runs from 16-24 pages, is a wonderful resource. It keeps a wide, accurate view of major environmental meetings and events, reviews current films, books, pamphlets, networks, reports, etc. It is definitely the best of its kind, and if you don't already receive it, get it. Like the rain, it's free.

High Country News, Box K, Lander, Wyo. 82520. $.35/copy, $10.00/yr (biweekly). Subtitled *The Environmental Bi-Weekly,* this feisty paper has been a major voice in the great gathering of positive energy for the natural world which is going on in Wyoming and Montana. In the amazing political double-talk surrounding ex-Wyoming Governor Stanley Hathaway's nomination as Secretary of the Interior, *High Country News* presented excellent coverage on the issue. (Of Hathaway, the *New York Times* commented, "Gov. Hathaway, as Secretary of the Interior, will make Mr. Morton look like Ralph Nader.") The newspaper does not limit its view to Wyoming and Montana, either. It moves easily around the country; if you read *High Country News* and *Rain,* too, you will be very well-informed indeed.

Planet/Drum. Planet/Drum Foundation, Box 31251, San Francisco, Ca. 94131. Membership, $10.00/yr. According to regional ecologist Peter Berg, *Planet/Drum* "is a network of correspondents. Fisher folk in Alaska and Maine, communes in North America and Europe, Japanese natural scientists, urban planetarians, African game preserve managers, Russian poets and ethnographers, American Indian medicine people." The seasonal bundle of information and visions that Berg assembles in *Planet/Drum* is satisfying material. It is tactile and visually provoking; it invokes a fourth-world or regional image, and moves out beyond the linear, over-quantified confines of Western "environmental resource management" into a field of natural magic and simple cohabitation with the earth. *Planet/Drum* makes tracks of vanguard thought — good food for environmentalists and ecologists alike.

Some other magazines and newspapers are reviewed here under their focus of interest, and many others exist which are not covered here, either because they are popularly known or extremely local in scope. Most large conservation organizations publish magazines, and so do some regional ecology centers. As you organize in various fields, you will naturally come across materials that are relevant to your current work. Of magazines not reviewed here, several are worth mentioning in case you haven't discovered them yet. *Organic Gardening and Farming* is one you've probably seen already; but *Prevention,* a magazine dealing with health and fitness, may have escaped you. Both are published by Rodale Press, Emmaus, Pa. 18049. *WIN Magazine,* Box 547, Rifton, N.Y. 12471 is a magazine of nonviolent social change and often runs articles on environmental and ecology-related issues. *The Futurist,* Box 30369, Bethesda Station, Washington, D.C. 20014 deals with issues of planetary future.

Media Access

A Handbook on Free Access to the Media for Public Service Advertising. Public Media Center, 2751 Hyde St., San Francisco, Ca. 94109. $1.00. This excellent how-to details clearly the process for getting your environmental issue aired on TV, radio, or in print. It is a very valuable tool in rousing public support for environmental action, and in educating the public on issues requiring immediate change. Public Media Center has conducted a wide variety of advertising campaigns and has media spots available on nuclear power which have already appeared on over 100 TV stations and 300 radio stations. Six TV spots and five radio spots on nuclear power and its dangers are available for rental and return or for sale from the Center. Sale prices are $5.00 per TV spot, $3.00 per radio spot, and $2.00 for postage. The ads were produced in conjunction with Friends of the Earth, Environmental Action and other public-interest groups and have elicited strong response wherever they have been aired.

Getting into Print. League of Women Voters, 1730 M St. NW, Washington, D.C. 20036. $.40. A good tool for working with the print media. The League also publishes *Make Publications Work for You* (free); and *Tips on Reaching the Public* ($1.25). Both are filled with solid advice on communicating your ideas.

A little over five years ago, WKAR radio, operating out of the Michigan State University Tape Network, began working on an environmental show. Today, the show, titled simply "Environment," goes out to over thirty Michigan stations,

eight of them public and the rest commercial. The show is oriented to local issues although it had an opportunity to go national through the public radio network. Jim Wiljanen, producer of the show at WKAR, believes that "Environment" has developed into a persuasive educational voice because of its regional stance, but that there is a real need for an environmental show of a country-wide nature, which should come from a network in either Washington or New York. Jim Wiljanen suggests the Environmental Protection Agency's pamphlet *Don't Leave it All to the Experts* (from EPA, Office of Public Affairs, Washington, D.C. 20460. Free.) as a good reference for groups interested in communicating environmental issues through the media. He is graciously open to helping groups who would like to start a similar environmental radio network in their region. Contact Jim Wiljanen, WKAR Radio, 310 Auditorium Building, Michigan State University, East Lansing, Mich. 48824 for more detailed advice.

Environmental Education and Organizing

Citizen Action by Odom Fanning. Harper and Row. $9.95 hardcover; $4.95 paperback. Mrs. Verna Mize grew up at the edge of then-crystalline Lake Superior. This book begins with the story of her disbelief, then horror, then action when she discovered how polluted her beloved lake had become. It is a good and inspiring story of individual responsibility toward the natural world. The rest of the book is a patchwork collection of materials, including "DDT: How It Was Banned," a short message on pesticides which notes their lethal effect, but does not explain satisfactorily why EPA still allows DDT's use in what it calls epidemic situations. In general, the book reports on a wide variety of large national and smaller regional conservation, preservation and environmental activist efforts, with an attitude that is well-intended yet lacking a real position, somehow neglecting to question deeply enough the effectiveness of some of what is touted as environmental change, especially government-sponsored actions. The book is worth reading for some of its anecdotal reportage on individuals, but as a guide to real transformation, it is a bit bogged in the status-quo.

A number of basic education and organizing tools are available from the

League of Women Voters, 1730 M St. NW, Washington, D.C. 20036, which can be helpful to the environmentalist as solid first steps to action. *How to Plan an Environmental Conference* (free), which evolved over a period of years from League work with land and water use seminars, can be effectively used in those and other areas of environmental educating and organizing. Because it does emanate from long, successful experience, the book is a very valuable tool. Another pamphlet, *Shaping the Metropolis* ($.60), comes from a conference on decentralization and contains some good material on that subject. *Channels for Change* ($.40) talks about regionalism and community control, and is a thoughtful digest. Other League pamphlets — on clean air and water, and use of the media — are reviewed here under those categories.

The Environment Film Review. Environmental Information Center, 124 East 39th St., New York, N.Y. 10016 is a wonderfully varied collection of films on the subjects of food, water, population, wildlife, weather, clean air, etc.

A useful environmental bibliography is available from the Public Interest Group, 2000 P St. NW, Washington, D.C. 20036. This group, which comes out of Ralph Nader's work, also issues a list of Nader-related publications which cover an amazing variety of environmental and consumer-oriented issues.

Organizing Macro-analysis Seminars: A Manual. Philadelphia Macro-analysis Collective, 4719 Cedar Ave., Philadelphia, Pa. 19143. $1.00. The concept of macro-analysis, developed by the non-violent Movement for a New Society, is of vital interest to environmentalists and ecologists working in an integrated, holistic and cooperative fashion to change the patterns of society. This book details a course for small-group discussion on the interrelation between ecology, our dealings with other nations, and domestic problems, and outlines strategies for social change which rise from an equalitarian social process. At a time when ecology and environmental groups may tend to isolate themselves into boxed categories, this expansive and focused course is worth investigating.

Organic Guide to Colleges and Universities. Rodale Press, Emmaus, Pa. 18049. $3.95. Compiled by Rodale's experts on organic gardening and environmental action, this book catalogues environmental and ecology-related curriculums in colleges and universities across the country, and also includes some very solid chapters on community gardening, organizing local food co-ops, land grant colleges and organic agriculture, and advice on how to get organic food into school cafeterias. As usual — Rodale Press is consistently conscientious in presenting material lucidly and carefully — this book is a nutritious digest for students who want to work on changing the environment as a way of life.

Opportunities in Environmental Careers by Odom Fanning. Universal Publishing and Distributing Corp., 235 E. 45 St., New York, N.Y. 10017. $5.75. This book, written by a science writer who has spent twenty years in the environmental field, including time in the Office of Environmental Quality, is considered *the* text in the field for those who want to enter into occupations like environmental management, earth sciences, recreation, and environmental design. It describes what is expected of one in those fields, and offers information on how to obtain jobs and what one can expect to be paid. Apart from these relevant facts and figures, the book has a slightly antique-flavor, and little sense of the vision of an environmental activist, but seems to concentrate more on the steady-job stability of the environmental bureaucrat. It is withal a good reference, recommended in the hope that career and paycheck don't get in the way of real change.

Conservation Directory. The National Wildlife Federation, 1412 16th St. NW, Washington, D.C. 20036. $2.00 (annual). A comprehensive nationally-oriented (it contains some international listings, too) directory which lists federal, interstate, state, and regional agencies, offices and commissions, plus colleges and universities which offer conservation curriculums. Brief descriptions of each group's functions and objectives are included. This is the most complete directory for use in the U.S.

Canadian Conservation Directory. Canadian Nature Federation, 46 rue Elgin St., Ottawa, Canada, KIP 5K6. $1.50 (annual). A good, regionally-oriented directory for use in Canada.

World Directory of Environmental Organizations. Sierra Club, 1050 Mills Tower, San Francisco, Ca. 94104. Out of print. The Sierra Club is hoping to reprint this excellent international directory soon, and meanwhile you can probably locate a reference copy at your local ecology center, university library, etc. It is by no means a "complete" listing of concerned groups, but does provide a firm base for communicating with major environmental groups in many countries, and includes a good smattering of small, more activist groups along with the larger organizations.

Simple Living

The Contrasumers: A Citizen's Guide to Resource Conservation by Albert Fritsch. Center for Science in the Public Interest, 1779 Church St. NW, Washington, D.C. 20036. Paperback, $3.50. This book details the planetary effects of material consumption, and offers specific suggestions for reducing consumption on individual, community, national, and planetary levels. CSPI also has a *Lifestyle Index* ($1.50). With its help, you can begin to evaluate the effect of your everyday consumption patterns. According to the *Index,* it takes one acre of strip-mined coal to burn six 100-watt bulbs for one year. It also points out that the Defense Department uses 6 percent of U. S. energy. This and other startling information should help you and your circle decide how to reduce your consumption.

Taking Charge by the Palo Alto Packet Committee and the Simple Living Project. American Friends Service Committee, 2160 Lake St., San Francisco, Ca. 94121. $1.00. The various addictions of consumerism are well explored in this friendly and thoughtful little book, which suggests that taking personal responsibility is the cornerstone for planetary change. *Taking Charge* asks questions like what goods and services do we use and rely on every day that were not generally available 75 years ago? If we could be doing any kind of work that we wanted to, would be continue in our present job? Community, food, child rearing, creativity and economics are a few areas investigated here, in a way that should prove very useful to groups of many ages.

Other Homes and Garbage edited by Jim Leckie, Gil Masters, Harry Whitehouse, and Lily Young. Sierra Club Books, 1050 Mills Tower, San Francisco, Ca. 94104. $9.95. The content of this book originated from the Stanford Workshop on Social and Political Issues, a group of engineers and students at Stanford University. Besides de-mystifying engineering concepts — a very good turn in itself since most folks have no idea whatsoever how all the machinery works, and why — the book gives very solid suggestions on converting individual and small-group lifestyle from high-velocity energy drain into self-sufficient use of natural energy. The natural design purist may take strong exception to some of the suggestions regarding building materials (polyurethane isn't exactly a commendable recommendation ecologically). However, the design aspect of the book does offer a strong survey and analysis of what architectural trends are ongoing, from Paolo Soleri's arcologies to Lloyd Kahn's work on shelters, and in general the book should prove very useful in putting readers back in touch with some principles of energy and self-recycling uses which have been progressively neglected for the past hundred years.

More Grass Roots Heroes

Editor's Note: Because the movement for environmental action is much larger than the confines of this book permit us to deal with, we include the following listing of the people who responded to our request for information.

United States

Alabama

Statewide — The Committee for Leaving the Environment of America Natural (CLEAN) is spearheading a two-state (Alabama and Mississippi) movement to stop the funding of the proposed Tennessee-Tombigbee Waterway Project, which would link the two rivers in northeastern Mississippi and western Alabama in a system of ten locks and dams. The battle against this project, with its potentially adverse effects upon the social, economic, and physical environment of the area, has been underway for several years.

Birmingham — The Environmental Law Society is working to have the state legislature pass a bill which would prohibit the sale of "no deposit-no return" beverage containers in this state.

Huntsville — The Alabama Conservancy and other citizen groups are battling against the construction of an interstate highway (I-565). The proposed highway would encroach on the Wheeler National Wildlife Refuge, cut through rich farmland, and then terminate within the urban community of Huntsville.

Alaska

Denali — The Denali Citizens Council has been organized to express citizen concern over conservation matters which affect Mt. McKinley National Park and the surrounding area.

Arizona

Statewide — Arizonans for Quality Environment have brought suit against the State Department of Health because of their failure to hold hearings before granting licenses to mining companies.

Alpine — Local citizens have worked for two and a half years to halt or significantly alter the Watts Timber Sale in Apache National Forest. This ongoing project is nearing a court hearing with the citizenry optimistic as to the outcome.

Arkansas

Little Rock — Workers with Arkansas Ecology Center are promoting a state bill which bans non-returnable beverage containers.

California

Northern California — Conservationists are fighting for "timber harvest plans" and to retain the use of mandatory environmental impact reports to protect forest areas.

Capitola — The Capitola Survival Committee, is opposing the McKeon Construction Company by requesting the State Coastal Commission to forbid the company from hooking up to the one existing sewer line any of its newly and partially built condominiums until a new line is built.

Carlsbad — Mrs. Lorene Callaway has established wildlife treatment and rescue centers in the San Diego area, the result of a 10-year effort.

Carmel — The Ventana Chapter of the Sierra Club has been working for the protection of the sea otter, and implementing a program of educating humans regarding the animal.

Doyle — The North American Predatory Animal Center, with a staff of three, is a research and education organization helping to establish an understanding of the predator's role in our environment and insure a place for him in our remaining wilderness.

Lake County — Efforts are underway to acquire the marshland area at the base of Clear Lake for a wildlife management area. This marshland is being threatened by real estate developers.

Lake County — Local citizens are blocking the exploratory well drilling on the slopes of Cobb Mountain. The drilling is for geothermal energy sources. The citizens want adequate environmental impact reports before any drilling takes place.

Lake County — The Warm Springs Task Force has effectively delayed for three years the construction of Warm Springs Dams.

Mendocino — In 1973, local citizens stopped developers from buying Jughandle Park. By inviting contributions to save individual flora and fauna in the area, enough money was raised to buy the land for a private park. It is presently being turned over to the state for management as a state park.

Mineral King — Local and statewide environmentalist groups are opposing the proposal to cede the Mineral King area to Disneyland for commercial exploitation.

Mojave Desert — Environmentalists tried unsuccessfully to stop the Bureau of Land Management from allowing the "World's Largest Motorcycle Race" to be held on federal land between Barstow and Las Vegas.

Oakland — The Rockridge Community Planning Council was successful in preserving the neighborhood's character by having the area rezoned to restrict new commercial development around a Rapid Transit station built in the community.

Orange — The Friends of Newport Bay are working for the preservation of open space and water fowl habitats.

Palo Alto — The local Sierra Club chapter opposes the reconstruction and enlargement of the Dumbarton bridge which would make the structure more conducive to an increase in commuter traffic.

Palo Alto — A small group has formed to see that surplus school lands are not sold to developers, but remain in public use.

Pismo Beach Dunes — A long-term battle is being waged against use of the beach area and the dunes area for recreational vehicles and camping.

Sacramento — The Save the Sutter Buttes Association is backing a plan for a wilderness preserve on 3,000 acres in the upper region of North Butte in the Sacramento Valley.

San Bernardino — The Defenders of San Gorgonio Wilderness united some 40 organizations and prevented a huge ski development from being built in the San Gorgonio Wilderness Area.

San Bruno — An organization of local citizens, Sane Transportation on the Peninsula (STOP), has been battling against the proposed construction of a freeway.

San Carlos — Citizen groups are working to have the city and San Mateo County buy 294 acres of wooded open space for a park rather than allowing real estate developers to buy it.

San Diego — Local citizens joined together to buy a small canyon in Mission Hills to be left as open space. They bought the canyon through assessment and then turned it over to the city for inclusion in the city park system.

San Francisco — People for a Golden Gate National Recreation Area worked successfully to establish a national park in less than two years.

San Francisco — Several local conservation groups including Friends of the Earth and the Loma Prieta Chapter of the Sierra Club are opposing the proposed expansion of the San Francisco Airport.

San Jose — A group of citizens opposes the construction of the Coyote Park Freeway — with proposed system of seven interchanges in eleven miles — which would help open the southern part of the county for development.

Santa Cruz — A group of citizens formed "Operation Wilder" to stop the proposed construction of a large housing development on about 5,000 acres of coastal beach and uplands.

Santa Paula — Friends of Santa Paula Creek was organized in 1972 to oppose a channelization project. In 1974 the courts ordered the project halted.

Santa Rosa — Spring Creek Citizens banded together to prevent channelization of Spring Creek with subsequent loss of private land. The result was a compromise with the city for a much smaller channel which has not yet been built due to lack of funds caused by the delay.

Saratoga — The Castle Rock group of the Sierra Club fought and won a battle against the proposed construction of a freeway.

Solano County — A local effort to preserve the Suisun Marsh resulted in the creation of legislation to protect this critical part of the waterfowl support area.

Tulare County — A citizen group stopped the construction of a Boise-Cascade Project near Three Rivers.

Visalia — Friends of the Earth helped a local group to prevent the building of a nuclear power plant in nearby Strathmore, California.

Willows — Local citizens continue efforts to have the U.S. legislature create the Snow Mountain Wilderness Area in a 37,000-acre roadless area west of Willows.

Yosemite — Year-round valley residents aided by long haired wanderers prevented the Park Service from building an auto bridge across the Merced River which would have also put a road through Leidig Meadow.

Colorado

Aspen — Citizens for Glenwood Canyon Scenic Corridor are opposing a proposed 4-lane Interstate highway and seeking designation for the canyon as a scenic corridor.

Denver — A group of women formed the Educated Consumers Organization to work with local consumers and supermarkets.

Fort Collins — The Colorado Student Lobby has introduced a bill into the state legislature which would ban non-returnable beverage containers.

Connecticut

Hamden — Project Standard Oil was created by six people who are working to stimulate participation by shareholders in the affairs of their company as it affects society and the environment.

Hartford — The Connecticut Citizen Action Group led an effort which has introduced into the State legislature a "container deposit" bill banning non-returnable beverage containers.

West Hartford — The committee to Save the Reservoir works to prevent Interstate 291 from going through the West Hartford reservoir lands.

Delaware

Newark — The Save the Coast Committee is fighting a battle against pamphlets issued by business interests who want a 1971 State Coastal Zone law repealed.

Florida

Statewide — Save Our Coast, a coalition of environmentalists, opposed the leasing of one million acres beneath the outer continental shelf on the Florida Gulf Coast for oil and gas exploration and production. They were unsuccessful in stopping the B.L.M. from selling the leases, but in 1973 the Sierra Club helped pass the Environmentally Endangered Lands Act which makes possible the purchase of such land.

Statewide — Citizens fought a statewide battle that stopped the construction of a regional jet-port near the Everglades National Park.

Statewide — Citizens are involved in statewide participation in the Florida Green Plan which describes and recommends proper environmental usage of existing undeveloped areas.

Gainesville — Local Sierra Club members continue to struggle against the Cross-Florida Barge Canal. For many years they also have urged designation of the Suwanee River as a national "wild and scenic river."

Jacksonville — Proposed phosphate strip mining in the Osceola National Forest faces growing citizen opposition.

Jacksonville — The local Sierra Club group is opposing bulkheading on the St. John's River by the St. Regis Paper Company, which they believe would constitute a navigational hazard at night.

Jacksonville — Environmentally aware citizens have launched a number of efforts, including establishing a food co-operative, sending petitions to the governor to pressure for state funding of solar energy projects, and an "Earth Week" festival with seminars, folk music, nature walks, etc.

Miami — Concerned citizens are battling to have the Florida Keys designated as an area of "critical state concern," thus preserving the Keys by requiring a development plan.

Miami — The Mangrove Chapter of the Izaak Walton League fought successfully to preserve 93,000 acres (mostly submerged) in Biscayne Bay. Their fight resulted in the creation of the Biscayne National Monument.

Orlando — Unwise highway planning stimulated by the construction of Disney World is being carefully monitored by local Sierra Club members.

Pensacola — Area residents are fighting for extension of the Gulf Islands National Sea Shore to protect contiguous lands that are under county jurisdiction.

Pensacola — Local citizens are joined in efforts to control the emission of air and water pollutants from the chemical plants located on the Escambia River.

Santa Rosa Island — The Save Our Beach group has brought suit against certain lease-holders of undisturbed areas of Santa Rosa Island who plan to construct motels and/or condominiums on the fragile sand dunes.

Tallahassee — Local citizens have formed the Sound Transportation Planning Coalition which opposes the widening of certain highways.

Tallahassee — The Big Bend group of the Sierra Club succeeded in obtaining "Wilderness Area" classification for the Bradwell Bay Wilderness Area in the Apalachicola National Forest and for the St. Mark's Wilderness Area in the St. Mark's National Wildlife Refuge. It is presently urging state purchase of Cape San Blas as an "Environmentally Endangered Land." The group also opposes a dam on the Apalachicola River that would endanger the flourishing oyster and shellfish industry in Apalachicola Bay.

Tampa Bay — The local group of the Sierra Club has been active in an effort to save Crystal Beach from efforts of the Army Corps of Engineers to deposit soil from dredging operations there.

Georgia

Statewide — Although the Okefenokee Swamp was a national wildlife refuge it had not been fully protected from many activities such as timbering and dredging. Such protection was a high priority goal of many conservation workers in the state and the goal was achieved in 1974 when the swamp was officially designated by Congress as a wilderness area.

Atlanta — Channelization threatened to destroy the Alcovy River swamp and this free-flowing stream. An educational campaign launched by the Nature Conservancy stopped this project in 1974.

Athens — Sand Creek in Clarke County was about to be channelized when local citizens developed a plan for a river park and nature center which has been approved in lieu of the channelization project.

Cave Spring — Local citizens prevented the U.S. Army Corps of Engineers from the channelization of Cedar Creek, a highly visible scenic stream which flows through the center of their town.

Chattooga River — The Georgia Conservancy initiated action to have the Chattooga designated a "Wild and Scenic River." This goal was accomplished in 1974.

Cumberland Island — Recognizing Cumberland Island as one of the two most outstanding undeveloped seashores along the Atlantic and Gulf coasts, the Georgia Conservancy initiated action to establish the island as a national seashore park, which was accomplished in 1972.

Douglas County — A five-year coordinating program directed by the Georgia Conservancy helped create the Sweetwater Creek Factory Shoals State Park in 1973.

Henry County — With the help of the Nature Conservancy, a unique 500-acre granite outcrop was purchased by the State of Georgia and the Panola Mountain Conservation Park was created in 1974.

Valdosta — In 1971, workers with the Georgia Conservancy were instrumental in defeating the Corps of Engineers' proposal to construct a dam on the Alapaha River.

Hawaii

Molokai — Using movies and still photos, Life of the Land was able to show a construction firm mining sand from a public beach below the high water mark in violation of the law, in an operation for which no permit has ever been issued. This mining has been going on for 15 years.

Oahu — Save Our Surf is a grassroots organization based on mobilizing politically and environmentally concerned surfers. It has been working with unexpected success to have a park established on the shoreline at Sand Island, Honolulu, instead of the industrial facilities which were planned.

Oahu — Life of the Land has since 1970 been opposing the building of an interstate highway on the island of Oahu which would cut through the only undeveloped valley, Moanalua. The group also opposes extension of the runway at Honolulu International Airport, and keeps a close eye on Hawaii State Land Use Commission dealings.

Idaho

Statewide — The State Sierra Club chapter is opposing construction of a dam on the Teton River.

Pocatello — The Citizens Environmental Council has been successful in having a bill introduced in the State legislature which will ban non-returnable beverage containers.

Illinois

Chicago — The Daniel Burnham Committee was an ad hoc group organized in 1965 to fight the Jackson Park expressway. The success of this action served as a focus in 1970 to defeat a proposed airport in Lake Michigan near the city.

Springfield — Students in the Sangamon State University "Wilderness Studies" course ventured deep into forests to collect data to determine if several pieces of land set aside by the Forest Service could be returned to their natural wilderness state and designated as a "wilderness area."

Winnetka — Ms. Louise B. Young is engaging in a fight against what she calls "Powerline Pollution" — the placement of extra-high-voltage (EHV) overhead transmissions in small rural communities and state forests. She aids various groups in educating the public to the hazards of EHV lines and in promoting research into the environmental effects of such lines.

Indiana

Attica — An energetic local group, Committee on Big Pine Creek, is making a concerted effort to prevent the damming of the stream and the subsequent inundation of geological phenomena.

Munster — For the past ten years, Ms. Irene Herlocker has acted as self-appointed guardian of what is believed to be the last remnant of wetland prairie in Indiana, the Hoosier Prairie.

Munster — The Save the Dunes Council has spent 22 years battling to protect a unique area along the shores of Lake Michigan, the Indiana Sand Dunes. They have accomplished legislation creating the Indiana Dunes National Lakeshore which preserves one half of the wilderness area, but seek to expand the area to protect it from developers.

Kansas

Flint Hills — Environmentalists are battling against agribusiness cattle interests and are seeking 60,000 acres of prairie for a Prairie National Park. This area, which contains virgin tallgrass prairie and supports viable herds of bison, elk, and antelope, is threatened by a new year-round system of cattle grazing which necessitates plowing the land to plant non-native grass.

Kansas City — The Ozark Wilderness Waterways and the Ozark Society (of Arkansas) were successful in preventing the damming of the Arkansas Buffalo River and the subsequent protection of the Buffalo by having it included in the national park system.

Kentucky

Lexington — Oscar Geralds, Jr., an attorney, started a movement which brought about Kentucky's first Wild Rivers Bill in 1971. Since then, he has successfully worked to protect and enlarge the bill.

Lexington — The Big South Fork Preservation Coalition is working to establish the Big South Fork National River and Recreation Area in Kentucky and Tennessee.

Louisville — The local Sierra Club group is involved in the establishment of the Three Forks of Beaver Creek Eastern Wilderness Area.

Nicholasville — A statewide action by a group called the Red River Gorge Legal Defense Fund, Inc. is fighting a proposed dam on the Red River in Eastern Kentucky which would periodically flood the famous Red River Gorge.

Louisiana

New Orleans — A group of citizens have filed a Federal lawsuit to prevent the destruction of marshes by the construction of a 54-mile-long beltway "loop" around the city, the Dixie Freeway.

Maine

Statewide — Efforts by the Maine Audubon Chapter have returned one half million acres of public timber lands to public control. A quirk in the agreements of the 1800's which gave control of this land to the large paper companies has been successfully utilized to force the return of the lands to the public.

Southern Maine — The Friends of Intelligent Land Use (FOIL) are working to stop construction of an oil refinery in southern Maine that threatens to spin off industrial and commercial overdevelopment on the coast of Maine.

Augusta — A local group, Friends of the St. John, are battling against the U.S. Corps of Engineers' proposed Dickey-Lincoln Hydro-electric power plant, which threatens thousands of acres of wilderness.

Portland — Maine Citizens for Returnable Containers are working to have legislation introduced in the state congress which would ban non-returnable beverage containers.

Portland — The Coastal Resources Action Committee is the major opponent of the use of the eastern coast of Maine as a site for oil off-loading and refining. They have been successful in several court challenges and at regulatory hearings.

Portland — The Maine Audubon chapter is opposed to the construction of the Westbrook Arterial Freeway which would fill the last remaining large salt marsh in Portland.

Stockton Springs — The Safe Power for Maine group is working against a proposal for a nuclear power plant on Sears Island, a wilderness island off the coast.

Maryland

Statewide — Passage of a "container deposit" bill in the State legislature is the goal of two groups, Sensible Citizens against Throwaways and Alliance for Returnable Beverage Containers.

Hollywood — Citizens' Coalition for St. Mary's County prevented construction of an oil refinery at nearby Piney Point.

Temple Hill — The Maryland Conservation Council united the efforts of several local groups and in 1973 stopped the construction of a 300-acre lake which would have submerged the Cedarville State Park and State Forest.

Massachusetts

Amherst — The Amherst Growth Study Committee, Inc. fought vigorously and vocally from 1971 to 1973 to stop the construction of a very large community development in East Amherst. Despite their efforts the development is being built.

Cambridge — The Douglas Street Tenants' Organization is opposing the building of a McDonald's drive-in restaurant in their neighborhood. They instigated a proposal before the city council which would prohibit the location of an "automobile-oriented fast-food establishment" in an area zoned for residential or office space.

Michigan

Alma — The local Sierra Club group promoted a fund drive and purchased 54 acres within the city which were slated to be sold to developers. The land will be made into a city park.

Escanaba — The Save Our Air organization made certain that a new Kraft paper mill built in the community controlled its odor pollution.

Lansing — The Michigan Student Environmental Confederation is working on a bill which would ban non-returnable beverage containers in the state.

Minnesota

Crystal Falls — Citizen organizations banded together to stop the construction of a fish ladder on the Presque Isle River. The proposal, which was defeated, would have cost the citizenry $1.2 million and destroyed much of the area.

Minneapolis — Citizens created a lobbyist organization, Project Environment, to educate the legislature and achieve improvement in the process by which environmental decisions are made, particularly through greater access and involvement of citizens. They have had a great effect on the passage of many environmental bills.

Minnetonka — Citizens Against Throwaways have gotten a "bottle bill" introduced into the State legislature which would ban non-returnable beverage containers.

Rochester — A group of local citizens worked to keep the Rochester Sanitary Landfill from being located in Olmsted County. Though unsuccessful in its attempt, they are now appealing to have the landfill removed due to pollution potential and existing leakage.

Mississippi

Statewide — Support for the Heritage program, a division of the Mississippi Game and Fish Commission, has aided in the commission receiving appropriations from the legislature to purchase acreage in wilderness areas of southern Mississippi.

DeLisle — Save the Bay, Inc. is battling against the E.I. duPont de Nemours and Company, Inc., which plans to locate a titanium dioxide plant on a pristine bay. No EIS is slated to be done and this group is suing duPont and the Mississippi Air and Water Pollution Control Commission for inadequate environmental studies of the area.

Jackson County — The Mississippi Wildlife Federation and the National Wildlife Federation filed suit in Federal court to halt the construction of Interstate 10 which is slated to go through the Mississippi Sandhill Crane Refuge in Jackson County.

Walthall County — Local citizens are in the process of halting a proposed Kraft paper mill from locating on the Bogue Chitto River, a natural and wild river.

Missouri

Statewide — The Conservation Federation of Missouri led a statewide citizen effort for appropriations, which resulted in the development of a Wildlife Habitat Management Plan for National forests in Missouri, the first such plan in the nation. The group also seeks funds for their "Design for Conservation" proposals, funds which would come from a one-eighth of one percent sales tax.

Statewide — A statewide battle against the U.S. Army Corps of Engineers led by the Ozark Chapter of the Sierra Club has prevented the damming of the Meramec River.

Statewide — Led by the Ozark chapter of the Sierra Club, citizens have brought pressure to bear on congressmen to support the designation of areas in Missouri as "wilderness areas." Missouri areas were not included in the first Wilderness Act, and this group of people are continuing work until legislation is passed which protects needed areas of Missouri forest from development.

Central Missouri — The grassroots campaign to establish the Cedar Creek Purchase Unit marks one of the few successful attempts to establish a public lands purchase unit in recent Forest Service history. Citizens now seek monies to purchase 50,000 acres over the next 20 years for multiple outdoor recreation use.

Upper Mississippi River — The Ozark Chapter of the Sierra Club is at the focus of the controversy over the replacement of existing Mississippi River locks and the dam at Alton, Illinois, with one four times larger in capacity.

Imperial — Efforts by the Mastodon Park Committee to establish a park in the Kimmswick Bon Bed are looking optimistic to the people involved in preserving this unique archaeological site.

Olivetti — A committee of citizens has been presenting workshops in Missouri towns which may be affected by a planned major nuclear reactor to be built for the Union Electric Company in central Missouri. The hope is that bringing information before the public will enable them to make a more informed decision on the nuclear power alternative.

St. Louis — Citizens are urging that the Weldon Spring Tract remain within the public domain. This area of 8,000 acres is owned by the University of Missouri which used it for research in agriculture and forestry. In 1974 the university declared the land as surplus and protests began by various state agencies and environmental groups over the possible withdrawal of this important urban "wilderness" area from the community.

St. Louis County — Local citizens led by the Eastern Missouri Group of the Sierra Club are organizing to press for a lower Meramec River Regional Recreation Area along thirty miles of the river. Parkland acquisition and repair of former gravel mining operations are their first targets.

Nebraska

Bellevue — Nebraskans for Returnables have gotten legislation introduced into the state legislature which would ban throwaway beverage containers.

Elkhorn — Local citizens are fighting against two proposed construction projects. One is the Lynch Pump Storage Unit, which would store electricity at the cost of millions of dollars and loss of prime wilderness land. The second is the Norden Dam Recreation and Irrigation Project, which would cause much damage to the wild Niobrara River in the effort to provide water to an already over-developed area.

New Hampshire

Concord — The Society for the Protection of New Hampshire Forest is working to preserve Sandwich Notch, a historic and natural area which is the last major White Mountain notch not in protective ownership.

Concord — The Environmental Coalition has established a statewide citizens' lobby on environmental legislation and government administrative decisions, including research capability, a telephone network, and ongoing public education program.

Concord — The Statewide Program of Action to Conserve our Environment (SPACE) is a volunteer effort by landowners and interested citizens to study and, where possible, recommend adopting new open space preservation methods, with emphasis on convincing landowners to take the lead.

Plymouth — Staff and students of the Holderness School have been cleaning up the Three Ponds-Carr Mountain area by removing trash and disassembling an abandoned fire watch tower that had become a public hazard.

Rockingham — Rockingham Recreational Roadways is a group involved with a project that turns abandoned railroad rights of way into a hiking, bicycling and recreation vehicle trail system. The ongoing project has met with success in their ventures.

New Jersey

Middletown — The Poricy Park Citizens Committee preserved for parkland the Poricy Brook region from encroaching developers.

Princeton — The state's Sierra Club has intensified their efforts to have New Jersey change their priority system for funding sewers in order to give higher priority to urban areas rather than sewering the countryside, which generates adverse secondary land-use impacts.

Tocks Island — The Save the Delaware Coalition has vigorously opposed the Tocks Island dam proposal for many years with effective results.

New Mexico

Santa Fe — The Santa Fe Community Action Organization is sponsoring a free seed program for eligible families who wish to start gardens.

Sunspot — Citizens have organized into New Mexico Clean Air and Water and are promoting "container deposit" legislation which would ban non-returnable beverage containers in this state.

New York

Deposit — Concerned Citizens of Deposit organized to force a local Celotex plant to measurably reduce their air pollution in the area.

New York City — A small group of people prevented the construction of a roller hockey rink on a parking lot site and pressured the Parks Department into creating a grassy park instead.

New York City — 200 people divided into eight task forces make up the Council on the Environment of New York City. These citizens prepared detailed recommendations on "Environmental Priorities for 1974-1984." The reports are being used in the formulation of regional as well as statewide policies.

Queens — The Woodhaven Residents Block Association is leading a fight to prevent the Long Island Railroad and the Metropolitan Transportation Authority from building a connecting rail link through Forest Park. The link would permit train traffic from eastern Long Island to take a direct route to Kennedy Airport — part of the Transportation Authority's plan for rail service to the airport.

Rossville — A local group, Bring Legal Action to Stop the Tanks (BLAST), concerned with the explosive potential of tanks storing liquified natural gas has successfully opposed the filling of two 14-story-high tanks on Staten Island.

Webster — The Monroe County Conservation Council has formed the "Delta Laboratories," a non-profit pollution testing laboratory and environmental watchdog.

North Carolina

Statewide — A number of citizen groups in the state have been working to protect natural areas. As a result, the Joyce Kilmer-Slickrock area is now an official Wilderness Area, and the Chatooga River has been declared a Wild and Scenic River.

Baldhead Island — The Joseph LeConte Chapter of the Sierra Club has filed an environmental suit against the U.S. Army Corps of Engineers and the developers of this tropical island off the coast of North Carolina.

Greenville — The Bartram Group of the Sierra Club proposed in 1971 the formation of a Southern Appalachian Slope National Recreation Area where the Appalachian Mountain Escarpment meets the Piedmont. Work continues on this project.

Raleigh — Citizens moved vigorously through the "Greenway Project" to make this city a leader in environmental matters. They urged the city to create a commission to continue work on a system of parks along the city's waterways, to initiate street tree plantings and land-use improvements.

Wilmington — The Cape Fear group of the Sierra Club is working to have Masonboro Island declared a state park.

Wilmington — Citizens created a local group, Citizens to Save Rockfish Creek. They stopped the channelization of Rockfish Creek by the U.S. Army Corps of Engineers.

Oklahoma

Durant — The state chapter of the Sierra Club has mounted opposition to the proposed Oklahoma Water Plan which would require damming all rivers in Oklahoma — even those presently designated as Scenic Rivers.

Inola — The Oklahoma chapter of the Sierra Club is working against the development of a nuclear power plant in this area.

Norman — Citizen organizations banded together and stopped the damming of the Illinois River and are now working to prevent unwise second home developments from marring the Illinois River and some of its tributaries in Oklahoma and Arkansas.

Stillwater — Citizens studied floodplain management on Boomer Creek in this city. Their plan was represented at a hearing on channelization of the creek (to be done by the Corps of Engineers at a cost of $3 million). The City of Stillwater has chosen flood plain management rather than channelization as a way to solve the problem of flood damage along the creek.

Oregon

Grants Pass — A local coalition is contesting the BLM's plan to liquidate all "accessible old growth" in drainage tributaries. The group wants to establish definitive criteria for evaluating management objectives on these marginal timberlands.

Lake Oswego — The Friends of Tryon Creek Park, Inc. saved 600 wilderness acres in the center of a metropolitan residential area which resulted in the Tyron Creek State Park.

Portland — The Oregon Environmental Council was instrumental in the passage of Oregon's "container deposit" bill. They have remained guardians of the law against container manufacturers who seek to change the bill which bans non-returnable beverage containers.

Ohio

Columbus — The Ohio Waste Watchers are working for a "container deposit" bill for this state.

Pennsylvania

Harrisburg — The Pennsylvania Alliance for Returnables is working to have "container deposit" legislation introduced into the State Legislature.

Rhode Island

Providence — Ecology Action for Rhode Island has gotten legislation introduced in the state legislature which would ban non-returnable beverage containers.

South Carolina

Columbia — The John Bachman Group of the Sierra Club has proposed establishment of a 70,000-acre national preserve of the swamp and bottomland forest along the Conagree, Wateree and Santee Rivers.

South Dakota

Statewide — Citizens' efforts pressured the State legislature to pass legislation which bans non-returnable beverage containers. This law will go into effect in 1976.

Statewide — The Committee for Preservation of Harney Peak convinced the U.S. Forest Service to deny a permit to build a tramway to the top of the 7,200-foot peak.

Badlands — Statewide conservation action is being conducted to establish a 64,250 acre grasslands wilderness in The South Dakota Badlands. If enacted it will be the Sage Creek Wilderness.

Black Hills — The Citizens Committee to Save the Black Hills blocked National Park Service plans to convert 175 acres into a 3,000 car parking lot for Mt. Rushmore.

Carpenter — The United Family Farmers are asking the Federal government to cease the funding of the Oahe Irrigation Project.

Texas

Statewide — Citizen pressure prevented the construction of the U.S. Navy's Sanguine project — which would involve laying a communications cable — after it was prohibited from laying the cable in Wisconsin.

Statewide — The Sierra Club has opposed for years plans for a massive water transfer scheme of moving water from the humid east of the state to the semi-arid west part. They actively oppose bond issues and work to inform the public of

the great economic cost and possible environmental destruction such a transfer would incur.

Houston — In 1959 ten people started Texas Beaches Unlimited which worked against tremendous odds to get an Open Beaches Act passed by the Texas Legislature. This group works to keep Texas beaches open to the public and helps with the problems of enforcement, littering, and erosion.

Houston — The Texas Conservation Council is dedicated to working for the establishment of parks and recreation areas including Padre Island National Seashore and a large Mustang Island State Park. The Council also is pressuring the state to purchase 221,000 acres of land adjacent to the Big Bend National Park which is being offered for sale.

Houston — The Co-ordinating Committee of Conservation Organizations worked hard for a Big Thicket Biological Preserve. Congress, however, passed an act which protected an area much smaller than the organization had fought for.

Houston — Many environmental groups are battling against the problem of over-development in the national parks such as Big Bend, Padre Island Seashore, and the Guadalupe Mountains.

Matagorda Island — Local residents with help from the National Audubon Society pressured the U.S. Air Force to suspend bombing runs on a practice range which borders the wintering grounds of the endangered whooping cranes.

Tennessee

Knoxville — The Tennessee Environmental Coalition is working to have a state "container deposit" bill introduced into the state legislature.

Memphis — Citizens to Preserve Overton Park won a five-year battle to ban an interstate freeway through a 342-acre urban park.

Nashville — Ten citizens formed the Radnor Lake Preservation Fund, Inc. Their public service project persuaded the state legislature to declare the 80-acre lake and surrounding area a "state natural area."

Utah

Warner Valley — The Clean Air Council of Southern Utah opposes the construction of a Warner Valley power plant. Though the local citizenry would pay for a large cost of the plant, the power will be sold for out-of-state use.

Virginia

Statewide — Citizens opposed to hydroelectric dams on the New River in Virginia have won a court-ordered stay of the license for the project. They now hope to defeat the proposed construction completely.

Arlington County — Citizen action under the leadership of Elizabeth S. Hartwell has managed to preserve the wilderness areas and marshes near Washington, D.C., after ten years of constant battles with various kinds of developers.

Chesterfield County — Local residents have maintained pressure on housing developers since 1971 to leave Swift Creek reservoir in a natural and unpolluted state as a public water supply.

Lynchburg — Citizens Against Nonreturnables is working to have a state "container deposit" bill introduced into the state legislature.

Vermont

Fair Haven — The State Federation of Garden Clubs persuaded the State legislature to declare billboards and throwaway bottles illegal in the state in 1973.

Washington

Olympia — The Consumer Lobby for Refillable Containers and the Seattle group of the Sierra Club are promoting the introduction of a state "container deposit" bill into the legislature.

Spokane — The Spokane Mountaineers are seeking wilderness classification of the Salmo-Priest area to protect endangered species which inhabit the area and to prevent the proposed clear-cut timber sale.

Seattle — Don Kneass has submitted a proposal to the Department of Ecology to establish a Washington Recycling Information Service. The service would use the media to inform the public how to recycle material, where to take it, etc.

Seattle — The Washington Environmental Council has an ongoing land-use committee which last year researched and wrote three pieces of land-use legislation.

Seattle — Environmentalists through the Nature Conservancy and in cooperation with the Governor's office are working to establish a bald eagle sanctuary on the Skagit River. This project involves buying various parcels of land from timber companies and private individuals.

Spokane — The Spokane County Shoreline Citizens Advisory Committee wrote up and has found acceptance for a Spokane County "Master Plan for Shorelines Management."

West Virginia

Statewide — Conservationists are working with groups in Virginia and North Carolina to stop the construction of the Blue Ridge Project by American Electric Power. The proposed dam and reservoir on the New River in Virginia will greatly affect the river system in West Virginia.

Statewide — Legal action initiated by various conservation groups forced recognition of the illegality of clearcutting as a management technique of federally-owned forestland. As a result of a 1973 court decision all timbering on the Monongahela National Forest has been halted pending appeal by the U.S. Forest Service.

Elkins — The West Virginia Highlands Conservancy and other groups are calling for a halt to construction on the present route of Corridor H, a segment of the vast Appalachian Corridor Highway system. Threatened by the project are a $10 million Federal fish hatchery, 17 clear mountain streams, and huge acreages of the Monongahela National Forest.

Randolph and Tucker Counties — An eight year fight by the West Virginia Highlands Conservancy finally bore fruit in December, 1974 when the 20,000-acre watershed of Otter Creek became an "instant" wilderness area under the Eastern Wilderness Areas Act.

Tucker County — Local citizens are attempting to block construction of a pump-storage dam and a 7500-acre lake in Canaan Valley.

Webster — The West Virginia Highlands Conservancy is fighting to save Shavers Fork River from strip and deep mining, clearcutting, logging road building, and resort construction. Protest over the destruction of the watershed continues.

Webster Springs — The West Virginia Highlands Conservancy has proposed the Cranberry Backcountry as a 36,000 acre wilderness area to be protected from the interests of coal-mining operations.

Weston — A local citizens' group, the West Fork River Watershed Association, is attempting to block a project by the U.S. Army Corps of Engineers to build a dam and reservoir on the West Fork River.

Wisconsin

Highbridge — The State Committee to Stop Sanguine prevented the construction of Sanguine — a Navy project involving 20,000 square miles which would be laid with underground cable for sending one-way messages to submerged submarines.

Wyoming

Statewide — The Wyoming Outdoor Council is spearheading efforts to have legislation introduced which would ban non-returnable beverage containers from being sold in the state.

Statewide — In 1971-72 the Laramie Wilderness Group led an effort to gain new wilderness areas. The area initially protected was the Medicine Bow National Forest and each year more areas are protected. Study teams are conducted by the Wilderness Society, Wyoming Outdoor Council, and the Wyoming Sierra Club.

Northeast Wyoming — The Powder Basin Resource Council is a grassroots rancher organization dedicated to informing the people about impacts from coal development, and to lobby for proper laws to protect their ranching interests.

Meeteetsee — The Meteetsee Preservation Organization was formed in fall of 1974 to battle against the construction of an Amax Copper Mine at nearby Kirwin.

Wheatland — A group of Wheatland ranchers have organized to inform the people and oppose a mammoth power plant to be constructed by Basin Electric.

Canada

British Columbia — The Okanagan Similkameen Parks Society is trying to get the park enlarged and have successfully set up a trust fund to purchase land for the California bighorn.

British Columbia — Conservationists are actively countering a grandiose Federal-Provincial-Corporate proposal for massive industrial development of the entire northwest quarter of this province.

British Columbia — Citizens in the Okanagan Valley successfully blocked a proposed ski development on Brent Mountain.

British Columbia — The Victoria group of the Sierra Club waged a vigorous and successful campaign to save a forest area of 13,400 acres from being logged.

Ontario — The Sierra Club of Ontario is promoting the immediate protection of the Missinaibi River through designation as a "provincial wild river park."

Ontario — Victorious action by the Terra Cotta and District Preservation Committee preserved the Niagara Escarpment and village community from the Consolidated Sand and Gravel Company which had begun high volume extraction.

Summerland — Citizens tried unsuccessfully to block the excessive channelization of Trout Creek.

Index